Creating Human Rights

Pennsylvania Studies in Human Rights

Bert B. Lockwood, Jr., Series Editor

A complete list of books in the series is available from the publisher.

Creating Human Rights

How Noncitizens Made
Sex Persecution Matter to the World

Lisa S. Alfredson

PENN

University of Pennsylvania Press
Philadelphia

Published by
University of Pennsylvania Press
Philadelphia, Pennsylvania 19104-4112

Printed in the United States of America on acid-free paper
10 9 8 7 6 5 4 3 2 1

Library of Congress Cataloging-in-Publication Data
Alfredson, Lisa S.
  Creating human rights : how noncitizens made sex persecution matter to the world / Lisa S. Alfredson.
      p. cm. — (Pennsylvania studies in human rights)
  Includes bibliographical references and index.
  ISBN 978-0-8122-4125-9
  1. Sexual abuse victims—Services for—Canada. 2. Women refugees—Services for—Canada.
  3. Women immigrants—Services for—Canada. I. Title.
  HV6593.C2A55 2009
  362.88—dc22

                                                          2008031615

Contents

List of Figures and Tables vii

List of Abbreviations ix

1 Introduction: The Sex Persecution Campaigns 1

2 Human Rights, Social Movement, and Asylum Seeking 30

3 Global Challenges and Opportunities for Sex-Based Asylum Seeking 81

4 Moving In: Asylum Seekers' National Rights, Resources, and Opportunities 112

5 "Use My Name": Noncitizen Identity, Decisions, and Mobilization 135

6 Universalizing National Rights: Political Confrontation and Cultural Framing 175

7 Making Sex Persecution Matter 226

Appendix: Comprehensive and Novel Aspects of Gender-Related Claims 267

Notes 269

Bibliography 283

Index 311

Acknowledgments 315

Figures and Tables

Figure 4.1. Refugee Determination Process   123

Figure 5.1. Core Campaign Network, Metanetwork, and External
Environment   173

Figure 6.1. Interrelatedness of Locus and Agent in Manifestations of
Violence Against Women   221

Table 2.1. Impact of Globalization on Human Rights   36

Table 2.2 Major and Minor Asylum Seeker Case Histories   74

Table 4.1. Development of Core Campaign Organizations   128–29

Table 4.2. Asylum Seekers from Campaign Group by Year
of Arrival   131

Table 4.3. Asylum Seekers from Campaign Group by Principal
Applicant Claim and Years Residency   131

Table 5.1. Timing of Public Claims, 1991–1997   139

Table 5.2. Mandate, Activities, and Access of Core Campaign
Organizations   170–71

Table 6.1. Campaign Network Hierarchy of Policy Values and Policy
Demands   179

Table 6.2. Expected Institutional Responses to Movement Goals and
Tactics   183

Table 6.3. Expected Public Responses to Movement Goals and
Tactics   183

Table 6.4. Pre-Campaign Period: Institutional Case-by-Case
Reform   188

Table 6.5. Generative Period: Reform Goals Plus Noninstitutional
Tactics   196

Table 6.6. Regional and Organizational Campaign
Representation   197

Table 6.7. Peak Period: Radical Goals Plus Noninstitutional
Tactics   205

Table 6.8. Peak Period: Reform Goals Plus Noninstitutional
Tactics   206

Table 6.9.   Decline: Radical Goals Plus Institutional Tactics   211
Table 6.10.   Decline: Reform Goals Plus Noninstitutional Tactics   214
Table 6.11.   Gender-Related Claims and Outcomes in the Early
              Years   216
Table 6.12.   Notable Claims Involving Social Group and Family
              Violence   218

Abbreviations

CACSW	Canadian Advisory Council on the Status of Women
CAR	Coalition aux Réfugiées
CCR	Canadian Council for Refugees
CRDD	Convention Refugee Determination Division
EIC	Employment and Immigration, Canada
ICCR	Interfaith Coalition of Churches for Refugees
ICHRDD	International Centre for Human Rights and Democratic Development
IRB	Immigration and Refugee Board, Canada
LSUC	Law Society of Upper Canada
NAC	National Action Committee on the Status of Women
NOIVMW	National Organization of Immigrant and Visible Minority Women
OECD	Organisation for Economic Co-operation and Development
OLAP	Ontario Legal Aid Plan
PDRC	postdetermination refugee claimant
RAM	Refugee Action Montreal
RHO	Refugee Hearing Officer
TAN	Transnational Advocacy Network
TCMR	Table de Concertation des Organismes de Montreal au Service des Personnes Réfugiées et Immigrantes
UDHR	Universal Declaration of Human Rights
UNHCR	United Nations High Commissioner for Refugees

Chapter 1
Introduction
The Sex Persecution Campaigns

The immigration officer came inside. He said: "Madame, when was the last letter you got from your husband? . . . Your lawyer, she talks about a letter that was written to you about a 'wedding dress.' What does it mean?" I said "Oh. This means that . . . if I don't stay here in Canada I have to go back with a wedding dress. But in our culture, when we die we dress in white. I am already married to him, why do I have to bring a wedding dress? This is it: for me to die in."
—Thérèse, refugee claimant, 1995

When I was in Saudi Arabia, I thought that women in other countries were more respected and more powerful. I was naive. I first realized my naiveté when they laughed at me at the airport when I said I have problems because I am a woman.
—Nada, refugee claimant, 1993

The persecution of women is irrelevant to the refugee status determination process.
—Randy Gordan, assistant to Immigration Minister Bernard Valcourt, 1992

I don't think Canada should unilaterally try to impose its values [on women's rights] on the rest of the world. Canada cannot go it alone, we just cannot.
—Bernard Valcourt, Canadian immigration minister, responding to demands to make refugee policy gender inclusive, 1993

Thérèse's and Nada's experiences are both typical and atypical for asylum seekers. All asylum seekers experience life in the balance as their eligibility for international protection as "refugees" is judged. Indeed, as one eminent refugee scholar captured so vividly, when it comes to issues of refugee recognition "the definitional problem . . . is not mere academic exercise but has bearing on matters of life and death" (Zolberg et al. 1989:3). Also typical is the "burden of proof" which inland asylum seekers bear (Schenk 1996). That is, far from being a simple process of doling out aid to victims, refugee determinations are organized in adversarial court settings in which individuals make claims, are questioned by officials, and must provide evidence that they have been persecuted. Their claims are then judged under national law as well as international standards and foreign policy considerations (Teitelbaum 1984). The atypical nature of Thérèse's and Nada's experiences, and asylum seekers like them, emerges in the explicitly politicized and very public nature of their claim making. They made claims at the time considered illegitimate, shared their personal stories of persecution with the mass media, and became the center point of campaigns to change refugee policy. Their actions in the early 1990s cast a spotlight on a previously invisible refugee movement, making national and international headlines and raising intense debates about the universality of women's rights. These women were seeking asylum from female-specific forms and causes of violence, and challenging historically gender-biased frameworks to get it. Their claims illuminated culturally relativist and sexist assumptions underlying the international human rights norms upon which refugee policy is based. In so doing, they not only triggered a radical shift in refugee policy worldwide, but facilitated an expansion of human rights as internationally understood.

Canada, where Thérèse, Nada, and dozens of other asylum seekers campaigned, became the first country to address women's rights to protection from female-specific violence as an interstate responsibility when it instated policy enabling asylum on what were then novel human rights grounds. Its March 1993 Guidelines on Women Refugee Claimants Fearing Gender-Related Persecution explicitly recognized violence against women as a serious structural human rights abuse and thus amounting to persecution, and laid out a detailed approach to incorporate such abuse within the five existing categories of persecution under international refugee law—race, religion, nationality, political opinion, and membership in a social group (1951 Convention Relating to the Status of Refugees). That is, human rights violations may occur due to the gender-specific treatment of women (e.g., domestic and sexual violence, persecutory gender customs and criminal codes), and for the purpose of refugee law this can be identified within particular races, religions, nationalities, political opinions, and social groups. Within a few years, the United Nations High Commission on the Status of Refugees, the European Union, and a growing number of states were following Canada's lead (UNHCR 2003).

Very little is known about this novel refugee movement, and even less about how it actually succeeded in making sex persecution matter. Policy outcomes have been treated primarily in a positivist manner, ignoring how and why they came to be and the actors and political processes that propelled them.[1] Of the hundreds of articles and chapters about the persecution of women that have emerged since 1993, the vast majority concentrate on the content of new refugee policies and relevant forms of violence against women (e.g., Macklin 1999, 2006; Musalo 2003; Goldberg 2000; Gilad 1999; Kuttner 1997; Young 1994), particularly legal analyses of domestic violence as grounds for refugee status (e.g., Schaffer 2001), and compatibility with human rights law and state sovereignty (Romany 1993).[2] The philosophical and legal basis for women's human rights, and specifically violence against women as a human rights abuse, has been even more widely treated (e.g., Charlesworth, Chinkin, and Wright 1991; Bunch and Reilly 1994; Cook 1994; Peters and Wolper 1995; Nussbaum 1999). This book looks beyond these critical but still limited legal and philosophical treatments. In contrast, it takes a deep look at *political processes* that catapulted the previously invisible issue of sex persecution onto the world stage and through which the parameters of what we think of as human rights were expanded and made viable—processes as yet little understood.

When considered closely, the success of this refugee movement is somewhat perplexing for academics, and particularly for those interested in understanding human rights change. The core of this movement was necessarily made up of persecuted, disenfranchised, homeless females—among the most powerless of the powerless in any context. And as indicated above in pointedly defiant statements by Canada's immigration department, this was no simple policy evolution but rather a fundamentally contentious political process involving both national and international considerations. Even more perplexing, applications of human rights to new populations are typically studied in downward movements of existing supranational norms imposed upon or absorbed into new national contexts through the help of transnational actors, while in this case, as this book shows, asylum seekers' national human rights claims preceded and indeed triggered developments and action supranationally. How then can we explain this case, and what are its broader implications?

By combining original empirical data and analysis of sociopolitical historical trends, this study offers the first comprehensive and systematic scholarly treatment of this new women's refugee movement and the challenges it posed to existing policy and norms, illuminating asylum seekers' little recognized political agency and grappling with paradoxes of their success. In so doing, it explains how this women's refugee movement succeeded in making sex persecution matter, and it illuminates theoretical implications for the political processes of creating human rights.

In this chapter I begin by taking a look at the policy model set by the Canadian Guidelines on Women Refugee Claimants Fearing Gender-Related Persecution. I then illuminate the central characteristics, triumphs, and paradoxes of the campaigns studied in this book, which I characterize as an "international trigger case" for human rights change. I conclude by introducing the analytical framework developed to approach human rights change in international trigger cases and laying out the structure of the book.

The Canadian Model

Canada's Guidelines on Women Refugee Claimants Fearing Gender-Related Persecution (hereafter the Guidelines), adopted by the Immigration and Refugee Board (IRB) in March 1993 under section 65(3) and (4) of the Immigration Act, transcend previous refugee law, policy proposals, and recommendations internationally in this area. At the tenth anniversary of the instatement of the Guidelines, Ruud Lubbers of the United Nations High Commissioner for Refugees (UNHCR) remarked: "Canada was the trailblazer in developing an asylum process that takes proper account of gender-related persecution. The IRB's Guidelines were the first of their kind, and led other countries to recognize the importance of devoting special attention in their asylum systems to the plight of refugee women" (UNHCR 2003). The Guidelines operate by instructing adjudicators to view refugee claims and the standard-setting 1951 Convention Relating to the Status of Refugees (hereafter the 1951 Convention) more broadly through a gender lens. The 1951 Convention defines a "refugee" as: "Any person who, as a result of . . . and owing to well-founded fear of being persecuted for reasons of race, religion, nationality, membership in a particular social group or political opinion, is outside the country of his nationality and is unable or, owing to such fear, is unwilling to avail himself of the protection of that country; or who not having a nationality and being outside the country of his former habitual residence as a result of such events, is unable or, owing to such fear, is unwilling to return to it."

Specifically, the Guidelines provide a gender-inclusive status determination framework through which adjudicators can justify granting refugee status to females whose persecution on Convention grounds—the five categories of race, religion, nationality, membership in a particular social group, or political opinion—is "related" to the gender culture of the society in which they live. This is evidently influenced by one's physical sex, as female and male gender roles are related to sexual status in particular societies or communities defined by race, nationality, political opinion, religion, or social group. The question is, how is this "relatedness" determined? To answer this question the Guidelines identify four crosscutting "broad categories" of persecution women may experience *as women*, any of which may be related to the five Convention reasons for persecution.

1. "Women who fear persecution on the *same Convention grounds, and in similar circumstances, as men* . . . although the nature of the harm feared and procedural issues at the hearing may vary as a function of the claimant's gender." That is, persecution may occur for similar reasons of race, religion, nationality, political opinion, or social group, but take forms that tend to be more specific to women, such as sexual violence, and may raise particular difficulties in the hearing room, such as claimant feelings of shame and hesitancy to discuss the persecution.
2. "Women who fear persecution for reasons solely pertaining to *kinship*." In such cases "persecution of kin" may occur to pressure women for information about the activities of family members, or because political opinions of family members have been imputed to them.
3. "Women who fear persecution resulting from certain circumstances of *severe discrimination on grounds of gender*, or acts of violence either by public authorities or at the hands of private citizens from whose actions the state is unwilling or unable to adequately protect the concerned persons." Here, females may be the target of policies and customs that amount to persecution, such as domestic violence and rape in war.
4. "Women who fear persecution as the consequence for failing to

conform to, or for transgressing, certain gender-discriminating religious or customary laws and practices in their own country of origin. Such laws and practices, by singling out women and placing
them in a more vulnerable position than men, may create conditions
precedent to a *gender-defined social group*." Here, policies and customs may or may not amount to severe discrimination but do single
out women and further impose severe punishments for nonconfor-
mity that amount to persecution (e.g., execution for adultery, stoning for violating a dress code).

This model builds upon earlier research by DeNeef (1984) and transcends the brief references and recommendations made previously in international documents, which are qualified, substantially elaborated, and
institutionalized.[3] The model encompasses "private" forms of violence from
which women so often suffer by identifying nonstate actors as potential perpetrators, and acts of omission by the state (failing to protect) alongside traditionally recognized acts of commission and public violence by state actors.
Attention is also drawn to evidentiary issues and problems in the hearing
room that are specific to females and problematize adjudicators' abilities to
evaluate information on both objective and subjective elements of claims.
Emphasis is placed on the need to recognize lack of documentation on violence against women and to make use of historical evidence about implementation trends regarding relevant laws, policies, and customs in countries
of origin.

Taking the above four general categories of persecution into consideration, adjudicators are advised to follow a six-step framework for analysis:
First, they assess the "particular circumstances which have given rise to the
claimant's fear of persecution," asking if the form of harm feared is one "directed at or experienced predominantly by women," such as: persecution related to kinship; severe discrimination against women; religious, social, legal,
or cultural norms affecting women; and "their exposure or vulnerability for
physical, cultural or other reasons, to violence, including domestic violence,
in an environment that denies them protection." Second, they assess "the
general conditions in the claimant's country of origin" regarding females.
This helps determine objectively the likelihood that the harm feared is legitimate by looking at the country's treatment of its female citizens historically
and currently. Is the "social and political position of women in that country"
likely to engender "the degree of discrimination likely to amount to persecu-

tion"? Are there laws and regulations oppressive to women or certain women, and "how severe are penalties for noncompliance?" What are the roles and attitudes of state authorities and nonstate groups toward inflicting, condoning, or tolerating violence against women, including domestic and sexual violence "as a means of punishing or reinforcing their dominance over other groups"? Third, they determine the "seriousness of the treatment which the claimant fears" by ascertaining if the form of harm "detracts from women's human rights and fundamental freedoms," and by using international human rights instruments "that declare the lowest common denominator of protected interests." The analysis thus adopts an explicitly human rights approach to interpreting "persecution" and assesses women's rights as human rights. Fourth, they assess whether fear of persecution occurs on any one or combination of grounds of persecution identified in the 1951 Convention refugee definition: race, religion, nationality, political opinion, membership in a social group. The harm feared that is *related* to gender must occur on one of these five grounds of persecution. Fifth, they consider the presence or absence of country-of-origin protection for the claimant. If state protection is evident, the claimant must seek the protection afforded by her own country. And sixth, they determine the well-foundedness of the claimant's fear of persecution under the circumstances that have been revealed, including the presence or absence of the "internal flight alternatives."

While the substance of the Canadian model has been highly praised, its form, as policy guidelines, has been the subject of some debate regarding enforceability. IRB guidelines have statutory basis in Canada under the Immigration Act. Their purpose is essentially to "foster consistency in what is a very decentralized system" (Young 1994:10). According to the IRB, guidelines are enforceable to the extent that: (1) Refugee, Immigration Appeal and Adjudication Divisions members are expected to "follow the Guidelines unless there are compelling or exceptional reasons for adopting a different analysis"; and (2) "individuals have a right to expect that the Guidelines will be followed unless compelling or exceptional reasons exist for departure from them"; but (3) they are not binding "in the sense that Members and Adjudicators may use their discretion in individual cases to follow a different approach where warranted, as long as the reasons for the departure are set out in their reasons for decision."[4] The Guidelines thus provide a forum and framework for identifying the kinds of persecution women may experience as women. They also act as a vehicle through which interpretations and procedural processes regarding such claims may be expanded over time. They facilitate the development of case law and documentation in this area and by their flexible nature are easier to amend than legislation, which must pass the approval of Parliament. Thus they remain open to future revisions and may expand in scope and application beyond their original purpose. Generally, by elaborating how adjudicators should interpret existing legislation, the Guidelines foster greater consistency in decision making. But to prevent inconsistency in decision making that could, at the same time, result from their nonbinding nature, adjudicators are required to document and justify their decisions and to demonstrate "compelling reasons" for departure from the suggested framework.

Since instatement the Guidelines appear to have been successfully enforced at least to the extent that acceptance rates of claims in this area have remained on par with those of conventional claims annually, at nearly 60 percent (IRB 2003). Interestingly, in more radical changes to national refugee laws following Canada's model, South Africa added the term "gender" and Ireland added the term "sex" to the definition of social group in the refugee definition, but these countries have been criticized for failure to enforce due in part to lack of explicit policy guidelines that lay out how to apply this legislative change and require adjudicators to justify their decisions.[5] In contrast, the parameters of Canada's Guidelines have been expanded since 1993. In November 1996 the Guidelines were officially updated to expand their application and better clarify complex situations adjudicators face. The 1996 update provides more explicit phrasing and explanation regarding domestic violence and other forms of violence by nonstate actors and further elaborates the appropriateness of the social group category of persecution for women. It also addresses change of circumstances in sending countries and how cultural, economic, and religious factors may affect claimants' internal flight alternatives (see Mawani 1997). Then in 2003 the IRB drew from the accumulation of jurisprudence to publish a compendium of select cases illustrating the application of categories, processes, and concepts central to the Guidelines, to further facilitate enforcement. However, the most effective policy form in this area may likely be the combination of both amendments to the refugee definition itself in national and/or international refugee law (adding "sex" or "gender" as a recognized Convention reason for persecution), alongside accompanying guidelines for implementation, and in this sense the Canadian model is not the end of the road but an essential guide toward it.

The Sex Persecution Campaigns: Characteristics, Triumphs, and Paradoxes

How were campaigns studied in this book linked to the instatement of the Guidelines, and what was their broader impact? Female-specific refugee claims had been made in Europe and North America prior to the campaigns studied here, but up through the 1980s gained little notice. Such cases were not publicized, were considered isolated and irrelevant and dealt with in an ad hoc fashion, for the most part rejected (see DeNeef 1984). It was in Canada in the early 1990s that the rise of asylum seeking by such women first became powerfully visible and influential.[6] The first asylum seekers to publicize their cases in Canada emerged in 1991, and by early 1993 dozens more were campaigning and awaiting decisions on claims, despite government's public rejection of the notion of female persecution. Asylum seekers who went public, whom this study tracks, originated from eighteen countries across six regions—Africa, Latin America and the Caribbean, Eastern Europe and Russia, the Middle East, South America, and Southeast Asia. They were publicly supported by a wide range of nongovernmental Canadian organizations, including refugee, human rights, women's, and community organizations.

Thérèse and Nada, quoted earlier, not only were key figures among the asylum seekers who publicly campaigned for refugee policy to be changed, but are also representative of the range of claims and tactics captured in the campaign. Like other asylum seekers studied, they exhausted institutional refugee status determination processes before taking public, noninstitutional action, demonstrating the ineffectiveness of existing laws considered gender neutral. Their claims further represent opposite ends of the spectrum of forms of violence against women evident among campaigners—from public violence inflicted or condoned by officials of a state, to so-called private violence inflicted by family members and the community in states that condone or turn a blind eye toward it. Reflecting the former, Nada fled a state-imposed penalty of public lashing for violating the female dress code (not wearing the veil in an Islamic country). Reflecting the latter, Thérèse's government and community denied protection from spousal beatings and death threats. Despite these differences, like all asylum seekers who campaigned, Thérèse and Nada argued that they are persecuted *because* they are female or *in ways specific to* females and so merit asylum from persecution based on sex. The intimate stories of domestic violence, rape, gendered torture, and criminalization made visible by the range of asylum seekers who went public throughout the course of the campaigns became test cases for a new gendered understanding of persecution in refugee law, where persecution is tantamount to serious, systematic human rights abuse.[7]

During this period, terms such as "sex persecution," "gender persecution," and "female persecution" were defined in neither policy nor academic discourse, but came to be used quite interchangeably in the media. The term "sex persecution" was prioritized by campaigners, therefore this book refers to their untitled campaigns as the "sex persecution campaigns." This reflects campaigners' primary policy demand that "sex" be inserted into the refugee definition of the 1951 Convention Relating to the Status of Refugees, as well as Canada's national refugee policy, as a basis of persecution alongside race, religion, nationality, political opinion, and social group. It also respects the use of French in Canada's bilingual population, particularly Quebec where campaigning was most intense; in French, "le sexe" refers to both gender and sex. Even in English the term "sex" was used more often at the time.

In retrospect, resulting policies worldwide tend to use variations on "gender persecution" (gender-related, gender-based) and provide descriptions relating the occurrence of such persecution to one's biological sex or sexual status, typically including references to "women" specifically. They then concentrate on describing the ways such claims may be "related" to the five grounds of persecution identified in the 1951 Convention. In short, currently there remains no concise definition even of gender persecution, but rather an elaboration of general causes and specific forms, particularly for women but with potential application to men as well.

As the definition of "persecution" in international refugee law is commonly equated with systematic, structural human rights violations carried out due to, and often through means specific to, one's inherent characteristics and/or beliefs (race, religion, nationality, political opinion, social group), I suggest "sex persecution" may be defined as systematic, structural human rights violations carried out due to or through means specific to the sex of the target. Gendered societal codes that target the female or male sex for certain abuses are cultural framings around sex as an inherent characteristic. However, when not referring specifically to the sex persecution campaigns or the broader concept of sex persecution, this book uses the most contextually relevant terminology. The term "female persecution" refers more specifically to the persecution of women and girls, the main population under debate in this area of international law, differentiated from "sex persecution," which may encompass both men and women. Indeed, after the Guidelines were instated jurisprudence did develop around male claimants (persecuted homosexuals, males threatened with sterilization, and so on). Finally, the term "gender-related persecution," which critics have characterized as vulnerable to narrow interpretations, refers to persecution specifically as recognized under policies later developed using that term.

The policy impact of this movement is difficult to overstate, being direct, broad, and deep, and from a political process perspective the paradoxes of its success are equally significant. The campaign's *direct* impact was evident and widely noted by politicians, activists, and practitioners, and indeed was credited in the text of Canada's 1993 Guidelines.[8] The sequence of events here is important from the standpoint of those who seek to understand how human rights change occurs, because it is important to understand who initiates policy and why. The Guidelines were instated in March 1993 at the very height of national policy campaigns, and they were geared toward campaigners' demands. The Guidelines marked a clear and radical policy shift; only eighteen months earlier the government had stated that the persecution of women was "irrelevant" to the refugee process and that more progressive Canadian women's rights were culturally relative, therefore Canada could not imperialistically "impose its values on the rest of the world."[9] Historically the government had for the most part simply rejected female-specific claims to refugee status. This policy shift also marked the first time a state institutionalized a mechanism through which it could condemn violence against women in foreign countries as human rights abuse, rather than ignoring it as a cultural prerogative.

The campaigns also had a far-reaching effect, as noted earlier. *Breadth* of impact was seen in the international media, which covered cases of individual asylum seekers in Canada as negative decisions on their claims were overturned and debated the policy implications. They ran provocative stories on the horror and prevalence of violence against women and the potentially vast implications of campaigners' demand that human rights to asylum be institutionalized for such a chronic worldwide social problem. Significantly, the day the Canadian government publicly announced it would comply with campaigners' policy demands, it also agreed to make representations to the United Nations on the issue.[10] It did not ignore but rather directly engaged with the international community in order to both justify and promote its departure from international law. Ultimately, the resulting Guidelines created a legal and moral prerogative for protection to be offered to foreign women victims of such violence.

In becoming the primary model for international developments in this area (UNHCR 2003), the Guidelines triggered no less than a radical shift in refugee policies and state responsibilities for women's human rights around the world. This is seen in the UNHCR's 2002 Guidelines on International Protection: Gender-Related Persecution Within the Context of Article 1A(2) of the 1951 UN Convention and/or Its 1967 Protocol Relating to the Status of Refugees (HCR/GIP/02/01, 7 May 2002), and in the 2004 European Union Council Directive 2004/83/EC. It is also evident in various national measures including gender-specific points in legislation (Ireland and South Africa), policy guidelines (Australia, Sweden, the United Kingdom, and the United States), gender-specific directives, handbooks, and work instructions (Austria, the Czech Republic, Finland, Germany, Guatemala, Lithuania, the Netherlands, Norway, Panama, Switzerland, and Venezuela), and draft proposals for policy guidelines (Ireland and Belgium).[11] These developments incorporate an expanded, gendered concept of human rights violations in tune with the concept of women's human rights as understood today. Women's rights to asylum were dramatically and globally expanded, as were subsequently the international understanding and legitimacy of women's human rights.

That the campaigns received not only national attention and debate, but also stirred intense international controversy by challenging historically entrenched structural challenges within international human rights law and practice is no small matter and signals the *depth* of impact. The movement arose not only despite but as a challenge to the absence of "sex" as a recognized category of persecution alongside race, religion, nationality, political opinion, and social group in the standard-setting refugee definition of the 1951 Convention. That is, they openly sought asylum on grounds not then recognized as legitimate. What is more, they sought an expansion in the categories of asylum at a time when restrictions against international migration were actually being tightened worldwide.[12] Not only, therefore, would this seem not to be a time conducive to refugee policy expansion, but in very real terms it translated into increasing restrictions on actual movement by asylum seekers—cutting off many asylum claims before they could even be made. Such prohibitive circumstances should surprise those skeptical of the genuine nature of these women's claims. It would be illogical for international migrants to fabricate stories of persecution on grounds historically considered illegitimate. Such migrants would be far more likely to succeed by fabricating stories of persecution using historically accepted legal arguments, rather than taking on the entire refugee system, particularly during a period of retraction. In fact, they would probably be even more likely to succeed by blending into the mass of invisible illegal residents. Significantly, these asylum seekers sought not only residency but *legitimation*.

Because the persecution that refugees flee is generally equated with serious, structural human rights abuse (Hathaway 1991b; IRB 1992), the historical blindness toward female-specific violence even in other human rights instruments would seem to make early sex-based asylum seeking practically impossible. Human rights law, its interpretation and application, has become considerably more gender inclusive since the period studied in this book, and its historically entrenched gender bias is now documented.[13] At the onset of the campaigns in 1991, already ten years after the instatement of the Convention on the Elimination of All Forms of Discrimination Against Women (which did not address gender violence), noted international legal scholars attacked the international legal system as fundamentally biased, saying, "both the structures of international lawmaking and the content of the rules of international law privilege men; if women's interests are acknowledged at all, they are marginalized. International law is a thoroughly gendered system . . . [which] privileges the male world view and supports male dominance in the international legal order" (Charlesworth, Chinkin, and Wright 1991:614). Scholars and practitioners now admit that gender bias ran through not only international law but also the human rights movement itself. Steiner and Alston go as far as to say that "it is instructive to contrast the vigor of the [human rights] movement in trying to 'eliminate' racial discrimination with its relative apathy until the last decade in responding to gender discrimination" (2000:159). Kenneth Roth (1994), executive director of Human Rights Watch, explained that even the most dedicated nongovernmental human rights organizations long neglected gender violence, perhaps due to the origins of the NGO human rights movement in concerns with classic types of politically motivated abuse such as the "prisoner of conscience." More damning however is the reality that even state-imposed sanctions against women for political statements and actions precisely on gender issues (such as stoning or whipping women who refuse to comply with gendered dress codes) were not previously considered "political." This lacuna long justified states in committing, condoning, or turning a blind eye toward violence against women—from rape as a strategy of war, to laws prescribing death for women accused of adultery or women whose accusations of rape cannot be proven, to chronic and widespread practices such as domestic violence, female genital mutilation, dowry deaths, and honor killings (see Cook 1994; Peters and Wolper 1995). It was not until nine months after the Guidelines were instated that a UN Declaration on the Elimination of Violence Against Women was adopted, which today has still not reached convention status. It was in this context of seemingly insurmountable barriers that asylum seekers made claims and challenged the then popular notion that the violence they faced was a cultural and state prerogative.

International implications were central to the way in which the campaign was framed, as this book later documents. Asylum seekers revealed culturally relativist and sexist eligibility criteria underlying Canadian refugee policy, but also as inherited from the standard-setting 1951 Convention and the utter silence of human rights treaties on this topic. The limits of international law in this area reified deeply entrenched beliefs that violence against women is permissible in cultures that condone it—a culturally relativist standpoint antithetical to human rights. This in effect justified the Canadian government's prior treatment of female-specific refugee claims as "illegitimate," despite Canada's otherwise progressive women's rights and humanitarian reputation. In this climate, campaigners criticized Canada not for failing to uphold international law, but rather for failing to uphold its own hard earned principles of gender equality when considering the rights of women more broadly. Canadians were surprised to learn that women's rights, as articulated through citizenship, were not considered human rights even by their own government. The Canadian media ran provocative headlines to this effect almost daily, such as "Is Sexual Equality a Universal Value?" (*Montreal Gazette*, 15 February 1993).

Canada is what I refer to as an international trigger case for human rights change because the standard it set was clearly both novel and widely influential in the global community. The sequence of events that transpired evidences, first, that contentious national political processes provoked by this refugee movement preceded the emergence of gendered rules of asylum supranationally and in other countries. Second, it therefore negates the possibility that an enlightened international policy or standard was applied nationally as part of a broader process of international norm diffusion or international human rights pressures upon states, contrary to current models of human rights change. Here, relevant international treaties were silent on the issue. Third, it rules out a simplistic assumption that, by reframing national refugee law to better match national values, international law did not matter to the state so much as its own values, as a realist interpretation might have it. Rather, the very politicized national debate was centrally concerned with the state's moral and legal obligations to defer to international law and other sovereign nations' cultural freedom. Finally, this sequence rules out an easy policy evolution emerging from an unpoliticized supply-and-demand interpretation (women needed asylum, and Canada could provide it), which some migration theories might suggest. Instead, this nationally targeted refugee movement and the contentious political processes surrounding it were clearly integral to refugee policy and human rights change, rather than simply benefiting from processes external to or preceding them.

The direct, broad, and deep impact of this movement poses a challenge to what Hannah Arendt in 1973 referred to as the fundamental paradox of human rights: those who need human rights protections the most typically have least access to them. As Arendt observed, this is perhaps no better exemplified than in the situation of refugees. Persecuted at home in countries where national citizenship rights fail to protect them from violence and international human right law goes unheeded, refugees seek foreign national protection but are often turned away precisely because they are noncitizens toward whom foreign countries have no enforceable obligation. The lack of international enforcement mechanisms for human rights undermines their potential precisely when most needed—when governments fail, or refuse, to protect their own citizens.

On closer examination, we can identify several legal justifications states use for not extending asylum to some who seek it, deepening the paradox. Some asylum seekers are denied protection because refugee policy covers only a selection of human rights abuses, for example including certain types of targeted violence against individuals while excluding situations of generalized violence (Plender 1989). Others are denied protection, even when human rights abuses suffered match refugee policy parameters, simply because states retain ultimate authority to grant or refuse asylum and often do so in a manner that promotes historically strategic political agendas (Teitelbaum 1984). And some asylum seekers are denied protection because not all abuses have been documented or internationally recognized as amounting to violations of human rights. From the viewpoint of states justifying their decisions, such violations are simply not "human rights" violations. But from a constructivist viewpoint, the array of human rights and our understanding of them are historically limited or incomplete, therefore some human rights abuses exist even if not yet recognized. In a final blow, asylum seekers' abilities to challenge exclusive parameters of national refugee law in foreign countries is of course limited by their status, since citizenship (which they lack) traditionally circumscribes political participation in national contexts. In sum, for refugees, what might more precisely be referred to as the citizenship–human rights paradox presents a double jeopardy. Home states may abuse their citizens while foreign states refuse protection to noncitizens, who are relatively powerless to evoke change in either context. The consequences for refugees in this study were dire; as Thérèse's lawyer explained, "In a country of 65,000 people, there is not a single shelter for victims of conjugal violence. And the courts there treat domestic violence as private family matters. So tell me, who will protect Thérèse?"[14]

The structural barriers set by traditional refugee, human rights, and citizenship parameters make the success of this refugee movement perplexing. How could women asylum seekers, long considered among the most powerless of the powerless given their triple burden as females, noncitizens, and persecuted individuals, overcome such deeply entrenched structural and historical barriers? Why did this previously ignored movement emerge and become influential at this time, more than forty years after the adoption of the 1951 Convention? What circumstances and strategies enabled noncitizens to successfully pressure for rights to international protection by foreign governments that have no binding legal obligations toward them? Through what means did women refugees become politically active and influential, and what exactly were their roles? How were the simultaneous limits of citizenship, refugee, and human rights law overcome and an expanded notion of human rights made viable, not merely in abstract statements of intent but in concrete institutional terms that exceeded existing international law in ways long obstructed by cultural relativism and fears of national imperialism? And ultimately, what light can this internationally significant case shed upon our understanding of how universal concepts of human rights may be changed and expanded? The convergence of human rights, refugee, and noncitizen politics in this case points toward underresearched and undertheorized areas in human rights scholarship, which in the current age of globalization are only increasing in importance.

Explaining Sex-Based Asylum Seeking: An International Trigger Case

Models of human rights change fail to explain how human rights were expanded in this case, which I have characterized as an international trigger for human rights change. This failure can be largely explained by three critical and interrelated limitations in current human rights scholarship. First, an empirical bias toward geographical versus substantive human rights expansions, that is, the spread of *existing* international standards versus the creation of *new* ones, leaving major gaps in the latter and affecting theory building. Second, an implicit normative bias toward supranational values as superior to national values. The role of national values in human rights change has received insufficient attention, perhaps overshadowed by the predominant claim in human rights scholarship that states' sovereignty is being undermined by more progressive human rights (whether new or old) and international pressures to adopt them. Third, despite dramatic demographic changes wrought by globalization, human rights scholarship has largely overlooked the significance of noncitizen politics for human rights, seeing instead only the converse significance of human rights for noncitizens. These limitations necessitate an alternate approach capable of grappling with human rights change that is in contrast, substantive, nationally precedented, and noncitizen based, and which can subsequently shed new theoretical insights.

From Geographic to Substantive Human Rights Change

The vast majority of empirical studies of human rights change focus on *geographical* human rights expansions in which existing international human rights law is imposed upon or absorbed into national settings, resulting in the creation or transformation of national laws. This is explained as the outcome of various pressures on states, including foreign policy, quiet diplomacy, sanctions and aid conditionality (Vincent 1986), humanitarian intervention (Wheeler 2000; Power 2002), international nongovernmental organizations (Korey 1998; Welch 2001; Bob 2005), human rights "regimes" involving intergovernmental bodies (Onuf and Peterson 1984; Donnelly 1986), Transnational advocacy networks including nongovernmental actors (Sikkink 1993a; Risse, Ropp, and Sikkink 1999), and global civil society more broadly (Brysk 2002). The processes through which such forces come into play have been described as involving a "norm cascade" (Sunstein 1997) in which international norms spread into national contexts (see Adler 1987; Haas 1990; Finnemore 1993; Katzenstein 1996; Klotz 1995; Sikkink 1991; Yee 1996), a "boomerang effect," in which local actors invoke transnational support (Keck and Sikkink 1998), and a "spiral model" of human rights change, in which international and local actors work together to exert pressure upon errant states (Risse, Ropp, and Sikkink 1999). This admirable body of work addresses the fundamental critique that the human rights system is strong in standard setting, as seen in the proliferation of human rights treaties and their adoption by large numbers of states, but fundamentally weak in enforcement. At the same time, the pervasive focus on implementation has unwittingly eclipsed empirical efforts to understand political processes through which human rights standards are developed and which is likely changing with globalization. Instead, work on the implementation of human rights necessarily and intentionally takes the norms in question for granted, typically focusing on well-established civil and political rights. In empirical studies, therefore, preexisting human rights standards are integrated into national contexts to become accepted national norms.

In contrast, in the case studied in this book the root problem was not inadequate enforcement of international standards but rather the inadequacy of international standards themselves. Violence against women had long been neglected in human rights treaties, a condition lamented in feminist scholarship particularly in the early to mid 1990s (Charlesworth, Chinkin, and Wright 1991; Bunch 1993; Cook 1994; Peters and Wolper 1995) and now widely documented by human rights scholars and activists. By 1993 the problem had just begun to be conceptualized as an international issue, primarily by women activists engaging in comparative work and including attempts to bring the issue to international forums. But it remained a side issue lacking international agreement and explicit standards. Generally, violence against women was still considered a cultural prerogative. So quite simply, there were no gender-specific international standards on violence to cascade down to states and little in the way of the international forces typically described as key to human rights developments. This is not to say that prior gains in human rights did not play a fundamental role in the case studied, for they were clearly compatible with an expanded agenda to protect women from female-specific violence. But they were not at the time sufficiently elaborated or agreed upon internationally to be grafted onto the national context, not to mention integrated into refugee law.

Human rights scholarship on *substantive* expansions of human rights is less developed, having been explored primarily by legal scholars following a positivist tradition. This has produced an extensive number of genealogies of international legal developments, but is largely devoid of political process analysis. More recently, constructivists in international relations have brought politics and nonstate actors to the forefront in studies of "norm building" or "norm emergence," although they offer relatively little empirical work in the area of human rights specifically. This emerging scholarship does not focus on international legal standards per se but rather on norms conceived more broadly as shared assessments. Here international norm building often refers to the spread of new norms across states or in agreements between states. Most studies use genealogy or process tracing to chart the adoption of similar national norms in different states, stressing the influence of "human agency, indeterminacy, chance occurrences, and favorable events" (Finnemore and Sikkink 1998:896). The little theorizing that exists in this area explains norm emergence as the first stage in the norm life cycle. Norms are the product of "international norm entrepreneurs" working from organizational platforms, especially nongovernmental organizations within larger international networks, who persuade a critical mass of key states to become "norm leaders." At the second stage, norm leaders socialize other states, creating a "norm cascade," until finally at the third stage the norm becomes internationalized or taken for granted (Finnemore and Sikkink 1998).

The essential downward international pressure upon states by international actors (international nongovernmental organizations [INGOs] and foreign states) and the focus on norm cascades and norm diffusion across states are reminiscent of geographic expansions of human rights. In this process, just as the latter takes existing *international* standards for granted, here researchers take for granted the substance of the new norms emerging in and across national contexts. Although they explain that "new norms never enter a normative vacuum but instead emerge in a highly contested normative space where they must compete with other norms" (Finnemore and Sikkink 1998:897), they do not offer empirical analysis of actual political discourses, framing processes and strategies that they note are needed to articulate the new norm and persuade states to become "norm leaders" in the first place. Neither do they analyze whether or how a new national norm may be framed and promoted as a morally universal "international norm" applicable in various countries or fit for international law, rather than simply a domestic norm worthy of imitation elsewhere. As one critic observes, "how persuasion occurs, how NGOs exert influence, and whether in fact these are the primary vehicles of normative change among states remain open issues" (Bob 2005:11). As a result, little empirical or theoretical attention is given to "norm resistance" (Elgström 2000) and the contentious political processes through which new norms are actually created, and in this sense work on the implementation of existing human rights is far more developed. This is surprising given that norm entrepreneurs are conceived as actors who offer new conceptualizations and cognitive framings of norms through a process of argumentation and persuasion. Indeed, perhaps the most captivating aspect of the idea of norm entrepreneurs is the question of how they actually "sell" their novel idea or convince states to buy into it. How do potential international norms get articulated *as such*, by whom, and through what processes? Why does this occur in specific times and places when many grievances have existed long before and have been widespread? At what point do existing national norms become conceived as fit for the international arena?

These key questions remain to be answered. Their relevance is perhaps no clearer than in the case of various "women's rights," which emerged nationally in many states while long remaining a cultural or national prerogative when considered internationally. I explore these questions specifically in a case that we know became internationally significant, thus in a sense taking for granted the later internationalization of the new domestic norm that resulted. This is possible because we know that subsequent international standards as well as national standards across a significant set of states were modeled after developments in Canada. Thus the question here is how and why specific Canadian women's rights were articulated *as human rights* in national refugee policy, in a case that triggered international developments.[15]

Rather than taking either international or national standards for granted, this book is concerned with the political and dialectical processes in early articulations of particular rights as human rights—that is, in a universal moral sense and a fit subject for international law—and how such articulations get institutionalized for the first time in states that become what Finnemore and Sikkink (1998) describe as "norm leaders." This necessarily involves close attention to political processes at the national level as "international norm entrepreneurs" influence a key state, although here "international" refers to the norm being conceived as international, rather than to entrepreneurs as necessarily international actors.

This captures a potential global standard's early articulation as a viable and legitimate human right in the moral sense and its early translation into institutional forms (law, policy, programs, and so on) demonstrative of its human rights viability. It explains how in some cases human rights experimentations at national levels may emerge, triggering more global acceptance and implementation. To be more precise, I refer to outcomes at this earlier stage not as "norms" but as internationally standard-setting precedents. This denotes the setting of new minimum levels of human rights protections around specific issue areas in a manner that, as a precedent, explicitly invites international dialogue and debate. In contrast, domestic change that does not make reference to international applicability or universality may provide an example of a new kind of right that other states may imitate, but does not explicitly engage in human rights debates or necessarily even use human rights language or theorize the rights in question as applicable beyond the domestic setting. For example, Finnemore and Sikkink (1998) describe the genealogy of women's suffrage from the late 1800s to roughly 1950 as a norm cascade as national rights in forty-eight states emerged, but do not refer to women's suffrage being conceived as a human right or universal right, nor do they mention or explain the later adoption of the right in the Convention on the Political Rights of Women in 1952.

In cases of human rights precedents set at the national level, then, if international consensus is later achieved and codified into international law (a kind of upward cascade), a new international standard is born. The eventual geographical expansion of the standard across national contexts (its wider implementation) internationalizes a norm. National precedents of international import may become trigger cases for consensus and standard setting. Such cases must be concrete and actionable, representing true political will around real expansions in human rights toward real beneficiary populations (new human rights protections enacted through policies for a previously neglected issue or group), rather than merely abstract statements of intent ("all people are created equal"), enlightened though they may be. This focus provides essential analysis at the neglected national level in early processes of norm emergence.

The articulation and first expression of institutional commitment to a new standard is as politicized and fraught with conflict as are the more widely documented political pressures to induce states to implement existing international rights. As demonstrated in protracted processes of international lawmaking between states, when states set international precedents they realize the import of international commitments they make and think ahead to the long-term costs and burdens of implementation. Indeed, the pioneering of new rights may even raise a higher degree of political conflict due to the greater risk associated with a lesser ability to predict outcomes when earlier precedents or models are lacking. This reality was well captured by one politician in this study, who early on dismissed the issue of sex persecution by saying simply that it "would be opening a whole can of worms."[16]

The significance of international trigger cases therefore rests on the following. First, an international trigger case depicts a type of human rights change with critical global impacts (substantive expansion of human rights), impacts more far reaching than those in more commonly studied types of human rights change involving the nationalization of existing international human rights. In the latter, human rights change occurs country by country, whereas the former affects the very shape of the international human rights agenda. International trigger cases are underresearched and undertheorized considering their potentially vast impact. At most they are taken for granted in historical and positivist accounts of human rights standard setting, or misconstrued as the acts of purely self-interested states. We need to understand the political processes through which states may come to articulate and project national rights into the international human rights agenda.

Second, trigger cases inherently describe exceptional outcomes: they set precedents, rather than following the norm. As exceptions to the norm, it may be less surprising if they involve different processes and outcomes and occur less commonly. Like the type of trigger case studied here, other human rights standards may be traced back to national political processes in strong states persuaded to exert their influence to shape the international human rights agenda.[17] This supports well-established theories in international relations in which international law necessarily follows state practice (Grotius 1964), but asks how national rights are conceptualized as international.

Third, as widely asserted today, globalization is changing the means, extent, and nature of world politics. The evolving affects on human rights standard setting, whether novel, rare, or common, certainly ought to be explored as part of the larger attempt to come to grips with the processes and impacts of globalization. Given the sheer dearth of empirical evidence in this area, such cases merit thorough analysis. At very least, the existence and significance of international trigger cases should bring some balance to human rights scholars' preoccupation with showing that human rights may influence sovereign states, since, after all, globalization is a two-way street.

From Supranational to National Values and Actors

The focus on downward international pressures for both geographic and substantive expansions of human rights supports a normative bias toward supranational values that this study challenges. Western human rights scholars commonly and fiercely assert that when states implement international human rights their sovereignty is undermined, weakened, eroded, compromised, or otherwise deteriorated, and generally for positive moral reasons (e.g., Henkin 1999; Shen 2000; Ayoob 2002; Schwab and Pollis 2000; for opposing views, see Welch and Monshipouri 2001; Donnelly 2004). This corresponds with broader theories of globalization, in which economic, political, and cultural trends are said to be undermining state sovereignty, though not always to positive effect (see Held and McGrew 2000, 2003). On this matter this book supports the somewhat dissonant arguments by Welch and Monshipouri (2001) and by Donnelly (2004), who argue that state sovereignty is not being undermined because states have never had complete control over international influences. In the case studied here, international migration by women fleeing female-specific violence was arguably not beyond state control. Prior to legal developments in this case, such refugee claimants were simply rejected as "illegitimate" refugees. According to available statistics, by 31 December 2002 a total of only 2,331 claims had been classified as "gender-related" in Canada, of which only 58 percent were accepted (on par with acceptance rates across categories), while 30 percent were rejected and the remainder withdrawn, abandoned, discontinued, or otherwise finalized (IRB 2003). This body of successful claims marks a major step forward but clearly not an unstoppable flood.

The decline-of-sovereignty conclusion, so fundamental to models of human rights change, also fails to account for cases in which national rights are equal to or more progressive than global rights and, far from being undermined, actually reify or influence the global agenda in a positive manner. It is vital to note that in this case asylum seekers did not consciously set out to claim "human rights," but rather to attain the female-specific legal protection already available to Canadian women. Canada, like many other countries that experienced a second wave of feminism in the 1970s, was far ahead of international treaties where violence against women was concerned. By the early 1990s Canada could boast laws and the cooperation of eight governmental departments prohibiting both public and domestic violence against women.[18] But asylum seekers like Thérèse and Nada, as noncitizens, needed to legally justify their right to such protection on human rights grounds. They therefore needed to promote an expanded conceptualization of human rights that reflect more progressive citizenship values. This book argues that, contrary to assumptions among Western human rights scholars, what international migrants really want are rights to specific benefits of membership in a foreign state. That is, "human rights" are a tool, not a goal in themselves.

And at times the national rights and benefits that migrants desire go above and beyond what international human rights have to offer.

As the importance of national change for larger global level developments is not sufficiently recognized, it is no wonder then that the processes and international significance of individuals acting nationally are also underexplored. Indeed, the increasingly heard distinction between "local" actors and transnational advocacy networks (TANs) assumes the former to be citizens wanting to address unfulfilled citizenship rights via recourse to supranational rights. TANs bring to local contexts the pressure of "international-transnational interactions among transnationally operating international non-governmental organizations (INGOs), international human rights regimes and organizations, and Western states" (Risse, Ropp, and Sikkink 1999:17). This leaves little space to account for local actors with transnational agency and impact.

This book argues that when considering cases involving international migration, the significance of nationally superior values and local actors with transnational impact becomes particularly evident. It examines an unrecognized case in which noncitizen asylum seekers made use of national values and had a novel transnational impact. This approach differs from influential human rights studies focusing on recent increases in noncitizen rights. Soysal's *Limits of Citizenship* (1994), Jacobson's *Rights Across Borders* (1996), Sassen's *Losing Control? Sovereignty in an Age of Globalization* (1996), and Benhabib's *The Rights of Others* (2004)[19] all explain rising noncitizen (guest workers, refugees, legal and illegal immigrants) rights as an outcome of the power of international human rights norms to undermine state sovereignty, largely agreeing with broader human rights scholarship. They further see noncitizen rights signaling the emergence of new modalities of membership that transcend the traditional institution of citizenship. These findings, certainly relevant in some cases, do not account for others in which actors seek to expand human rights, nor for the significance of noncitizen politics as such in human rights developments. In contrast this book explains asylum seekers' motivations, examines their transnational "signifying acts," or symbolic and strategic actions, through which they bring cross-cultural relevance to nationally and culturally rooted rights, and explores the collective mobilization tactics that compelled the government to adopt and internationally promote an expanded vision of human rights more in line with its national tradition.[20]

This case signifies a more symbiotic than hierarchical relationship be-

tween national citizenship rights and international human rights and suggests that noncitizens, a population only increasing under globalization, can
play an important and at times vital political role in these processes. The demographic changes wrought by globalization are in many states profound.
In 2005 one in thirty-five people in the world were international migrants,
and from 1990 to 2000 international migration accounted for 89 percent of
population growth in Europe and 75 percent in the United States (GCIM
2005). If the dynamic between national citizenship rights and international
human rights is a reciprocally shaping one in which the pressures of globalization are playing out, we need to better understand how it may be providing the means for new policy actors to push out the parameters of state
responsibility, and with what implications for the development of international human rights (versus merely impacts on citizenship). By remaining
attentive to citizenship–human rights dynamics, we can consider global
trends that may support or challenge noncitizen abilities to draw on either
or both sets of rights, illuminate more thoroughly the relationship between
these rights and their discursive and symbolic transformations, and more
accurately uncover the means—activities, alliances, moral and legal arguments, and political acts—through which human rights may be expanded.

The Way Forward

This study does not constitute a "test" of other explanations of human rights
change; the need for further theorization in this area suggests instead a need
to develop new hypotheses. This study therefore marks a step in the necessary development of a previously neglected area of refugee and human rights
research. The empirical evidence presented enables judgment of the generalizability of existing theories, demonstrating that other globally significant
cases remain to be considered and accounted for and suggesting other critical drivers and outcomes of human rights change. I see findings as comple-
menting and expanding the repertoire of human rights scholarship and
deepening our understanding of human rights change, while at the same
time illuminating and explaining a previously unstudied movement. This
book therefore pursues a dual analytical agenda.

First, to address a broader range of types of human rights change, I
argue, we need to overcome the false dichotomies that plague reigning theories. Chapter 2 examines in detail different types of human rights change in

the context of globalization theory to capture variations that current models neglect and then elaborates an analytical approach amenable to human rights change that is substantive, nationally precedented, and noncitizen based as described here. Specifically, I suggest we need to overcome the disciplinary divide between current models of human rights change and the wider field of social movement studies. The latter is a well-developed resource that unfortunately has not been consistently applied in studies of human rights movement and human rights change. Theories of social movement overcome the dichotomies underlying theories of human rights change by facilitating a systematic analysis of the relation between structure and agency. Social movement analysis isolates the emergence and decline of "political opportunity structures," "mobilizing structures," and "cultural framings" to explain when and how movements emerge and become influential (McAdam, McCarthy, and Zald 1996). The tripartite agency structure of social movements contains none of the methodological limitations of human rights studies that presuppose types and locals of actors and ideologies and can therefore overcome the dichotomies between geographical and substantive expansions, supranational and national values, local and transnational actors. The chapter lays out a means through which this framework may be applied to global human rights change, and more specifically to this case involving international migration, via embedding within the landscape of "migration systems" (Fawcett and Arnold 1987; Castles and Miller 1993; Zolberg, Suhrke, and Agnayo 1989) and by relating refugee policy making to human rights. This reveals the historically symbiotic structures of refugee law and lawmaking, as well as the physical and ideological landscape that asylum seekers must actively negotiate. I argue that the institutional logics of asylum seeking, which require asylum seekers to make claims and bear the burden of proof in host countries with various national traditions of rights, actually encourage and explain their agency in host countries in contrast to conceptions of refugees as victims and "forced" migrants. At the same time, the pressures of globalization are changing the global and national political opportunity, mobilizing and framing structures that asylum seekers rely upon to make successful claims. As a result, asylum seekers' claims may bring discordant national and international norms face to face, making asylum seeking a fruitful terrain for human rights developments.

The second analytical aim of the book is to operationalize this approach, exploring how the refugee movement in question made sex persecution matter. I draw on multiple sources of data and triangulate data sources in my analysis to reduce researcher bias, and employ the case study method to generate rich empirical description on a previously unresearched topic. Data was collected through archival and documentary research and field work in Montreal, Toronto, and Ottawa. Expert informants were identified through the "snowballing" technique whereby a point of saturation in the discovery of participants was reached, targeting primarily campaigners (asylum seekers, lawyers, NGOs, and community organizations) but also government officials. Extensive interviews were conducted, and case histories of asylum seekers who went public were compiled using a combination of interview data, transcripts of refugee hearings, direct observation during campaigns, media coverage, and policy reports. I studied the campaigns as they unfolded in real time while residing in Canada, and in repeat and lengthy return visits to Canada in later years. To further explore the campaigns, including the framing of a new norm and campaigners' policy advocacy, I compiled and analyzed mass media coverage and institutional campaign documents, as well as data on the evolution of international and national refugee law and policy, and a data set of precedent-setting gender-related refugee claims. Chapter 2 concludes by elaborating this methodology and identifying the asylum seekers at the heart of the study.

Chapters 3 through 6 go on to offer detailed empirical analysis that explains this successful international trigger case. I uncover and examine how this nationally powerful movement was contextualized within changing global structural constraints and opportunities that help explain its emergence. I explore political processes through which asylum seekers strategically compelled radical policy change, examining how the movement challenged the global context, its human rights construct, and existing norms, why noncitizens like Thérèse and Nada were able to make claims when they did, and the means through which they bridged national and international values. I consider how they paradoxically challenged internationally accepted limits of states' human rights responsibilities while reifying national-specific cultural values as relevant for the wider international community. The analysis brings us to the heart of this largely undocumented women's refugee movement, in particular evidencing and explaining the much overlooked political agency of asylum seekers with special capacities for the kind of transnational signifying work needed to drive national policy in an international direction.

Chapter 3 explores the changing structure of political opportunities, mobilizing structures, and cultural framings at the global level up to the eve of the Canadian campaigns. It draws on the feminist literature in international relations to map international structural factors and on archival research with primary documents to map and deconstruct the genealogy of soft law discourses on refugee women and the framing of women's refugee movement globally. This illuminates how, despite embedded structural constraints against women refugees, the very logic of status determination processes configures claim making as a linchpin for expanded interpretations of persecution, or human rights abuses. At the same time, key global structural trends suggest that by the early 1990s a critical balance had been reached between static and progressive conceptions of women's rights and between constraints and opportunities for refugee women.

Chapter 4 illuminates changing national-level political opportunity structures, mobilizing structures, and cultural framings critical to the emergence of the sex persecution campaigns. It illuminates the emergence of new resources, rights, and opportunities for women asylum seekers in Canada in the 1980s, including key changes in the domestic political climate that helped mobilize and bridge campaigners from refugee and women's rights circles, and the critical evolution of rights for noncitizens and women that facilitated and shaped the core campaign structure. Chapter 5 unveils why and how asylum seekers and supporters *decided* to campaign and the nature of asylum seekers' influence on other key actors and on the internal political culture of the campaign network as a whole. Asylum seekers' motivating factors as well as key aspects of their participation are illuminated as crucial to the campaigns, ruling out a simplistic conclusion that these asylum seekers were "forced" refugees and thus forced (nonpolitical) actors. Chapter 6 analyzes strategic interactions between the campaign network, the government, and the broader public, including physical and symbolic use of both national rights and values and international human rights and values. This identifies the different campaign phases and how actors actually mobilized policy reform and articulated what were at the time novel human rights in the substantive sense.

The combination of empiricism and theory here reinforces the relevance of gender, migration, and social movement studies to the burgeoning field of human rights and illuminates implications for theories of human rights change. Chapter 7 draws out global policy and theoretical implications for refugee women and women's human rights specifically and for human rights change more broadly. It is my hope that this study will advance understanding of this women's refugee movement and specifically how it made sex persecution matter, open renewed attention to potentially positive impacts of strong states and national values so often dismissed outright as "culturally relative" or "culturally imperialistic," and stimulate new interest in noncitizen politics within the human rights field, all with the aim of further engaging and facilitating the normative evolution of human rights under globalization.

Chapter 2
Human Rights, Social Movement, and Asylum Seeking

No [other] paradox of contemporary politics is filled with more poignant irony than the discrepancy between the efforts of well-meaning idealists who stubbornly insist on regarding as "inalienable" those human rights which are enjoyed only by the citizens of the most prosperous and civilized countries, and the situation of the rightless themselves.

—*Hannah Arendt,* The Origins of Totalitarianism, *1973*

How are human rights developed for specific populations that lack them? Human rights, and human rights abuses more broadly, are increasingly said to be both driven by and driving globalization (Schwab and Pollis 2000; Evans 2001; Brysk 2002; Howard-Hassmann 2005). Indeed, theories of globalization have had a marked impact on human rights scholarship. The following explores different types of human rights change in the broader context of globalization in order to capture variations that current models neglect. This illuminates how human rights scholarship has absorbed the false dichotomies that plague reigning theories of globalization and helps to explain the blind side toward significant cases of human rights change such as the one considered in this book. I devote significant attention to explaining this blind side, whose implications for theory have been ignored. Social movement analysis offers a means of overcoming these false dichotomies and needs to be brought more squarely into studies of human rights change. I elaborate an analytical framework for the human rights change considered in this book, applying well-established resources of social movement theory specifically to the structural context of international migration systems and refugee movement and exposing the links between refugee movement and human rights change. This enables a systematic examination of political processes in the case studied. The chapter concludes with a discussion of the research strategy.

Human Rights Change Under Globalization

Globalization drives economic, political, informational, cultural, and environmental trends that are increasing the interconnectedness of societies, cultures, and states around the world. Held and McGrew describe it as: "the expanding scale, growing magnitude, speeding up and deepening impact of interregional flows and patterns of social interaction. [Globalization] refers to a shift or transformation in the scale of human social organization that links distant communities and expands the reach of power relations across the world's major regions and continents" (2003:4).

In this, globalization is self-reinforcing; global forces drive the development of global level infrastructure that further facilitates and shapes global forces and trends. In this, increasing international interconnectedness makes international laws and norms increasingly relevant. The latter in turn increase interaction among the world's nations, creating and reinforcing common global patterns of interaction, understanding, and increasingly shared value systems.

Globalization also remains deeply contested, both praised and condemned due to competing perspectives regarding the overarching political agendas that characterize it. What Held and others characterize as "hyper-globalists" largely support the current neoliberal free-market ideological framework often said to drive modern globalization and see globalization optimistically as defining the modern era (Held et al. 2003). On the other hand, "anti-globalists" and neoliberal critics agree that major economic forces are key drivers of globalization but interpret outcomes as reinforcing the dominance of some states and cultures over others, deepening inequality and ultimately driving what are actually rather unglobal outcomes. In this context, Evans (2001:3) argues that in human rights scholarship, "while some studies have attempted to recontextualize human rights as an important aspect of globalization, most, if not all, adopt a neoliberal approach, which tacitly assumes that globalization presents new opportunities for strengthening human security (e.g., Donnelly 1993). Neoliberals tend toward a view of globalization that projects a vision of inexorable progress towards ever increasing levels of 'moral integration,' which parallels processes of economic integration, as normative and moral aspirations converge."

Less commonly, some scholars suggest human rights may actually be less effective under neoliberal globalization trends because purportedly "global" institutions actually reflect traditional, competitive statist logic. Some even posit that if globalization undermines state authority, as many neoliberals claim, "then international law, the law that governs relations between states, has less potential in regulating the practices of non-state transterritorial actors," with negative implications for human rights (Evans 2001:4; see Evans and Hancock 1998). Finally, globalization skeptics often argue that the idea of universal consensus about human rights may not bear out in reality. Rather, Western neoliberalism may treat its own culturally relative doctrine as universal while promoting new global class hierarchies (Evans 2001:4–5; Scholte 1996).

Only more recently has scholarship more explicitly addressed the relationship between globalization and human rights (Brysk 2002, 2005; Brysk and Shafir 2004; Howard-Hassmann 2005).[1] Howard-Hassman argues that the polarized debate about human rights is simply a false one, that whether "globalization as a process is 'good' or 'bad' is as irrelevant as arguing whether the transition from an agrarian to an industrial society in the Western world from the eighteenth to the twentieth century was good or bad. Many complex social changes occurred: some economies were strengthened, some were weakened. Some states rose, some fell. Some social classes and categories benefited, others sank into oblivion."

Indeed, globalization brings both human rights "opportunities and threats" (Brysk 2002). Brysk points toward the recent proliferation of empirical work that illuminates how evolving global trends impact our ability to *address* human rights violations as well as violator's ability to *violate* human rights. The former offers new opportunities to implement existing human rights norms in national contexts, limiting violators' capacities to violate. But at the same time, the latter presents new threats to human rights as new global forms and infrastructures for violations emerge, including abuses within global economic forces and within an increasingly complex system that is ever more difficult to manage. Brysk describes "optimists [who] suggest that transnational integration will empower citizen challenges to state power . . . while revisionists assert that globalization reiterates national and/or market exploitation" (Brysk 2002:7; see Falk 1995; Rosenau and Fagen 1997; Bhabha 1998; Burbach, Nuñez, and Kagarlitsky 1997; Brecher and Costello 1994; Mander and Goldsmith 1996). She also distinguishes between "globalization from above" in which international forces drive local changes and "globalization from below" in which local actors seek international support to achieve national human rights change. These processes have various impacts upon human rights, as shown in work by Hunter (1995) and Falk (1994). Still others see globalization as fundamentally transforming world politics "through changing identities, evolving social forms such as networks, and the diffusion of increasingly influential world institutional culture that includes support for human rights" (Brysk 2002:7; see Robertson 1992; Castells 1997; Meyer et al. 1997). Brysk concludes that "different elements and levels of globalization may produce distinct effects of empowerment, exploitation, and evolution" (2002:7).

Underlying these understandings of the relationship between globalization and human rights is the provocative and more widely held conclusion that globalization is undermining state sovereignty and therefore fundamentally transforming the nature and processes of world politics, both to positive and negative effects.[2] Human rights scholarship has absorbed the decline-of-sovereignty claim most wholeheartedly, observing that transformations of state sovereignty affect human rights opportunities and threats, and that human rights further undermine state sovereignty. States have less ability to protect their citizens from abuses by, for example, global market forces including international financial institutions and multinational corporations (Evans 2001), and from the use of global transportation and other technologies by nonstate actors for purposes such as international trafficking and the international drug trade (Brysk 2005). At the same time, states are the key implementers of human rights, and their authority to resist international pressures to conform to international human rights law is said to be declining. Thus, following the two-way process that globalization engenders, human rights (norms, laws, institutions, practices) reinforce globalization by undermining state sovereignty. Donnelly (2004:1) thoroughly documents the predominance of this claim among human rights scholars:[3]

International human rights obligations are regularly presented as assaulting (Mills 1998:10; Clapham 1999:533; Cardenas 2002:57), challenging (Aceves 2002; Butenhoff 2003:215–216), besieging (Weiss and Chopra 1995), undermining (Schwab and Pollis 2000:214), busting (Lutz 1997:652), weakening (Jacobsen and Lawson 1999), chipping away at (Kearns 2001:522), compromising (Krasner 1999b:125), contradicting (Forsythe 1989:6), breaking down (Bettati 1996:92), breaching (Lyons and Mayall 2003:9), perforating (van Hoof 1998:51), or eroding (Ayoob 2002:93; Henkin 1999:3–4; Lapidoth 1995) state sovereignty, which is portrayed as giving way (Aceves 2002:265), even surrendering (Lauterpacht 1968 [1950]:304–311), to higher human rights norms that "provide legal and moral grounds for disregarding the sovereign rights of States" (Shen 2000:435).

This is said to occur much in the same way that economic globalization is undermining state sovereignty and further opening pathways for the global market. It supports claims across a wide range of disciplines that suggest global forces, particularly the global economy but also trends such as the growth of global level institutions, global migration, global communications and information technologies, are weakening and fundamentally transforming state sovereignty.[4]

Such findings are all the more significant given that perhaps the greatest critique of the human rights system has long been its lack of enforcement power. There are encouraging signs that states can be persuaded to respect human rights, and in some cases forced to do so (e.g., the use of military intervention in cases of genocide). These means have become a major focus of study in the interest of developing empirically driven approaches toward ensuring state compliance with human rights and explaining outcomes. In this, the more nascent human rights scholarship that explicitly incorporates a globalization framework has begun mapping patterns of human rights violations and responses to them and identifying aspects of globalization that do or may challenge and empower the international human rights regime, including potentially fundamental changes to the way the international politics is conducted.

However, existing treatments do not present a comprehensive picture of the relationship between globalization and human rights because they primarily address only one of the two functions of the international human rights system, implementation (promoting, monitoring, and enforcing human rights), while largely overlooking standard setting (creating human rights laws and norms). The United Nations human rights system has been praised for normative strength, seen in the proliferation of international human rights declarations and conventions and their regular and repeated endorsement by an increasing number of states, while heavily criticized for procedural weakness (Donnelly 2003:135). Therefore human rights scholarship has increasingly turned toward the problem of implementation, with a proliferation of empirical work on how international human rights may be integrated into national settings. But in so doing, empirical studies largely assume the legitimacy of existing human rights standards, skirting the question of how the very substance of human rights continues to evolve. Perhaps this is a conscious effort to narrow what is already an enormous and complex field of study or to avoid raising complex issues that may undermine efforts to achieve implementation.

Beginning from the standpoint that human rights have achieved international consensus and universal legitimacy certainly seems a more powerful starting point for those seeking to promote and explain the diffusion and implementation of human rights. Indeed, human rights scholars increasingly discuss the "socialization of human rights in national contexts" (Risse, Ropp, and Sikkink 1999) and processes through which the cultural legitimacy of universal human rights can be established in diverse social contexts (An-Naim 1992). Typically these processes are said to include a combination of national and international pressures for states to conform, through which international human rights principles get absorbed into national settings.

The lack of empirically focused attention on how globalization affects *standard-setting processes*, or substantive as opposed to geographical expansions of human rights, creates a blind spot, with implications for both theory and implementation. To address this gap we need to consider substantive human rights change under the lens of globalization. How are global infrastructures and the increasing intensity and deepening impact of international interactions facilitating dialogue, information sharing, and participation in the identification and articulation of *new* rights? What are states' roles in this process? Is their sovereignty sidelined here too, and if so, is that negative or positive? What threats may globalization pose to the process of standard setting?

By human rights standard setting I mean the processes through which serious abuses to individuals' dignity, security, and well-being are identified as legitimate subjects of human rights discourse and set within the parameters and frameworks of protections in international human rights ideology and, ultimately, law. These parameters and frameworks evolve around the notion of universality, which Donnelly (2003:1) describes as consisting of both a moral and international normative aspect. Moral universality emerges when individuals are entitled to a right simply by being human, and this right is held against all other persons and institutions as one of the highest moral rights. International normative universality emerges when a right is actually accepted as an ideal standard through a strong show of international legal consensus among states.

Table 2.1 summarizes recognized opportunities and threats that globalization may pose to human rights implementation and also suggests a number of opportunities and threats that globalization may pose to the process of standard setting.

TABLE 2.1. IMPACT OF GLOBALIZATION ON HUMAN RIGHTS

Key functions of international human rights system	*Globalization impacts*	
	Opportunities	**Threats**
Implementation (monitoring and enforcement of global level rights)	New or improved global mechanisms for monitoring, reporting, pressuring, and enforcing rights, as well as for participating in implementation. Geographical expansion of existing rights into new national contexts.	New/expanded violations of rights facilitated by global infrastructures. Increasing complexity under globalization always ahead of learning. Sheer abundance of information and competing demands for attention overwhelm and paralyze a nascent human rights system. Limitations imposed by fetal global governance and continuing geopolitics. Paralysis or failure to keep pace with geographical expansions of existing rights.
Standard setting (identification and articulation of global level rights)	New or improved global infrastructures and international interactions that facilitate dialogue, information sharing, cross-cultural understanding, and participation. Expanded or new forums (nascent global civil society and global governance) that enable new actors to share views and information and to promote progressive articulations of rights. Increasing body of relevant legal precedents and international agreements upon which to build. Substantive expansion of "human rights" as internationally understood.	Paralysis arising from increasing number of international actors with different perspectives. Hidden assumptions and agendas behind international dialogues and imbalance of political power among states in nascent (or absent) forms of global governance. Paralysis, cultural bias, or retraction of substantive understandings of human rights.

In the area of implementation, the growing body of empirical studies suggests globalization influences human rights practices through a variety of means, including: facilitating the spread of international norms into new national contexts (e.g., Adler 1987; Haas 1990; Finnemore 1993; Katzenstein 1996; Klotz 1995; Sikkink 1991; Yee 1996); pressures exerted through foreign policy, quiet diplomacy, sanctions, and aid conditionality (e.g., Vincent 1986); humanitarian intervention (e.g., Wheeler 2000; Power 2002); the work of nongovernmental organizations (Korey 1998; Welch 2001); international or transnational nongovernmental actors (Sikkink 1993a; Keck and Sikkink 1998; Risse, Ropp and Sikkink 1999); and global civil society more broadly (Brysk 2002). The sum total of such international means and actors have been described as constituting "transnational advocacy networks," or TANs. TANs encompass international actors, institutions, and foreign governments who support domestic actors and are now widely considered essential to successful domestic struggles for human rights (Risse, Ropp, and Sikkink 1999). Consequently, human rights change in national contexts is conceived as an outcome of pressures exerted by globalization that enable international human rights to undermine state sovereignty—compelling states to implement human rights and decreasing their ability to refuse. This observation is taken to its extreme in the case of noncitizens, whose increasing access to rights in financially and politically powerful states (whose sovereignty might be thought more resistant to external influence) is said to evidence the power of human rights to weaken or transfigure the institution of citizenship through which states traditionally set parameters for membership and access to human rights protection. New "postnational," "transnational," and "flexible" forms of membership are said to be emerging, oriented around international rather than national rights (Soysal 1994; Jacobson 1996; Benhabib 2004:217).

In contrast, human rights scholarship concerned with standard setting has long been predominantly positivist, although recently new constructivist accounts of standard setting and "norm building" have emerged. In the former, standard setting is understood as occurring at the intergovernmental level among state members of international bodies, resulting in the creation of international law. International law refers to formal contracts between states that arise through negotiations between specific state parties and/or within intergovernmental organizations made up of member states. Scholarly work on human rights lawmaking focuses on processes through which treaties are negotiated and agreed upon by states and international bodies, most commonly tracing the genealogy of resulting, often cumulative legal developments. State representatives at the United Nations and including appointed members of working groups propose subjects of human rights, seek input and data, compile information and reports, propose legal solutions, and negotiate human rights laws and declarations.

In more recent work, members of intergovernmental bodies are increasingly seen to be influenced by transnational activists, nongovernmental organizations, and global civil society, which provide information, make policy recommendations, raise media awareness, and lobby key international players (e.g., Korey 1998; Welch 2001; Brysk 2005), although opinions on NGO impact are divided. Transnational advocacy networks (Sikkink 1993a) are also said to include "international norm entrepreneurs" who persuade key states to adopt new norms in national practice, at times prior to their institutionalization in international law, becoming "norm leaders" that socialize other states and diffuse the norm across the international arena (Keck and Sikkink 1998). Constructivist work on norm emergence and diffusion takes us a step earlier in the standard-setting process.

In all these processes globalization is inherently considered a positive force. It is evident that new or expanded global infrastructures, forums, and international interactions facilitate dialogue, information sharing, crosscultural understanding, and participation in standard setting and norm emergence. A wider range of actors can more than ever before share views and information and participate in the elaboration of human rights, not least as seen in the expansion from 56 state members of the United Nations in 1948 to the current membership of 191, each increasingly susceptible to nongovernmental pressures.

Critical analyses of the United Nations system in recent years also suggest some negatives. The Sixtieth Anniversary UN Reform Project underscores the threat of paralysis arising from an increasing number of international actors with different perspectives, needs, and wants resulting in blocked or stalled negotiations on key treaties. In recent debates over "Asian values," for example, Asian countries articulated an alternative approach to human rights that, while accepting the universality of human rights, reaffirms the sovereign authority of the state and asserts human rights founded on explicitly Asian traditions. Some political scientists observe the continuing reality of geopolitics and the danger of potentially hidden assumptions or agendas behind new norms and laws that emerge due to the imbalance of political power among states in what is at most a very nascent form of global governance, even if they do support the ideal of universal human rights.

These are all fairly intuitive and significant impacts of globalization upon human rights standard setting, which can be inferred from relevant scholarship. A remaining gap emerges due to lack of empirical research on actual processes through which states are persuaded to articulate particular rights as explicitly international in nature rather than merely national. Processes of identifying, articulating, and promoting particular visions of rights as "human rights" are not the same as processes of formulating and negotiating those articulations into international treaties. International norms and laws are preceded by the very process of generating knowledge about and identifying particular issues *as legitimate subjects of international concern.* The founder of modern international law, Hugo Grotius (1964) recognized that historically international law always follows changes to social and political norms, rather than preceding them; in other words, it is the codification of existing forms of behavior and practice (see Evans 2001:54). But in the creation of the United Nations a paradox emerged. The UN engages with ideas about a future normative order and in this sense may fail to reflect the reality of current practice (Watson 1976). The process of identifying issues relevant to this future normative order is thus inherently and intensely political as it involves promoting and selecting some issues as worthy of international codification and not others. Equally contentious is the process through which individual states may develop, through national political processes and domestic struggle, the political will to engage with and promote particular issues internationally and to generate viable institutional options for the promotion of those rights that demonstrate their potential. The empirical study of this level of human rights development, substantive expansions of human rights in international trigger cases, has been sorely neglected.[5] Even constructivist accounts, including work on TANs, while referring to persuasion fail to explore actual processes (Bob 2005), including the articulation of new norms within relevant national and cultural frameworks, and the ways this framing evolves to respond to "norm resistance" (Elgström 2000). They take for granted the new norms in question, examining their spread across states but not the political struggles to articulate and develop norms in a manner convincing to states.

What are the political processes that drive state norm leaders to identify and articulate particular violations of human dignity and security as legitimate subjects for global human rights and to promote them as such? This question is key to understanding why states may invest in promoting global issues of seemingly lesser concern to national security (such as women refugees), or issues that in the long run may even cost them, how they choose some issues and ignore others, and how the changing nature of world politics under globalization is affecting these processes.

I suggest that globalization is transforming what is essentially a dialectical and political process of conceptualizing preexisting national rights as legitimate subjects for human rights. In this process, sovereign states and domestic political processes maintain a critical if not dominant role both in shaping the articulation of new rights conceived as "universal," and later promoting these rights at the international level. At the same time, globalization increasingly makes previous human rights advances the subject of wider national debates involving civil society and, in so doing, influences the nature of popular participation and the shaping of later human rights agendas. Participation is spreading from the intergovernmental and international level down to national and even local levels where civil society is increasingly educated about human rights and may seek not only to get their own governments to implement human rights, but to promote particular visions of human rights. This feeds into processes of global standard setting and subsequently the potential expansion, paralysis, or retraction of human rights as internationally understood. Therefore, not only does globalization facilitate the emergence of the much discussed *transnational* and global forms of civil society aimed at influencing standard setting at the international level and transnational forms of advocacy networks aimed at influencing national implementation of rights. But as well, *national* constituencies play a fundamental role in shaping the stances states bring to the international bargaining table, as well as the stances of other transnational actors that may become influential at that level (international NGOs). Altogether, although not all states will ultimately be equally influential, the increasing interaction between local and global, near and distant players, forces and pressures that globalization heralds is likely to increase state participation in standard setting and to create new sources of pressure upon states to articulate and promote what may be nationally specific or nationally foreign rights as new, refined, or expanded international standards.

This process evidently has not only potentially positive outcomes but also potentially negative outcomes. Although human rights scholars, practitioners, and activists loudly proclaim the achievement of international consensus on what are subsequently considered "universal" human rights, the developing paths for participation and input into the shaping of human rights can also result in biased human rights agendas geared toward the interests of the more politically and financially powerful states and in conflict-ing or contracting human rights agendas. The dominance of Western state agendas on human rights historically has been well documented and engaged in both positive (see Donnelly 2003) and negative light (see Evans 2001), al-though implications for claims that human rights are undermining state sov-ereignty have not been addressed, nor have the potential impacts of changing world political processes under globalization more broadly.

In this book, the suggested approach toward understanding the rela-tionship between human rights and globalization does not necessarily con-tradict claims that human rights are undermining or eroding state sovereignty, but it does nuance them. Human rights *may* be eroding state sovereignty in certain respects and, more likely, to different extents and ef-fects around different types of issues in different parts of the world. Indeed, it is debatable that states are undermined if pressured to better comply with particular values they themselves promoted based on national experience. So perhaps more accurately, state sovereignty is being *transformed* by new obli-gations to comply with human rights, as Donnelly has suggested (2004). He argues that state sovereignty has in practice never implied absolute state con-trol over a territory but, rather, its decision-making authority. When states choose to comply with international pressures, it may be within their author-ity and often their interests to cooperate. Similarly Welch and Monshipouri argue that "to adapt national sovereignty to the requirements of human rights is fraught with paradoxes. Although the number of states that have rat-ified human rights instruments has increased, ratification cannot simply be equated with compliance. Without states' consent and actions, no funda-mental obligation to protect and promote human rights can be fulfilled. An effective and strong state can, in certain situations, be a precondition for the respect and promotion of human rights. . . . Similarly, an effective and ac-countable state has the potential to withstand the negative pressures of the globalizing trend" (2001:375).

We need to look more closely at how state sovereignty continues to play a major role in setting human rights *agendas*, in potentially negative or posi-tive ways, and how its role in this may be transformed and evolved under globalization. In this sense the approach here contrasts with a purely opti-mistic, universalist approach that takes agreements among states as evidence of international consensus, casts dialectical outcomes as imposing interna-tional rights upon errant or nonobliging states, and concentrates on how er-rant states are compelled to conform. This is a "top-down" process in which the international community pressures for national change, or a "bottom-up" process (perhaps a misnomer) in which national actors claim preexisting international rights and garner the support of international actors—the so-called "boomerang effect" (Keck and Sikkink 1998). Rather, the approach here brings a universalist flavor to realist, neoliberalist, and globalization skeptics' interpretations of the impact of globalization on human rights, which see human rights agendas driven essentially by geopolitics and world markets, lacking truly global or universal moral underpinnings. Realists and globalization skeptics "stress the continuing power and significance of national governments to regulate international flows" (Steiner and Alston 2000:1307) and to shape international agendas. A universalist spin on this casts global universal normative aspirations as one possible positive outcome of state influence; biased origins do not necessarily mean biased or unworthy outcomes.

The approach here therefore builds on both state-centered and universalist approaches, illuminating a third, rather intuitive, impact of globalization upon human rights: the increasing extensity, intensity, velocity, and impact of interactions between state-level and international-level rights, values, and actors bring new opportunities for human rights to be substantively developed and expanded, or as the case may be, contracted and withdrawn from the international arena. In this process, not only may human rights increasingly influence state compliance and change the face of national rights, expanding the reach of human rights around the world, but so too may states, national rights, and national values increasingly influence the shape of human rights as internationally understood.

Underlying this approach are premises about the nature and origins of "universal" human rights that are largely institutionalist and constructivist. Historically there is an impressive array of moral and political philosophies on the origins of human rights, including "natural rights" theory,[6] "human needs" approaches (Maslow 1970), and more recent "capabilities" (Nussbaum and Sen 1993; Nussbaum 1997) and "constructivist" approaches (Donnelly 1985; Finnemore and Sikkink 1998). Constructivists claim norms emerge through dialectical processes rather than by justifying categorizations or natures of rights from purely moral and philosophical standpoints. Relevant approaches include theories of "overlapping consensus" (Rawls 1996; Donnelly 2006), foundationalist approaches (Donnelly 2003), and dialogical and iterative processes of achieving intra- and intercultural legitimacy (An-Naim 1992). A constructivist approach has universalist moral aspirations but explains our understanding of human rights as nevertheless historically and culturally contingent. It is therefore attentive to the diversity, complexity, and historical variability of cultural and historical factors that shape these universal aspirations. Consequently, as An-Naim explains, "normative universality in human rights should neither be taken for granted, nor abandoned in the face of claims of contextual specificity or cultural relativity" (2002:79–80). Donnelly describes the "relationship between human nature, human rights, and political society" as "dialectical": "Human rights shape political society, so as to shape human beings, so as to realize the possibilities of human nature, which provided the basis for these rights in the first place. . . . The essential point is that 'human nature' is seen as a moral posit, rather than a fact of 'nature,' and a social project rooted in the implementation of human rights" (2003:16).

To this context this book brings analysis of the neglected political processes through which national rights become conceived and promoted as "universal" and provides substantiating evidence. I examine an internationally significant case that helps us better understand how rights are actually battled out, negotiated, and agreed on at the neglected national level in the context of globalization. "Universalization" of rights, in my reading, is essentially a process of "globalization" of rights, where cultures and states increasingly interact, cooperate or compete for control over and the building of consensus about dominant international norms and their diffusion across global society. Ideally, outcomes should reflect a more consensual than competitive process, but ultimately the "good" of the resulting norms are what matters insofar as they increase rather than decrease respect for human life. I focus more specifically on understanding how substantively new and expanded human rights are made viable through national example. In this respect, globalization not only may empower or challenge implementation of existing human rights, but may also reveal the deficiencies and limits in the substance of human rights at any point in time and generate new possibilities for improving, expanding, and refining this substance. I examine political processes through which debates about new human rights were generated in an internationally significant case, involving new and broader ranging actors enabled through previous rights gains at both national and international levels, rights whose interaction is driven by globalization. The attention to national political processes is certainly therefore not exclusive of global forces and trends; it is conceived as part of larger globalization processes that bring national and international arenas face to face and through which new and expanded human rights are generated.

When we examine cases in which the substance of human rights is expanded and made institutionally viable, keeping one eye on the reality that formulations of international human rights are historically contingent, we find that in some cases, far from being undermined by human rights, the significance of states, national rights, and national values emerges as strongly as ever both as a vehicle for and example of possible formulations of human rights. Human rights may be changing the nature of state sovereignty and citizenship, but so too are the latter changing human rights. This points toward a much more dialectical and at times symbiotic relationship between national and international rights and pressures (strategies and actors) emerging under globalization. Human rights are historically contingent, and we need to better understand how globalization is affecting not only implementation and state sovereignty, but the limits of human rights themselves and the political processes through which we determine, agree on, and change those limits.

The increasing complexity of national and international level interactions also brings new actors into the process of substantive expansions in human rights. The dictatorship of the enlightened, in which a relatively few but progressive heads of state negotiated new rights for individuals at the world level in the post-World War years, may be changing. National civil society today (like the global civil society of transnational actors) is more educated about rights, more enabled to participate in dialogue and to press for preferred visions that its members want their own government to promote as internationally relevant. They understand more clearly than ever the links between individuals in one state and the rest of the world in which it is no longer enough to have rights protected at the state level; rights not protected internationally are rights at risk in a global society. Finally, national civil societies today are more culturally diverse, and their multicultural members wield more rights that give them greater political voice, than ever before. This facilitates a greater number of perspectives in national politics that become relevant for global human rights.

The implications of the world's increasingly multicultural national populations have not been engaged in scholarship on human rights standard setting despite the dramatic rise in numbers and economic and political influence of international migrants. Global migration trends suggest a force with which we have barely begun to contend. In 2005 the Global Commission on International Migration reported to the United Nations that there are over 200 million international migrants, counting only those who have lived outside their country for more than one year and including 9.2 million refugees. This is equivalent to the population of the fifth largest country, Brazil, or one in thirty-five people in the world. And their numbers are increasing, up from 82 million in 1970. Moreover, from 1990 to 2000, international migration accounted for 56 percent of the population growth in the developed world; it accounted for a whopping 89 percent of population growth in Europe and 75 percent in the United States. In 2004, immigrants sent home up to $300 billion in informal remittances and about $150 billion in formal transfers of remittances, the latter alone amounting to almost triple the value of official development assistance and the second largest source of external funding for developing countries after foreign direct investment (GCIM 2005). Finally, noncitizen migrants are increasingly exerting their "right to rights," as the 2005 and 2006 mass protests in the United States and in France and a proliferation of academic work on the rise of noncitizen rights attest (Brubaker 1992; Soysal 1994; Rees 1995; Bulmer and Rees 1996; Boeri, Hanson, and McCormick 2002). Politicians, academics, and often panicked publics increasingly observe pressures exerted by noncitizens, both legal and illegal, for greater access to social, political, and economic rights in advanced industrial countries as a challenge to the limits of state-defined citizenship parameters that subsequently get undermined (Soysal 1994; Jacobson 1996; Sassen 1998) or expanded (Benhabib 2004) and as a challenge to national economic and political security.

This book explores how, through their presence in foreign countries and increasing access to rights and resources, noncitizen politics may also constitute a new source of pressure on the limits of human rights. Noncitizens may be key candidates for triggering national debates about the limits of human rights as internationally understood, with their firsthand experience of variations in rights across countries and their ability to lend or withhold cultural legitimacy regarding host country formulations of rights and values that contrast with international standards (being narrower or wider). While there may be many motivations for doing so, two self-interested reasons are to encourage the improvement of world standards for application to their countries of origin and to themselves as marginalized populations with limited access to rights reserved for citizens in host countries. In this way they may play important roles in shaping long-standing debates about the international legitimacy of conceiving select national values as universal rights, particularly in host countries with financial and political power in the world community and subsequently with greater clout to influence the international human rights agenda. This turns the age-old battle against cultural relativism on its head and describes a process opposite to that most commonly studied by human rights scholars: here culturally specific national rights are not necessarily the enemy of universal rights as popularly and commonly implied, nor are national values and state sovereignty necessarily undermined by human rights. Rather, universal rights are themselves still evolving, and to further this process we need to be attentive to culturally specific formulations of rights that may help to push out the frontiers of human rights. Noncitizens can help us to do this.

Noncitizen politics can be explored in the shaping of "institutionalized cultural rules"; in an institutionalist perspective, the institutional structure of society "creates and legitimates the social entities that are seen as 'actors.' That is, institutionalized cultural rules define the meaning and identity of the individual and the patterns of appropriate economic, political, and cultural activity engaged in by those individuals. They similarly constitute the purposes and legitimacy of organizations, professions, interest groups, and states, while delineating lines of activity appropriate to these entities. All of this material has general cultural meaning in modern systems and tends to be universal across them, so that all aspects of individual identity, choice, and action . . . are depicted in the institutional system as related to the collective purposes of progress and justice" (Meyer, Boli and Thomas 1994:9).

Noncitizen contributions to political debates about cultural legitimacy become viable and meaningful precisely because of their noncitizen status, rather than being necessarily limited by it. By making claims on states, noncitizens raise questions about which rights ought to be made more universally accessible and morally relevant. Of course, not all noncitizens can or do raise such debates or become influential upon doing so, so we need to better understand how and when they do.

Social Movement for Human Rights: An Analytical Framework

Having laid out the principles guiding the case studied here, characterized as *substantive*, *nationally precedented*, and *noncitizen based*, an alternative approach to analyzing it is now needed. Social movement theory, which enjoys an older and more well established tradition than theories of human rights change specifically, can be fruitfully and systematically applied to overcome the false dichotomies that currently characterize human rights scholarship.

Social movement analysis has long been used to explain social and political change occurring in national and local contexts, and it is now increasingly applied to more transnational movements.[7] Human rights change of the type considered in this book is inherently global, although necessarily involving nationally rooted actions and mobilization; that is, theoretical and policy impacts are transnational in nature, and target audiences and core actors are both national and transnational.

Social movement theories explain how the structural context is used and resources and ideologies mobilized around particular collective identities and aims, including policy aims. They identify the structural context while also focusing on the *agency* of policy actors, that is, the *use* of the structural context.[8] McAdam, McCarthy, and Zald's (1996) widely credited approach describes actors' use of *political opportunity structures, mobilizing structures*, and *framing processes*. This represents a synthesis of two previously separate bodies of social movement theory, New Social Movement (NSM) and Resource Mobilization (RM) theory, resulting in a structural-historical and identity oriented approach that is also attentive to institutional and noninstitutional resources and their strategic use. NSM theory focuses on the long term—*why* movements develop—postulating this question is best understood at the macro level as *new* political identities coagulate around changing social grievances corresponding to broad sociopolitical and technological changes of postindustrial societies. Movements are essentially cultural struggles for control over the production of meaning and the constitution of collective identities (see Melucci 1989; Touraine 1981; Nedelmann 1984; Offe 1985; Habermas 1987). RM theory concentrates on short and intermediate term variables and the processes through which *preexisting* grievances are translated and mobilized into goals and action. It explores, for example, the necessary preexisting and developed resources, *how* resources and political opportunities are operationalized, participant recruitment, strategic political-entrepreneurial interaction between movements and existing political processes and structures (see Tilly 1978; Gamson 1975; Oberschall 1973; McAdam 1982; McCarthy and Zald 1979).

According to McAdam, McCarthy, and Zald (1996), the structure of *political opportunities* describes the variety of institutional structures and informal power relations in a given issue area, which shapes the interaction of collective interests and institutionalized politics. *Mobilizing structures* refers to the particular formal and informal structures or "vehicles . . . through which people mobilize and engage in collective actions" (McAdam,

McCarthy, and Zald 1996: 3), such as NGOs or legal structures and institutionalized claim-making processes. And *framing processes* describe the ways culture, identity, and politics are "framed" for a particular political purpose within or as a challenge to the structure of salient ideas and ideologies. These dimensions provide various opportunities and constraints for individuals and groups to engage in successful political actions and thus shape vehicles for action, ideas and identity, institutional structures, and power relations. The aims and outcomes of their endeavors may be broad social change, and/or particular vehicles encouraging social change, such as legislation and policy. They also operate in a context where national and international discourses, norms, and institutions may interact. The effects of globalization are pertinent to nationally rooted social movement and policy processes because globalization helps shape "institutions as cultural rules giving collective meaning and value to particular entities and activities, integrating them into the larger schemes. . . . [The] patterns of activity and the units involved in them (individuals and other social entities) [are] constructed by such wider rules" (Meyer, Boli, and Thomas, 1994:10). Wider rules or environments include those of (1) world society and its dominant rules and ideologies, as well as the organizations and professions that structure these, that is, those emphasizing world level human rights ideologies; (2) universalistic ideologies and scientific doctrines that may also be worldwide and involve general or universal claims to authority; and (3) arrangements that in fact aggregate to the world level because of common clauses or diffusion processes, that is, because interrelations among nation-states make changes widespread, such as ideas, politics, and practices regarding women's rights (Meyer 1994:30).

Political opportunity structures, mobilizing vehicles, and framing processes are *changing* structures (e.g., under the influence of globalization, which creates standardizing human rights law, international and ethnic organizations, and ideologies of multiculturalism linked to citizenship and women's rights), and this explains the emergence, development, and subsequent nature and extent of influence by political actors in a specific time and place. As structures and cultures change, new opportunities and constraints for political action emerge. Changes occur both over the long term as the result of broad historical change and the development of new meanings and identities (NSM theory) and in the intermediate-term mobilization of resources and political opportunities to address grievances (RM theory), affecting national and international levels and their interrelations.

What social movement theory needs for application to the global level is fairly simple: (1) No explicit designation of actors as assumed citizens; and (2) an institutional and patterned map of typical interactions and relations within the global arenas involved in particular movements studied. This enables us to draw reasonable boundaries around the otherwise insurmountable task of analyzing all possible global factors and actors and to produce a more feasible framework for inclusion of particular factors and actors as more critical and worthy of attention than others.

Following these two caveats, the parameters of social movement theory may be applied to the more specific contexts of asylum seeking and the political action and policy process under consideration by laying out the landscape of "international migration systems"—global to national arenas, patterns of interaction, institutions, and actors—as well as their relation to human rights. By so doing, the collective identity of asylum seekers, and the stable and changing nature of the structural context (political opportunities, mobilizing structures, framing processes) where asylum seeking takes place, can be explored and its use by asylum seekers analyzed to determine factors shaping the rise of sex-based asylum seeking and its human rights impact.

Social Movement and Asylum Seeking: The Institutional Logic of Migration Systems

To understand political processes of human rights change that occurred through international migration and refugee movement in particular, we need to lay out the institutional and political systems asylum seekers traverse and key premises about their roles as actors within these systems. I suggest that the refugee policy-making process as captured in "migration systems" theories that emerged in the 1980s can be viewed essentially as a political process that brings domestic needs, interests, and culturally relative norms face to face with international events, "universal" norms, and international actors. Therefore refugee policy making and the asylum seeking central to it constitute fruitful political terrain for negotiating national and international rights, at times resulting in fundamental political and policy challenges.

Migration Systems and Refugee Policy Development

The standard-setting refugee definition provided in the 1951 United Nations Convention Relating to the Status of Refugees identifies a number of the characteristics of refugees and the conditions characterizing the refugee's situation. Most states have developed national refugee policy around this definition. Asylum seekers falling outside this definition may not only remain invisible to our conception of just what a refugee is or what "makes" refugees, but may have their chances of survival seriously threatened. Policies themselves "make" some asylum seekers into formal refugees eligible for protection, while excluding others. The issue of refugee policy development is thus a serious matter, but the political processes and agendas behind an "international politics of migration" only began to be deeply engaged in the 1980s (Hollifield 2000; Loescher 1989; Zolberg, Suhrke, and Aguayo 1989). This was driven by a major theoretical shift in migration studies, which moved away from a causal model (push-pull, demand-supply) to one that incorporated micro- and macrostructural mediating factors.

Resulting collectivist and institutional theories view migration as historical phenomena deeply influenced by globalization, particularly relations between sending and receiving countries and the emerging global economy (see Castles and Miller 1993:19). The idea that migration is structurally determined fostered much more complex, realistic, explanatory, and predictive models of international migration that were more conducive to understanding and predicting not only voluntary migration but forced migration as well. Only then did migration theory begin seriously considering the role of receiving countries in creating or sustaining root causes of refugee flows and in shaping and controlling refugee flows through policy, rather than simply responding to them.

Macrostructural determinants of national and international migratory processes generally include economic and political historical relations and trends between sending and receiving countries and on a global level. They include large-scale institutional factors such as the political economy of the world market and interstate relationships (see, e.g., Bohning 1984; Sassen 1988; Mitchell 1989; Fawcett 1989). International migrations are seen as "embedded in larger geopolitical and transnational economic dynamics" (Sassen 1998:8; 1988). Thus analysts have attempted to identify "the dynamics of the transnational capitalist economy, which simultaneously brings both 'push' and the 'pull'" to migration (Zolberg, Suhrke, and Aguayo 1989:407), economic and political relations and power asymmetries between countries, and prior links between sending and receiving countries, such as colonization, political influence, trade, investment, or cultural ties (Portes and Borocz 1989).

The regulatory laws and structures of both sending and receiving countries also shape international migration flows, while overarching international agreements and conventions help shape both flows and state responses. Zolberg, Suhrke, and Aguayo (1989) refer to the "international refugee regime" as the institutional and policy structures and the ways they were developed in response to changes in the migration system—flows of people, relations between countries, sending-country causes and receiving-country responses—internationally since World War II. It consists of international bodies at global and regional levels, such as the United Nations High Commissioner for Refugees (UNHCR) and the European Commission on Human Rights, and the human rights principles they support (Zolberg, Suhrke, and Aguayo 1989). These create international pressure for state conformity to international human rights conventions and agreements (Sassen 1996), while human rights instruments and organizations exert increasing influence on international and national refugee law (Hathaway 1991b). They also offer individuals legitimacy as "persons" rather than "subjects" of states, thus enabling claim making and potentially conflicting with state-circumscribed parameters of responsibility limited to citizens (see Sassen 1996, 1998; Jacobson 1996; Soysal 1994).

National refugee regimes reflect relations between the migration system as a whole and particular institutional and policy subsystems at the national level, both of which evolve and change over time (Boutang and Papademetriou 1994). Countries have evolved different national responses to the broader migration system, and their immigration and refugee policies subsequently help shape that broader migration system, for instance by compelling, opening, or closing off avenues for international migration. Therefore Boutang and Papademetriou suggest national level migration systems be defined as "the particular combination of types of population flows between countries of departure and arrival . . . along with the rules regulating these flows, and their administration." This definition "allows the interplay of institutional variables to be given an important role," while recognizing that migration policy is highly dependent upon the system in which it operates, suggesting a definition of migration policy as "a subsystem of the migration system." As a subsystem, it "reflects the content of the system, and at the same time is an essential component of its dynamics." The ways receiving-country responses *are formulated* must therefore be understood within the overarching migration system. Migration policy is concerned with controlling "the effects of the migration system and, to some extent . . . the magnitude of international migration movements." But it faces constraints arising "from the nature of the system" and from "the policy's being only a subsystem, which limits what it can achieve" (Boutang and Papademetriou 1994:20).

In this context national immigration policy comprises all actions taken by central and local government on the basis of regulations under the rule of law: treaties, agreements, laws, regulations, and administrative instructions, as well as measures concerning the foreign immigrant population and its descendants (abroad or in the host country). Such regulations may be clear-cut, but the variables of the system itself are not and cannot be controlled. These variables include the attitudes of countries of origin, all refugee flows in time of war, and the influence of interest groups and political parties (Boutang and Papademetriou 1994:20). Other macrostructural factors include interstate relations affecting modernization and anticolonialism, and the globalization of technology and communication (Fawcett and Arnold 1987; Zolberg, Suhrke, and Aguayo 1989; Castles and Miller 1993).

The migration systems approach (Fawcett and Arnold 1987) binds macrostructural approaches together with microstructural approaches developed earlier in sociological studies. The approach is premised on the concept of global interdependence in which linkages between the sending and receiving countries play significant roles, including "state to state relations and comparisons, mass culture connections and family and social networks," exchanges of information, goods, services and ideas (Fawcett and Arnold 1987:456–457). The sets of relations making up international migration take place "not so much . . . between compartmentalized national units as within an overarching system, itself a product of past historical development" (Portes and Borocz 1989:626). The migratory process or system is essentially the result of interacting macro- and microstructures (Castles and Miller 1993:22). Prior to this approach, refugee movements were largely regarded as unpredictable and unstructured events triggered in sending countries. Seen within the larger migration system, "refugee movements, like other international population movements, are patterned by identifiable social forces and hence can be viewed as structured events that result from broad historical processes" (Zolberg, Suhrke, and Aguayo 1989:vi). For example, legacies of colonialism play a major role in civil war and mass displacement, while ex-colonial relationships between countries may result in special treaties and policies on the movement of people between those countries.

The migration system can be summarized as explaining refugee movement through four contiguous elements, each of which must be addressed in this study of sex-based asylum seeking: (1) supranational trends and institutions affecting sending countries and involving receiving countries in relations between states; (2) particular national circumstances and events (including those influenced by international factors) causing refugee-creating situations and underpinning the ways sending countries address them; (3) particular responses of receiving countries in either addressing root causes or dealing with resulting flows through policy; and (4) microstructural determinants of individuals' motivations, needs, and opportunities to seek asylum. Each of these four mediating dimensions shapes or creates "refugees," both in real terms and in discursive or policy terms.

To explain refugee policy development, the first three dimensions have been explored most rigorously. These involve foreign policy considerations and national political agendas arising from the domestic climate, needs, and security measures. Teitelbaum demonstrated three fundamental influences of interstate relations: foreign policy affects international migration; international migration may be used (stimulated, restrained, facilitated, or regulated) as a tool of foreign policy; and foreign policy may reflect the changing constituency of countries due to past migrations (1984:433). For example, most national refugee definitions as well as the 1951 UN definition were formulated around the prevailing Cold War political climate. Refugee policy in Western democratic countries at that time was largely intended to protect persons from countries under communist domination but also to advance anticommunist ideology. International relations and the political agendas of Western states were crucial influences on the UN refugee definition, which was drafted primarily by Western states and initially applied to European countries, the USSR, and the Far East (Melander, 1988:9). It encouraged migration from those countries at a time when communist countries made exit increasingly difficult. International migration policies and practices address "unwittingly or not, both domestic and international issues that have to be dealt with in the domestic arena" (Sassen 1988:7). Receiving countries' chosen policies and attitudes toward migration, and the fluctuations and trends they exhibit, further affect migratory trends. Other key dimensions of refugee policy development include the relative weight of humanitarian concerns (Dacyl 1992), domestic pressures such as pro-immigration lobbies, increasingly from settled immigrant and ethic communities (Baubock 1998), and global pressures to conform with international human rights standards and regional agreements (Sassen 1996 and 1998; Soysal 1994).

In contrast, studies of microstructural determinants of migration have been relatively narrow. They typically look at immigrants and their patterns of assimilation and incorporation once resident in host countries and the economic, social, and political consequences of their presence, often from a sociological perspective (Portes 1995). They neglect motivations, means, and political impacts of asylum seeking and do not explore the relation between international migration and the making of policies, looking instead at existing policies and rights used by international migrants.

The lack of attention to political processes and impacts of asylum seeking upon receiving countries may be a symptom of the fact that, despite the shift to structural theories of refugee movement, refugees are still popularly characterized as forced migrants. This forced image seems to preclude individual agency and political action, detracting from our understanding of why and how refugees seek asylum and their impact on the evolution of refugee policy and underlying sociopolitical norms. The relationship between asylum seekers and refugee policy development is instead characterized as indirect: structural or root causes of refugee movements create the need for particular refugee policies; refugees themselves are only the symptom of those root causes, pawns of history rather than individuals whose actions help drive recognition of new policy needs. Paradoxically, structural theories of migration in the 1980s coincided with rising levels of international migration in the post-World War years and contributed to an attitudinal shift that may have obscured even refugees' sending-country politicism (Zolberg, Suhrke, and Aguayo 1989). In an earlier approach, Matthews (1972) described degrees of "conflict situations" in receiving-country refugee policy decisions, arising from a combination of asylum seekers' actions and receiving-country stances. Refugee actions in sending countries may be either politically active (e.g., persecution of a political dissident) or politically passive (e.g., persecution of an ethnic minority who has not engaged in political actions), while receiving-country stances toward particular events in countries of origin may be either political (e.g., political interest or agenda in events) or primarily humanitarian (e.g., no apparent political agenda). A combination of politically active refugees and political receiving-country stances produces high conflict policy decisions, possibly obstructing policy change. A combination of politically passive refugees and humanitarian stances produces low conflict policy decisions, easing policy change.[9] Although this approach stopped short of discussing asylum seekers' potential politicism in the receiving country, it did capture asylum seekers' politicism as a key element.

The new structural theories shifted the policy focus toward mediating factors with the aim of *preventing* refugee-creating situations from arising in the first place. Preventative approaches respond not only to humanitarian concerns, but also to the perceived need to limit refugee inflows and cope with the pressures of globalization. Since the early 1980s this has been marked by, for example, increasing overseas humanitarian aid and conflict mediation in foreign policy, but also by the imposition of visa requirements on people from high refugee-producing countries, aircraft carrier sanctions (to prevent airlines from accepting persons without valid identity papers), and general tightening of entry rules and regulations. Humanitarian aid and conflict mediation may be seen as positive preventative measures, but restrictions on asylum seeking may actually stifle the political and "social change function" that refugee movements may serve in sending countries. The preventative approach seeks to avert refugee flows but takes into account neither the role of refugee movement nor that of receiving countries in creating and shaping refugee movement: "[It] ignores the historical connection between social change and refugees. To avert flows would be the equivalent of trying to oppose social change. . . . To stifle change may freeze a repressive social order or contribute to systemic social inequalities. In the longer run, both conditions are likely to produce their own refugees (Zolberg, Suhrke, and Aguayo 1989:262).

Change in the refugee definition is a natural and desirable outcome of broader processes of social change. Social conditions change or are newly recognized as producing new types of refugees, thus a good refugee determination framework is one that can respond to the changing times.[10] Refugees are part and parcel of forces of social change, and so are the policies that encourage, enable, or prevent refugee movement. By "voting with one's feet," a refugee may alert the international community to human rights abuses in countries of origin (Hathaway 1991b). Increasing global interdependence and the growing salience of human rights codes should make this easier, rather than harder, for asylum seekers. But preventative policy approaches, concerned as they have been with preventing refugees from entering host countries, may remove some of refugees' symbolic political force. Once seen primarily as symbols or direct outcomes of problems in sending countries, asylum seekers are now cast as problems for receiving countries. International migrants are increasingly blamed for contemporary social problems in receiving countries—from increasing racial tension and unemployment to overburdened welfare states. There is paradoxically more talk about what governments should do to keep refugees out than on what governments should do to foster preventative social and political change in sending countries or to better respond to individuals who are nevertheless forced to seek asylum.

We need to enlarge conceptualizations of refugees' social change function. In fact, under conditions of globalization, individual opportunities and capacities for "voting with one's feet" in legitimate political actions may actually be increasing. Refugees' social change function may occur not only in sending countries but also in receiving countries where their claims may conflict with national policies as well as political ideologies and agendas. They may touch upon deeply held social values and social tensions within receiving countries as well as sensitive interstate relations and conflicting perspectives of how countries and their populations see themselves within the international system. That is, for refugee policy to evolve, social and political change needs to occur in receiving countries as well. Receiving countries that politically support or turn a blind eye to the actions of repressive regimes are challenged when individuals from those regimes seek asylum. Their presence and claims may raise political debates, for instance about receiving-country practices and agendas in relation to sending countries about the accuracy of information about sending countries or about our understanding of human rights violations in cross-cultural contexts.

To round out the migration system landscape, we need to address the political impact of asylum seeking upon policy making as a contiguous part of it.[11] For instance, we cannot assume that the circumstances with potential to compel individuals to act will actually result in individual actions, nor can we assume how individuals will act and to what effect. While explaining migration as structurally determined and thus essentially rational acts or reactions to the structural environment (macro and micro), we need to more specifically account for the *individual* fleeing persecution as something more than a response to his or her environment—but rather as an actor who makes decisions and takes risks and who as part of a shared collective identity may move and shape his or her environment. We can probe the migration system further to flesh out refugee roles as agents of social change in policy-making processes and the relation between refugee policy and human rights specifically. The migration system helps shape structural determinants of individuals' needs, abilities, and opportunities to seek asylum, receiving-country responses to asylum seeking, and subsequently the shapes flows ultimately take.

Establishing a Viable Collective Identity

There has been insufficient attention to the complexity of asylum seekers' roles as they navigate the migration system and sometimes push out its boundaries. They are at best considered the pawns of history caught up in broader structural events, victims who become charity cases in another country, or at worst the greatest mass of con artists in history—illegitimate refugees. To better understand the politicized nature of refugee systems from the point of view of asylum seekers, we must examine the ways asylum seekers, through their agency, involve receiving countries in sociopolitical debates and moral issues surrounding their flight, and how their actions may negotiate the refugee system in necessarily political ways to challenge prevailing norms and policies.

The migration system constitutes the structural context for political contests over identity and rights that asylum seekers physically traverse and the institutional rules and norms that asylum seekers negotiate. The terrain of asylum seeking meets that of policy development in receiving countries, which is part of international and national refugee systems. This structural context comprises an "institutional logic" and contributes to the "institutional structure of society [that] creates and legitimates the social entities that are seen as 'actors.' That is, institutionalized cultural rules define the meaning and identity of the individual and the patterns of appropriate economic, political, and cultural activity engaged in by those individuals" (Powell and DiMaggio 1991; Meyer, Boli, and Thomas 1987:9). This institutional structure legitimates and enables asylum seekers' political action.

To account for and explain asylum seekers' political and policy roles in receiving countries, asylum seekers must be understood as *collective actors* and *central components* of the institutional structure and cultural rules of the international migration system. Refugee claim making is a collective enterprise driven by persecuted individuals establishing their identities within politicized status determination processes in order to access relevant rights. We can identify and explore essential stages in establishing a viable collective identity corresponding with social movement theory.

Under international refugee law asylum seekers are obliged to present their case in both individual and collective terms, and their claims must evidence human rights abuse tantamount to persecution. Therefore the first stage in establishing a viable collective identity is for asylum seekers to demonstrate that their *grievances are structural*. This means demonstrating that the problem—for example female-specific violence—is chronic and likely to reoccur for particular peoples or groups (it is not a one-off).

Second, asylum seekers must demonstrate an *individual association with a collective identity around the particular grievance*. That is, they identify themselves as individual targets of that structural persecution, and their refugee claim is based on this individual association with the structurally persecuted group. Refugee law requires that asylum seekers identify their personal experiences of persecution within a broader structural experience of persecution by similarly structurally situated people. During the refugee determination process, asylum seekers are questioned closely about the structural nature of their persecution and asked for evidence of their individual persecution around this association. Failure to provide adequate answers and evidence to link their individual claims to the collective level results in rejection. However, we cannot assume that during status determination processes asylum seekers will succeed in framing their personal experience within structural causes of persecution. They may present only their individual experience (e.g., "attempts were made on my life"), or as is common in some cultures, they may describe structural persecution of a collective group but not refer to their individual experience (e.g., "my people are persecuted"). The ability to present a claim using evidence or persuasive arguments as to both its structural element and the individual's link to it is a prerequisite to earning formal refugee status. The political and collective aspect of claim making is particularly important when claimant experiences do not fit refugee eligibility frameworks. Claimants need to explain why theirs is a chronic, not just an individually experienced, problem.

Third, to win claims, asylum seekers must draw on appropriate and available ideologies and ideas as moral and legal resources to argue for access to collective rights. This dimension is interesting and significant as it brings different cultures and layers of legal and ideological arguments into contact. As indicated earlier, asylum seekers draw on a complex system of international and national law. They further raise debates about culture and the rights of particular groups (for example, women) in both sending and host countries, the latter often overlooked. This process underlines that refugee policy is framed by historically and culturally specific ideas about rights and their justification through affiliation to group identity or membership. The changing pool of available ideologies and salient ideas under conditions of globalization alter the opportunities that asylum seekers may have to argue for their collective rights. Host country populations may benefit indirectly from politically backing an ideology that supports not only asylum seekers but themselves as members of a common group, such as women in gender-stratified societies.[12]

Fourth, to frame their claims in a successful manner asylum seekers need to make use of host country resources and support—financial, legal, and material. Many of the resources asylum seekers may access have traditionally been considered the reserve of established residents or citizens, such as legal aid, welfare, housing, rights to membership in local organizations and associations, freedom of speech, and rights to national police and civil protection under the law. Legal council is the most obvious support for asylum seekers to frame their experiences appropriately, and increasingly important are public or community groups, for example, material and emotional support provided by nongovernmental organizations to see claimants through the claim process. Residents may not be personally affected by the same grievances and may not have a personal stake in taking political action around particular issues except insofar as their employment may involve dealing with the affected population. On a broader political level individuals and organizations may benefit indirectly from politically supporting a common ideology that benefits them as members of a broad (even global) group. The changing context of available resources, support, and potential mobilizing structures in a particular host country may increase or decrease asylum seekers' abilities to make influential claims (or to make claims at all) and to influence policy in a particular time and place.

Fifth, influential asylum seekers strategically use emerging political opportunities in order to draw on appropriate ideology and resources to make their claims and contest negative decisions. That is, the timeliness of certain types of claims is very important not only to generate political access (actual rights in law), but also to seize moments when opponents may be more vulnerable to certain debates and conflicts and may respond in a conflict-avoidance or more cooperative manner than in other periods.

Failure of persecuted groups to be recognized in receiving-country policy and practice not only returns individuals to the situation where their life may be at stake, but also reduces the possibility for exit for other people suffering the same structural persecution. Yet by seeking asylum and making claims these individuals alert the international community to serious collective problems in the sending country. In some cases, even if they do not win asylum, the issues raised by their claims may mobilize discussion of possible political action on other fronts, for example, increased NGO and humanitarian aid, or even foreign policy actions by the potential host country.

Agency and Structure: Linking Refugees and Human Rights Change

This view of asylum seekers as collective actors—formerly invisible as such within migration system theory—forces an elaboration of migration systems in order to properly see asylum seekers within a system comprised of interdependent parts. Interdependent agents are both instrument and effect of a specific but changeable context—in this case, the migration system context, which is prone to shifts in the structure of political opportunities, mobilizing vehicles, and framing processes. Seeing asylum seekers as collective actors within this interdependent framework enables more precise discussion of the structural context and institutional logic framing their social and political change function. Five key principles capture this relationship.

Asylum seekers face a conflict between theory and opportunity in institutionalized status determination processes. Theoretically, all persecuted individuals have the right "to seek and enjoy asylum" in other countries, according to Article 14(1) of the Universal Declaration of Human Rights (1948). However, not all persecuted individuals enjoy the same opportunities to seek asylum in the first place, and once asylum is sought, receiving countries maintain the authority to determine whether asylum seekers actually have the right to receive asylum (in order to "enjoy" it). That is, the right to seek asylum is no more than the right to be considered a candidate for "refugee" status as interpreted by sovereign states in national refugee policy and along lines delineated in international refugee law (Plender 1989).[13] The first problem is that both international law and states' interpretations favor some types of refugees over others. Second, in the face of this, the burden of proof in determinations of status falls upon refugee claimants. According to the 1951 Convention refugee definition, claimants must show "well-founded fear of persecution." Proof of persecution contains objective and subjective elements, and applicants are responsible for both. Objective elements refer to "objective circumstances that give rise to the fear," while subjective elements refer to the claimant's genuine suffering from fear of persecution (Schenke 1996:8). But not all claimants enjoy the same availability of information and support to prove their cases, nor to present information in an environment suitable to their needs.[14]

Conditions that pit theory against opportunity may seriously obstruct persecuted individuals' ability to act effectively in order to be recognized as genuine refugees, a status that transfers state responsibility for an individual's welfare from one country to another. Yet at the same time the structural context makes the *act* of seeking asylum a linchpin for expanding the refugee definition in policy. The institutional logic of asylum seeking requires claimants to base their claims on human rights violations amounting to persecution and to demonstrate a well-founded fear of persecution, typically in an adversarial judicial setting. When untraditional claims are made, there is a potential for policy makers to be alerted to the need to adapt refugee policy to changing realities. Women who seek asylum from sex persecution, considered "illegitimate" throughout the greater part of institutionalized asylum-giving history, engage in a contest over identity concerning rights and state responsibilities, framed by historically specific contexts and opportunities to do so.

What opportunities enable some asylum seekers to attain asylum and not others? Starting at the most basic level, individuals must have opportunities to seek asylum in the first place, that is, the capacity to leave their country and also to request refugee status from a host country. They then need opportunities in the receiving country to make and (if necessary) challenge decisions on their claims. Opportunities therefore refer to a combination of macro and micro level factors shaping international migration, as identified in migration systems theories. These are structural circumstances that may not only trigger but also shape and facilitate or constrain international migration flows, for instance, global economic trends, decolonization, modernization, and other interstate or international level trends. They include laws permitting free movement in the sending country, potential asylum seekers' financial and/or human resources (i.e., contacts, particularly relevant for immigration to distant counties), international refugee law and receiving-country refugee laws and determination systems, and political relations between sending and receiving countries. These create the structural contexts of constraints and opportunities for certain migrants in particular times and places. Factors also include the resources international migrants can access once inside receiving countries, described earlier as including access to legal counsel, evidence regarding widespread persecution in sending countries, welfare benefits such as housing and community organizations that offer information and advocacy, and the particular rights associated with residence in the receiving country, such as constitutional and civil rights.

Opportunities to challenge negative decisions, though rarely discussed in migration or refugee studies, refer to the specific structures of refugee law and status determination systems, including the resources made available to claimants (judicial setting, legal representation, housing, medical care) that not only help shape successful claims (see Tuitt 1996; Paul 1992) but also claimants' abilities to challenge negative outcomes. The more closed an immigration system is, the more it constrains asylum seekers' chances of being accepted. Similarly, the more open a particular system, the greater opportunities asylum seekers will have to challenge it. The same is true for less tangible aspects of international migration systems that affect particular types of claimants and claims, for example, systemic bias toward refugees arriving from particular countries due to political relations between sending and receiving countries (see Fawcett and Arnold 1987), receiving countries' use of immigration as a tool of foreign policy (Teitelbaum 1984), general attitudes toward international migration in receiving countries, and the salience of human rights and citizenship norms in receiving countries or as forces undermining state sovereignty (see Sassen 1996). We may also add factors less commonly associated with status determination processes—those that will affect *policy influence.* Policy influence typically requires opportunities such as access to substantive rights and means (resources and opportunities) of participation in the host country; salient ideas and interests in the receiving country, which are relevant to ideologies underlying particular claims (e.g., ideas and interests embodied by the women's movement, or particular ethnic communities and/or public opinion concerned with international politics giving rise to refugee flows); and vulnerability of the establishment at a given time or on relevant political issues (e.g., domestic discontent toward a particular government, factions within political parties, and inherent or rising institutional weaknesses).

The contest between theory and opportunity in the making of refugee claims is influenced by the structural context asylum seekers must negotiate and the resources available to negotiate effectively. Resources are legal, ideological, and material. They may include, for example, particular rights as refugee claimants and also as temporary residents in the host country awaiting decisions on claims; empirical evidence about conditions in the country of origin (to "prove" persecution); ideological support in the host community or culture; accessibility of financial, legal, and material aid; and social support by nongovernmental organizations and individuals in the host community (e.g., social services provided by ethnic community associations). These may create leverage points for asylum seekers facing the conflict between theory and opportunity.

Asylum seekers are rational versus forced actors affecting the migration system. A defining feature of the migration system is the interdependency of its parts. Asylum seekers, as central *components* of the migration system, its refugee regimes, and human rights underpinnings, are both *instrument and effect* of that system, not merely shaped by but shaping it through their decisions and actions. This is recognized in migration systems theory insofar as refugee policy is often said to respond to refugee flows and also to shape them. It differs from migration theory, which is popularly interpreted as describing refugees as "forced" migrants. The forced characterization implies that legitimate refugees do not make conscious or rational decisions that may influence their migration prospects; rather asylum seekers lack control over macrostructural causes of persecution and thus are simply forced to seek refugee status. The many barriers to access that asylum seekers face, the dangers and risks they take in flight and in refugee camps, have been documented, and without doubt many asylum seekers may describe themselves as unwilling participants in larger structural events and circumstances. The influence of asylum seeking upon the broader structural context is considered almost inevitable, not a factor of individual asylum seekers' actions in a political context but of their forced collective roles as pawns of history. Hathaway (1991b) and Zolberg, Suhrke, and Aguayo (1989) made substantial contributions by identifying the role of refugee movements in drawing attention to the occurrence of human rights abuses and constituting part of broader processes of social change in sending countries. However, asylum seekers' influences on the broader international migration (for example, the rules and patterns of asylum) are not considered.

However, we know that individuals risk their lives and the safety of their families by attempting to seek asylum, a choice that not all are willing to make, since some choose to remain in the country of origin despite opportunities to leave. We also know many rejected refugee claimants do not launch appeals but simply evade deportation and remain in the host country illegally, rather than risk having their appeals overturned and deportation enforced. Asylum seekers' *willingness* to make use of opportunities to seek and achieve asylum is a question neglected in refugee studies perhaps because their traditional "forced" image suggests that claim making by desperate people is not a choice. Although some have contested the "forced" definition (Zolberg, Suhrke, and Aguayo 1989:30), asylum seekers' capacity to weigh risks of various kinds and make choices even under difficult circumstances still tends to be overlooked. Moreover, despite the shift from push-pull to systems theories there is still a marked tendency to concentrate on factors in sending countries pushing asylum seekers out, while ignoring the importance of opportunities and constraints in receiving countries.[15] If asylum seekers are presented with opportunities and constraints upon seeking and receiving asylum, they may be confronted with decisions about the kinds of risks they must be willing to take to achieve their goal. Are they willing to make untraditional types of claims that are less likely to be accepted? Would they rather attempt to fit their claims within more readily accepted eligibility parameters by distorting the evidence? Would they be willing to challenge negative decisions on their claims (a surprising number of claims are abandoned or withdrawn at some stage of the determination process), or would they rather simply defy deportation and disappear into the masses of illegal migrants? Would they be willing to take noninstitutional measures, such as going public, to challenge decisions? Or would they fear the possible negative repercussions, for themselves or their families back home, of revealing their identity and location? These considerations may often depend upon whether asylum seekers have the necessary opportunity to become aware of the possibilities in the first place and ultimately to be able to go act on them (for example, knowing one's legal rights, having a good lawyer, having community support, good evidence, public sympathy, and mobilization potential).

Asylum seekers are creations or objects of refugee policy, as well as agents of refugee policy development. Asylum seeking is a symbol of processes of social change begun in the sending country and moving into the receiving country through individuals who react to serious grievances by seeking protection from another state. The asylum-seeking "terrain" meets that of policy development in receiving countries precisely through the refugee claim-making process.

What we think of as "legitimate refugees" is a product of our times despite the ahistorical structural nature of the persecution by which policy attempts to identify them (racial, religious, political, nationality, and social group). Policy that defines "refugees" reflects historically specific biases that affect refugee selection processes and exclude many refugees who may have legitimate claims in modern terms. By the same token, the modern structural context also offers opportunities and constraints of various kinds that affect asylum seekers' abilities to make successful claims and alter the terms of their inclusion in host countries.

Refugee policy develops in both a radical and an incremental fashion. It reflects historically specific sociopolitical processes and the changing needs of refugees or changing opportunities to make claims. Most powerful but less common is the reinterpretation of the Convention itself. For example, radical refugee policy change occurred when the African Union changed its refugee definition (based on the 1951 Convention) to include refugees of civil war (Convention Governing the Specific Aspects of Refugee Problems in Africa, art. 1, 1969). More commonly, refugee policy tends to develop incrementally through new interpretations and applications of the law. This is evidenced in the resilience of the 1951 Convention refugee definition in most national refugee policies. Where the 1951 Convention definition has been unable to accommodate new kinds of refugees, legislation recognizing "extra-Convention" refugees has been added in many states. Sweden first introduced the category of "B status" or "de facto" refugees in the 1960s, creating temporary ad hoc measures to cover refugees of social-political crises without precedent in the 1951 Convention. Many countries followed this example and created extra-Convention categories. Canada allows entry to "nonstatutory" refugees through ad hoc "designated classes" and on "humanitarian and compassionate" grounds (Immigration Act 1976, 1993). The UNHCR recognizes persons in "refugee-like" situations, extending aid to those fleeing civil war and famine.

Even more common is the use of national case law arising from individual asylum seekers who challenge the existing eligibility criteria to reshape the interpretation and application of the Convention. As the significance of refugee jurisprudence (to varying extent in different countries) is generally recognized, it is only logical that we should acknowledge asylum seekers' political roles in the evolution of jurisprudence and the development of legislation based on it.

Asylum seekers are actors working with changing *political opportunities.* If asylum seekers are not solely forced actors by virtue of being compelled to seek asylum, we can explain their movement as, in part, that of rational actors working with political opportunities that arise in changing structural contexts. McAdam, McCarthy, and Zald's theory of collective action (1996) identified actors' use of political opportunity structures, mobilizing structures, and framing processes as central to successful social change. These same dimensions enable or constrain asylum seekers in making claims, establishing a link between their individual experience and a collective group of persecuted individuals, and successfully proving the legitimacy of their claims. The structure of political opportunities shapes whether and how asylum seekers may take their claims from the individual to the collective level.

Several striking dimensions of the contemporary world may constitute changing opportunities for asylum seeking on a broad level, including the growth of regional and international conventions and agreements and the increasing salience of the human rights principles they support. Human rights codes prioritize the individual or person and provide legal and moral tools to challenge states' sovereign right to violate human rights and to exclude aliens from their territories. In this context "the individual emerges as a site for contesting the authority (sovereignty) of the state because she is the site for human rights" (Sassen 1998:8). Asylum seekers' claims to the legitimating discourses of institutionalized human rights and notions of personhood lend them options and some means for agency.

Other key changes wrought by globalization include the increasing application of citizenship rights to noncitizens, and noncitizens' increasing ability to access and claim citizenship rights (Soysal 1994; Jacobson 1996). Like other migrants, inland asylum seekers are exposed to the political, social, organizational, and resource environment of the host country as they make claims and await decisions on them. This provides asylum seekers a range of institutional and noninstitutional resources and opportunities, for instance, to make full use of judicial institutions and be represented by lawyers paid for by the state. Not all asylum seekers get equal access to all types of rights, and some enjoy few rights at all, remaining instead in detention centers. But many others access a range of rights through to the appeals process, rights of association, and freedom of expression.

International and national dimensions increasingly intersect within the context of globalization, marked by increasing interaction between national and international level systems (see Held and McGrew, 2000), and subsequently between national and world level institutional norms and logics that legitimate individual actors (see Meyers 1994:30). Asylum seekers' agency in refugee policy development is in no small part a factor of strategic opportunities available through receiving countries and worldwide norms. We can explore how asylum seekers acquire the means and legitimacy to challenge exclusion from host countries despite increasing restrictions on refugee movement in recent years. Like other types of migrants, they frequently access an array of rights, resources, and avenues for participation in host societies. These strategic opportunities emerge out of changing international and national refugee regimes, status-determination processes, and national possibilities for mobilization. For instance, the nature and infrastructure of Canada's refugee regime, its common law tradition and pluralistic inclination toward policy making are important for successful challenges to refugee policy. Canada has a progressive humanitarian reputation with a relatively high rate of refugee acceptance. It is a country rich in resources and has an increasingly multicultural identity. It values jurisprudence and in politics tends to avoid conflicts, resulting in a consensual style of policy making. Yet it was previously hostile toward female-specific refugee claims. What key opportunity structures converged or changed to better enable asylum seekers' politicism and influence at that historical moment?

Strategic opportunities are linked to the salience of particular ideas (Edelman 1971), here regarding responsibilities and rights of states, individuals, and groups of people or collective identities that are increasingly transnational or global in nature. They are heavily influenced by national politics and citizenship rights, increasingly by international politics and supranational rights, principles, and standards, and by the interaction between the two. While they may provide new legitimacy to individuals, enabling their claim making, they also raise conflicts. At this interface collective identities (sharing similar structural experiences of persecution) stand between culturally relative and universal rights, both of which present potential obstacles and opportunities and are intimately linked through the changing globalization context.

Asylum seekers specifically use and encourage the interaction between citizenship values and human rights under globalization. Asylum seeking raises fundamental questions such as: Which rights will be safeguarded as "universal" rights on specific issues? When should citizenship rights be considered universal (applicable to noncitizens)? When should human rights outweigh cultural traditions? When or in which state should asylum seekers have rights to benefits associated with citizenship? Asylum seekers, by their unique position between states, inherently raise debates about culturally relative rights versus human rights. In practice, cultural relativism underpins interpretations and applications of the universal standards upon which refugee policy is based. Thus in some cases asylum seekers may be denied protection despite legitimate human rights violations. In other cases, when claims challenge international refugee law, they may extrapolate culturally relative rights of citizens in host countries to thicken the use of human rights principles. In both scenarios, asylum seeking raises moral and political debates in receiving countries regarding *which* culture, *which* country, and *which* rights will ultimately be used as touchstones for interpretations and applications of human rights. Asylum seekers can help determine the outcome of such debates by claiming a right to choose which universal cultural morality they believe in, starting with a rejection of those values that offend or harm them in countries of origin. The right of a sovereign state to commit, condone, or ignore what an individual member of that state considers to be human rights violations should never be considered a culturally relative right in the international domain if that individual rejects it. Asylum seekers make an expressly political choice by seeking membership in a foreign country that upholds the rights they are seeking.

Negotiating National and International

In sum, the conceptual and analytical framework offered here provides a means of exploring political processes behind human rights expansions facilitated specifically through national refugee politics and asylum seekers' roles in such processes. In this, noncitizen capacities are conceived as an outcome of institutionalized cultural rules and structures of society taking on both international and national frameworks. The types of rules and structures in this case fundamentally involve the international migration and human rights system with its levels and types of actors, rights, structural opportunities, and bureaucratic eccentricities.

The political nature of asylum seeking suggests one way the citizenship–human rights dialectic may result in an expansion of human rights and state responsibilities. Asylum seekers' role in and use of the structural context may be both symbolic and institutional/strategic. Their importance for symbolic politics (Edelman 1971) involves the interpretation and creation of meaning and understanding of identity. Their strategic institutional influence involves bringing political situations to light and helping to convince states to adopt appropriate policy.

Identity for asylum seekers is both self-defined and state-defined. Both definitions are important, and together they highlight the distinction between informal and formal status and the significance of their interaction for policy making. Refugee policy identifies potential beneficiaries of state protection and their rights according to basic state responsibilities explicit and implicit to the policy. Feeding into refugee policy development are policy actors' willingness and opportunities, which arise from informal and formal rights inherent to contracts and relations between states and individuals in the global system, and between the state and citizens or residents, through which asylum seekers may mobilize and legitimate their claims.

We can explore opportunities to seek asylum and challenge the refugee determination system, alongside willingness to successfully make use of these opportunities in both tangible and intangible, symbolic and strategic aspects.

Asylum seekers have symbolic self-defined identities as refugees and institutional or state-defined identities as "legitimate" or "illegitimate" refugees. Opportunities and constraints include institutional structures and resources (or lack of) and other tangibles, as well as salient ideas, trends, and other intangibles. Asylum seekers and supporters may use ideas and ideology in "symbolic politics" (Edelman 1971) as well as strategic tactics through the use of law, media, and other instruments for public and government persuasion. McAdam (1996) describes symbolic and strategic actions as types of "signifying acts" used by collective actors to influence social and policy change.[16] In this book, I refer to *transnational signifying acts* in order to encompass the fundamental conflict and negotiation of national and international values and rights at the heart of the sex-persecution campaigns.

Conditions for effective policy advocacy by noncitizens are an effect of changing political opportunities and their use by individuals whose identity and roles in relation to receiving states have also been changing. Transformations occur both symbolically and strategically, as in changing relationships between noncitizens and states, noncitizens and residents, and citizenship and human rights. In this the dynamic between asylum seeking and policy development is also political, involving struggle and conflict and describing an important overlooked dimension of refugee policy development. Refugee policy is not only a vehicle for protecting states and preventing flows or providing aid to passive beneficiaries, but potentially a vehicle for making use of or even expanding states' human rights responsibilities. Asylum seekers may use the existing structural context as a vehicle to overcome constraints and restrictions in receiving countries and in human rights law. Both scholarly and popular discourse tends to be either panicked at this likelihood, saying that the system is prone to abuses by illegitimate refugees, or protective of legitimate refugees' structural vulnerability and "forced" image. The migration systems approach overlooks the international migration system as one of developing opportunities or constraints that asylum seekers *must* negotiate and *may* successfully and legitimately challenge. It neglects the political process involved in asylum seeking and claim making, which is essential to understanding policy needs and influences under globalization.

Seeing asylum seekers as *actors* removes them from the "forced" image in which the individual actor disappears and refugee movements are seen as irrational and unstructured events, yet without making the illogical assumption that individuals who challenge the refugee system are opportunistic voluntary migrants and thus illegitimate refugees. The forced-voluntary distinction is problematic for political dissidents who choose to be political activists in their home country and thus do not quite fit the "forced" definition (Zolberg, Suhrke, and Aguayo 1989:31). It is also problematic for untraditional asylum seekers; for instance, refugees of economic persecution are not recognized under the 1951 Convention and thus are considered voluntary migrants or illegitimate refugees. Due to barriers against their acceptance, untraditional asylum seekers challenge the very systems within which they seek protection. In some cases they may strengthen claims to state protection by taking voluntary political action in the receiving country, for example, making the rejection of their claims public to elicit national sympathy and public pressure in support of their claims. But paradoxically, the more asylum seekers challenge the system the more they may appear as calculating individuals who are not really forced migrants at all. We need to dispense with the artificial distinction between "voluntary" and "forced" migrants and explore how asylum seekers may use political opportunities for legitimate reasons to push out existing refugee eligibility frameworks. The rationale of seeking asylum is based not on how well they fit existing refugee law, but on membership in a collective persecuted group with shared identity and grievances and varying structural opportunities, resources, and potential strategies for redress—all important factors mediating the migration system. Thus, just as the "voluntary migrant" category is now subject to historically structured processes that qualify individualistic explanations of migration, so should refugees be distanced from the "forced" category and seen as individuals acting within given opportunities and constraints.

Implications involve more explicit recognition of pressures on both international law and national policies, including noncitizen access to rights and policy-making processes, and a mutually informative dialectical relationship between international and national rights themselves. A crucial dynamic of the asylum-seeking process is its role in the evolution of interstate responsibilities, which occurs when international and national norms are brought face to face through the making of refugee policy. Asylum seekers straddle international human rights and citizenship norms, making use of rights and resources at both levels in order to seek asylum. The *representative* nature of their claim making in foreign national contexts raises political conflicts between universal human rights and culturally specific citizenship rights. While refugee regimes may expand and contract in the liberalness of their approach over time, the debates and political conflicts that asylum seeking may provoke occur at the frontiers of current debates about just what human rights are and about the limits of state responsibility and state sovereignty under conditions of globalization.

Social movement theory enables us to examine political processes of human rights change free of false dichotomies and preconceptions entrenched in reigning theories of globalization, human rights, and nation-states. Applied to the context of international migration systems and refugee movement in particular, as relevant for the case examined in this book, the institutional and political structure and key actors emerge. The tendency to overlook asylum seekers' political roles in receiving countries necessitated a more detailed examination of this group of individuals as potential collective actors embedded within the international migration system. The key principles regarding the relationship between refugees and human rights change suggest why and how asylum seekers may make the transition from being self-recognized refugees to state-recognized refugees in ways that involve bringing national and international values face to face, forcing a negotiation of the two.

Of course, policy influence specifically and human rights change more broadly may not *often* be a direct result of asylum seeking by individual claimants, and certainly cannot be conceived as an easy process. But certainly asylum seekers' representation of a collective identity paired with the possibility of collective influence through claim making over time suggests a political and ideological challenge. The following chapters explore this challenge and how it succeeded in the case of sex persecution, examining global and national contexts, emerging opportunities for asylum seeking, and policy advocacy and the ways asylum seekers negotiated and made expressly political use of them to make gender persecution matter.

Research Strategy

To gather data for the type of analysis described in this chapter, oriented around complex sociopolitical processes about which there is little prior research, the qualitative case study approach is most appropriate. The case study method is advantageous for generating rich data on topics for which research resources are limited, particularly complex social phenomena (Yin 1994). It is invaluable in generating thick description (Burgess 1984), reducing researcher bias by enabling subjects to develop their own interpretations (Critcher, Waddington, and Dicks 1999:72), and allowing unanticipated themes to emerge (Pollitt et al. 1990). The case study method is subsequently considered a fruitful means of generating theoretical insights (Bryman 1988).[17]

A variety of data sources was needed to suit these aims and to compensate for the dearth of previous research, and a triangulation method of data analysis was used. Yin explains: "the most important advantage presented by using multiple sources of evidence is the development of *converging lines of inquiry*, a process of triangulation" (1994:92). By offering multiple sources of evidence with different perspectives, and diversifying the methods by which they were obtained, triangulation reduces the chances of researcher bias in the interpretation of data and increases the internal validity of the study. Many perspectives pertaining to factual details of the campaigns were gathered from a variety of sources to present a more holistic and reliable account of events, and to tease out significant recurring themes. Converging lines of inquiry here meant that the conditions, nature, and strategies of asylum seekers' participation in policy processes were illuminated. Because a successful case was chosen in which asylum seekers played a role, evidenced in their claim making and going public, the data was not searched for proof of their participation per se, but rather to elaborate why, how, and to what extent and effect asylum seekers participated, and the conditions under which this was possible and influential. This included considering why asylum seekers *chose* to participate and to what extent they acted on their own behalf or were represented by advocates. An important aspect of addressing this last point was looking at why some asylum seekers considered not participating. Examination of considerations against going public and of obstacles to claim making and policy advocacy that asylum seekers needed to overcome supports an interpretation of asylum seekers' agency rather than forced actorhood.

The effect of asylum seekers' participation cannot be divorced from overarching campaign processes and collective claim making, but multiple qualitative indicators relating to the success of policy influence strategies as they in fact involved individual asylum seekers (indeed, reinforcing asylum seekers' centrality to chosen strategies) provide some measure of asylum seekers' influence. In this the case is not representative of asylum seekers generally; rather it describes why and how particular asylum seekers helped shape policy as an illustration of influences on policy processes, the transformation of state responsibilities, and human rights agendas.

Research methods included the compilation of individual asylum seeker case histories, expert interviews with core campaigners, a survey of women's shelters, examination of NGO and government documents, analysis of mass media coverage, analysis of a data set of gender-related jurisprudence, historical documentary techniques, as well as direct observation during my residence in Montreal before, during, and immediately after the campaigns.

The main focus of the case study is the core of the campaign network in Canada between 1991 and 1996, in campaigns leading to instatement of the 1993 Guidelines and in follow-up campaigns leading to the revision of the Guidelines at the end of 1996. At the heart of the campaign network is a series of asylum seekers making public their refugee claims. Individual claims thus also constituted individual case studies, or embedded units of analysis, of the claim-making and campaigning processes, which could then be viewed as a whole. Claimants were linked through common supporters (Canadian residents) in a loose network structure. Analysis of individual claimant case histories thus considers individual claims and campaign experiences and also examines them within the campaign as a whole. The case study also takes into account how the structural environment—an intersection of international and national contexts, historical and current trends and changes—affects claimant abilities to influence refugee policy. It explores both how asylum seekers influenced policy and why they were able to do so at that particular historical moment.

Case histories of twenty-six asylum seekers from eighteen countries across six world regions were compiled, including the twenty-three asylum seekers who engaged in public pressure tactics and three who made private appeals to the immigration minister through or backed by campaigners during the campaign period between 1991 and 1996 (see Table 2.2). Of those who engaged in public pressure tactics, or went public, a total of twenty women from fourteen different countries constitute major case histories and the main focus of attention in this study due to substantial data attained with multiple sources of corroborating evidence. The remaining three asylum seekers who went public, along with the three who did not go public, had more minimal case history information and therefore constitute minor case histories drawn upon in a more limited fashion. Some asylum seekers used a pseudonym when they went public (e.g., in interviews with the press, editorials, and public speeches) and left instructions with supporters regarding how to release information about them; others were candid about their identity. In this study a high degree of confidentially and respect for claimant wishes was ensured in all cases. Many of these claimants wished to return to a life of tranquillity and peace after undergoing traumatic processes involved in seeking asylum, exacerbated by the ordeal of having to challenge their cases publicly. Quotations and viewpoints of asylum seekers are referred to by first name (real or fictitious).

TABLE 2.2. MAJOR AND MINOR ASYLUM SEEKER CASE HISTORIES

Major case histories		*Major case histories*	
Name	**Country of origin**	**Name**	**Country of origin**
Ferdousi	Bangladesh	Hindra	Trinidad and Tobago
Anna	Bulgaria	Lee	Trinidad and Tobago
Nadia	Bulgaria	Phagawdeye	Trinidad and Tobago
Ginette	Cameroon	Taramati	Trinidad and Tobago
Angela	Dominica	Kapinga	Zaire
Maria/Miranda	Guatemala		
Azadeh	Iran	*Minor case histories*	
Fatima	Lebanon	**Name**	**Country of origin**
Ines	Peru	Sandy	Germany
Olga	Russia	Zahra	Iran
Nada	Saudi Arabia	Ana	Mexico
Liza	St. Vincent	Amina	Somalia
Thérèse	Seychelles	Kissoon	Trinidad and Tobago
Dulerie	Trinidad and Tobago	Fatima	Turkey
Basdaye	Trinidad and Tobago		

Note: Some names are pseudonyms.

Individual case histories are analyzed in Chapters 4–6, which include data on claimant characteristics, scenarios of female persecution and corresponding claim types, descriptions of asylum seekers' institutional and extrainstitutional actions and their relationships with supporters, campaign chronology and details in individual case histories and as a group, and direct quotes and political commentary regarding asylum seekers' situation, beliefs, aims, and demands. These case histories are representative of asylum seekers in the campaigns since, according to supporters and the media, the cases identified constitute *all* claimants who received substantial media attention as part of the campaigns. They were all initially ineligible for refugee status due to their circumstances, timing, and experiences of persecution. They all arrived in Canada between 1984 and 1991, were initially rejected, resorted to public activities, and subsequently formed a collective body with specific policy demands. These asylum seekers are representative of the *broader* population of claimants (those who did not go public) in that they constituted test cases for later claims and jurisprudence; their stories reflect a range of forms of sex persecution, from traditionally "public" to "private" and involving diverse scenarios such as country of origin, location of the abuser and relation to the asylum seekers (family, in-laws, community, government officials, sometimes following the claimant to Canada), and claim-making processes. However, these claimants were different from claimants emerging *after* the Guidelines were instated, not only in taking public pressure tactics but also because of administrative complications they faced precisely because they initiated claims *before* the Guidelines were instated. For example, under Canadian law an individual can only make one refugee claim and cannot introduce new evidence at a later time, therefore some asylum seekers could not introduce new (second) claims after the Guidelines were instated. Consequently, as later chapters explain, many of the women studied were ultimately accepted into Canada by the end of the campaign period but on humanitarian grounds rather than 1951 Convention refugee status, while several remained in appeals processes and one was deported. For these women, being accepted or rejected was fundamental to their survival. In the broader picture, regardless of legal status ultimately attained, their claims and actions remain fundamental to political changes that occurred.

The process of identifying and compiling evidence for individual case histories necessitated a variety of methods, including searching newspaper archives, identifying and interviewing advocates and supporters, tracking down leads from interviews, and studying organizational and official archives. Data sources included asylum seekers' official case files and other institutional documents (e.g., sensitized Personal Information Forms), case synopses attained through lawyers and NGOs, press packages, interviews, and media coverage. As noted, access to information was uneven; claimants who received the greatest media coverage were most accessible, and among these some also had the greatest contact with supporters who could provide additional information.

Expert interviews were conducted with actors in Toronto, Ottawa, and (primarily) Montreal where campaigns took place, including all but one of the organizations in the core advocacy network and the majority of the main participating lawyers, as well as several secondary campaign participants and government sympathizers.[18] Campaign participants were diverse in profession. Interviews were undertaken with lawyers, international, national, and local level refugee, human rights, and women's NGOs, refugee claimants, IRB officials, and government researchers. Interview schedules were individually tailored to suit professional backgrounds and thus best elicit the kinds of information interviewees could offer. A semistructured interview schedule was used to enable respondents "to develop their own perspectives and agendas. . . . This reduces the chances that the researchers will impose their own prior pattern on the evidence" (Pollitt et al. 1990:184). The experts interviewed provided an alternative to the paucity of published information on the topic and provided "elite" or insider accounts of the campaigns. Interviews served to: identify policy actors; to describe undocumented asylum trends, the particular claims and their movement through the Canadian refugee system; and to describe the campaign process (participants, aims, strategies, chronology of campaign generation, height, and decline), interviewee's roles, relationships between asylum seekers, supporters, and the government, and opinions on the resulting Guidelines. The diversity of interviewees contributed a wide range of perspectives and holistic view of campaigns, asylum seekers, and processes, raising a variety of themes and generating rich descriptive data. To complement interview data, a survey was administered to women's shelters in Montreal, Toronto, and Ottawa. The majority of respondents were secondary campaign participants (not part of the core advocacy network). The survey sought to illuminate and describe trends in the shelters' experience with international migrant women, specifically asylum seekers; asylum seeking scenarios, of those who resided at the shelter; and the shelters' participation in and views on the campaigns and Guidelines.

Mass media coverage, press packages, and press releases were researched and analyzed to identify campaign participants, to add to case histories of individual asylum seekers, to provide a chronology of campaigns and strategies, and to facilitate discursive analysis of the public evolution of campaign language and symbols. Newspapers that covered the campaigns included all major and some smaller (local) papers, with a predominance of papers located in Quebec and Ontario.[19] Institutional documents were also analyzed, including government consultations and conference reports, press releases and speeches, IRB papers, reports, and statistics on claims. I received special assistance from the IRB Working Group on Women Refugee Claimants, the editorial board of RefLex (a legal database of refugee jurisprudence), and the government under the Access to Information Act.[20] Nongovernmental archives included correspondence with the immigration minister, internal reports, and policy documents. Institutional documents proved a relatively abundant source, providing details and chronology of government and nongovernment stances, demands, and responses. Finally, the historical and policy literature on international migration and Canada's refugee regime and the nascent literature on female persecution were also analyzed. Historical documents were consulted regarding factors shaping the "refugee" in policy and the asylum-seeking process, including historical descriptions and analysis of the international refugee regime and migration system, Canada's refugee regime, and trends for women in particular. Although information on female persecution is limited, a body of literature developed quickly since 1993, primarily in international human rights and refugee law and including policy literature and institutional documents.

Analysis of asylum seeker participation considers not only their extrainstitutional actions (campaigns), but also their institutional actions within the Canadian immigration system before, during, and after the instatement of the Guidelines. Analysis of a wider set of claims derived from legal jurisprudence complements the case study and analysis of institutional actions specifically. Jurisprudence on 147, or 100 percent, of "notable" gender-related claims and court decisions between March 1993 and November 1996, as cited in RefLex (Canada's national legal database of refugee jurisprudence) was analyzed. "Notable cases" are those that break legal ground, either expanding or challenging previous decisions on similar cases. Turning to this broader pool of claims (that is, beyond those who went public) enables analysis of claimant influence on the Guidelines via the growth of jurisprudence in later years. Jurisprudence is examined qualitatively and quantitatively for characteristics and trends exhibited under the Guidelines in the early years.

It is helpful to put this jurisprudence as well as the individual case histories in the wider context of refugee claims made during the same period.

The newness of the "gender-related" refugee category makes information on such claimants more manageable than for refugees of racial, religious, nationality, political, or social group persecution because there are simply fewer of them. However, this newness also creates difficulties in terms of availability and quality of data. Information obtained through the Access to Information Act in 1995 prior to the release of government data identified 2,500 gender-related claims since 1993, broken down by countries of origin and status of claims (positive/negative/pending). But by the end of 1996, and the end of the campaign period studied, the IRB reported a total of only 1,200 gender-related claims, with no information on countries of origin. This discrepancy is likely due to improved methods of identifying claims. The latest public data indicates that by 31 December 2002 the IRB finalized 2,331 gender-related claims since 1993, accepting 1,345 and rejecting 691, while a further 295 claims were either withdrawn, abandoned, discontinued, or otherwise finalized (IRB 2007). Annually, gender-related claims have constituted 1 to 2 percent of all refugee claims in Canada.

The 147 gender-related RefLex cases constituted approximately 8.2 percent of all IRB cases identified as gender-related in the same period, and 100 percent of gender-related cases in the RefLex database. More important, they constitute significant and influential jurisprudence. RefLex represents refugee case law based on the criteria below; its cases were searched for gender-related claims. The gender-related jurisprudence analyzed in Chapter 6 therefore represents a range of case scenarios and novel applications of the Guidelines, and the development of types of claims and decisions on them over time.

RefLex case selection criteria:
- Cases in which court decisions depict a "novel approach to law," with an emphasis on cases where reasons for the decision are set out in a clear and concise manner
- Cases reflecting the application of established legal principle to a novel fact situation
- Cases where reasons for decisions are representative of a number of decisions decided on a specific issue from a particular country, or decided in a particular IRB region
- A balance of positive and negative cases and a selection from each of the IRB provincial offices
(RefLex Policy, memorandum, 1)

All data collection was undertaken with sensitivity to issues of *mapping, access, representation,* and *confidentiality,* which affect the nature and reliability of data obtained. Campaigns were organized around a series of individual and groups of asylum seekers making their claims public. The core policy advocacy network studied was therefore comprised of asylum seekers who went public and their supporters. Studying a particular campaign involves locating and getting access to key informants or campaign elites—the only sources of information about the campaigns from the perspective of *core* campaigners who are irreplaceable. Highly publicized cases were identified and interviews scheduled to gain access to the network of advocates and asylum seekers. Interviews were first conducted with supporters who according to press coverage appeared most frequently involved with cases and public pressure tactics. At each interview other core supporters were identified and follow-on interviews were arranged. A network structure best describes the nature and organization of the campaign, which was nonhierarchical, diffuse, and diverse in constituency and types of action or strategies used. A nominalist sketch of overarching and subnetworks of asylum seekers and supporters was thus mapped. Laumann and colleagues describe a nominalist delineation of network boundaries as a process by which "an analyst self-consciously imposes a conceptual framework constructed to serve [her] own analytic purposes" (Laumann, Marsden, Prensky 1983:23). In this approach "network closure has no ontologically independent status. There is no assumption that itself will naturally conform to the analyst's distinction; the perception of reality is assumed to be mediated by the conceptual apparatus of the analyst, be he (or she) an active participant in the social scene under study or an outside observer" (22).

The chain of contacts was mapped until information about participants and events became saturated and overlapped extensively among interviewees. At this point, the network could be mapped through a realist approach in which "the investigator adopts the presumed vantage point of the actors themselves in defining the boundaries of social entities. That is, the network is treated as a social fact only in that it is consciously experienced as such by the actors composing it" (Laumann 1992:20–21). This produced a map of the larger metanetwork of support, nationally and regionally, and of the core network of supporters and asylum seekers. Core refers to those most involved with, and indeed leading, campaigns. This was a relatively small cluster of individuals from diverse professions of varying mandates and expertise, including nongovernment, semigovernment, international, national, and local human rights, refugee and immigrant, women's, and religious organizations, as well as lawyers. Supporters involved with a particular claimant but not the core advocacy network are referred to as secondary supporters, with whom several interviews were conducted for information on involvement, campaign descriptions, other actors, and claimants. Secondary supporters not involved with claimants could be said to include sympathetic government authorities, especially members of the IRB Working Group on Women Refugee Claimants. They did not campaign and were not regarded by core actors, but were seen as making key contributions by drafting the Guidelines and participating in consultations and conferences about the Guidelines. Other secondary supporters were reached via a survey sent to women's shelters in Montreal, Ottawa, and Toronto, as women's shelters were involved in the campaigns in higher numbers. The core and metanetwork is depicted in Chapter 5.

Chapter 3
Global Challenges and Opportunities for Sex-Based Asylum Seeking

Everyone has the right to seek and to enjoy in other countries asylum from persecution.

—*Article 14(1) of the Universal Declaration of Human Rights, 1948*

The question is whose criteria defines legitimate fear for refuge recognition purposes? Why is it decided that persecution on the grounds of race or religion may lead to "well-founded fear" followed by international assistance, while women who are burnt to death have no rights of protection? Why is a girl who is threatened by violence and who attempts to escape by fleeing from her country, not part of the UNHCR's responsibility? Since neither national governments nor international bodies offer the right to protection and right to life [for these women], this is their underdevelopment and their shame.

—*Lucy Bonnerjea*, Shaming the World, 1985

To appreciate global constraints and emerging opportunities for women asylum seekers we must begin by examining gender biases historically underpinning international refugee and human rights law and the manner and extent to which they may be reified or changed in national contexts. We can then consider more recent global developments that shifted the structural context for asylum seeking by women and constituted critical building blocks for policy changes in the early 1990s. The fundamental shifts seen in this global history of women refugees paints a landscape of emerging global political opportunities, mobilizing structures, and cultural framings that were essential for national level policy challenges that later occurred.

Invisible Women: Traditional Refugee and Human Rights Law

International law does not make explicit any gender distinction with regard to asylum rights, thus in theory men and women are subject to the same rights and rules of status determination. These rules are loosely defined, and perhaps purposefully so. Most important, according to Article 14(1) of the 1948 Universal Declaration of Human Rights (UDHR), the determining factor of the "right to seek and to enjoy . . . asylum" is the experience or threat of "persecution" in the country of origin. But what exactly constitutes "persecution"? The UDHR provides no definition of this key concept. The subsequently instated 1951 Geneva Convention Relating to the Status of Refugees (1951 Convention) and its 1967 New York Protocol define the "refugee" as "Any person who, as a result of . . . and owing to well-founded fear of being persecuted for reasons of race, religion, nationality, membership in a particular social group or political opinion, is outside the country of his nationality and is unable or, owing to such fear, is unwilling to avail himself of the protection of that country; or who not having a nationality and being outside the country of his former habitual residence as a result of such events, is unable or, owing to such fear, is unwilling to return to it."

This definition identifies five reasons asylum may be granted—persecution occurring due to one's race, religion, nationality, political opinion, or social group—but again fails to define persecution itself. There are thus no definitional parameters regarding the nature of persecution (e.g., what extent or degree of injury must be caused before violations amount to persecution? Must injuries be physical, mental, or any violation of human dignity?), the forms it may take (e.g., torture, imprisonment, inhumane punishment, deprivation, starvation?), or the particular groups affected (e.g., particular races, religions, nationalities, political opinions, social groups?). Signatory states reproduce the 1951 Convention definition in national refugee legislation, also leaving persecution undefined (see Hathaway 1991a; Schenk 1994). When making refugee determinations, states therefore build explicitly on international law but due to its vagueness also enjoy leeway to determine exactly whether individual experiences actually amount to persecution.

The fact that structural causes of persecution are identified rather than the nature of "persecution" itself, the forms it may take or the particular groups affected, indicates an intent to characterize persecution quite broadly as a threat to human characteristics considered essential or central to one's being. Rights such as equality of race, religion, nationality, political opinion, and social group are universally held human rights under the UDHR, and thus persecution has increasingly been equated with serious structural human rights violations (Hathaway 1991b; 1994:108),[1] while the proliferation of treaties that address particular human rights issues over the past fifty years, such as those on minority rights, aid decision making in refugee cases. The use of broad structural causes of persecution as a key element of the refugee definition further makes possible the recognition of newly persecuted groups (races, religions, and so on) over time as situations arise and change (Zolberg, Suhrke, and Aguayo 1989:25).

At the same time, compared to the much broader range of human rights in the UDHR, the refugee definition is also clearly delimited by the identification of only five structural causes. A second delimiting element in the definition is the requirement that persecution be individualized. That is, the Convention does not entitle all members of a particular race, religion, nationality, social, or political group to asylum even if that group is known to be persecuted—only those who can demonstrate a "well-founded fear" of persecution directed at them individually. The third delimiting element is the requirement that individuals demonstrate that they are "unable . . . or unwilling," due to the fear of persecution, to avail themselves of any internal flight alternative within the country of origin. These three mutually qualifying features of the refugee definition—structural causes of persecution, individualized basis, and flight alternatives—legally preclude large masses of persecuted individuals such as victims of random violence, while in theory opening the way for certain persecuted individuals who are most in need. Thus refugee law treads a fine line between universal and particularistic categories and concerns. Universalism won out through the categories of persecution equated with human rights rather than very specific forms and targets of persecution, while the specification of five particular causes of persecution, the individualized nature of persecution, and lack of flight alternatives serve to particularize and delimit the refugee definition.

What some see as a *necessarily* loose refugee definition is evidently open to both progressive, expansive readings and regressive or narrow readings. In light of this reality, the 1951 Convention recommends that "governments continue to receive refugees in their territories and that they act in concert in a true spirit of international co-operation in order that these refugees may find asylum and the possibility of resettlement" (Recommendation IV.D). But in leaving ambiguities to be fleshed out in national law and state practice, a lack of international consensus on the refugee definition has emerged, as most countries subject the UN definition to qualifications that address regional problems (Plender 1989:63, 64). In Western countries claims of persecution are determined on a case by case basis, unlike countries that experience mass intraregional exoduses of people, as in Africa. Under common law tradition, further definitional variations emerge from judicial precedents on individual cases that legally broaden or tighten the application of the refugee definition. And in some countries, de facto asylum (right to residence for asylum seekers but not via refugee status) is also offered for reasons that fall outside the 1951 Convention, on an ad hoc basis that reflects regional and ideological realities of the receiving country, particularly during times of severe crisis. De facto refugees are those who, although they fail to meet Convention criteria, do not wish to return to their country of origin due to general political conditions there (Plender 1989:67).

It is important to note that the process of legally recognizing some claimants as refugees and rejecting others reflects and reifies cultural and political attitudes toward asylum seekers. Applicants rejected through established institutional processes, women being no exception, may be seen as having made "illegitimate" or false claims, or as being less worthy of need than others. They may be seen as having failed (perhaps consciously) to avail themselves of existing internal flight alternatives or mechanisms for redress. They may be seen as not actually fleeing "persecution" or human rights violations on established structural grounds (for example, those fleeing generalized violence during civil war; economic persecution; or sex persecution). Or, even if they fit established structural causes of persecution, the severity or particular form of the violence they face may not be considered tantamount to human rights violations. Within this system women face three major obstacles that are exacerbated by sex: the gendered "public/private" divide inherent to international law; gendered dependency; and a gendered cultural divide.

The Gendered Public/Private Divide

Constraints against asylum seekers attaining legal refugee status, and the opportunities for overcoming them, are deeply influenced by the gendered structural context of international law. Legal discourse, writes Klare, mirrors "systematized symbolic interaction," it "informs our beliefs about how people learn about and treat themselves and others." This includes "ways of thinking about public and private" (Klare 1982:1358, 1361), which subsequently may fluctuate and be revised. There is now a vast literature on the structure of the public/private divide and implications for women in society, ranging from issues such as women's caring and unpaid labor, to violence against women, to gender in international relations. Until the 1970s, female-specific violence within most countries was considered part of the private sphere beyond state responsibility,[2] and until the mid to late 1990s there was little to no discussion of violence against women as an interstate responsibility. Failure to apply equally the laws of asylum to women and men in accordance with UDHR Articles 2 and 14(1) is rooted in the gendered public/private divide in international law (see Beasley and Thomas 1994; Cook 1994; Schenk 1994; Peterson and Runyan 1993; Sylvester 1994; Charlesworth, Chinkin, and Wright 1991). International law and lawmaking have neglected and marginalized the female experience, resulting in what Charlesworth and colleagues call a "thoroughly gendered system . . . [which] privileges the male world view and supports male dominance in the international legal order" (Charlesworth, Chinkin, and Wright 1991:614).

This includes states' interpretation and application of the UDHR, which does not explicitly recognize female-specific violence as a human rights violation and in this sense also reflects the statist demarcation between public and private. States are the "public faces in the global system" (Walker 1994), while what goes on within states, and in particular by nonstate actors, has traditionally been considered private. This is partially explained by the fact that prior to the 1945 United Nations Charter, human rights violations were a matter of domestic jurisdiction. The UN Charter represents the intent to "assert an international interest" in the human rights of individuals by formulating standards of conduct, encouraging compliance with standards, and condemning egregious examples of noncompliance. It includes the creation of international cooperation in "promoting and encouraging respect for human rights and for fundamental freedoms for all without distinction as to race, sex, language, or religion" (Riggs and Plano 1988:240–241). But the UDHR is based on the principle of state responsibility with its origin in "the demarcation of spheres between the sovereign state and the individual in a social contract relationship" (Romany 1993:90). Cook explains that state responsibility in international law "makes a state legally accountable for the breaches of international obligations that are attributable or imputable to the state. In other words, only a state and its agents can commit a human rights violation. Nonstate actors are not generally accountable under international human rights law, but the state may sometimes be held responsible for human rights violations" (1994:21).

Subsequently, human rights protection has traditionally referred to the "public" realm of state governance and excluded the nonstate or private realm (see Romany 1993 and 1994).[3] Similarly in refugee law, human rights violations were traditionally violations perpetrated by the state or by actors of the state (see Romany 1994:90).

Many forms of violence against women are, in contrast, considered "private," committed by "nonstate actors." Private violence is most often described as violence within the traditional family structure where it supports and perpetuates the gender hierarchy at its most basic level. But this hierarchy is typically reflected in gender relations underpinning the public sphere of state and society. Moreover, the separation between public and private sectors is manifested "to different effects" in different societies (Cook 1994:6). Charlesworth (1994) explains that what is public in one society may be private in another but that which is the women's domain is the one consistently devalued. This combination of public/private demarcation and differentiation in cultural manifestations creates special problems for the protection of women's human rights, both within and between states.

Within some states condemnation of violence against women (public and private) grew markedly since the 1970s (see Dobash and Dobash 1992). *Between* states, female-specific violence only gained government attention beginning in the 1990s.[4] This lag epitomizes the "false separation of ethics" between foreign and domestic policy when it comes to violence against women, apparent in the historical fact that "no state has ever proposed sanctions, economic boycotts or war against another for its treatment of its female citizens" (Ashworth 1986:3). Many states have developed an infrastructure to act as intervening third parties, preventing and penalizing violence against women in their own countries, but continue to treat such violence as noninterferable in other countries, including in the case of refugees.[5] Refugees fleeing female persecution bring domestic and foreign policy face to face, and this is battled out in refugee determination processes, jurisprudence creation, and refugee policy development.

The public/private divide has traditionally informed readings of "persecution" in refugee law and impacted each of the three key characteristics of the refugee definition: the fit between existing *forms and causes of persecution* and women-specific experiences; women-specific experiences of protection or *internal flight alternatives*; and women's ability to establish *well-founded fear* or an individualized basis of persecution.

The persecution women flee may occur in *forms* of human rights violations typically dismissed within the five Convention grounds of persecution. Ironically, violence against women has been regarded as "the issue which most parallels a human rights paradigm and yet is excluded": "it involves slavery, it involves situations of torture, it involves terrorism, it involves a whole series of things that the human rights community is already committed to [fighting but] have never been defined in terms of women's lives" (Bunch cited in Friedman 1994:20).

For instance, the rape of women as a tactic of war aimed at destroying the "purity" of a racial or ethnic group could in theory be conceived as persecution on the grounds of nationality or social group, but traditionally has not. The view that rape (the *form* of persecution) is a "private" rather than public or state matter has precluded consideration of the structural basis of the persecution.

In other cases, women may flee persecution on the grounds of sex, falling outside the five existing Convention grounds or *causes* of persecution. Persecution occurring due to structural status as females has traditionally been precluded because such causes of human rights violations are not recognized and do not match traditional reasons men are persecuted. Sex-specific elements have generally been considered irrelevant to refugee claims worldwide, as epitomized in a statement by an Australian refugee hearing officer, who remarked: "Now, you make two claims: one is on your rape and one is on your religion. The rape question is not a Convention-related issue, therefore we will not discuss that question. We will go straight into the religion question."[6]

In other cases, officers have not merely dismissed gendered elements of claims, but made judgments on female claimants' proper cultural roles as a justification. For example, in one widely publicized Canadian case involving violation of a gendered dress code, the officer stated that the claimant should "show consideration for the feelings of her father" and "abide by the laws of general application she opposes" (see Young 1994).

More often than male claimants, females generally face a paucity of documentation in which to find evidence regarding the occurrence of persecution generally and the lack of state protection or internal flight alternatives (IFAs), evidence such as the conditions for women and statistical data on the incidence of violence in the country of origin. Even more damaging, evidence of generalized violence and IFAs may not even be deemed necessary if violence against women is considered culturally relative, that is, if states in particular cultures are believed to have the right to withhold protection under their own cultural rules.

Women's lack of access to proper documentation is compounded by the difficulties of providing hard evidence of a *well-founded fear* of individualized persecution. The requirement that claimants be responsible for proving that their fear is well-founded, the "burden of proof," consists of both subjective and objective elements. Objective elements include objective circumstances that give rise to the fear, while subjective elements refer to the claimant's genuine suffering from that fear. Whether or not immigration officers are aware of country-of-origin conditions, claimants must demonstrate well-founded fear of persecution. While this requirement puts the onus on claimants and creates an adversarial setting, it also supports a system described as allowing people to become directly and immediately involved in the process of calling attention to affronts to human dignity in their home state (Hathaway 1991b). They can make claims and bring their own evidence to bear upon decisions.[7]

Gendered Dependency

Access to claim-making and case-law-creation processes is stratified despite what should be an inherent recognition that "Persecution is, in fact, a violation of one's human rights, whether the claimant is a woman, man or child" (Liebich 1993:2). It was not until the early 1990s that women asylum seekers' socioeconomic disadvantages, both in their home countries and in receiving-country status determination processes, began to be noted. Women refugees' real and assumed dependency on male relatives prevents them from emigrating, may lead to what has been dubbed "sponsorship abuse," and ultimately prevents them from making their own independent claims.

Fewer women than men are able to migrate internationally, and those that do predominantly travel with a male family member who represents the family in claim-making processes. Women face structural disadvantages in all entry categories. For example, Boyd (1987, 1994) and others have shown that Canada's immigration and refugee system, considered one of the most progressive and open in the world, favors those who are or have been financially independent or have particular skills considered marketable— excluding women's unpaid labor, traditional skills, and contributions to society. This is balanced by a high rate of admissions for the family class or sponsored relatives. In the late 1980s Boyd showed that even among refugees, whose financial situation and skills are supposed to be irrelevant, women are overwhelmingly not accepted on humanitarian grounds (as Convention refugees, designated classes, and humanitarian refugees) but rather through landed immigrant classes, in particular the "family class" (dependent family members of status immigrants or refugees) where they outnumber men by 50 percent. As in other countries, dependents do not make their own claims, therefore if the primary applicant is rejected or deported, his sponsored relatives are as well. The sponsorship system can additionally lead to abuses of power. In 1990 Canada's National Clearinghouse on Family Violence produced a report on sponsored women who are battered (MacLeod and Shin 1990) showing that women dependents of sponsors who are abusive often become trapped in the situation, fearful of being deported to their country where they face persecution if they leave their abusive sponsor. At the same time, they are fearful of attempting to change to refugee status because their failure to make a refugee claim upon entry weighs against their credibility, often resulting in rejection and deportation (see MacLeod and Shin 1990; Pope and Stairs 1990).[8]

The Cultural Divide in Status Determinations

The manner in which refugee determination hearings are conducted and case law generated is shaped by gender biases that have traditionally favored male claimants. Barriers to recognition of female persecution thus occur not only in legal discourse and interpretations, but in how refugees are treated in refugee determination hearings. Gender bias underlying adjudicator and immigration officers' cultural framing often prohibits women from effectively proving the cause, individualized basis, and lack of flight alternatives. Women are less heard, less supported, and less understood during determination processes.[9]

Some cultural divisions affect all refugees, including women, despite disparate national, ethnic, and racial backgrounds. In particular, they face many stress-producing factors that can affect the telling, and hearing, of claims. Karola Paul, chief of the Promotion of Refugee Law Unit of the UNHCR Division of International Protection, produced an influential report in 1992 observing that refugees are often in a psychological "state of emergency" in the first days after arrival in a foreign country, making communication difficult during claim-making procedures. The claimant may be euphoric, "almost incoherent in communicating her joy at having escaped humiliation and persecution." Following initial euphoria, the claimant may be so depressed by uprooting from the country of origin and the traumatic events experienced that she becomes reserved and withdrawn and has difficulty producing information. These situations are particularly difficult when the persecution experienced is not commonly recognized and adjudicators do know not what type of information to look for (Paul 1992:11).

Claimants also commonly lack understanding of the status determination hearing, in particular the condition "that they have to *substantiate* in the first hearing all measures of persecution that they *individually* have been subjected to in order to avoid the credibility issues which can arise when new information is presented after the hearing" (Paul 1992:12, emphasis added). The particularized evidence rule, under which claimants must show that persecution that is general in nature (i.e., affecting all or groups of women in their country of origin) has affected them in particular, is difficult to comprehend in many refugees' non-Western cultures. Paul explains that "for refugees who come from cultures where the individual does not count as such but only as part of a collective, the individualized notion of persecution is hardly understandable"; claimants often describe in general terms the situation in the country of origin and "in terms of what has happened to her family, clan or tribe" rather than the persecution she herself experienced or is in danger of experiencing (12).

Claimants may not understand the questioning of refugee hearing officers, who seem to doubt well-known generalized persecution in the country of origin. They may even consider questioning by officials as a negative signal and may decide to be careful of what they say, becoming fearful and defensive or nervous and aggressive. Some refugees come from situations in which authorities do not accept dissonance, where their opinions are not wanted by officers of rank. Attempts to retrieve precise and "to the point" information from claimants may actually be interpreted as an order not to speak or explain further (Paul 1992:13).

As refugees, females also face particular difficulties presenting their claims because refugee officers may not understand that they may come from cultures in which it is "uncommon that women speak in public, i.e., outside the confines of their family collective. If a woman wishes to state something, a man from her family will represent her interests" (Paul 1992:14). And even if the refugee officer does encourage female claimants to speak, her own cultural rules may inhibit her from speaking. When represented by a male family member, she may not have her experience of persecution expressed. Refugee hearing officers describe the presence of female claimants as being "in the background," or as if they are not really there at all.[10]

When females do have the opportunity to tell their stories, the hearing room environment has not traditionally been sensitive to either gender or culture. For example, females may come from societies that highly value a woman's sexual honor as representative of the honor of her family. In some cases, a woman "who admits during the hearing that she has been sexually mistreated or even raped during detention would normally have to take her own life in accordance with the traditions of her home country in order to restore the honor of her family. . . . For a woman, the hearing itself therefore puts into question the norms and values to which she was accustomed in her country of origin. This fact will be aggravated if the hearing officer is a man. For Tamil women, for example, it is forbidden to be alone with a man in a closed room" (Paul 1992:14). Loyalty to family and cultural values may also inhibit a woman from divulging information about persecution perpetrated by kin. In some cultures family members may inflict severe violence, or even death, upon women to punish them for transgressing social mores and sullying the family honor. In other cases, women may feel ashamed that they are betraying gender-specific traditions (e.g., female genital mutilation) or male cultural rights (e.g., the right to beat one's wife), even if they disagree with such traditions.

Facing such inhibitions, female claimants may introduce vital information only as a last resort to avoid deportation. Sadly, information introduced late in the refugee process has low credibility and often still results in a negative decision: "the tragic consequence is that many women who have suffered severe persecution do not obtain refugee status. . . . What embitters these women most is that the shame is now out in the open but their 'sacrifice' was superfluous because it did not protect them from deportation or continued persecution" (Paul 1992:15). If rejected and deported, persecution by family, extended family, or community members in the country of origin may be heightened by the divulgence of information, considered further betrayal of family honor.

Research has shown that the culture among refugee hearing officers is also affected by stress-producing factors, as well as individual cultural and gender biases. Officers' abilities to make sound judgments can be affected by stress associated with the emotional/psychological exhaustion of day-to-day hearing of traumatic events and by cultural confrontations that may result when officers' own values are cast into question. Such stress may lead to feelings of disgust and indifference and to a tendency to favor less demanding asylum seekers (Paul 1992:16). Additionally, officers may not understand gender roles and practices of other cultures or the ways cultural values may inhibit claimants from presenting information in the way officers desire (Liebich 1993).

All of these barriers inhibit female claimants from making and verifying the merits of their claims. In Canada, as in other countries, jurisprudence accounting for women's experiences was scant before the late 1990s, therefore the meaning of persecution was derived from the experience of male claimants. Canada's 1993 Guidelines later explained: "The existing bank of jurisprudence on the meaning of persecution is based on, for the most part, the experiences of male claimants. Aside from a few cases of rape, the definition has not been widely applied to female-specific experiences, such as infanticide, genital mutilation, bride-burning, forced marriage, domestic violence, forced abortion, or compulsory sterilization" (para.7).

Instruments necessary to overcome these barriers to female-specific claim making would ironically not develop until greater opportunities emerged for women to make refugee claims more generally.[11]

Emerging Opportunities for Sex-Based Asylum Seeking

Several global trends become apparent during the 1980s, which generated both pressure and political space for the needs of refugee women to become more visible. First, the demographics of migration shifted worldwide, including a broad "feminization of migration" (Castles and Miller 1993), as a result of both changing *needs* and growing *opportunities* to migrate. Second, a marked evolution in the discursive framings of female refugees' experiences occurred in "soft law" (intergovernmental recommendations, resolutions, statements, and so on).[12] Third, the extent of violence against women began to be recognized globally at the same time that cultural feminism was gaining ground, resulting in a nascent shift toward a broader framework within the women's movement: human rights. These three trends brought about essential changes in global political opportunity structures, mobilizing structures, and cultural framings for women asylum seekers.

The Feminization of Migration

The feminization of migration refers to "the increasing role in all regions and all types of migration" that women have played since the late twentieth century, "one of four major international migration trends characterizing the modern world, including globalization of migration, acceleration of migration, and diversification of migration" (Castles and Miller 1993:8). It is believed to have resulted from the particular affects upon women of rapid changes arising from decolonization, modernization, and uneven development. Though women are still underrepresented, their numbers have increased in areas that men traditionally dominated, such as labor migration and as principle applicants. Among refugee populations the change was even more dramatic as women simply became visible. Dubbed "the forgotten majority," policy makers were surprised to learn that females typically constitute at least 50 percent of any uprooted people (UNHCR 2006), indeed that some refugee movements are predominantly female due to the fact that able-bodied men are often the last to leave their countries and the first to return (UNHCR 1995). Additionally, increasing numbers of women refugees mirror the dramatic worldwide increases in refugee movement generally since the 1970s. Asylum applications in highly industrialized countries of Europe, North America, Australia, and Japan rose from some 100,000 in 1983 to over 800,000, in 1992. The total number of applicants recorded between 1983 and 1992 was approximately 3.7 million in these countries alone (UNHCR 1993). By the end of the decade the total number of people of concern to the UNHCR, including refugees and internally displaced and stateless persons, reached a high of nearly 22 million. Since 2000, a slowdown in asylum applications in highly industrialized countries has led to the leveling off of the number of applicants awaiting decisions on claims to about 840,000 in 2004. In 2005 refugees totaled 9.2 million worldwide, although persons of concern to the UNHCR rose 13 percent from 2004, to 19.2 million (UNHCR 2005).[13]

Increasing volume and dispersion of women across entry categories raise new issues both for policy makers and for those who study the migratory process, in particular regarding the implications of links between ethnicity, class, and gender for the migration process and for ethnic community formation in host countries as it feeds into the migratory cycle (Castles and Miller 1993:8).[14] The feminization of migration is integrally related to factors influencing the globalization, acceleration, and differentiation of migration, but the ways females are affected, their mobility and opportunities, are different from men in many respects. But studies of female migrants have tended to focus on the role of female migrants in the family (see Morokvasic 1984), both in settlement and adaptive processes and in camps (see Fincher et al. 1994). This may reflect women's concentration in the "family class" among advanced industrialized receiving countries (UNHCR 1995). Immigration policy played a large role in shaping women's concentration in the family class by not valuing women's particular labor skills and failing to create conditions suitable for hearing women's refugee claims (UNHCR 1995).

But female migrants not only strengthen migratory cycles already underway through family and community roles, they also raise new policy considerations by leading *new* migration cycles and migrating for reasons different from males. These aspects of the "feminization of migration" received relatively little attention. Root causes of refugee movement have long been considered the same for women and men: gross human rights violations, war, and natural disasters. Receiving countries' influence upon refugee movement (e.g., through colonization, military involvement, political links, the Cold War, trade, and investment), refugee camps, and refugee resettlement has also been considered the same regardless of sex. But considered more closely, all of these may have particular implications for females. Such gendered differences became increasingly visible in practitioner policy reports, academic studies, and finally, soft law discourses during the 1980s.

Global Evolution of Soft Law Discourses

The influence and significance of international "soft law" has been widely debated due to its nonbinding nature, in contrast with legally binding "hard law" of international declarations, conventions, and treaties. While potentially a disadvantage, its nonbinding nature is also commonly regarded as a strength because it enables "the incorporation of conflicting standards and goals" as new or innovative legal developments emerge, by providing "states with the room to maneuver in the making of claims and counterclaims" (Chinkin 1989:866). Although states may disregard it, soft law may reflect and strengthen international lawmaking trends and create expectations for state behavior (Reisman 1988:374). Ultimately, soft law may provide a foundation for the development of "hard law." The development and ways that soft law discourses have been framed around women refugees generally and female persecution specifically may either constrain or facilitate opportunities for sex-based asylum seeking.

The discursive evolution of key issues and root causes of female-specific persecution occurred in roughly three contiguous and ultimately incomplete phases up to the early 1990s, characterized by gender neutrality, gender difference, and a nascent gender inclusivity.[15] Under traditional refugee policy and programs, considered *gender neutral*, the concerns and needs of women refugees were largely overlooked and little data about them existed (Morokvasic 1984). In 1989 Genevieve Camus-Jacques's groundbreaking work on women refugees showed that the number of female refugees generally exceeds that of males but "cultural patterns oblige women to remain 'invisible' to foreign male eyes," explaining why the UN High Commissioner for Refugees in the late 1980s reported that in a visit to Afghan refugee camps in Pakistan he "did not see any women." Through extensive work in refugee camps, she explained that invisibility was "a much deeper issue than a simple question of custom. . . . Refugee women encounter specific problems regarding protection, assistance, and participation in decision-making. The following remarks are unfortunately not based on statistical data, for the simple reason that such data on refugee women do not exist. In spite of the recognition that women and girls constitute most of the world's refugee population, policy-makers and field-workers still do not have the proper information which would enable them to implement adequate protection and assistance for refugee women or to allow them a greater voice in decisions regarding their lives" (Camus-Jacques 1989:141–142). Women refugees in camps were systematically overlooked in data collection, policy, and research, resulting in unbalanced policies and services (see Camus-Jacques 1989; Martin-Forbes 1992; Moser 1991). They were similarly overlooked in receiving-country status determination systems and settlement programs (Boyd 1994). Fincher and colleagues concluded that refugee women's invisibility was an effect of a more general "taken-for-granted view that women are the appendages of either protective males or the patriarchal state" (Fincher et al. 1994:150). Policies intended as gender neutral were, in effect, gender blind.

The illumination of women refugees was greatly facilitated by that of gender variables in international development. Esther Boserup's critical work in 1970 revealed that economic and welfare failure was related to gender-blind policies and programs. Development was a trigger issue that made women's equality a more global concern as opposed to nationally focused, contained, and culturally specific, as the economic repercussions of underdevelopment could be felt across borders. By 1975 the issue of gender in development reached the international level with the United Nations Decade for Women, which targeted "Development, Equality, and Peace." Concern emerged regarding development needs of women and children in refugee camps, where the majority of refugees are located. With this virtually new attention to gender in refugee studies in the early 1980s (Buijs 1993), women refugees became known as "the forgotten majority" (Camus-Jacques 1989). It was observed that alongside the same needs for physical protection, assistance, and participation in decision-making and status determination as men, women refugees in transit, in refugee camps, or facing cultural assimilation and role change in countries of asylum also face different risks and difficulties.[16] Women's invisibility had resulted in a tendency to treat their problems and needs reactively rather than proactively. Their needs were generally explained as a factor of some special vulnerability as females, rather than a result of relations between men and women in society.

Analysis of female persecution first appeared in the work of Swedish researcher Connie DeNeef. Her study, carried out between 1978 and 1984, was the first of sexual violence against refugee women and its effect on status seeking, eligibility, and determination processes. DeNeef analyzed refugee women's claims and situations and identified four categories of persecution particular to them in which sexual violence "may have played a role in the flight from the country of origin in any variety of ways." These lay the groundwork for international soft law that later developed.

1. Persecution based on a woman's political convictions, where the persecution is expressed through sexual violence (rape, sexual assault, torture methods concentrating on the genitalia, and the like). DeNeef explains, "Both for men and women in a number of countries sexual violence is an integral part of the methods of torture." Here torture is considered in a gender inclusive rather than gender neutral manner.

2. Persecution of a woman for "not conforming to the cultural traditions in the country of origin which prescribe a certain behavior for women," for example, "decapitating or stoning women who have committed adultery in some Islamic countries."

3. Persecution of women as both a strategic and symbolic act of war, where persecution is manifested through "the threat of, or through actual sexual violence against women" as an expression of conflict (or way of deciding conflicts) between different political or religious groups. Rape is used to hurt an entire group through humiliation, resulting social disintegration, and the introduction of ethnic impurities from resulting pregnancies.

4. Persecution of unprotected women, for instance women "who have fled [their country] because of conditions of war or of a reign of terror," where persecution is expressed through sexual violence because

such women may be "exceptionally vulnerable" due to having been "deprived of the men's traditional protection and hav[ing] lost their status of wife" (DeNeef 1984:6–7).

This groundbreaking work identified violence particular to women refugees for the first time. While the study did not explore women's motivations for seeking refugee status, it revealed the necessity for status determination systems to be aware of female-specific forms of persecution and deterrents women face against speaking about such experiences (particularly to male immigration officers), such as trauma and cultural taboos. References to an early report of DeNeef's research (prior to its 1984 publication) appear in regional and international discussions in the 1980s. The first mention of persecution as defined by DeNeef occurred at a 1980 UN roundtable designed to address the needs and risks arising from refugee women's "special vulnerability as women." The theme of vulnerability was to remain central to international discussions and debates about the nature of the persecution women face.

Two years later the European Parliament submitted a motion for a Resolution requesting that the 1951 Convention be reopened for the first time since its instatement in 1951, "for the purpose of including the word 'sex' therein on the same basis as the words 'race, religion . . .'." The motion also acknowledged the gendered nature of violence women experience by calling attention to interpersonal dimensions (beyond the traditional individual-state dimension). It stated that "extortion" and "inhumane treatment" may be perpetrated by either state authorities or nonstate actors, the latter when women infringe the moral or ethical code imposed on a social group to which they belong on the basis of cultural or religious traditions (Provision A). The motion also explicitly recognized that women's cultural infringements "do not constitute offences or crimes under provisions of international criminal law or United Nations agreements" (Provision B). This removes blame from the victims and redirects attention to the persecutors. The recommendation suggested subordination and persecution or "inhumane treatment" of women occurs because of their status as women within society, and because those who subject them to such treatment "belong to the same social group" and are thus "[immune] from criminal proceedings" (Provision C). It finally noted that the 1951 Convention "disregards persecution on the grounds of sex" (Provision D). The motion raised critical debates about cultural relativism and state sovereignty, and was rejected.

A new motion suggested persecuted women may be recognized as a particular "social group" within the 1951 Convention's five existing grounds of persecution, rather than through sex as a sixth category of persecution. In so doing, it emphasized the symptoms of sexual divisions in society rather than their structural causes. The motion passed on 13 April 1984, identifying "sexual violence against refugee women" within camps or by soldiers, border officials, or other state-related authorities (as DeNeef's categories 1, 3 and 4).[17] States were also advised that they may recognize women as members of "a particular social group" if they fear cruel or inhuman treatment for having transgressed the social customs of the society in which they live. This strategy was upheld by the Dutch Refugee Council (DRC) in a policy recommendation that same year, and by the UNHCR Executive Committee in 1985, each with slightly different definitions.

The Dutch Refugee Council's 1984 policy directive on refugee women was the most far-reaching, stating: "persecution for reasons of membership of a particular social group, may also be taken to include persecution because of social position on the basis of sex. This may be especially true in situations where discrimination against women in society, contrary to the rulings of international law, has been institutionalized and where women who oppose this discrimination, or distance themselves from it, are faced with drastic sanctions, either from the authorities themselves, or from their social environment, where the authorities are unwilling or unable to offer protection" (Advisory Committee on Human Rights and Foreign Policy 1987).

Here the social group to which women may belong is defined by "social position on the basis of sex." The persecution they face may be a consequence simply of sex, particularly when institutionalized discrimination against women is opposed or when women seek to "distance themselves from it." The DRC remained at the forefront of related policy discourses throughout the 1980s, with the Dutch delegates acting as a prime mover within their capacity as members of the UNHCR Executive Committee.[18]

In April 1985 a Subcommittee of the Whole on International Protection issued a report recognizing that "there are situations in which refugee women face particular hazards due to the mere fact that they are women" (para. 1). Its "Note on Refugee Women and International Protection" (EC/SCP/39, 8 July 1985, 36th Session) recognized the danger of "violation of their physical integrity and safety" in camps or in transit, particularly the threat of sexual abuse, including sexual exploitation, rape, and prostitution, through extortion, brutality, and abduction (para. 2, 3). These are violations women may experience once they become refugees, rather than causes of their refugee flight. The report observed that in such situations refugee women should have "right to equal treatment," but that neither the 1951 Convention and New York Protocol, nor the Statute of the Office of the UNHCR, "makes a distinction between male and female refugees, the basic assumption being that all refugees, irrespective of their sex, face the same problems and will be treated equally. In practice, however, the effects of the international refugee instruments and of humanitarian principles may be vitiated for some refugee women because the social conditions of women in a particular society may not permit their full impact to be felt" (para.4).

These limitations were observed to persist because of "prevailing attitudes" in both "countries of asylum and/or origin" (para. 5). As well, the report recommended that the UN follow the European Parliament resolution advocating use of the "social group" category: "As regards women who face harsh and inhuman treatment because they are considered as having transgressed the social mores of their society, consideration should be given by States to interpreting the term 'membership in a particular social group,' as mentioned in article 1 (A) (2) of the 1951 United Nations Refugee Convention, to include women belonging to this category."

However, the UNHCR Executive Committee did not accept this interpretation due to state objections on two counts. First, the interpretation of social group was too broad and, they argued, "could lead to a wider interpretation of refugee status for others. This interpretation is, after all, based on 'persecution' due to the transgression of certain social customs and not due to the status of the individual who does so." Second, the interpretation was rejected as a "condemnation of certain social customs" in some states.[19] These responses attempt to separate the status of women from the gender roles they are expected to embody. Recognition of women's greater protection needs due to a presumed inherent vulnerability, both as women and as refugees (those already recognized as such, not those seeking asylum) had won agreement relatively easily; it corresponded with traditional images of women as passive and requiring male protection, not necessarily because of their position in society as females but because of their inherent nature as females. Negotiation over "transgressions of social mores" on the other hand was more protracted; it raised the question of whether social mores themselves are persecutory toward women and based on women's status in society and whether a woman not *already* a refugee (in camps or in transit through dangerous territory) should be granted refugee status on such grounds.

The UNHCR Executive Committee resolved the problem of implicating states and cultures by passing a directive on Refugee Women and International Protection (36th Session, A/AC.96/671, 1985), including the brief statement "that States, in the exercise of their sovereignty, are free to adopt the interpretation that women asylum seekers who face harsh or inhuman treatment due to their having transgressed the social mores of the society in which they live may be considered as a 'particular social group.'" The UN's position was, unsurprisingly, criticized for going both too far and not far enough. States objected that too many women would arrive on their doorstep ("floodgate fear") and that the directive is culturally imperialistic. On the other hand, the provision appears only in a subcommittee report that advises and is not binding upon states, is impossible to monitor, and whose wording further emphasizes state rights to determine whether violence against women is considered a cultural right. It is also limiting in its characterization of violence against women; unlike characterizations of persecution in the 1951 Convention, here the suggested interpretation of social group identifies a woman's own transgressions as the defining cause of the persecution, rather than her inherent belonging to a social group. Only women who have "*transgressed* the social mores of the society in which they live" (emphasis added) can be considered persecuted, leaving out those that may choose not to transgress (due to fear of persecution), but rather to flee the country. This suggests that the social mores are not themselves persecutory or discriminatory, that only certain punishments for infractions are. This fails to reflect either the basis of social custom within politicized socially stratified societies or the potential for "transgressions" to be political acts. Instead, the persecuted individual is cast in a criminal light, transgressing codes rather than fighting for their rights. Finally, only "public" forms of female persecution are identified, thus a state must be directly implicated in the persecution through national laws and through individuals acting in an official capacity or as a representative of the state. Private violence is not a consideration.

However, like other UN documents the 1985 directive is discursively significant at the international level as it helped to make the issue worthy of international attention. The UNHCR Executive Committee reiterated its commitment at its thirty-ninth session in 1988, issuing Conclusion No. 54, "Refugee Women," recognizing both the "particular hazards, especially threats to [refugee women's] physical safety and sexual exploitation." A 1990 subcommittee "Note on Refugee Women and International Protection"

(EC/SCP/59, 28 August 1990) called upon international treaties for the civil, political, social, and cultural rights of refugee women embodied not only in refugee-related documents but also in human rights instruments. It recognized that "international protection of refugees also requires a human rights approach based upon equity, and refugee women should be informed about their rights as refugees and as women" (para. 65). It notes in particular the 1966 Human Rights Covenants, the Nairobi Forward Looking Strategies on the Status of Women (1985), and the UN Convention on the Elimination of All Forms of Discrimination Against Women (1979), all of which uphold right to equality regardless of sex (para. 8 and 9). The 1990 report also refers to causes of persecution as "severe gender-based discrimination," without reference to transgression of social mores as prerequisite. In a comment on the need for proper documentation, the document notes that "severe discrimination . . . may justify the granting of refugee status" (para. 18), explicitly naming for the first time persecution *based on* gender: "It is important that decision-makers involved in the refugee-status determination procedures have at their disposal background material and documentation describing the situation of women in countries of origin, particularly regarding gender-based persecution and its consequences."

Unfortunately, gender-based persecution remained undefined, while physical violence and discrimination were said to arise from circumstances common to refugees (male and female), and "not [from the] fact that they are subject to such violations of their rights" (para.14). Human rights violations against women refugees are not associated with sexual status, but rather, once again, with their increased vulnerability as refugees and females. And most damagingly, paragraph 17 explicitly states that international protection will *not* be readily extendable to all persecuted or at risk refugee women because "the universal refugee definition contained in the 1951 Convention and its 1967 Protocol relating to the Status of Refugees does not include gender as one of the grounds for persecution which will lead to refugee status being granted." The document instead stresses forms of female persecution resulting from increased vulnerability, reiterating Conclusion No. 39 (1985) on the social group category for persecuted women.

The 1991 UNHCR Guidelines on the Protection of Refugee Women, toward which the above report had been geared, addressed issues of concern to refugee women more generally, making a brief but relevant remark regarding female persecution. It identifies violence against women as a symptom of the need for economic and democratic development in the countries of origin.

It surpasses the 1985 UN Resolution by stating that women "fearing persecution or severe discrimination on the basis of their gender should be considered a member of a social group for the purposes of determining refugee status. Others may be seen as having made a religious or political statement in transgressing the social norms of their society." Here the term "gender-based persecution" is not used, rather recourse to the social group category of persecution is emphasized, but a move is made toward a more political interpretation.

These international developments contain both limitations and possibilities. It is not clear that international developments influenced the development of national jurisprudence in following years, or if existing jurisprudence was uncovered when international interest grew. The first comparative study of relevant jurisprudence emerged only after Canada's 1993 Guidelines were instated (Leiss and Boesjes 1994) and did not include cases prior to the late 1980s. It did however uncover and compare ten to twenty cases each in the Netherlands, Germany, France, and the United Kingdom (only summarily reviewing Canada and Belgium), identifying six common themes that surpass the international recommendations: persecution *arising from* or involving sexual violence, grave discrimination, guilt by association, women breaking norms and values of society, women carrying out odd jobs (for political causes), and political activism. In Canada as in other countries "persecution" is not defined in the national Immigration Act but derives its meaning through case law and interpretations of former precedents (OLAP 1994). National case law, its development and application, may be a vehicle through which new interpretations of persecution develop, setting precedents for other cases to draw upon. Prior to the development of Canada's 1993 Guidelines, refugee cases involving female persecution are for obvious reasons difficult to trace. There was no such category to be monitored, while relevant cases would emphasize the aspect of claims likely to be accepted under traditional frameworks, such as race or nationality. Moreover, aspects of claims considered irrelevant to the final decision are not usually recorded if a decision is positive.[20] But in theory, women could receive asylum through membership in a particular social group in accordance with the UNHCR's 1985 Conclusion. In 1987, two women were accorded Convention refugee status in Canada on the basis of "political opinion" in opposing Iranian laws governing dress (*Shahabaldin v. MEI*, 1987) and on the basis of belonging to a "particular social group" comprised of "single women living in a Moslem country without the protection of a male relative (father, brother, husband, son)" (*Incirciyan v. MEI*, 1987). The success of these cases may reflect growing international recognition of the special vulnerability of women refugees and the harsh punishments they face for deviating from accepted gender roles in society. They may also reflect anti-Islamic sentiments in the 1980s, as the acceptance of particular types of refugees is believed to send political messages to sending countries (Teitelbaum 1984). But positive cases in which gender was a primary factor remained uncommon and difficult to monitor, possibly reflecting inconsistent use of the 1985 UN recommendation by adjudicators, as later observed by IRB officials.

A 1992 IRB survey of women refugees in Canada from the top five sending countries between January 1990 and September 1991 serves as an alternative source of data on the prevalence of female persecution as a reason for flight prior to the instatement of the 1993 Guidelines. The survey captures refugee women's perspectives on "causes of flight," rather than causes corresponding strictly to the five 1951 Convention categories, with the intent of establishing if female violence had occurred as an important element of flight. A main cause identified was "female violence," which unfortunately was not defined (neither explicitly including nor excluding private violence). According to the findings, 4 percent of all female refugee claimants from the top five sending countries at that time named female violence as a reason for flight. This was before claimants could reasonably hope to be accepted on such grounds, suggesting it would be in their interests to instead identify a traditional reason for flight (the five persecution categories). Notably, the report further comments on the difficulties of documenting such cases, saying: "the incidence of female violence (including sexual assault, rape and forced abortion) is probably much greater than has been recognized here. According to a recent study, most women refugee claimants feel highly uncomfortable discussing such issues with officials involved in the refugee process. Many experience great shame and, due to family or cultural expectations, often choose to avoid the repercussions of disclosure" (IRB 1992:7).

Although only 4 percent of women in the study identified female violence, it ranked sixth out of a total of fourteen potential forms of persecution.

Violence Against Women as a Human Rights Violation

While progressive national developments (the Dutch Refugee Council) and emerging international discourses may have been important for female asylum seekers' emerging opportunities in Canada, other changes were also necessary to encourage sensitization, documentation, and acceptance of such claims. To this purpose, a crucial global trend was the growing salience of ideas and legal norms concerning women's human rights, specifically regarding violence against women, which emerged in the early 1990s.

As we have seen, recognition of women refugees by the international community grew suddenly and rapidly in the 1980s and did encompass some types of violence women experience, although the debate was never quite settled as to the structural causes of these experiences. By the early 1990s the stage was set for refugee women to be able to draw from the language of "women's human rights," which some activists claim had been moving into national and regional levels "at a pace that far exceeded that of any previous movement on behalf of women internationally" (see Friedman 1995:31). Groundbreaking feminist work in several fields broadened the definition of violence against women and internationalized it, stimulating the emergence of a new discourse.

Internationalization affected conceptualizations of both forms and causes of violence against women. Discussion of global causes first grew from attention to negative female-specific effects of gender-blind development programs and policies (for example, Beneria 1982; Sen and Grown 1988). This was followed by research attending to the gendered means and effects of, for example, militarism and war (Enloe 1989), the rise of nationalism and fundamentalism (Yuval-Davis and Anthias 1989; Jayawardena 1986), humanitarian aid and refugee policy (Moser 1991; Camus-Jacques 1989; Martin-Forbes 1992), and international relations more broadly; (Peterson and Runyan 1993; Sylvester 1994; Grant and Newland 1991). Violence against women was in itself finally recognized as an obstacle to development in the early 1990s (Bunch and Carrillo 1990). These researchers argued that gender hierarchies pervade not only state but also interstate relations, perpetuating and promoting the violent subordination of women that occurs through gender inequality and gender-blind state, societal, and family politics. The resulting interdisciplinary discourse describes structural processes and foundations that shape how states have long interrelated in ways that reinforce and exacerbate gender biases, while virtually ignoring these gendered processes and consequences. Violence against women must be understood as having root causes not only within specific cultures and contexts, but within the superstructure of interstate relations (Peterson and Runyan 1993). Unless confronted, it may be perpetuated internationally through the growth of the global market and international community, the globalization of information and other technologies, development, colonialism and the subsequent rise of anticolonialism, nationalism, and militarism (see Giles 1996; Grant and Newland 1991; Sylvester 1994; Peterson and Runyan 1993). Consequences include the growth of the international sex trade, child prostitution and mail-order brides, rape in war, and severe gender discrimination in fundamentalist regimes. This has been explained in various ways, but as Kandiyoti (1990) observed in a review of discourses up to 1990, different perspectives on women and nationhood in postcolonialism share "recognition that the integration of women into modern 'nationhood', epitomized by citizenship in a sovereign nation-state, somehow follows a *different* trajectory from that of men." This trajectory may create or amplify the violent subordination of females or may bring a new sense of state and interstate responsibilities for gender inequality.

A crucial dimension of the growing literature on violence against women was the novel international perspective arising from local grassroots women's endeavors in developing countries and multicultural projects by ethnic minorities in advanced industrialized countries (Schuler 1992). In 1990 Isis International produced a survey of documentation on violence against women during the 1980s, identifying over 650 entries from around the world, 350 from Latin America and the Caribbean alone. In countries like Canada, the United States, and Britain, women's movements became increasingly multicultural in all sorts of ways (see Schuler 1992). They described different experiences of violence women of different cultural and ethnic backgrounds face, exacerbated by discrimination in accessing resources, protection and rights within majority cultures. Schuler explains: "the discovery of gender violence . . . took different paths in different parts of the world, but in general, it emerged in the context of activism and research on issues related to the social status of women and their right to participation. . . . [I]n Europe and North America [it] coincided with the early stages of feminist theory development. In other parts of the world the convergence of development, human rights, and feminist praxis produced the framework for discovering the nature, forms, extent and pernicious effects of violence against women" (1992:5).

Increasingly, women in different countries also began working together, broadening conceptualizations of violence against women and types of redress: "coalitions and networks based in Europe and North America tended to be more specialized—concentrating on one form of violence such as rape—than those in the Third World where groups often coalesced to work on a variety of issues simultaneously" (Schuler 1992:5). Merging definitions, the Asia Pacific Forum on Women, Law and Development described "gender violence" in a way that could be applied to the divergence between male and female experiences of globalization: "any act involving the use of force or co-ercion with an intent of perpetuating/promoting hierarchical gender rela-tions" (APFWLD in Schuler 1992:5). The Canadian Advisory Council on the Status of Women in 1991 provided an equally broad definition: "Violence against women is a multifaceted problem which encompasses physical, sex-ual, psychological, and economic violations of women and which is inte-grally linked to the social/economic/political structures, values, and policies that silence women in our society, support gender based discrimination, and maintain women's inequality" (CACSW 1991).

Violence against women made it onto the agenda of the 1985 Nairobi conference largely at the prodding of nongovernmental organizations, "al-though not yet on the same scale as other development issues" (Schuler 1992:4). That year the UN General Assembly passed its first resolution recog-nizing the significance of violence in the home and the need for "concerted and multi-disciplinary action" (Res. 40/36 of 29 November 1985), though not evoking women's human rights. In 1991 the Expert Group Meeting on Vio-lence Against Women reported to the UN Commission on the Status of Women and the Economic and Social Council, proposing a Draft Declara-tion on Violence Against Women. In it they affirmed "that violence against women is a violation of human rights," and recognized "that violence against women is also a manifestation of historically unequal power relations, which have led to the domination over and discrimination against women and the prevention of their full advancement." Violence against women was recog-nized as an obstacle to the achievement of equality, development, and peace. The report called for a more expansive definition of violence against women and women's rights by the United Nations, and a clear commitment in the international community to the eradication of violence against women (EGM/VAW/1991/1). This was one of the earliest UN reports to use a "women's human rights" argument over nondiscrimination.

The nascent literature on "women's human rights" that began to emerge in the 1990s went beyond recognition of forms of violence against women in different countries to look at explicitly how and why it is maintained through the underlying legal structure of states in an interstate system. Romany (1993) argued that by relegating state responsibility to spheres of social life consid-ered "public," the legal structure succeeded in casting "women as aliens" within their own countries, lacking basic citizenship rights and protections in social spheres considered private. State interpretations and applications of international human rights law have generally been part of the system that supports underlying causes of violence against women. Women's human rights would not be protected if women did not enjoy basic citizenship rights, nor would they receive international protection for violence considered "private" and beyond state responsibility, as seen in traditional refugee law. If amended, receiving countries should not simply respond to female-specific human rights violations causing refugee flight, but address the overarching system that supports causes and prevents redress of such violence.

In North America, international migration studies in the late 1980s and early 1990s also began touching upon violence against women (Bonnerjea 1985; Heise 1989; Pope and Stairs 1990; Greatbatch 1989; Indra 1987). Like intergovernmental documents described earlier, they relied primarily on equality and nondiscrimination doctrines and largely focused on sexual violence in refugee camps. Work also emerged on the relation between domestic violence and refugee sponsorship systems (Pope and Stairs 1990), raising questions about abuse fostered within receiving countries through gender-biased refugee systems. On the other hand, as seen earlier, intergovernmental documents on refugee women lacked a solid human rights framework and built on traditional images of women as passive and vulnerable rather than situating their persecution within a sociopolitical structural context, and they largely lacked parallel grassroots political action. These were aspects the fledgling women's human rights movement could access, creating the potential for further expansion in refugee policy and underlying human rights discourses in the 1990s.

Asylum Seekers' Global Symbolic and Strategic Challenge

The legal and administrative framework of asylum seeking reveals both gender-neutral and gender-specific constraints derived from the refugee definition itself, from the public/private division in international law, and from resource limitations and cultural framings. Within the institutional logic of asylum seeking, however, the role of asylum seekers themselves in interpretative processes also emerges as they are required to make individualized claims and carry the burden of proof. Asylum seekers must prove that their fears of persecution are well-founded on subjective and objective, individual, and collective grounds, and in doing so they may bring new human rights abuses to light. In theory, international law balances the rights and roles of asylum seekers and states in interpretative processes surrounding the meaning of persecution, which determines whether individuals will in fact be eligible to "enjoy" asylum once they have sought it.

But the public/private demarcation in statist discourse informs international law, state interpretations of persecution, and the extent of state responsibility for human rights violations giving rise to refugee flows. This may negatively affect female claims that challenge the demarcation between "public" and "private," and between foreign and domestic responsibility. Appropriate theoretical and policy frameworks may help adjudicators to more equitably hear claims involving female persecution, but until institutionalized the significance of claim making and the growth of jurisprudence looms large. Jurisprudence enables new legal interpretations to be developed. Traditionally, however, stratified access to equitable refugee determination processes and lack of relevant documentation for women, alongside the public/private divide and gender-biased status determination processes, have fostered predominantly male-based jurisprudence. This vicious cycle exaggerates the burden of proof facing female claimants. On one hand it perpetuates the fundamental contradictions between externally imposed identities and actual experiences of asylum seekers by obstructing their credibility, and on the other hand it may necessitate their greater action. These claimants must work harder to find alternative ways of proving the merits of their claims, including, as later chapters will show, taking both institutional and noninstitutional actions.

The dearth of well established theoretical and administrative frameworks for refugees fleeing female persecution necessitates both theoretical revisioning "from above" and practical developments "from below." Both are essential, mutually shaping and reinforcing. On one hand, states must establish a framework for determining whether the experience of individuals seeking asylum amounts to persecution. Development from below occurs through claim-making that confronts the political boundaries of state responsibility, as in this case untraditional women refugees overcome disadvantages to foster the growth of case law. Such claimants face formidable structural barriers to "seeking and enjoying" asylum, thus becoming more than ever political actors who must seek strategic means to overcome constraints in receiving countries.

Asylum seekers therefore face and pose symbolic and strategic challenges within status determination processes. Despite structural barriers we can see a potential forum in which asylum seekers can bring to light the occurrence, forms, and nature of female experiences of persecution. Interpretative processes involved in claim making and the development of jurisprudence help drive the institutionalization of untraditional definitions of persecution. In this the state is a vehicle for expanding interpretations of human rights, while interaction between national and international legal and moral norms facilitates claim making that fuels the need for new interpretations. But women asylum seekers need structural opportunities to better access and influence interpretative processes. The illumination of the invisible majority as migration became increasingly feminized brought with it a discursive evolution in soft law. Not surprisingly, the most readily accepted image of persecuted refugee women was that of vulnerability. This went hand in hand with recognition of sexual violence, particularly against women in transit and in camps who had lost their traditional status as wife. A later shift occurred toward viewing female persecution as the result of women's "deviance," suggesting their actions were not political but criminal (if harshly punished) in their societies, and that a woman complying with persecutory laws is not persecuted. This cast the political nature of women's flight into voluntary, irrational, or indeed criminal actions. With the exception of the European Parliament's rejected 1982 motion for a resolution, policy recommendations up to 1992 tended to focus on "public" violence against women, excluding violence by nonstate actors. Conclusions and recommendations concentrated on images of women as vulnerable, passive, and deviant. These themes have their rightful place in categorizations of female persecution but fail to get to the root of the persecution and rights to protection.

The apparent conflict between conceptions of women as *nonpolitical* (e.g., violence as a factor of women's innate vulnerability) and as *deviant* (transgressing cultural mores) is one endemic to women's position in modern transformations of society. Feminist writers on race and ethnicity and on international relations have remarked that as the cornerstone of many ideologies of national identity, women often find their rights as citizens defined by their female-specific role as cultural markers, such that their needs and identities are equated with those of the nation and culture in which they live (Yuval-Davis and Anthias 1989), and not their individual needs or needs as women. Often highly praised as "mothers of the nation," their guarded rights become a catch-22 hinging on both national and gender stereotypes that may fragment basic human rights principles. This is no less true for women seeking asylum in a foreign country, where they have long been perceived as symbols of cultural continuity, bringing with them categorical belief systems, values, and culture-specific traditions and social structures.

Refugee-creating factors in the global system have increasingly thrown women into positions where they seek asylum, have opportunities for their needs to be recognized, but continue to face stereotypes in both sending and receiving countries. This prevents recognition of causes of refugee movement particular to females. Human rights discourses provide a logical vehicle for such recognition, to evoke state responsibility beyond the immediate citizenry and beyond culturally relativist conceptions of women's rights as citizens of other countries. The refugee policy and human rights discourses discussed here were important stepping stones for Canada's March 1993 Guidelines, and also for other important developments in state responsibilities for women's human rights later the same year. In June 1993 the fourth World Conference on Human Rights took place and was the first ever to address women's human rights. That year the United Nations accepted the draft Declaration on the Elimination of All Forms of Violence Against Women (GA Res 48/104, passed 20 December 1993, ratified in 1995), and for the first time appointed a UN Special Rapporteur on Violence Against Women. Canada's Guidelines must be understood, like each of these developments, as part and parcel of a global women's human rights movement that emerged and began to gather strength in the late 1980s. But the Guidelines and their advocates also contributed to the movement. At these and other international gatherings IRB Chairperson Mawani promoted the Guidelines as a strong example of a women's human rights protection mechanism. In fact, the Guidelines may be described as an early attempt "to move beyond mere visibility for women's human rights to actual accountability for abuse," a call made by women's human rights advocates through the 1990s (Friedman 1995:31). The Canadian Guidelines build upon, transcend, and institutionalize earlier frameworks and typologies of female persecution, bringing together the strands of feminist theorizing and research described and making them actionable. They reinterpret international human rights and refugee law and apply it to national refugee policy, explicitly using the language of women's human rights, with direct effects for persecuted women and the women's human rights movement. The debates surrounding their development, and their successful outcome, contributed to a surge of work in the 1990s on women's human rights, state responsibility, and more specifically, female persecution.

The international structural context, asylum-seeking system, and trends illustrated are key to stimulating and enabling activism from below on the part of asylum seekers themselves and were important for the later growth of the refugee movement in Canada and its policy impact. We turn now to policy developments in Canada, in particular the dynamics of government-nongovernment interaction and the role of asylum seekers. How did the development of the Canadian Guidelines breach the impasse of "mere visibility for women's human rights to actual accountability for abuse"? How was the state compelled to accept responsibility for persecuted female noncitizens and to institutionalize an explicit commitment to women's human rights? These questions are addressed in the following chapters.

Chapter 4
Moving In: Asylum Seekers' National Rights, Resources, and Opportunities

> *Every individual is equal before and under the law and has the right to the equal protection and equal benefit of the law without discrimination and, in particular, without discrimination based on race, national or ethnic origin, colour, religion, sex, age or mental or physical disability.*
> —Canadian Charter of Rights and Freedoms, 1982, Section 15

The gendered international structural context of political opportunities, mobilizing vehicles, and approaches to framing migration, discussed in Chapter 3, interacts with and affects national migration systems, which in turn further shape international migration trends. The resulting institutional logic of asylum seeking, refugee determination, and policy-making processes makes asylum seekers' policy agency viable. As a "subsystem of the migration system" (Boutang and Papademetriou 1994:20), Canada's migration system, its policies, and the ways they are formulated must now be examined to identify changes in national political opportunities, mobilizing and framing structures that preceded and facilitated the sex persecution campaigns. The following depicts the Canadian context and asylum-seeking process; identifies critical changes in national opportunity structures in the 1980s and analyzes how they facilitated the development of the campaign network; and consequently introduces core campaigners including asylum seekers and supporters. I argue that newly emerging opportunity structures shaped imperatives and mobilization prospects for refugee policy change, which in Canada is typically a "high risk" policy area (Dirks 1995), during what was essentially a period of increasingly restrictive immigration practices under an unsympathetic government.[1] In particular, these nascent opportunities directly and indirectly bolstered women asylum seekers' institutional claim making as well as their noninstitutional actions, the latter including public actions to influence the institutional context itself.

Canada's Refugee System and the National Climate

Jurisdiction over migration is one policy area beside agriculture in which federal-provincial authority has been shared since Confederation in 1867.[2] Unlike the United States and Australia, Canada has never had a federal organizational base devoted exclusively to immigration and refugee matters. Rather, immigration has historically been combined with other policy and administration areas, primarily expressing security or labor priorities (Hardcastle et al. 1994:106). The federal government has historically been hesitant to raise debates, make legislative changes, or commit itself to a long-term vision regarding immigration, even avoiding contentious issues in parliamentary debates over proposed legislation by instead using Orders in Council to modify regulations and procedures (Dirks 1995). During the 1970s, provincial interest in migration authority grew markedly as immigration, through selection criteria and levels, became a tool for protecting regional and language rights (Simeon 1987:265–267).

Unlike federal and provincial governments, nongovernmental organizations (NGOs) always sought greater involvement, legitimacy, and authority in international migration matters. Although the real extent of voluntary sector influence upon refugee policy making has not been ascertained,[3] its humanitarian interest in immigrant and refugee matters has long been recognized as a significant dimension of Canada's refugee regime and has become fundamental in the provision of services (Hawkins 1972; Ruddick 1994). NGOs have historically been involved in national immigration consultations, representing the interests and needs of immigrants and refugees regarding entry levels, composition, and social services during and after status determination. Their historical involvement also depicts the increasing number, types of involvement, and issue interests of ethnic organizations, immigrant and refugee advocacy groups, and other humanitarian groups in Canada over the years (Hawkins 1972; Chapman 1994; Ruddick 1994). In the immediate postwar years church involvement was institutionalized in overseas activities including screening and selecting refugees (Hawkins 1972:303). Federal government financed their activities until the early 1950s, but support tapered off as government began institutionalizing its own professional system of management (Dirks 1995:101). In particular, government no longer wanted nongovernment agencies to handle the selection of immigrants and refugees abroad. By 1960, voluntary organizations were strongly redirected toward family reunion and inland resettlement operations. A labyrinth of inland services for immigrants and refugees developed, but with little guidance in relation to the federal government's immigration program and with little interorganizational structure (Hawkins 1972:304).[4]

A confluence of internal and external pressures led to deep changes in Canada's migration system in the late 1970s and the 1980s, which fostered NGOs' greater advocacy power, coordination and inclusion in consultative style policy making, as well as greater rights and opportunities for international migrants. Dramatic changes in international migration coincided with economic downturn and restructuring of economies and subsequent changes in Canada's refugee law. By the 1970s, a changing immigrant and refugee constituency and volume brought mounting pressures and a radical reassessment of policy. International migrants increasingly arrived from less developed countries, and illegal migration steadily rose, two scenarios that the government was not equipped to manage. In response the 1976 Immigration Act was passed, stressing educational and employment preferences over racial determinants as the major criterion for status determination in order to address Canada's need for economic growth (Hawkins 1971:52). Section 7 finally formalized intergovernmental authority, requiring the immigration minister to actively consult with the provinces to determine annual immigration levels (see Boyd and Taylor 1990:37), while section 3(d) requires the government to cooperate with the voluntary sector particularly in the provision of settlement services.

The 1976 Immigration Act distinguishes three different classes of immigrants: independent immigrants, family class, and refugees. This gave refugees, for the first time, statutory recognition as well as inland status determination procedures, by far the most controversial aspect of the act. Previously, although Canada had ratified the 1951 Convention Relating to the Status of Refugees, refugees and those in "refugee-like" situations were admitted through ad hoc provisions or Orders in Council that "suspended normal immigration regulations and routines and permitted relaxed criteria for screening and processing to be substituted" (Dirks 1995:61). And like other countries adhering to UN conventions on refugees, Canada was not previously concerned with asylum seekers claiming refugee status from within Canada or at its borders. Unlike refugees resettled from overseas, inland asylum seekers do not undergo screening and selection processes by overseas officials and thus may lack travel documents and generally raise very different management issues. Regularizing acceptance of such refugees changed Canada's refugee regime from a system oriented toward "resettlement from abroad," to a country of "first asylum," opening Canada to a much larger pool of potential refugees (Dirks 1995).

The Immigration Act was weak in defining long-term objectives for Canada, and by the early 1980s its operational structures were already proving cumbersome, particularly in the area of refugee determinations. Canada was experiencing a tremendous increase in refugee claims, for which it was ill prepared to deal. From the 1970s to 2000, the annual number of inland refugee claims grew at a remarkable rate. In 1976 only about 600 inland refugee claims were made, of which approximately 60 percent were accepted as Convention refugees (see Dirks 1995:77). In 1986, 18,280 inland claims were made. These thousands of inland claimants were further confronted with "a cumbersome, multi-step process" including appeals that could provoke long delays (Knowles 1992:173). By May 1986 some 23,000 claims were backlogged, and just three years later that number reached nearly 50,000 (see Malarek 1987:104).

Significantly, these dramatic changes also coincided with a period of profound identity crisis and structural vulnerability in Canada. Canada's domestic sociopolitical climate in the 1980s and early 1990s has been described as one of turmoil unlike others; Canadians exhibited what has been described as a dramatic "decline of deference" (Nevitte 1996), a reallocation of authority (Rosenau 1992) or shift from "a devotion to authority to cynicism and self-assertiveness" (Flanagan 1982:408), quite unlike the high degree of trust and cooperation traditionally characterizing Canadian attitudes toward government. Individual and group rights, and Canadian identity itself, were hotly contested. Conflict over French/English citizenship rights *within* Canada became complicated by increasingly organized nonregional and nonlanguage interests, such as First Nations, women, and ethnic minorities. This coincided with increasing conflict over Canada's place in the world and the identity of its population as Canadians. The Constitution, free trade, welfare state devolution, women's rights, and international migration dominated the national agenda.

Constitutional debates raised fragile Canadian identity issues internally, the most extreme being the specter of Quebec's separation from Canada. Controversy evolved around how the Constitution was to set out the division of powers between federal and provincial governments, and subsequently how status and powers should be divided among the provinces. Quebec's insistence on special status as one of the two founding cultures of Canada pitted French Canada, or French Quebecers, against the "Rest of Canada." Canadian nationalists and Quebec sovereigntists became increasingly polarized and unable to reach agreement on government proposals in 1982, 1987, and 1992.

Constitutional debates also evoked demands by nonregional and non-language interests whose needs were being overshadowed by the French/English question. Two fundamental vehicles for such demands were the government's policy on multiculturalism and the 1982 Canadian Charter of Rights and Freedoms. Multiculturalism was brought to the fore in the 1970s by Prime Minister Trudeau to recognize the racial and ethnic diversity of Canada within a bilingual framework. Knowles comments: "In a sense it was both the logical child of official biculturalism and a polite gesture to non-English and non-French Canadians, who now made up a significant source of potential support for the Liberal Party" (1992:169). In 1972 a minister of multiculturalism was appointed and a Multiculturalism Council and Multiculturalism Directorate were established within the Department of the Secretary of State. In 1988 Prime Minister Mulroney established a separate ministry for multiculturalism and in July of that year Bill C-93, the Canadian Multiculturalism Act, was passed.

The Canadian Charter of Rights and Freedoms arose out of the Constitution Act of 1982, which provided for a domestic amending process that as Simeon explains, "bypasses federal-provincial relations and makes salient identities and interests that are nonregional—that are, indeed, hostile to regionally defined interests" (1987:268). The charter, and more specifically the equality rights section fought for by NGOs, was both instrument and effect of changes in Canadian attitudes toward government. The Constitution and Charter of Rights and Freedoms "not only define the relationship between the individual and the state, and between various parts of the state, but also include principles defining the relationships between various collectivities or groups of people" (CACSW 1992:57).

Processes of establishing the charter also "demystified the federal-provincial process for many groups." Mechanisms were set in place giving greater attention and legitimacy to NGOs and nonregional issues in intergovernmental relations, in particular the use of the legal system and court rulings (Simeon 1987:268). Greater NGO pressure could be, and was, brought to bear on federal government and federal-provincial relations. The Charter of Rights and Freedoms and the ideology of multiculturalism were important for citizens generally and for specific groups, as Cairns explains: "The Charter brought new groups into the constitutional order or, as in the case of aboriginals, enhanced a pre-existing constitutional status. It bypassed governments and spoke directly to Canadians by defining them as bearers of rights, as well as by according specific constitutional recognition to women, aboriginals, official language minority populations, ethnic groups through the vehicle of multiculturalism, and to those social categories explicitly listed in the equality rights section of the Charter. The Charter thus reduced the relative status of governments and strengthened that of the citizens who received constitutional encouragement to think of themselves as constitutional actors" (1988:121).

According to section 27, the charter must be interpreted in a manner consistent with the aims of multiculturalism, described as "reaffirming two fundamental human rights in Canadian society—the right to be different (preserving culture) and the right to remain the same (receiving equal treatment)" (Agnew 1996:145; see Elliot and Fleras 1990:65).

Nationalism and sovereignty encouraged public panic over rising international migration levels, but multiculturalism as a defining feature of Canadian identity gained increasingly organized support. The Canadian Multiculturalism Act passed in 1988 recognized and promoted multiculturalism as "an invaluable resource in the shaping of Canada's future" (section 3[2]). It drew upon the Canadian Human Rights Act, (1977, amended 1983), which provides that "every individual should have an equal opportunity with other individuals to make the life that the individual is able and wishes to have, consistent with the duties and obligations of that individual as a member of society" (preamble). Multiculturalism was increasingly accepted as encompassing nonethnic identity groups in a broad "politics of identity" (Kymlicka 1998:9)

At the same time, international migration matters were becoming a real priority for government and publics for the first time. Support grew for multiculturalism and recognition of the importance of international migration in founding and building Canada (settlement, agriculture and industrialization) and its constituency, past and future. By the mid-1990s, 16 percent of Canada's population was foreign born, more than twice that of the United States (see Kymlicka 1998). Government support for marginalized racial, ethnic, and immigrant populations had increased substantially. International migration remained high on the government agenda and indeed is now considered crucial to offset Canada's aging population and declining birth rate. International migrants saw their status and legitimacy rise in many respects, including rights as Canadians or potential Canadians with citizenship rights.[5] The Charter of Rights and Freedoms was fundamental for the latter, gradually being applied to most people within Canadian territory: citizens, denizens, and noncitizen residents and visitors.

Skyrocketing international migration levels led government to download more service provision to private and voluntary sectors in order to cope and brought increasing coordination between NGOs and government in service provision (entry, advocacy, and settlement services). The proliferation of NGO activity in the international migration sector, which also included new action on women refugees' issues, mirrored NGO growth in other areas as part of the government's concerted move toward a more mixed economy of welfare (see Chapman 1994; Ruddick 1994). Thus both government departments and services and NGO services grew, bringing new relations with government, in policy making and implementation, status determination and settlement issues (Dirks 1995:102). By the 1990s government was boasting NGOs as an integral part of its immigration and refugee regime. Government services and investments continued to expand, including the development of "arms-length" government or quasi-government organizations. Some organizations, primarily nonsecular, were created or remained independent of government funding. To coordinate this growth, secular and nonsecular umbrella groups emerged. With the growth of international migration NGOs that occurred, the sector as a whole became increasingly fertile, involving professionals and highly articulate activists skeptical of government but able to move government funding to their advantage and have a strong voice in politics and policy. They have been increasingly regarded with a high degree of legitimacy. As Hardcastle and colleagues observe, Canada's humanitarian NGOs "have played a role disproportionate to their size" (1994:117). This is in no small part due to the energy and capabilities their membership.

It contributed to what Adelman and colleagues (1994) have described as a refugee policy-making situation in Canada characterized by "the tension between two embedded dynamics: a 'nation-building statism,' involving policy management by governmental elites according to an agenda which legitimates state action and promotes national goals, and a 'pluralistic' social and political structure which enables particular social pressures to bear on the process." Interests include political parties, organized labor, business, ethnic minorities, humanitarian interests, environmental interests, ethnocentric anti-immigration groups, and public opinion. Refugee policy making became increasingly vulnerable to pluralist intrusions (Adelman et al. 1994:121).

During this time, refugee NGOs also became deeply influenced by the women's movement. What some have referred to as the "Third Wave" of feminism in the late 1980s and the 1990s marked the onset of a more concerted effort to incorporate different experiences of multiculturalism, race, and ethnicity. This produced an inherent critique of more essentialist or universal conceptions of the female identity, particularly as previously formulated around the experiences of upper- and middle-class white women. The more poststructuralist bent of feminist theorizing and action during this period emphasized the discursive power and ambiguity of gender terms and categories. Yet, even while moving toward a theory of "cultural feminism," the increasing diversity of the feminist movement in turn reified the impetus for theorizing and action around concerns common to women globally, such as female-specific violence. That is, the search for a universalizing framework remained constant and indeed became prominent in the women's human rights movement that had emerged powerfully by the tail end of the 1990s (see Chapter 3). All this had important impacts for refugee women in Canada, as previously disparate refugee and women's organizations began to take on board refugee women's issues. And gains achieved by earlier feminist "waves," including the incorporation of legal obligations on gender equality in both the 1982 Canadian Charter of Rights and Freedom and the 1977 Canadian Human Rights Act, were important for women's organizations generally and refugee women's organizations specifically. The Canadian charter contained key equality provisions for women, culminating in section 28, which states that "Notwithstanding anything in this Charter, the rights and freedoms referred to in it are guaranteed equally to male and female persons."[6]

A Patchwork of State Responses: Mobilizing Advocacy and Asylum

In this context the state instituted a patchwork of responses to the refugee crisis, which ultimately served to increase asylum seekers' political leverage, antistate mobilizations generally and within the core campaign network studied here. The following analyzes these responses, revealing the evolution and state of the Canadian refugee system up to the eve of the campaigns and the parallel emergence of rights, resources, and opportunities for asylum seekers to navigate and challenge this system. It draws examples and implications for claimants fleeing female persecution and concludes with impacts on members of the core campaign network specifically.

The Administrative Response: Increasing Processing Delays

Canada has generally been more successful coming up with short-term administrative solutions to international migration than long-term legislative solutions (see Cox and Glenn 1994:290–291). In the early 1980s these involved imposing a nonuniversal visa system requiring visas for visitors from countries likely to produce illegal migrants and carrier sanctions for airlines carrying passengers without proper documentation. These moves reflect the worldwide turn toward what has been ironically termed a preventive approach to the refugee problem, in this case preventing individuals from seeking asylum. But as processing delays continued to grow, government fell back on adjustment of status tactics, initiating a mass clearing of backlogged claims through two Administrative Review programs without simultaneously taking steps to prevent future buildups. In order to address a backlog of 23,000 claims the first program granted amnesty to all claimants entering Canada before 21 May 1986. The backlog took several years to process while new claims accumulated under the still inadequate system, prompting a second backlog clearance program in 1989 to deal with some 50,000 claims (see Dirks 1995). Administrative alternatives such as applications for Minister's Permits on Humanitarian and Compassionate grounds became increasingly popular. These offer residence through the immigration minister's personal review and authorization in individual cases. Humanitarian and compassionate applications can be made any time through what was then the Employment and Immigration Commission, an administrative body.

These administrative solutions added to processing times of claims. Backlogs took years to clear, and last resort Minister's Permits and Humanitarian and Compassionate class applications added another layer to determination processes. But as well, these developments created alternatives and time for rejected claimants to seek support and information. In this study, lawyers interviewed described processing delays and their effects upon claimants. One commented: "Sometimes cases were postponed, even three years. . . . This affects people. Living in a country for four or five years, waiting for your case, you meet someone and start another life, you have children, and then you are refused! Those people then go in appeal and wait another year."[7] Others noted that cases could run between four and eight years.[8] While typically a cause of great instability and anxiety for claimants, such delays may provide opportunities to become established in Canada, make contacts with Canadians, attain support, learn how the system works and how to challenge it. This capacity was enhanced by other changes to the refugee system implemented around the same time.

The Judicial Response: New Rights and Increasing Mediation

A new judicial approach was developed that granted individual rights to refugees such that they could not be turned away without full oral hearing. This profound change had been advocated by voluntary sector organizations since the early 1980s. But the greatest influence and determining factor was a landmark decision handed down by the Supreme Court of Canada in the case of *Singh v. MEI* in 1985, the same year that the Canadian Charter of Rights and Freedoms came into effect. Dirks observes that with this decision "the long and rancorous debate over oral hearings came to an abrupt close. . . . As a result of this judgment, the government introduced amendments to the Immigration Act in Parliament in June 1985" (Dirks 1995:82). In the *Singh* case, failure to grant refugee claimants the right of full oral hearing, even at appeals stages, was found to be a constitutional violation according to charter (Knowles 1992), despite the fact that the individuals in such cases were not Canadian citizens or permanent residents. This had a number of profound implications.

First, recognizing right to oral hearing through the 1982 Canadian Charter of Rights and Freedoms in effect equated asylum seekers' rights with those of Canadian citizens (Knowles 1992:174). Institutional recognition of the charter as a basis for refugee and immigrant rights expanded and solidified in subsequent years. In a 1995 speech to the international judicial conference in the United Kingdom, the Immigration and Refugee Board Chairperson declared: "All claimants have the protection of the Canadian Charter of Rights and Freedoms, concerned as it is with life, liberty and security of the person" (Mawani 1995a). Second, between 1985 and 1989 Canada's determination system changed radically to meet new requirements raised by the *Singh* decision. Bill C-55 (Refugee Reform Bill), proposed in May 1987, altered the entire structure of the refugee department from an administrative to a quasi-judicial branch with autonomous decision-making power. In 1986 the

Immigration and Appeal Board was expanded and by 1988 refugees came to enjoy the benefits of an adjudicative status determination model involving full oral hearing, review, and appeals processes. In 1989 when Bill C-55 came into effect, the new system was renamed the Immigration and Refugee Board (IRB). Operating independent of Employment and Immigration Canada (EIC), adjudicators and lawyers became mediators between the state and refugee claimants.

The application of the charter to noncitizens and the resulting status determination process both distanced claimants from the administrative arm of the state and provided rights and opportunities to debate the legitimacy of claims. The fact that a refugee claim setting a judicial precedent actually drove through the above changes itself indicates the potentially profound impact noncitizen claimants can have upon policy and policy making, and consequently upon noncitizen rights and state responsibilities.

The individualized aspect of the asylum-seeking process also fostered the growth of rights for particular *groups* of asylum seekers, as refugee jurisprudence grew. Women seeking asylum from female persecution benefited from the new access to rights and opportunities. Under the new system the first precedent-setting decisions on female persecution emerged in 1987.[9] Later, the growth of such jurisprudence was no doubt aided by the development of special working groups within the IRB, in particular the Working Group on Refugee Women (Gilad 1999). However the new system still suffered certain disadvantages, particularly for untraditional types of claims. Its decentralized structure could foster inconsistency in decision making (see Young 1994). More widely recognized, the adjudicative model made expeditious hearings virtually impossible and added considerably to the costs of processing refugee claims (Knowles 1992:174). The status determination process proposed in Bill C-55 involved three claim-making stages. Later a "fast-track" class was added, enabling applicants from designated countries or suffering obvious persecution to be granted refugee status at the first stage. Figure 4.1 depicts the full range of "possible pathways" in refugee status determination processes in 1995 and through the campaign period. It indicates the complexity and extent of procedural options, including access to appeals with full oral hearing at federal and Supreme Court levels. As critics later pointed out, in effect the proposed system was not three-tier, but potentially involved a lengthy seven stages (see Knowles 1992:174; Young 1997:9–10) that increased the backlog of claims. It made essential the second special administrative review for backlogged claims, but vast numbers of new

Figure 4.1. Refugee Determination Process: Possible Pathways for Inland Asylum Seekers

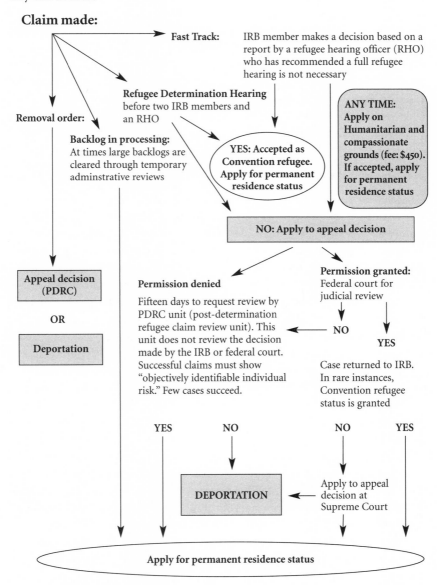

Source: Adapted from Community Legal Education Ontario, Immigration Fact Sheet, 1994. Schema depicts the process in effect to 1995.

claimants entitled to review continued adding to the backlog. Like previous backlogs, this may have increased the likelihood of claimant contact with nongovernment services and support, including appropriate lawyers. Thus the triple effects of this cumbersome system were to increase both the ways asylum seekers could gain entrance (possible pathways) and their rights to make claims; to increase delays and add to time spent living in Canada awaiting decisions and coming into contact with Canadian residents as sources of support; and to fuel antigovernment responses and increase refugees' support base. We turn now to the last of these, followed by a description of the consequences of all three in the cases studied.

The New Right: Restricting Refugee Flows, Mobilizing Dissent

Canada's system was still acclaimed for being strong on refugee rights, but was increasingly criticized for catering to illegal immigrants and "illegitimate" refugees who might take advantage of a time- and money-consuming process. The pervasive New Right political atmosphere undoubtedly fueled these criticisms. More pointedly, as Knowles notes, "it raised the question of whether it was possible to manage an immigration program when aliens were given the same rights as Canadian citizens" (1992:174). Thus Canada's immigration system also became increasingly restrictive in a number of ways, in turn triggering a backlash as antigovernment sentiment increased among NGOs and other refugee supporters. Given Canada's international migration NGOs' heritage of fragmentation, the development of stronger links between organizations themselves is important. The restrictive aspects of Bills C-55, C-84, and C-86 were pivotal in this respect. These bills were controversial and unpopular; they empowered immigration officers to interdict and refuse admission to undocumented arrivals and to require the departure or deportation of those who overstayed visas or otherwise failed to meet immigration requirements or satisfy asylum eligibility criteria. Interestingly, such measures were intended to crack down on "illegitimate" refugees while at the same time amnesty was granted to thousands of others and individuals enjoyed rights to oral hearing and judicial review.[10]

In contrast to governments' mixed responses, NGOs became more directed and organized. They were increasingly concerned with refugee legitimacy being compromised by management problems, saying that these bills endangered legitimate refugees' ability to be accepted. The bills met considerable sustained opposition by NGOs, the immigration bar, church groups, immigrant associations, and unions (Young 1997:8). The legislation was passed in 1989 but the consequences of NGO dissent were long lasting, as it was highly organized. Voluntary sector dissent as an outcome of government's constraint tactics has been noted (see Young 1997), but its implications have been underexplored. From the mid to late 1980s this historically fragmented sector mobilized and organized to an extent unprecedented in Canada, involving a range of advocates opposed to the proposed legislation. Major vehicles for this were no doubt umbrella groups such as the Canadian Council for Refugees (CCR) and Table de Concertation des Organismes de Montreal au Service des Personnes Réfugiées et Immigrantes (TCMR), which later became members of the core campaign network studied, both of which were either created or formalized in that period. Rivka Augenfeld, TCMR president, described the legislation as a mobilizing force for the TCMR, refugee groups generally, and for the network that later formed around women seeking asylum from female persecution: "It was in opposition to the legislation all those years ago that we really got organized, when we had Bills C-55 and C-84. The legislation, as far as we were concerned, was not what we had hoped, so we mobilized, we worked very hard to present our . . . parliamentary briefs and our senate briefs. We worked very hard and the network developed out of that."[11]

Augenfeld remarks that for the CCR, in which TCMR is a member, "it was the same thing, it was around the legislation, Bills C-55 and C-84. The CCR had a sort of quantum leap in this time, when the office became an office."[12] The network Augenfeld mentions linked Montreal based refugee organizations as well as organizations across provinces, through national umbrella groups. In coordinated opposition, the network brought into contact a variety of people and groups working with different international migration issues through various approaches: those "more interested in the settlement part," and those "more interested in the protection part of it . . . those who do *rights.*"[13] It also involved new organizations whose membership not only spoke for refugees but was made up of refugees, such as the Montreal Refugee Coalition.

The implications of this mobilization and coordination are manifold. They increased the international migration voluntary sector's strength and legitimacy and that of refugees themselves. Like the judiciary system, increasingly coordinated NGOs took on more of a mediating role between refugees and the state, both in policy advocacy and case work. This was both instrument and effect of the growth and increasing support of other voluntary sector groups throughout the decade. Augenfeld describes: "the big thing we accomplished here over the years, something that people don't even realize now because it seems so obvious, was to bring people together from different political stripes, different opinions, right across the spectrum from left to right."[14] Characteristics of core NGOs in the campaign network that later developed during the sex persecution campaigns are depicted in Table 4.1. Core NGOs were comprised of traditional refugee/humanitarian groups and women's organizations. The former included the Canadian Council for Refugees (CCR), International Centre for Human Rights and Democratic Development (ICHRDD), Refugee Action Montreal (RAM), and Table de Concertation des Organismes de Montreal au Service des Personnes Réfugiées et Immigrantes (TCMR). Women's groups included the National Action Committee on the Status of Women (NAC), National Organization of Immigrant and Visible Minority Women of Canada (NOIVMW), three women's shelters catering to immigrant and multicultural women, Flora Tristan, Women's Aid, and Multi-Femmes, as well as one mainstream women's shelter, Auberge Transition. Each of these organizations experienced three important trends in the 1980s: (1) growth and institutionalization; (2) the bridging or integration of international migration and women's issues within the organizational mandate; and (3) the development and diversification of political status and advocacy strategies in the increasingly mixed economy of welfare, as government contracted out service delivery. These organizations also represent a wide range of types of service organizations, from frontline service, to umbrella groups for advocacy, education, and research, operating at local/community, provincial, national, and international levels. They have a wide range of funding relationships to government (complete, partial, and none) as well as political access to government (high, medium, and low). They include the most prominent, largest, and most influential national and/or umbrella groups on human rights, refugee issues, women's issues, and immigrant women's issues in Canada. In the 1980s these organizations developed crucial organizational foundations, resources, interests, capacities, and strategic frameworks to successfully mobilize a new issue niche combining refugee with women's issues and organizations. They also developed and expanded specific advocacy skills and forms of influence.[15] The following chapter examines characteristics of these core organizations in detail in relation to their stated motivations for joining the sex persecution campaigns.

The confluence of changes in Canada's political climate and migration system also affected opportunities for asylum seeking and claim making by the refugees later involved in campaigning. Like other asylum seekers, they experienced: (1) increasing opportunities to make use of emerging resources and to gain political leverage vis-à-vis the state; and (2) the mediation of the judiciary and of an increasingly coordinated NGO sector. On one hand, backlogged refugee claim processes translated into longer waiting periods for asylum seekers residing in Canada. At the same time, increasing advocacy by the NGO sector around refugees' newly institutionalized rights facilitated successful claim making. Finally, increasing coordination among the NGO community facilitated their mobilization around noninstitutional claim-making processes.

Asylum seekers involved in the campaigns experienced increasing opportunities to get into contact with and make use of emerging resources, rights, and support networks, all of which affected their ability to effect institutional and noninstitutional challenges. These claimants arrived in Canada between 1984 and 1991 while refugee backlogs were building up and being cleared. Some experienced a significant time lapse between year of arrival and first independent refugee claim—up to ten years. For some, this delay was partly influenced by the types of first claims that were made, which included claims both as sponsored and as principal applicants. Seven of twenty claimants who went public were sponsored by spouses or boyfriends upon arrival. They made independent refugee claims only upon breaking the sponsorship contract. These cases usually involved domestic violence, and sponsorship was broken for various reasons: the woman left and divorced the husband; husbands or boyfriends withdrew sponsorship as punishment for their leaving the relationship; or the sponsor was deported or chose to leave to evade criminal charges of domestic assault.

In the case of deportation, sponsors' claims were sometimes caught in backlogs, creating a delay between arrival and rejection. In cases of women leaving relationships, the time allowed for their growing awareness of rights and resources for protection in Canada was likely to have been important. This is common among Canadian citizens who experience domestic violence. The 1993 Violence Against Women Survey reported that only 24 percent of women abused by a marital partner used social services and only 26 percent reported violence to police. Reasons for not seeking help included shame or embarrassment, being too afraid of their spouse, or not having anyone to turn to (Statistics Canada 1994). As MacLeod and Shin (1990) reported in a study of immigrant women's use of shelters for women who are battered, these factors are even more important for women from other

TABLE 4.1. DEVELOPMENT OF CORE CAMPAIGN ORGANIZATIONS

Refugee and humanitarian NGOs

	CCR	ICHRDD	TCMR	RAM
Focus	Refugee issues (inland and overseas, policy and administration)	Human rights and democratic development	Refugee entry, settlement, and integration, some policy advocacy	Refugee issues, primarily entry and settlement
Year formalized	1977/1978, volunteer effort; formalized in 1988	1988	Early 1980s	1985, first paid staff
Women's issues an interest (year)	Working Group on Refugee Women, 1985; became a core group in 1988, Refugee Women's Issues.	Women's human rights part of mandate from the start; targeted as a *domestic* issue in 1992	Member of CCR Working Group on Women Refugees, 1988.	Member of CCR Working Group on Women Refugees, 1988; focus on refugee women, networking, policy advocacy in 1993
Government funding	Yes, for specific activities on short-term basis (unstable)	Yes, "arms-length" or "independent" NGO initially created and funded by government	Yes, from various departments for specific activities on short-term basis (unstable).	No, ecumenical group funded by Protestant church but operating independently since 1992

Women's NGOs

	NAC	NOIVMW	Women's Aid	Flora Tristan	Multi-Femmes	Auberge Transition
Focus	Women's issues, general	Immigrant and visible minority women	Women's shelter	Immigrant women's shelter	Shelter for women of different races and ethnicities	Women's shelter, Montreal
Year formalized	1972; institutionalized, 1980–1988	Formalized in 1986	Late 1970s	1986	Early 1980s	Late 1970s
Refugee women's issues an interest (year)	Increased attention to visible minority, ethnic, and immigrant women's issues since 1988.	Always; more attention to immigrant women and settlement issues than entry issues	Sensitization toward the needs of immigrant women, late 1980s	Always; sponsorship abuse a particular focus in late 1980s	Always	Increasingly catering to women of different ethnic and racial origins, mid-1980s
Government funding	Yes, through Women's Program and Secretary of State. Other: membership fees, donations	Yes	Yes	Yes	Yes	Yes

cultures where violence may be accepted and state protection not offered and who may not be aware of their rights and resources in the host country. They are also relevant for other types of claimants who either do not apply for refugee status upon arrival, or who do not mention female-specific forms of persecution during the refugee application process because they are ashamed of their experience or unaware of its importance for their eligibility. Delays in claim processing provide opportunities to gain resources necessary (knowledge and support) to decide to leave abusive partners, make such claims, and potentially challenge negative decisions.

What is known as "change of status" applications arising from the above scenarios occurred a further two to three years after sponsorship breakdown, likely due to the time required for the immigration office to review sponsorship status, determine residence eligibility, and issue deportation notices. During this time women had opportunities to make contacts and gain support and resources they later used to challenge decisions on their claims. Upon making independent refugee claims they entered another waiting process involving reviews, hearings, decisions, and appeals.

But for one exception, a claimant who arrived as a student and two years later applied for refugee status when her country of origin circumstances changed, the remaining eleven claimants made their first refugee claim as principal applicant. Of these the majority (seven) applied for refugee status immediately. This is important because the longer claimants wait, the more the credibility of their claims is in question. Only three claimants applied between two to three years after arrival. Tables 4.2 and 4.3 present the distribution of sponsored and principal applicants by three characteristics: year of arrival; time lapse between arrival and first claim as principle applicant (PA); and years of residency before going public. So, for example, in the second column of Table 4.3, five of the women made principle applicant (PA) claims between two to three years after arrival. Two of these were in change of status claims, and three were the first claims ever made by the applicants.

Claimants who applied immediately and were rejected, as well as those who applied later, experienced various forms of female persecution, from domestic violence to gender-related political persecution. They entered the same processes of hearings, rejections, and appeals that previously sponsored claimants faced, and they tended to face delays of between one and five years. Like claimants who were initially sponsored, their length of stay in Canada provided opportunities to find and use resources necessary for challenging negative decisions and going public. Before going public, thirteen (68.4 percent) of these claimants had lived in Canada between two and five years, five (26.3 percent) had lived in Canada between five and ten years, and only one (5.3 percent) for less than a year. Alongside need, the significance of time lapses between making refugee claims and going public may well have been the discovery of necessary resources and opportunities.

TABLE 4.2. ASYLUM SEEKERS FROM CAMPAIGN GROUP BY YEAR OF ARRIVAL

Year of arrival	No. of asylum seekers
1991	8
1990	2
1989	2
1988	3
1986	1
1985	2
1984	1

Source: Major case histories of claimants who went public, 1991–1997.

TABLE 4.3. ASYLUM SEEKERS FROM CAMPAIGN GROUP BY PRINCIPAL APPLICANT CLAIM AND YEARS RESIDENCY

Years	No. of asylum seekers by years between entry and PA claim	No. of asylum seekers by years residency before going public
0-1	7	1
2-3	5	6
3-4	3	4
4-5	1	3
5-6	1	1
6-7	0	1
8-9	2	2
9-10	0	1

Source: Major case histories of claimants who went public, 1991–1997.

Refugee resources and rights, and particularly those for women refugees, were developing precisely during the period of these asylum seekers' residency. They gained rights to full oral hearing, recourse to the Canadian Charter of Rights and Freedoms, and a host society with declared multiculturalism and human rights commitments. They could access a broad range of organizations and memberships whose capabilities and particular interests later provided a crucial framework for the emergence of specialized networks concerned with female persecution. The majority of claimants who went public came into contact with *both* NAC and one of six different women's shelters. Many were in direct contact with the CCR, the ICHRDD, RAM, and NOIVMW. Some went through a number of lawyers until arriving at one attuned to female-specific issues. Shelters were particularly important sources of information about asylum seekers' rights and resources, providing referrals and offering sanctuary and emotional support. These contacts were among the most important for the women when going public, rather than an exhaustive list of organizations with which the women were involved, which were often quite numerous. Some women received direct support from community organizations, church groups, and even schools they or their children had attended.

Some claimants came to Canada expressly to escape female-specific violence in their countries and made claims to this effect well before the Guidelines were instated. Others, primarily those in sponsorship situations, had no initial intention of making such a claim. On the contrary, some hoped that moving to another country would bring a fresh start to their troubled marital relationships, only to see problems intensify. Others were neither sponsored nor explicit about the female violence upon entry, although they later claimed they had purposefully fled it. They may have been initially unaware of the potential to make such a claim or afraid to discuss their abuse. These were likely influenced by long-term residence and contact with organizations and individuals.

Some in this situation may well have realized they could make gender-related claims by seeing other cases going public with the support of powerful organizations in late 1992 and early 1993. This coincided with the end of the last administrative review program, announced in 1991, and the introduction of another restrictive immigration bill (C-86). The combined effect was a deportation panic and a rush of claims among those in dire situations who needed to formalize their status in Canada. This brought to NAC's doors a mass of asylum seekers, among them fifty facing female persecution, including fourteen of the women who later went public.[16]

Conclusion: Setting the Stage

While Canada's refugee crisis did not reach the proportions that European countries faced, it became hugely unmanageable and ushered in a period of public panic, controversy, and conflict between government and NGOs. The Conservative government was unable to find adequate long-term solutions, issuing instead a confusing blend of responses with both disadvantages and advantages for asylum seekers. This weakness coincided with a turbulent domestic political climate generally; in Canada the 1980s are typically described as years of political turmoil and identity crisis, increasing restraint in government spending, rising refugee panic, and restrictive immigration practices. This domestic political climate deeply affected attitudes toward government, multiculturalism, and international migration, and also set the stage for the emergence of important new rights, resources, and collective interests for asylum seekers. This combination of factors helps explain how refugee opportunities for migration, rights, and resources paradoxically expanded in critical ways during a period of cutbacks and constraints on immigration.

Government's patchwork responses provided incentives and opportunities for both asylum seekers and advocates to exploit the increasing structural vulnerability of the establishment. A crucial vehicle for asylum seekers was increasing mediation between refugees and the state in status determination processes by a new semijudicial system with an active Working Group on Refugee Women and by an increasingly fertile and coordinated NGO sector with overlapping interests in women's and refugee issues. This combination of forces created political opportunities and an organizational or resource basis for campaign networks concerned with Canadian responsibility for female persecution.

Implications for the asylum seekers later involved in the campaigns were manifold. Direct effects on institutional and noninstitutional avenues for action include the growth of new institutional rights, resources (material and ideological), and political access, as well as increasing opportunities to make use of resources and emerging interests due to the rise in processing delays. Indirect effects include the nature and structural vulnerability of Canada's political climate and refugee regime as well as the rising organizational strength of nongovernmental supporters, who were increasingly diverse and coordinated. These trends preconditioned the mobilization of a final emerging resource and opportunity: new working relationships between asylum seekers and Canadian residents in policy advocacy situations. The following two chapters explore how the core campaign network was generated, how members related to each other, what their motivations and aims were, how the network operated internally and in relation to the external environment, and to what effect.

Chapter 5
"Use My Name": Noncitizen Identity, Decisions, and Mobilization

I remember when my lawyer in 1992 wrote an article and she told me she is not going to use my name. I said "No. I want you to use my name." . . . *And whenever my lawyer tells people, she calls and she says: "I told them to use your name!"*

—Thérèse, refugee claimant, 1995

The importance of ideas and ideology, and their formal and strategic expression by actors attempting to influence the external environment, cannot be understated. McAdam explains: "Mediating between opportunity and action are the people and the . . . meanings they attach to their situations" (1982:48). It is important to understand why actors act in the way they do, and this means not taking for granted their decisions and the intended course of a campaign. In the following, I explore why and how asylum seekers and supporters got involved in campaigning, even when risks were involved, and with what implications for the internal political culture of the campaign network that coalesced. In so doing I seek more specifically to uncover (1) whether asylum seekers were essentially "forced migrants" without options, dependent on the goodwill of the state or desperate to challenge it, or if indeed they sought options and made rational political decisions to act on them; and (2) what roles asylum seekers played in shaping the ideology, aims, and participation of key supporters, and the larger structure and political culture of the campaign network. This emerges through detailed analysis of asylum seekers' and supporters' identity, decision making, and interactions.[1]

The internal political culture of the campaign network not only shapes its membership and organization, but their core ideology and aims in relation to the external environment (the public and government). By exploring why and how actors decided to get involved in public pressure tactics, their belief systems and corresponding aims are illuminated. Jenkins-Smith and Sabatier explain, "public policies/programs incorporate implicit theories about how to achieve their objectives . . . and thus can be conceptualized in much the same way as belief systems. They involve value priorities, perceptions of important causal relationships, perceptions of the state of the world (including the magnitude of the problem), perceptions of the efficacy of policy instruments, etc." (1994:180). We can draw out actors "deep core policy values" (Sabatier and Jenkins-Smith 1993; Jenkins-Smith and Sabatier 1994), which link identity and ideology to underlying policy aims and strategies. The first section below reveals how asylum seekers conceptualized and approached noninstitutional actions—"going public"—exploring the personal and political considerations that informed their decisions. These crucial factors mediated between the need for safety as a driving force behind their flight, supporters' influence upon asylum seekers' decisions and opportunities, and asylum seekers' actual willingness to engage in radical tactics to secure asylum. The second section looks at how core supporters' participation, policy values, and approaches to achieving them were influenced by how they conceptualized the relation between their own belief systems and the asylum seekers they met. It reveals factors predisposing supporters toward participation and how contact with asylum seekers served as a linchpin between their "deep core" ideology and participatory action. Implications of asylum seekers' involvement are discussed in the final section, with a schematic presentation of the campaign network.

Asylum Seekers "Going Public": Benefits and Risks

To understand asylum seekers' role in shaping the nature and structure of support, we must begin with an inquiry into why asylum seekers went public. First, an obvious point is that, failing institutional means to secure safe asylum, the life and death situations that refugees may face if deported provide a predominant motivating force for noninstitutional action. Second, among a typically resourceless and relatively politically powerless population, actually pursuing noninstitutional action requires opportunities and support. I shall return to these two crucial factors later and begin by questioning both as sufficient in themselves. This is important because overreliance on the former may support the idea that real refugees must be primarily "forced" actors to whom receiving countries simply respond or else illegitimate refugees rather than political actors in their own right within receiving countries. Overreliance on the latter may similarly exclude the political role of asylum seekers, instead explaining policy change primarily as result of activism by Canadian residents advocating *for* asylum seekers, rather than *with* actors who have various options and participate in decision making.

Empirically, problems with both explanations emerge when we consider that generally asylum seekers receive support and advocacy from a variety of sources (e.g., refugee, ethnic, and community organizations that offer entry and settlement services) and for a number of reasons before, during, and after claim making. Yet the actions typically taken with such support are a long way away from "going public" to campaign for individual and collective claims to be accepted. Similarly, the traditional "forced" image of refugees, desperate to attain entry, does not explain the extremely small number of rejected refugee claimants who do or will go public. That is, one could suppose that huge numbers of desperate, forced refugees would resort to public pressure tactics, but in reality this is rarely the case.

As McAdam and other collective action theorists have observed, neither grievances (such as persecution) nor opportunities and support structures are sufficient to explain the generation and influence of collective action. Grievances, opportunities, and organizational readiness may have little influence at a particular time if potential actors are unable or unwilling to make use of or exploit them (see McAdam 1982, 1996). In this case, going public became a central pressure tactic and constituted a driving force behind policy demands, so we need to understand why asylum seekers would make their intimate life stories public knowledge and what would be involved in making such a decision. Their *willingness* to go public must be explored. What were the decision-making processes that mediated between grievances and opportunities on one hand and actions that asylum seekers may or may not take because of or through them on the other?

Deciding to Go Public

Looking at the asylum seekers who shared intimate life details with the public through mass media over the course of the campaigns reveals important personal and political considerations behind their decisions and actions.

These claimants went public from a range of female-specific experiences, raising a variety of case-specific complications that would shape why and how public action was chosen and at particular times and with a range of potential outcomes.[2] All contributed directly to the public debate and pressure brought to bear upon government. Strong commonalities can be seen in the ways and extent that claimants went public, within which we can look for important elements informing their decisions to go public in the first place. All provided personal testimony of their experiences as persecuted women and also as claimants discriminated in Canada's refugee system. Going public raised contentious debates about persecution and rights to protection in Canada *as refugees*. The grounds for their acceptance under any refugee category (race, religion, nationality, political opinion, social group) subsequently set important precedents.

Of twenty-three women who went public, seven claimants individually sought and received particularly extensive media attention, speaking at press conferences, giving interviews, and/or writing editorials. Three of these women (Dulerie, Nada, and Basdaye) had their cases concluded during the campaigns and before the Guidelines' instatement in March 1993, while the remaining four (Ferdousi, Taramati, Thérèse, Ginette) were concluded after March 1993 and during a second campaign phase aimed at achieving proper implementation of the Guidelines (see Table 5.1). All of these high coverage claimants went public individually, but two of them also publicized their claims together with a group of twelve other claimants at press conferences in January and February 1993. This latter group of simultaneously publicized cases also included, therefore, women who received less individual press coverage, but significant collective coverage. This group was drawn from an even larger group of fifty asylum seekers that had sought the support of NAC, a core campaign organization.[3] A final three asylum seekers who went public did so individually but received relatively less public attention (forming minor case histories in this study), and this may be explained in part by their timing; two spoke at press conferences held prior to the organization of the larger campaign (Ana, Sandy), and one went public at a downturn in the campaign when the issue was largely waning in the public interest (Kissoon).

All the women worked with and through supporters in order to voice their stories. Some chose pseudonyms to protect their identity, but others did not.[4] Several were particularly open about their experiences, accepting to be photographed and generally making extra efforts to be accessible to the media and other interested individuals and potential supporters. At least one was emphatic about not hiding her identity and experiences, in a sense claiming due credit and strength for the difficulty of the choices she made and actions she took. Others were interviewed by the press, under alias or not, several during campaigns but after being accepted. It is notable that of the fifty women known to NAC, thirty-six never went public at all.

TABLE 5.1. TIMING OF PUBLIC CLAIMS, 1991–1997

Campaign Onset	First Campaign Peak		Second Campaign Peak and Decline
Ana	Anna	*Tamarati*	*Taramati*
Sandy	Nadia	*Thérèse*	*Thérèse*
	Angela	*Ferdousi*	*Ferdousi*
	Maria/Miranda	Dulerie	Ginette
	Azadeh	Nada	
	Fatima	Basdaye	
	Ines		
	Olga		
	Liza		
	Hindra		
	Lee		
	Phagawdeye		
	Kapinga		
	Kissoon		

Source: Major and minor case histories.

Considering those with the greatest media attention, it is evident that decisions to go public, and to do so in particular ways, were made both for personal and political reasons deeply intertwined in what we might call identity politics. This describes ways of thinking about self within the world. It involves recognizing self within social and political contexts and power structures and from that recognition and the understanding gained from it either reconstructing (on one's own terms) or reifying self-identity.

Choosing to use real or invented names was one way of expressing sociopolitical identity, which claimants made use of in different ways and based on various considerations. When asked if she would prefer to use another name in an interview for this study, Thérèse stated without hesitation: "You are using *my* name." She explained that she was "not talking lies," people would hear her story, and there should be no suggestion that her story could be untrue by hiding behind a false name. "Some people don't want to use their name. I don't care. . . . You can use "Thérèse" . . . I remember when my lawyer in 1992 wrote an article and she told me she is not going to use my name. I said 'No. I want you to use my name.' And she said most of the women use another name. That they come to this country and they use another name, they don't use their *own* name. And I said: 'You use my name.' And whenever my lawyer tells people, she calls and she says: 'I told them to use your name!'"[5] Revealing the truth or reality of life experiences, and standing behind her words by revealing her identity, appears as not only a self-affirming process, but also a cathartic process as the reality of abuse and persecution is publicly recognized. Identity as a persecuted individual invokes the intimate details of the persecution. Thérèse explains: "Back home we don't talk about that: our rape, our abuse, everything. We just close our mouths. So I don't know, I changed a lot since I've been here in Montreal. Like, I never keep secrets now. Everything that comes, I just say it. [I talk to] anybody who calls me and says, 'I am doing this and I want your help . . .' It's hard when I am talking about it still, but after that I get over it. I used to have headaches when I used to finish telling everything, but now I don't get it anymore. And I used to cry a lot, but now I do just a little bit. It doesn't hurt as much."[6]

The need to constantly reassert and prove one's identity by revealing personal experiences is basic to the refugee determination process. To be recognized as a "refugee," identity must be proven through the personal experience of structural persecution and lack of protection. But for claimants like Thérèse, structural invisibility of the persecution as such, and subsequently their identity as persecuted individuals, initially prevented protection both in their home countries and in Canada. The experience of not being believed and not having concerns taken seriously is for asylum seekers a humiliating and often infuriating process, particularly when revealing personal abuse is a major emotional challenge to begin with. For Thérèse, revealing her identity went hand in hand with the structural nature of the abuse she experienced, and as she describes above, the ways it had been enshrouded in a culture of secrecy that was self-perpetuating and isolating for victims. Voicing the truth was both a personally liberating, if often painful, process and an act keeping strongly in mind the similar experiences of other women, the "we" who "don't talk about . . . our rape, our abuse . . . ," in the Seychelles Islands.

The lengths to which such claimants went to prove their identity also went far beyond the confidential closed hearing room status determination processes that all refugee claimants must undergo. Expressing her truth about self and society became increasingly important for Thérèse after being rejected by immigration authorities. Her struggle was not only about conditions in home countries, but about conditions in Canada. Thérèse's adamancy emerges not only as a strategy to influence and reverse the decision on her claim, but also as a crucial part of reclaiming a sense of integrity after being disbelieved in Canada. Describing the dismissive treatment she received from Canadian immigration authorities, Thérèse again asserts the truth of her story against disbelief in its reality or validity. "On the immigration side there is nothing that you can say that they were really there for you. . . . They are very rude, they don't think that they are like us, like you. They just take pity on you. I don't want them to take pity on me, but just to think: if it were *you*, or your family! And I have a lot: everything that is written, everything that is in my file, it is *true*. It's not something that was made up. It was true. But they didn't look at it. Their idea was just that 'we have to deport her, and that is it.' "[7]

Taking the opposite approach with regard to revealing her identity, but no less emphasizing the structural nature of the violence experienced, was perhaps the most well known claimant of all. Despite the most widespread, even international, coverage, including numerous interviews by journalists, this claimant never revealed her name or showed her face to the public while arguing her case. The pseudonym she chose was "Nada," in some languages signifying "nothing" or "zero." Concealing her identity while going public was intended to protect her privacy and safety as well as that of her family in Saudi Arabia. But Nada's portrayal of herself as a woman without an identity was also a powerful image of the treatment of females in Saudi Arabia. She claimed persecution on political grounds for opposing the formal and informal laws of her society on roles and behaviors appropriate to females, in particular the dress code. Nada described the required chador, or veil, as literally rendering women faceless and identityless. Refusal to comply would result in public flogging or stoning as well as the private punishments inflicted by family. She explained: "Wearing the veil made me feel dirty. It made me feel faceless and bodiless, like some sexual object in the street. I felt like I was nothing. I was not a human being. So I decided I would not do it anymore. I would rather stay home all day. I preferred to be stoned rather than to be without an identity" (Nada 1993).

In Canada, in the only photograph Nada allowed to be taken for use in the media, she appeared modeling the traditional abaya, which conceals the body and face. After her claim was accepted and after the campaign period Nada participated "as herself" in the National Gender Consultations between NGOs and government. Nada's nameless and faceless identity as she portrayed herself to the Canadian public suggested the invisibility of persecuted women in the Canadian refugee system. Her appeals to the public were moral and political, highly intelligent, eloquent, and educational. Like Thérèse she brought both foreign and domestic blindness to her person, as an individual and as a woman, to light. "When I was in Saudi Arabia, I thought that women in other countries were more respected and more powerful. I was naive. I first realized my naïveté when they laughed at me at the airport when I said I have problems because I am a woman" (1993). The dismissive treatment Nada received upon arrival in Canada was mirrored during the oral hearing of her refugee claim. Nada was refused refugee status based on the assertion that she should not disobey the laws of her society and family. The adjudicator in her case stated: "The Claimant would do well, like all her compatriots, to abide by the laws of general application she opposes, and to do this under all circumstances, and not only, as she has done, in order to study, work or to show consideration for the feelings of her father, who, like everyone else in her large family, was opposed to the liberalism of his daughter."[8]

As later recognized when this decision was reversed, it disregarded the discriminatory nature of laws that target females, and the persecutory nature of punishments inflicted for transgressing these discriminatory moral and legal codes, in this case public lashing or stoning. It also took a typically patriarchal stance in stating that Nada, a grown woman, should defer to her father's wishes.

Nada was particularly emphatic about the hypocrisy inherent in a culturally relative approach to determining refugee status eligibility. In an editorial written for the *Ottawa Citizen* in March 1993 she described: "Throughout the agony of waiting for my case to be determined, many issues were raised in the media. The minister of Employment and Immigration, Bernard Valcourt, argued that Canada should not intervene and impose its cultural values. He was missing the point."

At the same time, Nada was concerned with the likelihood that going public, while challenging cultural relativism in women's human rights, would provide ammunition for racist public responses toward the treatment of women in Arab countries. Diana Bronson from the ICHRDD, one of Nada's primary supporters, explained how the campaign was prepared before Nada decided to use a pseudonym. Nada had gone into hiding, remaining in Canada illegally after receiving a deportation order. Letters and documents had been prepared and the campaign was set to go public, when Nada changed her mind. "I asked her again: 'Are you sure you are ready to go through with this? The media is going to use every anti-Arab stereotype you ever heard, they are going to be talking about veiled women in the Arab world, they are going to want to know all your personal stories, they will not stop at anything to know everything that is personal about you, they will ask you insulting questions, and there may be repercussions back home, for you or your family. Are you sure?' And she said, 'No.' "9

This depiction of factors involved in the decision-making process vividly illuminates the very real reasons many asylum seekers may choose not to go public, despite the urgent and life-threatening situation and pressures they face. Why then did Nada ultimately choose to go public? Her decision was a political one wrapping together personal need for safety with her beliefs about women's rights in her own country and, interestingly, also with what Nada felt were Canada's political responsibilities for the persecution she faced. It also prompted her to choose a pseudonym in order to protect her family. The incident that triggered her final decision involved a Bulgarian musician who had been granted refugee status because of a fan who happened to be the daughter of an influential federal bureaucrat. Journalist Andre Picard concluded his column on the story saying: "We turn back women who are being beaten by their husbands but a white guy got in for a song." Working closely with Nada, Bronson described: "I don't know if I showed this article to Nada or if someone else did, but she got wind of it. She got so mad at the federal government that she decided to go public, for sure. So we went public."10

The political nature of Nada's decision was made clear in her criticism of the Canadian government's attempt to shirk responsibility for violence that it claimed was cultural rather than political. This she counterposed against the extreme realities of life for women in Saudi Arabia:

The discrimination and repression I lived with in Saudi Arabia had political and not cultural roots. When governments impose a certain set of beliefs on individuals, through propaganda, violence or torture, we are dealing not with culture but rather with political expediency. To claim that such practices are cultural is dangerous, if not racist. . . . When a woman walks down the street in Saudi Arabia without a veil and the *Mutawwni'in* (religious police) flog her, this is not cultural, it's political. Who gave permission to the *mutawwi'in*? The government. . . . I'm suspicious when I hear the Canadian government expressing concern for cultural integrity. . . . When women are publicly flogged for wearing perfumes or cosmetics imported from the West, do westerners protest about cultural imperialism? (Nada 1993)

Here Nada points out again that the treatment and recognition women receive both in Saudi Arabia and in Canada are structural issues, the instability of women's human rights a form of "political expediency." Thus pressure was put on Canadian Immigration to recognize human rights violations against women, not as an act of compassion and pity but as the act of a socially responsible and accountable state within a global system, where states already influence one another and state politics and cultures are intertwined.

Like Nada, other claimants also expressed concerns that going public could further jeopardize their safety and that of their family. This could occur in three ways, each of which might be affected by choosing to use either real names or pseudonyms. First, going public could notify violent family members of the claimant's location. For this reason, one woman's case was publicized *after* her claim was accepted, in order to support the ongoing campaign, and even then her name was not revealed.[11]

Second, going public could endanger the lives of claimants' children, either through violent family members tracking them down, or through custody battles in Canada or between claimants in Canada and family members in the country of origin. In cases of domestic violence, the extent to which violent men may go to track down their partners is well recognized. Despite the geographical distance, this can be true for asylum seekers as well. When Dulerie fled to Canada with her three children after seventeen years of violent abuse by her husband, he followed, was allowed entry, and was subsequently convicted in Canada eleven times for assault and death threats and finally deported. Another case involved a Bangladeshi woman, Ferdousi, married at age eleven to a man twenty years her senior who beat her for eighteen years. They arrived together in Canada with three children. Ferdousi's husband threatened to marry off their two daughters, ages eleven and thirteen, and to kill Ferdousi or drive her to suicide if she should call the police and get him deported. Men in many countries have custodial rights over children, making his threat very plausible. When charged with assault and uttering death threats in Canada he failed to appear at trial. The family remained in hiding, both from Canadian authorities and from Ferdousi's husband whose location remained unknown, while fighting to overturn their deportation order.

This ties into a third type of risk raised by going public and using real names: amplifying dangers faced back home if the claimant is still rejected and deported. For example, having divorced her husband and failing to return with him to Bangladesh, Ferdousi would no longer be accepted by her family. Without the means to support herself, she would be at the mercy of the community. The fact that cases had been publicized could get back to family members, community, and the government. In some countries, social ostracization for having defied social norms may be accompanied by physical forms of punishment, and both could be enhanced by the shame the woman brings to her people (leaving a husband, dishonoring the family name, and defying social norms).[12] In countries where women have little means to support themselves, social ostracization can be dire.

These examples suggest asylum seekers, and particularly those with children, must have great impetus to attempt every possible means to secure safety; those who went public were willing to take the above risks, most did not use their own names, but a few who received the greatest publicity did. Being mothers may also have served a strategic purpose; mothers may provoke greater public sympathy and support than childless women, particularly when they allow photos to be taken, a consideration in favor of trying the strategy. Of the seven most publicized cases, five involved children.

But public pressure tactics always remained a last resort strategy after careful consideration and, as indicated earlier, many women refugees known to NAC did not go public at all. Such tactics tended to be used after all institutional options had been exhausted and deportation orders had been issued, in an attempt to overturn negative decisions. The fourteen women who went public collectively had been rejected or were in the final stages of appeal and were or could soon be facing deportation. At least three were in hiding, the date of deportation having passed.[13] The last resort aspect was a strong indicator that these asylum seekers' *needs* outweighed the risks and unpleasantness of going public. But it also served the strategic purpose of highlighting failures of the Canadian refugee system.

The fact that some claimants went public after receiving deportation notice but before exhausting all appeals processes (in one case), or that some claimants *wanted* to go public earlier on (in at least one case), while others ultimately chose not to go public at all, indicates the influence of other considerations mediating between need and public actions. In at least one case a rejected claimant went public while still in appeals processes to overturn the negative decision on her claim. Under a pseudonym (so as not to interfere with the appeal) the claimant went public with the group of fourteen claimants, asking NAC to publicize that she made the decision "to make her story known in order to help the Minister reconsider the Guidelines regarding gender-related problems in some countries, including her own."[14]

The fact that others chose not to go public at all indicates many mediating considerations and often competing priorities that won out. It also shows that pursing refugee status on untraditional grounds, an expressly political act challenging the refugee system, was not always the only recourse and was not always considered most desirable. Entry could sometimes be sought through other types of status that, while perhaps not accurately reflecting reasons for international migration and not challenging the status quo in that regard, nevertheless achieve individual aims to secure safe asylum. At least thirty-six claimants who sought NAC's assistance at that time considered going public but ultimately did not for various practical and technical reasons, together with personal and political considerations and risks discussed above. Handling the cases, Flora Fernandez, of the Executive Committee, Violence Against Women Unit, NAC, and director of Women's Aid, explained that some women chose alternative solutions where possible, such as marriage to Canadians, in order to avoid the media and risk of rejection in this uncertain area of refugee policy. Others still in determination processes (appeals) reportedly decided "not to push more at that time" out of fear that publicity could negatively influence decisions, even though the likelihood of receiving positive decisions was extremely low to begin with.[15]

Another last resort strategy was going into hiding from Canadian authorities after receiving deportation notice. That is, remaining as an illegal immigrant. While not necessarily uncommon among asylum seekers generally (the real number of illegals residing in Canada is unknown), what was unusual was the choice to *publicize* the fact of being in hiding, speaking to the media *before* going into hiding (announcing the intention) or *while* in hiding, thus blatantly defying and challenging Canadian law. This may be regarded as a form of civil disobedience. Their claims had already been rejected. These "illegals" were seeking institutional recognition of their right as part of a collective identity to remain in Canada, even if it meant jeopardizing actually staying hidden. Announcing the fact of being in hiding was also a powerful way of conveying to the public the depth of desperation and realities of persecution faced. Thérèse explained: "I had three choices: Go in hiding; leave the country; or go in hospital because I was suicidal. I was telling my sister, 'If you don't send the letter, the journal showing there is no protection for women in our country, I will throw myself under the metro.' And always [my lawyer] was saying, 'No, no, you must be brave, you have been so brave always, you can keep on—braving.' "[16]

As many asylum seekers and supporters have commented, "going underground" is a last resort because it creates a life of insecurity and risk, without legal rights to work or to health and welfare benefits, in constant fear of being discovered and deported. Ginette went into hiding after her claim to refugee status and her humanitarian and compassionate appeal were refused, she had gone public, and the immigration minister refused to intervene. In hiding she told reporters: "I'm really in a state of despair. I really don't know what to do. Living in hiding is no life at all."[17]

Going into hiding did have strategic advantages which some claimants made use of. During her twenty-one months in hiding, Nada sought out people both sympathetic and in a position to help her remain in Canada legally. It gave her the time to go public in a well-orchestrated and effective manner by providing a time of reflection and planning not available to others facing the urgency of upcoming deportation who would not consider going underground, like Thérèse. Nada's campaign was well thought out and prepared. Receiving the greatest media attention of all those who went public, Nada in many ways lay a road map that other claimants and supporters later used to pressure the government. During and after Nada's campaign, the ICHRDD offered campaigning advice to other groups based on its experience with Nada.[18]

As indicated, the desperation inherent to "last resort" strategies provided forceful images of Canada's refusal to provide protection, while highlighting structural considerations that link personal identity to collective grievances and potentially collective rights. Although at the time the fourteen claimants who collectively publicized their claims received less individual press attention, the collective nature of their claims provided a strong example of the macrostructural and cross-cultural nature of female persecution. These fourteen claimants arrived from twelve different countries: St. Vincent, Bulgaria, Guatemala, Zaire, Seychelles, Dominica, Trinidad and Tobago, Bangladesh, Iran, Turkey, Peru, and Russia.[19]

Thérèse's depiction of her last press conference—after fighting for status one year before the Guidelines and one year after, being deported to a third country with her children, detained, rejected, and sent back to Canada for deportation to the Seychelles Islands—is more than ever an emphasis on structural persecution and rights. She went public both collectively (in the group of fourteen) and again individually. While in detention she decided to do individual press conferences a few days before final deportation. She describes the experience of telling her story to the media, and how she approached the topic when confronting the public: "So we had the press conference. Twelve o'clock I arrived with Father Robert, Glynis [Williams, coordinator, Refugee Action Montreal] was there, we stepped out of the car and I saw a big white van and Father Robert said: 'You know what it is, it is for you, the CBC [Canadian Broadcasting Corporation].' The room was all packed, people all around, so many journalists and my friends. And when I started to tell my story, I just said, 'I don't know the meaning of abuse. Abuse is a culture.' "[20]

Like Nada, Thérèse's depiction of how she went public was a story of defiance and desperation, but also careful reflection on the conditions and structural reasons for the abuse suffered and rights to asylum from it. Thérèse emphasizes the cultural rootedness of domestic violence, which prevented protection in her country of origin.

From the testimonies of all the women, it is evident that going public was not simply a "forced" outcome of their needs. It was a conscious decision involving many considerations that tied together personal experiences, identity as a persecuted woman and as part of a broader persecuted group and ethnic minority in Canada, and status as "invisible" refugees in Canada's refugee system. It also took into account children and other family members, as well as abusers' abilities to track them down. These mediating factors are significant, first, because making personal and political decisions and acting on them challenge the notion of refugees as simply forced migrants and beneficiaries of foreign aid, lacking political agency. Second, for the public, asylum seekers' decisions and actions brought real human faces to abstract notions of political and structural persecution, making a strong bid for accountability on the part of both sending and receiving countries. They were both symbolically and strategically forceful.

Public pressure tactics were no doubt a last resort option for all the women concerned. However some went public before going underground, while others found themselves having to go underground in order to create time and opportunity to go public. As we shall see, supporters had mixed feelings about how to combine these strategies. Some preferred to leave public pressure as a last resort, while others hoped to avoid claimants' need to go underground by keeping that as a last resort. For claimants, in either case, going public followed the failure of institutional options but was mediated by important decision-making processes about self and family, structural representation and collective identity, and sending- and receiving-country responsibility. To take these processes for granted would be to discredit asylum seekers' abilities to seek out options, understand their situation and identity in relation to the broader political context where social constructions occur, think through possibilities and consequences, and make informed decisions.[21] Subsequently it would discredit their role in national policy making (despite their noncitizen status). These processes illuminate that asylum seekers are, first, political actors and symbols in seeking membership in a host country and, second, refugees according to the outcome of their claims and challenges.

Needs and Opportunities Affecting Asylum Seekers' Decisions and Actions

Willingness to go public is only one of several necessary elements shaping asylum seekers' decisions and actions. Both personal and political considerations, in Canada and in the country of origin, were important motivating factors in this respect and were expressed in various ways. Here we return to two other extremely important and mutually informing factors: primary individual *needs* for safety and *opportunities* to pursue alternative means to attaining safety when institutional methods fail. The first puts constraints and pressures upon asylum seekers, the second presents options and strategies.

The number one motive and goal of seeking asylum from female persecution is need for immediate safety. It is a driving force behind willingness to go public, mediated by important decision-making processes discussed. It must be understood in its structural context, arising from fear of persecution *and* lack of more desirable alternatives. The violence feared may take a range of forms from more to less traditionally "public" in nature, but all must be structurally rooted in and encouraged, condoned, or ignored by society and the state. Because of the structural embeddedness of the persecution, seeking asylum is itself, according to the refugee definition, a last resort option.

We have seen how asylum seekers linked personal experiences to the political structural context in identifying themselves with a persecuted group and claiming collective rights. But their *expression* of experiences (or fear) of persecution and perceived lack of alternatives is itself important for several

reasons. It is informative and pathbreaking in that it reveals forms of persecution previously unrecognized as well as the often undocumented lack of
protection in sending countries. It is also a powerful tool of public persuasion, as the following chapter shows. Finally, their life stories and the *telling*
of life stories highlight tremendous courageousness in the face of extreme
danger and uncertainty, which itself merits attention. By no means is the
amount of space that can be devoted to their life stories sufficient. The affi-
davits, argumentation, and court decisions on the broader data set of cases
published in RefLex, discussed in Chapters 2 and 6, tell similar experiences of
persecution and thus easily, though unfortunately, illuminate a shared desperation. The claimants quoted here regarding experiences and fears of persecution provide an idea of the extreme nature and complexity of their
situations and the tremendous fears and urgent needs they shared. Some, like
Nada, have already been discussed in a sufficiently detailed manner that the
issue of need has already been touched upon.

As indicated, different forms of persecution seemed to influence how
these asylum seekers went public. Those forms least recognized institutionally and consistently formed the basis of the greatest proportion of types of
claims made public, for obvious reasons that they faced greater obstacles to
attaining refugee status.[22] These involved intrafamilial or domestic violence,
which brings the personal and the political together at its most insidious
level. Of the seven cases with the greatest individual media attention, only
Nada's involved public rather than domestic violence. However, as in many
other cases, the persecution Nada faced was condoned by her family who
therefore deprived her of one source of protection in her home country.
Nada and the other women's experiences of persecution exemplify opposite
ends of the range of *forms* of female-specific violence that may amount to
persecution, both ends being culturally accepted human rights violations
and thus structurally rooted. Of the fourteen asylum seekers who went public collectively in February 1993, eleven involved domestic violence. One involved female genital mutilation, which may fall under a broad definition of
domestic violence as any violence inflicted or enforced by family members.
Once case involved both domestic violence and "guilt by association" (familial relation to political dissidents).

Such cases involve fear of persecution by a husband and/or in-laws. In
one complicated, individually publicized case, the suicide of the claimant's
abusive husband while in Canada incited fears of persecution by in-laws in
Cameroon. In statements to the press Ginette explained that her husband

called police to resolve a domestic dispute: "he thought the police would arrest me because that's what would happen in our country. But when the police saw how badly I was beaten, they arrested him instead." She fled to a women's shelter while he was in jail. After his release, discovering Ginette had left, "he mailed a letter to his family in Cameroon saying his wife was responsible for his death," then "stabbed himself in the stomach, doused his body with gasoline and set himself on fire." Ginette subsequently received death threats from her husband's family. She explained: "his family is very powerful and they can do what they want. They could kill me with a machete and nothing would happen."[23] Ginette went public after her humanitarian and compassionate claim was turned down, the immigration minister refused to intervene, and her request to remain in Canada until the Federal Court could hear her appeal was rejected.

Taramati's situation was also complicated. She fled to a women's shelter after two years in Canada, applied for refugee status, and saw her husband deported to Trinidad for repeated physical assaults. But two years later, while her claim was still being held in a backlog, her ex-husband married a Canadian and was accepted in Canada. Ironically, Taramati's own claim was no longer considered credible because her husband no longer posed a threat to her in Trinidad. Beside the unfairness of the situation, in which a convicted criminal was accepted into Canada and not his victim, Taramati's future in Trinidad looked grim after having left her husband. To the press she stated: "I'm scared to go back, because of my in-laws."[24]

Dulerie's case raised similar difficulties. She fled seventeen years of domestic violence involving rape, beatings including use of razors and knives, having her head slammed into a car door, and other forms of abuse now considered torture. From Trinidad, Dulerie's husband continued to threaten her in Canada, saying he would "chop her into little pieces." Such threats, in letters and in phone calls that Dulerie taped, served as evidence in her claim for refugee status based on the risk she currently faced and lack of protection she had formerly experienced in Trinidad. After her acceptance she said to the press: "If they had sent me back, I would have killed myself. If I had gone back to Trinidad my husband would have killed me, so one way or another I would have been dead. Now it's like being dead and waking up again. I feel like I'm alive again."[25]

Other claimants described similar stories involving lack of protection in countries of origin. Basdaye described: "Even if you get in touch with the police back home, it's different from here in Canada. If it's a husband beating a

wife, the police don't want to get involved. They just say it's a family problem."[26] Another claimant, known as "Lee," whose leave to appeal was granted
by the Federal Court in the first decision of its kind, stated: "I was terrified
for my life and felt that escape from Trinidad was my only hope. My husband
beat me on a regular basis, sometimes several times per month. He generally
used his fists, beating me so ferociously that I often could not see through the
swelling in my face. . . . He had begun using weapons and I felt that it was
only a matter of time before he killed me."[27]

Domestic violence is difficult to directly contrast with more public
forms of persecution, as in Nada's case, but seems to have encountered
greater resistance in refugee determination claims both before and after the
Guidelines were instated. Thus the likelihood of such claimants going public
to challenge negative decisions was higher. As indicated earlier, several such
claimants who went public were later ordered deported, for a second time,
provoking further campaigning.

Public persecution involved, in Nada's case, public flogging upon return
to Saudi Arabia. Another claimant, Miranda, whose persecution was the result of her previous husband's political actions, explained: "my oldest child
and I face great danger in Guatemala. The authorities could take me or my
child in an effort to force my first husband out of hiding."[28] Ines, from Peru,
already had evidence of authorities' intent to persecute her for the actions of
her relatives—her head was scarred from being doused with quicklime. Yet
her claim had been rejected as illegitimate because her husband was the political activist, not her.[29]

Willingness and need to go public are not in themselves sufficient to
foster collective action. Surely the opportunities and structure of support
also further shaped asylum seekers' decisions and actions. Information and
awareness, contacts, mobility, and politicization, along with a host of other
mediating factors, may be important influences on whether and how asylum
is actually sought through noninstitutional actions. Thus we would expect
the structure of support that developed to inform or reaffirm asylum seekers' decisions to go public. Support takes many forms: moral, emotional, and
ideological (i.e., political framing processes about self, rights, and collective
identity); material and human resources (i.e., organizational, human labor,
political and legal knowledge, access to media). The various forms of support
may work toward and present asylum seekers with strategies for achieving
the primary aim, safety. It involves both offering advice and support and the
means and tools for claimants to go public.

In terms of decision making, asylum seekers who went public were from the onset affected by their unfamiliarity with the external environment and their lack of information. Transnational migrants face language barriers as well as legal and administrative systems and social and political customs with which they are unfamiliar and which constrain their abilities for action. These asylum seekers were no exception, although some had resided in Canada for several years. Simply making an independent refugee claim (aside from going public) can be difficult. This may be enhanced for female asylum seekers, who face cultural barriers particular to their gender (Paul 1992). It is particularly amplified for those fleeing forms of persecution not traditionally recognized. They are less likely to receive spontaneous and pertinent information and advice through typical interaction with the immigration system, including government, nongovernment, and legal counsel who themselves lack information or sensitivity concerning the particular group. Added to these constraints are the psychological traumas and fears that refugees often face and which gender-related experiences of violence are particularly likely to foster (see Chapter 3).

Sponsored or dependent asylum seekers already in Canada face particular concerns. These asylum seekers fall into two categories: those currently in status determination processes, often lasting several years, and those already accepted through the claims of family members, whose sponsorship agreement later breaks down. For those whose persecution occurred within the family, transnational migration of the whole family may appear as a panacea that is later proven illusory. Indeed, the pressures of status determination and integration may cause an escalation of violence (MacLeod and Shin 1990). Thérèse falls into the category of those engaged in status determination processes with a sponsor when the need to make an independent claim became apparent. "I came to Canada in September 1991 to join my husband, even though we had problems. I had pressure at home, and his political problems. I thought my marriage will work, because I left all the political and social problems back home. By coming here, things got worse, I realized I was wrong."[30] Others came to Canada with violent spouses because they had no option to separate or divorce under the social norms of their home countries. Repercussions could include not only escalation of violence, but social ostracization, losing guardianship of children, inability to earn a living or find support due to gendered divisions between paid and unpaid work, and even legal punishment.

A common misconception among battered immigrant and refugee

women is that they will automatically be deported if sponsorship is with-drawn, for example if separation or divorce is sought (MacLeod and Shin 1990). They lack information and support to make their own claims. But the greater problem for the asylum seekers studied was the lack of information and advice about the nature of their particular claims. Both those battered women whose husbands' claims are being determined, and those already ac-cepted as dependents, may be unaware that they have sufficient grounds to make their own claims or that their own stories of persecution are impor-tant. Standard immigration procedures at the time of the study did not in-form, advise, or encourage women to make their own claims (Paul 1992).

For Thérèse and her children, lack of information and fears raised by dependency on her husband's refugee claim had serious consequences. Ini-tially, she did not make use of protection Canadian police could offer because she feared it would interfere with the status determination process, while she also was unaware that she could make a claim of her own: "one day my boy called the police because [my husband] threw the telephone at me, and hit me. [My son] called and when he told me he called the police, I went to hide and I didn't want the police to see me. . . . My mind said: You are here, im-migration is a big deal for you; if you start to get involved with the police, you will not get a chance with immigration. This was in my mind! So I said to myself: You better keep quiet![31]

Often increasing desperation forced asylum seekers to take action, re-gardless of lack of legal information about consequences or alternatives to deportation. The greatest providers of information were, in most cases, women's shelters and private legal counsel. But like women's shelters, other organizations helping asylum seekers who went public were often not tradi-tional refugee organizations. They included churches, ethnic community groups, advocacy groups, and frontline service groups. Nada sought help from NOIVMW (geared toward immigrant and minority women already es-tablished in Canada) and the ICHRDD (not typically involved in domestic refugee claims). Thérèse and Tamarati contacted the CCR (a refugee group) and ICHRDD (a human rights group) through chance encounters on the street with individuals who referred them to these organizations.[32]

Thérèse is a good illustration of the variety of contacts and influences informing an asylum seeker's decision and of their outcome. Two events con-vinced Thérèse to seek help: the escalation of her abuse and finding out that her husband had been sexually abusing her children. Upon discovering the latter she sought advice from various sources and received different opinions about what to do. She contacted Youth Services and talked with a psychiatrist, who helped her understand the abuse of her children and suggested how she might prevent her husband from being alone with them. These professionals were unable to advise her on immigration problems when she inquired. According to Thérèse, the president of one association she had joined advised: "'Why did you have to come here? Why you didn't stay [in Seychelles]? This was your chance for breakup!' I said: 'I don't know, I followed my husband here, I didn't know what was happening with the family.' And [the president] told me: 'Keep quiet until you have everything with immigration, then I will help you.'" Thérèse did "keep quiet," but her husband's abuse intensified when she confronted him about abusing the children. When she requested a separation, he threatened to kill her. He was arrested by Canadian authorities, and when he was released and his refugee claim was rejected, he continued to threaten her. He was deported in handcuffs due to his criminal behavior. "He wanted me to pay for the rejection of his claim, even though I had nothing to do with it. . . . Even when he was back home he still threatened to kill me because he was jailed here in Canada and rejected, so I had to pay." When Thérèse received a deportation notice and explained her situation to immigration authorities, she was granted leave to reapply on humanitarian and compassionate grounds. Knowing there was no protection from domestic violence in the Seychelles Islands, she reapplied but was rejected. Fearful of returning to her country, where her husband continued to issue death threats and police protection was unavailable, she sought advice from a priest. "I told the priest what I want to do, and he said it's the wrong idea: Why don't I take my money and go back to my country? . . . But I said to him 'I will do anything I have to do to save the lives of my children.'"[33]

Ultimately the decision was hers to make. She opted to fight her case even it if entailed going public, which core supporters subsequently offered her the means to do. In a chance conversation with a woman she met while waiting for a bus, she was advised to contact the CCR, which subsequently put her in touch with a new lawyer and others in the campaign network.

The ways and extent that supporters shaped asylum seekers' decisions and actions reaffirms the roles of the latter as political actors. Supporters not only provided critical information, means, and moral support for going public, but also respected and supported asylum seekers' decisions. Analysis of supporters' views reveals that (1) they emphasized giving asylum seekers the final say and respecting asylum seekers' choices, and (2) asylum seekers made rational and strategic decisions when presented with options or strategies.

Asylum seekers' decisions to go public involved strategic considerations shaped by and also shaping the internal environment of supporters, as part of two-way structures of influence.

Glynis Williams (RAM), who worked closely with Thérèse, expressed an often-repeated attitude among core supporters regarding influencing claimants' decisions and actions:

I am reluctant [about claimants going public] until, first of all, you have a whole group that is agreed that this is the only option and that we have to go this route. I also think it is the person themselves who has to make that decision because I have been involved in some cases over the years, of people who got very dependent on you to make the decisions about what was the right thing to do—and that is a killer, emotionally. People have to determine their own lives, and if you don't push them to make some of their own decisions, because it is a hard decision, they live with it. Once they are in the media, that information will be sent back to their country; you can't hide people for too long; and there is simply a limit to what we can do. So that is something the people have to think about themselves.[34]

Similarly, Bronson (ICHRDD) emphasized to Nada the consequences of going public (as discussed earlier), and also Nada's ultimate power of choice: "We had always said 'whenever you want to back out that is fine, but you are the one who will have to say it, because you are the one who will have to pay, you and your family, if things turn out badly against you, if you lose.' Because that was all I could say. 'Maybe we will win, this is my best bet, this is my educated guess on what will happen to you. . . . And we will do whatever we can if they deport you and you are thrown in jail: we will write letters, we can make diplomatic representation. But we can't save your life.' "[35] Thérèse and Nada chose to go public like the others, weighing possible losses against possibilities of success and the best available recourse of action. Bronson emphasized going public as a "last resort" strategy presented to Nada. "It was fairly obvious to me, though I was quite naïve and ignorant of the immigration system and how it worked at that time, that if we got public attention on her case, she would win it. And that would be the *only* way she would win it. And that I knew in function of my background and my understanding of politics."[36]

Rivka Augenfeld (TCMR) described media use in more negative terms, as a last resort strategy and one not suitable for most asylum seekers, despite powerful public impact: "It is not usually good to do case work through the media. You leave it to the end to use as a last resort because if you haven't exhausted the other avenues [government] will say 'You haven't given us a chance yet.' And the media is hard because you need a case that stands out, and the person in question and the family in question has to agree and has to be able to explain what is going on. And the media does not always pick up the points that you think are the important ones. . . . Of course, people always respond to these individual stories. . . . But you also have to think 'how many times can you actually do this through the media?' "[37]

Hesitancy to use the media indicates that key NGOs in these cases were against pushing asylum seekers to go public, for a variety of reasons. However, they did see the advantages and power of using media appropriately.

Lawyers also were firm on keeping media as a last resort strategy. Only after at least four separate requests/claims were rejected did Ginette's lawyer state: "I have good contacts in the immigration department, but I was told (yesterday) that the Montreal department won't change its mind. The only thing I can do is appeal to the public to try to help her."[38]

However, conflict did emerge among supporters when it came to claimants going into hiding, and particularly concerning when they should go into hiding. Many supported decisions to go into hiding, either to allow an opportunity to campaign, or upon the failure to overturn decisions through campaigning in particular cases. One lawyer for several of the publicized cases declared: "You must never give up. The secret: never give up. Even if it means saying to the woman, 'go into hiding.' "[39] However supporters were clearly aware that hiding was no long-term solution. A women's shelter that housed seven of the fourteen claimants who went public, including some who had gone into hiding, commented: "We didn't say in any case that is the solution. I don't agree with it because I do not think that it is really life. . . . Maybe, when there are women who don't have a choice but to go underground while some decisions are being made; but we don't want to do that again in the future."[40]

Women's shelters that supported such decisions and provided residence were adamant that if possible it should be a last resort, behind going public. They emphasized the conflict in strategy among supporters, which emerged in several cases regarding *when* a claimant should go public. At least one women's shelter felt strongly that contrary to some lawyers' advice, claimants should go public *before* being ordered deported or going into hiding, indicating less faith in government making acceptable decisions under only pressure from institutional channels.

Another core campaign organization similarly emphasized that if possible, going underground should be avoided unless public pressure tactics fail or there are no opportunities to use public pressure tactics sooner. "I am always amazed because my experience of going underground is that you have no resources, no access to money, so who is paying? Is it a long-term strategy? . . . As far as government is concerned you are not a drain on the public purse any more, and if you are not a danger they are probably happy if you get lost. But you have no status, you have no future, what do you do with health care, if you've got children either here? You have no way to protect them or put them in school—or if they are overseas they are never going to get here. It is a terrible limbo situation. Though maybe it works in the short term, I don't know."[41] That is, despite its negatives, being in hiding before going public had strategic advantages as discussed earlier in Nada's case. In such cases, a member of one NGO noted, "It would work in the short term if you are working on something and yet they have determined to deport somebody. It seems to me you have got to have some card up your sleeve still . . . that you hope that time will help you deal with."[42]

Public pressure was a last resort choice shaped by the two-way structure of influence between asylum seekers and core supporters. Asylum seekers' decisions to go public were heavily influenced by external support and advice and by the desperation of their situations. But neither need nor opportunities and support were sufficient to foster action. It would be a gross oversimplification to say that asylum seekers take certain actions simply because they are forced out of desperation or that supporters simply act/make decisions for them. Rather, asylum seekers are rational, strategic actors interacting with their structural environment of opportunities and constraints and exercising choices within it, often in an incremental or trial-and-error manner. Going public came to involve both personal and political factors in decision making by asylum seekers, alongside strategic decision making informed by the options supporters offered. Asylum seekers had to weigh the possible risks of going public, including further endangering themselves and their families, against needs, alternatives, opportunities, and beliefs about identity and rights.

Mobilizing Ideology into Action: The Structure of Support

Why did supporters get involved and what role did asylum seekers play in shaping the structure and nature of support they received? This question can be explored by looking at the onset and development of core supporters' involvement with the issue of sex persecution generally and public pressure activities specifically. I draw on qualitative analysis of supporters' explanations and descriptions of their involvement, in relation to the following factors: profession and organizational type; previous experience and predisposition toward the issue; core ideology; and how supporters linked ideology with particular asylum seekers with whom they came into contact.[43] Analysis reveals a clear link between the translation of supporters' deep core ideology into participatory actions, and supporters' coming into contact with particular asylum seekers at a time when perceived potential or interorganizational support for successful actions was high. Deep core values are defined as "the highest/broadest level" in a hierarchy or value set of beliefs. They include: "basic ontological and normative beliefs, such as the perceived nature of humans or the relative valuation of individual freedom or social equality, which operate across virtually all policy domains; the familiar left/right scale operates at this level" (Jenkins-Smith and Sabatier 1994:180).

All core supporters' deep core values were in some way predisposed toward issues raised by asylum seekers' claims (having women and/or refugee centered mandates), but their profession, organizational type, and previous experience alone fail to explain why they engaged in advocacy on this issue when they did. When asked why they got involved with the policy campaigns, core supporters commonly identified one of two reasons. Both reflect deep core values, and both revolve around contact with individual cases as the critical factor that mobilized core supporters' deep core values into actions: (1) individual asylum seekers' structural representation (a particular case or set of cases was illustrative or representative of a broader problem—violation of women's rights as human rights violations—due to women's structural inequality worldwide, which raises Canada's responsibility under international human rights law); and (2) individual asylum seekers' immediate needs (a particular claimant's experience was a type of persecution chronically ignored in the Canadian refugee system due to inherent structural inequality, placing that particular claimant in a dire situation). The following considers reasons for involvement among supporters, whose profession, organizational type, and previous experience can be grouped in to three categories: umbrella advocacy organizations, frontline service organizations, and lawyers. This identifies and explains supporters' justifications in relation to key mediating factors and evidences the criticality of asylum seekers for supporters' decisions to get involved. In so doing it also provides deeper description of the core constituents of the campaign network and, as this network became the prime mover for the issue of sex persecution in Canada, sheds light on why and how advocacy first arose.

Umbrella Advocacy Organizations

As umbrella organizations, the TCMR, CCR, ICHRDD, and NAC do not typically engage in frontline service work with individuals and communities. Rather, they approach social issues with macro level aims of policy change, education, research, and interorganizational work. Among these groups, the *exemplary* nature of individual cases was crucial. Participation was based foremost on a case or set of cases considered representative of violations of women's human rights, indicating Canada's responsibility to provide protection under international law. Rivka Augenfeld of the TCMR explained: "Normally we do not take on individual cases, unless those cases are illustrative of an issue. Some cases carry a wider issue with it, so we get involved. Everybody needs help but as a coalition we can't get involved in all cases and take them all on, so we tend to decide when we get involved based on what issue it represents. So with Nada, for example, it was the whole wider issue of gender persecution." Describing the downside, Augenfeld remarked: "unfortunately, it is always around some desperate case. It is unfortunate that there has to be somebody's life on the line."[44]

A small number of the asylum seekers—particularly Nada, Taramati, Dulerie, and Thérèse—provided the initial impetus for supporters, who in espousing the cause and developing policy aims and strategies for one asylum seeker later got involved with others. Advocacy for the *issue* was always linked to advocacy for particular cases. Nada also provided the political impetus for the ICHRDD's involvement, although they generally take on neither individual cases nor domestic issues. Their involvement was precipitated by a chance encounter at a semipolitical social event. Nada (whose claim had already been rejected) was introduced to Diana Bronson, ICHRDD media relations officer, who offered to look into the situation and "invest time and energy in it" upon approval by Edward Broadbent, the president. "Nada came here, she told me her story. I thought that it merited our attention . . . because we saw it as an international human rights issue . . . I thought it was a brilliant illustration of how women's rights are not considered to be human rights: that her rights were massively violated in Saudi Arabia was not enough for the Canadian Immigration and Refugee Board to determine that she was a refugee. It did not matter that her rights as a woman were denied to her."[45] Nada's experience illustrated both lack of state protection (in sending and receiving countries) and women's human rights violations. It also illustrated a particular form of female persecution contributing to the ICHRDD's strategic decision to support her and not others at the time. This is apparent in Bronson's depiction of how, again through a chance encounter, she met Taramati whose situation involved domestic violence. Meeting Taramati prompted Bronson to consider advocating for individuals fleeing more private types of female persecution, including not only Taramati but also Dulerie whose case had recently been publicized without ICHRDD support: "I met Taramati on the street one day, completely by accident . . . she asked me where to find [a street]. I offered to walk her to the corner. . . . And we got to talking. It turned out to be Taramati. She ended up telling me her story on the street corner—about how she had been threatened by her husband, how she had two children, how she was in hiding and she was going to a [women's shelter]. I came into work that morning and I said I thought we should take on the three cases: Nada, Taramati, and Dulerie."[46] However, strategic considerations hinging on the different forms of persecution the women faced prompted the ICHRDD to pursue the cases separately. The ICHRDD became involved with Nada, but decided not to simultaneously advocate for Taramati and Dulerie. "Mr. Broadbent's political judgment was: No, let's go with Nada . . . because it's the easiest thing for them to swallow. The Canadian government cannot go against an argument of equality. They can still argue that domestic violence is a private issue, a cultural tradition, whatever they want. . . . At that time [domestic violence as a human rights violation] wasn't at all clear either in . . . the government's head or among human rights groups."[47]

The ICHRDD did later advocate for claimants facing domestic violence. In both cases the combination of contact with asylum seekers, the ICHRDD's preestablished ideological commitment to women's human rights, and strategic considerations prompted their participation. Dulerie was the earliest of the three to publicize her case (in July 1992); she did so through women's shelters and was the only one not in direct contact with the ICHRDD at the time. For the ICHRDD, not accustomed to frontline service work and lacking experience with the particular asylum seekers, contact with asylum seekers appears to have been crucial to participation. However the ICHRDD first pursued the case with the strongest legal arguments—the public nature and nondiscrimination argument in Nada's claim.

NAC is another powerful organization that generally deals with macro level issues and which at the time lacked experience with sex persecution. NAC got involved through Taramati. Contact occurred through overlapping membership on NAC's executive board and Women's Aid, the shelter where Taramati was residing. Following Taramati's deportation notice in February 1992 (scheduled for October of that year), NAC formed a special committee to address the issue of persecution. As head of the Violence Against Women Unit in the Executive Committee of NAC, Flora Fernandez explained that Taramati's deportation was delayed with the support of NAC, "and after, in the Executive Committee of NAC, we spoke about the [case] and we understood that big problems would arrive, and we started to prepare."[48]

NAC's involvement grew after making statements to the media and as refugee claimants began arriving at its Toronto office. NAC's initial organizational inability to cope with the situation was overridden by the structural nature of the problem and the deep emotional and ideological affinity for these women's situation. Fernandez explained that as an umbrella group NAC would not typically advocate for individuals, but that these women "came in a group": "[After] we went to the media . . . women who had this problem went to the Toronto office of NAC. The people arrived and arrived! They cried, and it was a very emotional time for us—for NAC and for me too. We felt a great responsibility. But NAC is a lobby group. We don't have the infrastructure to work on . . . individuals' problems; we can't give [frontline] service too. But we saw [the individual problems] as a group of problems . . . those women came in a group. So for that [reason] I took the decision to take the cases. I had about fifty cases. Of those, we publicized fourteen."[49] The fourteen cases publicized as a group in February 1993 arrived from various shelters where the women were residing and through women presenting themselves at the NAC office.

From the onset, NAC was a strong supporter of women fleeing all forms of female persecution, from more to less public, recognizing their structural and representative nature and also individual asylum seekers' paramount need for immediate safety. NAC had been committed to ending violence against women since the 1970s (Vickers, Rankin, and Appelle 1993). However, asked about the influence of the campaigning process on NAC's mandate, Fernandez expressed a clear sense of achievement and benefit for NAC internally as it expanded its scope. "We are very proud about that. We worked so much—it was crazy. We don't have the resources, we don't have the money, and we have too many people who wait with only hope, about what we can do. It was not in our 'mission.' . . . We didn't have any [extra funding for it]. We had only solidarity with the women. Only that. It was hard to go with all that pressure, all on a deadline. In another way, we learned the importance of the media."[50]

NAC's broadened mandate became a source of pride for the significance of the task itself, their achievements under difficult circumstances, and the effectiveness of some of the strategies learned to galvanize public support. Like many core supporters, NAC lacked sufficient financial resources for additional (new) activities, relying instead on human and nonmaterial resources. NAC's preexistence and predisposition toward the issues were fundamental products of rising opportunities and resources experienced during the 1980s (see Chapter 5), but it did not take on this new policy issue as result of new resources or expertise on the issue. Like other organizations, the expansion of organizational mandate occurred before new resources and expertise were available. Augenfeld (TCMR) described the importance of links between women's and refugee groups for the technical information the latter could provide, but still observed that NAC's involvement developed before its expertise: "When some of the cases went public, the network of women's organizations really got involved. And when NAC got involved, they got a lot of exposure. NAC got involved with a commitment to shepherd those cases that they adopted. But they had to learn about the ins and outs of immigration: how things work, the nitty-gritty. They had to learn about that because it is not as simple as it seems at first glance."[51] Expanded mandates were typically enabled through heavy reliance on extra volunteer labor and overtime. Individuals contributed personal time and energy, in addition to offering free services to the asylum seekers. According to explanations provided by core supporters, emotional and ideological affinity for the issue alongside the urgency of individual asylum seekers' situations were paramount, motivating supporters to transcend resource limitations.

Frontline Service Organizations

In contrast to the larger, umbrella organizations that tended to get involved because particular cases were exemplary and they had not previously come into contact with cases of a similar nature and urgency, frontline service organizations often experienced the opposite. As service providers, women's shelters and organizations working with immigrants and refugees dealt with the target population on a more daily basis and saw these asylum seekers in terms of their individual needs first and foremost. They equated particular cases with the general problem but saw each as one of many such cases due to their more regular contact with them. They identified the failure of the Canadian refugee system rather than the existence of sex persecution as motivation for getting involved, because the latter was taken for granted or continuous in their experience. Therefore, rather than discovering exemplary cases suited to a new issue area, these supporters experienced new needs and opportunities to pursue policy change through these exemplary cases. They saw an increase in the number of women in this situation, with whom they came in contact; and new opportunities to engage in policy advocacy around this issue.

As expected, women's shelters became involved by providing frontline services to refugee women who sought shelter (residence) with them. At least seven women who went public had been residing at women's shelters. Asked why they campaigned in 1992 and 1993, Elizabeth Montecino, director of the Flora Tristan shelter, succinctly stated, "We were involved because we had such cases at that time . . . [some] were residents here."[52] The involvement of women's shelters was particularly important not only in providing crucial day-to-day support services, but also because some of the larger advocacy organizations, such as the ICHRDD, were not at the onset strategically inclined to take on cases involving "private" violence. These shelters tended to be strong public supporters, and through them asylum seekers often came into contact with NAC, which helped publicize claims.

What then was the difference between the asylum seekers who went public and previous asylum seekers encountered by shelter workers? With fifteen years experience at Women's Aid, Flora Fernandez argued that the problem of sex persecution was recognized long before campaigns began in the early 1990s. She explains Women's Aid's use of public pressure tactics at that time as a factor of increased need for immigration and refugee policy change following the Conservative government's increasing restrictions on migration in the late 1980s. Deportation of women fleeing domestic violence, she contends, "was not a problem until after the Conservative Party arrived, and for sure with Immigration Minister [Benoit] Bouchard [1986–88]. He made very Machiavellian moves against refugees . . . and very big manipulation in the media. After that the problem for women who leave conjugal violence was like the maximum result."[53]

Earlier, while formal rules guiding entry did not exist, relaxed criteria were reportedly applied in some cases in which a woman's sponsor had become abusive and return to the country of origin was deemed unsafe. But increasingly restrictive immigration policy during the 1980s (see Chapter 4) cut off ad hoc solutions and loopholes. Asylum seekers residing at shelters in this study began to be ordered to be deported. Meanwhile the rising backlog of asylum seekers awaiting decisions during the 1980s and early 1990s contributed to an increase in the number of immigrant women residing in the shelters studied and increased the average duration of their stay.[54] This increased women's shelters' contact with women fleeing persecution, increased obstacles to policy change, and made policy change all the more necessary.

Comparing women's shelters' previous and later experiences, we can see how the emphasis on state responsibility changed, policy goals evolved, and new interorganizational support was attained. At Flora Tristan, public sensitization work (educating the public) and pressure activities in 1991 were argued primarily in terms of sponsorship abuse. New advocacy frameworks including ideological and institutional support emerged around later cases; while often still involving some form of sponsorship abuse, domestic violence was contextualized within human rights discourses and discrimination toward women in the refugee system. Earlier cases also enjoyed little external support aside from lawyers. Cases publicized after 1992 under the broader issue of sex persecution enjoyed the interest of larger organizations and umbrella groups, as well as many supporters among the public at large. For frontline service groups, the political support and legal know-how that umbrella advocacy organizations could provide were important. Shelters joined campaigns not because the particular asylum seekers were new to the shelter; rather they joined because system failure seemed to be increasing and new opportunities were arising to advocate for such women within a larger context of activism. To address system failure, they became convinced that the law needed to be changed to account for women's structural experiences. As Montecino explained, as the problem "is going to repeat, it is going to . . . create other social problems. We can't save energy, money, or anything without letting the problem get poor. So, I think that the immigration structure has to be revised with the times. . . . Reality doesn't correspond with the law."[55] The Flora Tristan shelter worked to educate the public and work with asylum seekers, giving twenty-six media interviews, participating in twenty-one conferences, twenty-six meetings, and eleven student sessions between April 1993 and March 1994 (Maison Flora Tristan 1994). Last but not least, shelters campaigned because public pressure seemed the last chance for these women to remain in Canada. In all cases, safety from violence and deportation remained the paramount short-term goal and policy change the long-term secondary goal.

RAM, a frontline organization working with refugees in entry and settlement processes, also became a core supporter through cases involving domestic violence. But unlike women's shelters, RAM did not have previous experience with such cases. It had knowledge of the immigration system and an ideological predisposition toward work with women refugees. Emphasis on advocacy increased when its board was restructured in 1992. Contact with particular asylum seekers in 1993 precipitated its participation, first peripherally (in Nada's case) and then directly (in Thérèse's case). RAM coordinator Glynis Williams explained of the core campaign network: "Some people knew one another [previously], but the rest of us got pulled in . . . the push really came more from the individual cases." She described public support arising from "people like Nada, coming forward from out of the blue, on her own initiative. . . . She was articulate enough, though she didn't get accepted at first, but she knew that women's issues are at a very different stage in our country than they are in Saudi Arabia."[56]

In this sense RAM was more like the larger umbrella groups without previous experience, but like women's shelters in focusing on the acuteness and immediacy of individual asylum seekers' situations and perceiving new needs and increased opportunities for advocacy. "We noticed that when other issues around refugees were not being picked up or people were just getting in a 'compassion fatigue,' that around Nada's case when that finally broke and was quite successful . . . we had a broad range of groups that had an interest in the subject, that were not just refugee organizations. Whereas, I think it is fair to say that on other kinds of cases there has not been the kind of broad spectrum of organizations that were affected by the issue, that were involved, as there were in this case: women's groups, women's shelters, groups that are increasingly seeing immigrant or refugee women seeking their support. That was a whole new network of people that got involved and took up the refugee cause."[57]

Increased opportunities for action, from the point of view of refugee and humanitarian organizations, arose from the interest of women's groups, rather than the other way around. Umbrella groups similarly expressed the significance of support by women's groups, as indicated earlier, however for achieving outcomes rather than precipitating their own involvement.

Lawyers

Like RAM, lawyers occupied an interesting position between groups and asylum seekers, nonservice and service (frontline) oriented groups. This was reflected in their combined emphasis on immediate needs of clients and the exemplary nature of their cases. One of the most vocal and active lawyers during the campaigns, Marie-Louise Côté was in a special position having held several different posts within the immigration system: immigration officer (border official), Refugee Hearing Officer (RHO) presiding as a neutral party during the refugee hearing, adjudicator, and finally a lawyer in private practice. This provides a well-rounded perspective on the immigration system and the particular types of claims. As an adjudicator between 1989 and 1992, she explains: "I had been expecting to see these cases, it has been my interest for a long time, so as an adjudicator I was just waiting for those cases to appear. One did appear one day, a very clear gender case. It was a woman, 'Caroline' . . . and she was claiming that she was afraid of going back because her husband had been abusing her, and she was saying that her country would not protect her. This, back then although it is not long ago, seemed to be like: 'how can you *ever* expect that this would be accepted!'"[58] While clearly on the look out for an exemplary case, she recognized that the challenges faced and posed by such claims within the immigration system were fundamental to the *invisibility* of such cases within the system. Earlier, as an immigration officer at the border, her experience was common: male refugees tended to do the talking, women tended to be silent and not make their own claims. As an RHO and later an adjudicator, she observed: "Some lawyers would dare to present the case going along a gender-based claim, but they would not say it like that necessarily. More often than not it would be presented . . . under the 'social group' category, which as one of the five grounds of the Convention is fine. But when a case was presented, it was received with a lot of skepticism." Côté took Nada's case, which had been referred to her by the ICHRDD. She noted that she had thought it was interesting but "didn't get into it until Nada phoned." She offered her services free to Nada and became a core supporter in the network that developed, representing approximately forty such cases over the next three years.[59]

Other lawyers had extensive previous experience through dual work in immigration and civil law specializing in domestic violence. They tended to work on cases of sponsorship breakdown before 1993, and later on gender-related persecution under the Canadian Guidelines (including cases that may or may not involve sponsorship complications). Among lawyers interviewed, clients were most often referred by women's shelters. One lawyer with thirteen years' experience with domestic violence cases and extensive involvement with refugees who went public likened the lawyer's role to that of an orchestra conductor: able to direct people as to how to use the law, but not being the primary power behind change. As she described it, her role was in the legal battle, attracting media attention, and providing individuals and organizations with information on how to proceed, "on writing letters and press releases, what journalists to talk to, how the law works, how different procedures work . . . and who else can be of help." She emphasized solving individual women's cases more than their exemplary nature and corresponding policy goals. Rather than looking out for exemplary cases she made use of emerging opportunities to assist such women, in particular the availability of resources and women's increasing willingness to use them, stating: "The greatest trend: women are leaving clandestinity. . . . Things have changed because of women's groups, and because immigrants themselves started to get organized. . . . Women victims of violence now have more social services and phone contacts. There are more refugees in women's shelters. Women's shelters phone me. [Refugee women] more often leave their homes than in 1983, 1984, 1985. I had one or two per year, back then. Over the years ten has been the most [per year]. That is because they are more aware of resources that exist. They go to the resources, and the resources put them in my path."[60]

The Internal Political Culture of the Campaign Network

We have seen some differences and many commonalties in the ways supporters became involved with public pressure tactics, and some of the factors involved in how asylum seekers made decisions about going public. Several important conclusions may be drawn from this. First, asylum seekers were politically conscious actors making decisions and advocating for themselves and as representatives of a persecuted group. This was revealed particularly in how they decided to use noninstitutional strategies to challenge negative decisions on their claims. The desperate need for asylum and the options supporters could provide were mediated by asylum seekers' personal and political considerations—how they viewed themselves in relation to the world and to a collective identity, their rights and politicization, and risks they were willing to take.

Being noncitizens did not negate these actors' desires or abilities to challenge policy, rather it increased their need for policy change in order to be granted refugee status. Although need was their primary motivating factor, and they did rely on opportunities and support to challenge the receiving-country refugee system, they were neither simply "forced" out of desperation to make such challenges nor "illegitimate" refugees abusing the system. They made rational and strategic choices around a legitimate political debate regarding their own identity and right to state protection. This involved identity politics, which is both symbolic and strategic. It involved thinking about self in relation to society, states, rights, and responsibilities. It involved taking into account the risks, options, information, and means supporters could provide. And, although neither citizens nor permanent residents, it involved accessing a range of host-country resources. Asylum seekers were deeply embedded within what needs to be recognized as a complex political process; they were not merely beneficiaries of aid or schemers seeking personal benefit without political legitimacy. In sharing their stories and decisions through institutional claims and noninstitutional interactions with the media, asylum seekers in turn could become symbolic and political instruments of persuasion and actually influence the public and government (see Chapter 6).

Second, asylum seekers were not only conscious political actors, but also key mobilizing agents among supporters. Their willingness and determination to seek support and take noninstitutional actions was crucial for mobilizing Canadian citizens and permanent residents and binding them together in a common cause. In looking at how core supporters conceptualized the relation between beliefs and participatory action, asylum seekers' symbolic and strategic roles emerged. In all instances core supporters became involved through contact with asylum seekers willing to go public. Asylum seekers' needs and structural representation mediated between supporters' ideology and deep core policy values, opportunities for collective action and strategic means, and actions actually being taken. The violence and lack of protection they experienced represented the broader problem of women's structural inequality as citizens around the world, raising Canada's responsibility under international human rights and refugee law. The structural inequality they experienced in Canada's refugee system increased the urgency of their need for external support as their claims were rejected. Emphasis upon one of these two reasons for participation tended to correspond with organizational type, experience, and approaches to advocacy. Supporters who took up the issue because particular cases were "representative" tended not to have had direct experience with actual women in these situations. Some may have been aware and on the lookout for such cases, but compared to frontline service organizations and to some extent to lawyers, awareness and involvement were fairly new among the larger umbrella and advocacy groups. Their interest was sparked primarily by particular claimants whose exemplary cases

Table 5.2. Mandate, Activities, and Access of Core Campaign Organizations

Refugee and humanitarian NGOs

	CCR	ICHRDD	TCMR	RAM
Locale and mandate	National umbrella organization for refugee groups (150+)	Human rights organization (international focus, based in Canada)	Montreal umbrella group coordinating refugee organizations	Frontline community service for refugees
Activities	Education and networking forum for nonprofits; policy advocacy via meetings, correspondence, and phone contact with government, and via media *Rarely advocates in individual cases	Mainly international advocacy, mediating between governments and NGOs/citizens; occasionally domestic issues *Rarely advocates in individual cases	Research/education on refugee rights; develop and coordinate NGO settlement services; foster understanding between society and migrants; policy advocacy, especially via CCR. *Rarely advocates in individual cases	Intervention in entry processes; networking, education; policy advocacy via national umbrella groups (ICCR, CCR, TCMR) *Advocacy in individual cases
Political access	High political and media access; serve on government working groups (IRB Advisory Committee; UNHCR consultative status), regularly advise government on policy and practice, participate in consultations	High political and media access, including leadership of a former party political leader as president (Broadbent)	Moderate political access, particularly on a regional level, and with IRB in Montreal	Moderate/low direct political access; operates primarily on local level, advocacy through umbrella groups

Women's NGOs

	NAC	NOIVMW	Women's Aid	Flora Tristan	Multi-Femmes	Auberge Transition
Locale and mandate	National umbrella organization for women's groups (500+)	National umbrella organization for immigrant and visible minority women's groups	Immigrant women's shelter; frontline community service	Immigrant women's shelter; frontline community service	Immigrant women's shelter; frontline community service	Women's shelter; frontline community service
Activities	Primarily lobbying federal government on legislation and policy. Education and research *Rarely advocates in individual cases	Education and research; policy advocacy *Occasionally advocates in individual or representative cases	Residence, counseling, and support; policy advocacy via national and provincial networks *Advocacy in individual cases	Residence, counseling, and support; research and education; policy advocacy via provincial and national networks *Advocacy in individual cases	Residence, counseling, and support; policy advocacy via provincial and national networks *Advocacy in individual cases	Residence, counseling, and support; policy advocacy via provincial and national networks *Advocacy in individual cases
Political access	High political and media access	Moderate access to government and media	Low government access, moderate media access	Low government access, moderate media access	Low government access, moderate media access	Low government access, moderate media access

provided an opportunity to pursue an important ideological and political issue. In contrast, women's shelters and other frontline organizations perceived rising needs and new opportunities to advocate for a longer term solution to such cases, with which they had previous experience. For them, individual life histories of the women they worked with may have been representative of the issue generally, but many individuals, in their own experience, were representative. What moved them to action was the immediacy of particular women's situations and their willingness to try new strategies to attain entry, coinciding with perceived possibilities for new types of advocacy and its potential for success. Lawyers fell into both groupings.

Finally, asylum seekers played a crucial role as binding agents among supporters. Supporters strengthened and formalized links between each other by getting into regular contact over particular asylum seekers. This was facilitated by several organizational cross-memberships and supporters who wore more than one hat within their organization, serving bridging roles. Asylum seekers only occasionally worked directly with other asylum seekers, although most went public within the same six months, some simultaneously. Together these asylum seekers and their supporters constituted the core campaign network. The constituency of the network was diverse (umbrella, advocacy, and service, within and across issue niches and with various specialties within issue niches) and controlled a wide and strategic mix of capabilities across local, national, and international levels. Core advocacy organizations' locale and mandate, activities, and political access are presented in Table 5.2. This diversity facilitated the mobilization of an equally diverse range of secondary actors and the public. Secondary actors comprise those who gave public support but were not involved at the planning and organizing level, or who worked through core actors rather than directly with the asylum seekers. They included member organizations of NAC (over 500 women's groups), the CCR (over 150 international migration groups), NOIVMW (representing immigrant and "visible minority" women's groups), and the TCMR (Montreal's ethnic, community, international migration groups). National organizations also provided links to Canadian offices of the UNHCR and Amnesty International and to political contacts within Canadian government. Other networks of secondary supporters spun off local organizations—women's shelters tapped into the shelter network and other women's groups, lawyers linked into formal and informal legal networks, refugee and ethnic minority groups reached out to client populations' local schools, communities, and politicians. Secondary supporters partici-

Figure 5.1. Core Campaign Network, Metanetwork, and External Environment

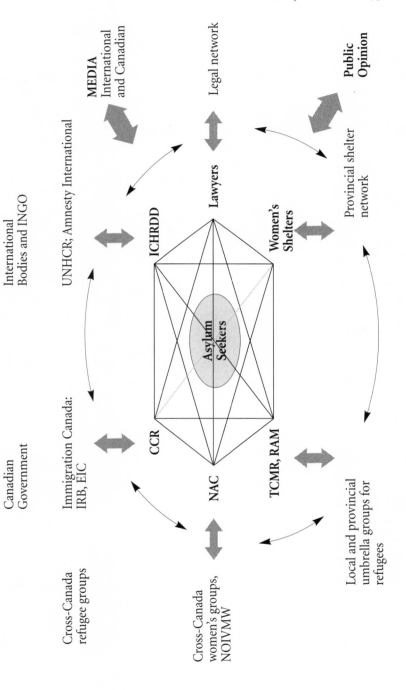

pated by (for example) signing petitions, faxing and writing to the immigration minister, attending press conferences, and providing direct support services to asylum seekers.

Figure 5.1 portrays the campaign network schematically and depicts some important characteristics of its internal political culture. Unlike coalitions, the network structure accounts for relationships among individuals (not members of an organization) and organizations, rather than solely between organizations (Gerlach and Hine 1970). Networks are also more fluid or less organizationally formal. The "clique" structure depicted here portrays asylum seekers' centrality, the density of linkages among supporters, and their links to secondary actors.

In the process of deciding to campaign and forming the campaign network we can see that asylum seeking occurs within a structural context of reciprocal or mutually shaping relationships between asylum seekers, the structure of support, and the ideological and strategic frameworks and opportunities through which they ultimately act. The campaign network also illustrates relationships between citizens or permanent residents and noncitizens, relationships not territorially defined or exclusive, and not imposed upon but developed with noncitizens. Through the campaign network's resources, capabilities, and tools, we can see how asylum seekers might gain additional political leverage and influence in policy-making processes. We turn, in the following chapter, to these processes.

Chapter 6
Universalizing National Rights: Political Confrontation and Cultural Framing

I ask you: if we don't listen to women now, when are we going to listen to them? When are they going to be taken seriously? Women around the world are suffering, and governments use all their powers not to develop, but to repress their people. . . . This is the time for Canada to take a stand for the human rights and fundamental freedoms of oppressed women.

—Nada, *refugee claimant*, Ottawa Citizen, *11 March 1993*

In the period leading up to the campaigns, emerging rights, re-sources, and collective interests provided important opportunities and build-ing blocks for asylum seekers and their core supporters, while relations between asylum seekers and supporters shaped actor participation and the core campaign network's internal political culture as a whole. We now need to understand how subsequent campaigning processes influenced the exter-nal environment. Which framing strategies and tactics mobilized the public and reversed government responses? How and to what extent did national and international rights and discourses influence campaign demands, strate-gic choices, and outcomes? What impact did asylum seekers specifically have upon political processes and outcomes?

Underlying the following analysis is McAdam's concept of "strategic framing processes" or "signifying acts" (1996). Framing processes typically constitute "the conscious, strategic efforts of movement groups to fashion meaningful accounts of themselves and the issues at hand in order to moti-vate and legitimate their efforts" (McAdam 1996:39; see also Snow and Ben-ford 1988 and 1992; Melucci 1989; Touraine 1981). Thus it describes ideology and identity as movement resources. McAdam's expanded concept of "signi-fying acts" observes that the ways ideologies and demands are developed and articulated by actors constitute important actions and tactics in themselves, both in influencing and responding to the external environment. Signifying work reflects movement-environment relations that shape one another over time, serving at least four broad purposes: attracting media attention, particularly of a favorable nature; mobilizing public support; constraining the social control options of the environment it wishes to influence; and influencing public policy and state action (McAdam 1996:353).

The first section below uncovers the plurality and hierarchy of more to less radical campaign goals, policy demands, and pressure tactics characterizing the campaigns, and considers expected state responses to them according to social movement theory. The second section analyzes strategies and political processes in action at each stage of the campaign, uncovering campaigners' evolving and strategic interaction with the state and public, and the overall pressure and impacts brought to bear.[1] The final section considers asylum seekers' ongoing institutional influence by analyzing a database of precedents set in the first years under the Guidelines.

Campaign Characteristics and Expected External Responses

Priorities and Demands: Balancing Safety, Time, and Representation

As shown previously, core supporters' involvement in the campaigns stemmed from a combination of factors including contact with asylum seekers, previous personal and professional experience, and new opportunities for action perceived to be constructive. Underlying these factors were deep-core values that, upon contact with asylum seekers, resulted in two fundamental reasons why supporters' got involved: individual need for immediate safe asylum and individual representation of a structural issue and persecuted group. Asylum seekers also stressed both needs as individuals and rights as part of a group as reasons for going public. Reflecting these two basic motivating factors, leading campaign priorities were to respond to individuals' immediate needs for safety and to long-term collective or structural needs for safety. But what was the priority assigned to each? Different policy demands could be made that would satisfy either immediate or long-term structural needs, or both, depending on priority and perceived potential for attainment. Indeed, actors faced a crucial dilemma regarding the conflict between shorter and longer term priorities as interaction with the state evolved. With immediate safety as the overriding priority, we would expect ends to be more important than means. Policy change under this scenario is only one means for securing asylum. Using existing legislation, asylum may be sought on a case-by-case basis using whatever means available to ensure individual safety (including ad hoc and non-Convention status), without regard for consistent application in future cases. In the medium to long term ends and means may merge if judicial precedents are set and promote incremental policy change, but the likelihood and time frame for this are unclear, leaving consistent outcomes in future cases unknown. On the other hand, policy goals may be ends in themselves, promoting safety for current and future asylum seekers by addressing immediate individual needs consistently over time as part of a structural group. The question was, how or to what extent could policy change be sought without compromising immediate individual needs if the external environment was resistant to more immediate structural change?

In fact, a number of different policy demands were made during the course of the campaigns corresponding to campaigners' dual priorities. Rather than fragmenting or diffusing campaign pressure, as might be expected, the evolution and negotiation of different demands ultimately served a strategic purpose (see below). This can be explained in part by actors' common "deep core" ideologies. Jenkins-Smith and Sabatier (1994) describe "deep core" ideology among policy advocates consisting of "basic ontological and normative beliefs . . . which operate across virtually all policy domains," and giving rise to a hierarchy of "near core" and "secondary core" policy values with corresponding demands. Near-core policy values describe "basic normative commitments and causal perceptions across an entire policy domain or subsystem" (Jenkins-Smith and Sabatier 1994:180). The next level in the hierarchy takes into account secondary aspects of the belief system within a specific policy domain. At this "secondary core" a large set of narrower beliefs come into play, for instance regarding the seriousness of the problem or the relative importance of various causal factors in specific locales, policy preferences regarding desirable regulations or budgetary allocations, the design of specific institutions, and the evaluations of various actors' performance (181). Common deep-core ideology can bridge near-core and secondary-core policy values, enabling policy actors to prioritize and also to shift strategically from one to another should the need become apparent. For instance this may occur due to "policy learning" as new technical information or beliefs emerge regarding the substance, means or possibilities of policy change. In this view, shifting policy demands may be a strategy for, rather than a threat to, policy advocates' unity or influence (Jenkins-Smith and Sabatier 1994).

Table 6.1 presents the campaign network's policy value hierarchy with corresponding policy demands. Most closely reflecting actors' underlying deep-core values concerning women's protection from violence as a fundamental need and right, near-core policy values were shaped equally by asylum seekers' immediate individual needs and their structural representation. Corresponding legislative change would provide immediate recourse for all such asylum seekers as soon as possible and remain effective in the long term (immediate needs plus structural representation). All core actors expressed such legislative change as the ideal outcome. Actors' secondary-core policy value was to secure safe asylum for the greatest possible range of persecuted women within a specified short-term time frame. This would respond to the immediate needs of as many current asylum seekers as possible, by enacting a more moderate policy framework to support future asylum seekers. At this level, time demands remain constant and increase conflict, while policy content demands change and reduce conflict. None of the activists made this their initial demand or fought for it exclusively, but all supported this pragmatic option at some point and attempted to achieve and ensure proper implementation. This suggests campaigning asylum seekers' immediate safety was indeed paramount, creating a degree of openness toward policy strategies and enabling a shift in policy demands. The third tier of the hierarchy represents a "no policy change" approach. Here, actors did not seek policy change but challenged the system on a case-by-case basis. Safety could be sought under Refugee Convention status (by setting gender precedents or relying on nongender elements of a claim), or outside it (e.g., extra-Convention categories such as humanitarian and compassionate grounds). None of the core actors were supportive of this option exclusively. Although several precedents had been set through it, increasing restrictions on international migration seemed to be badly affecting individuals' likelihood of success through these means—indeed, it was the series of negative decisions on such claims that triggered activism for policy change.

Corresponding policy demands posed different challenges and subsequently evoked different types and degrees of resistance, and can be categorized on a continuum from radical to reform. The demand for legislative change corresponding to near-core policy values was a *radical strategy* because it would rephrase the 1951 Convention refugee definition in Canadian refugee policy (adding "sex" or "gender" as a grounds of persecution) and be more binding on the state. This was the highest policy aim in the hierarchy presented and evoked deep resistance by the government from the start. In contrast, the *reform strategy* would bypass the need to change the wording of existing refugee legislation by instead "adding on" new policy guidelines that mandate and explain a relevant reinterpretation of the law. This suggests that the interpretation and application rather than the substance of existing legislation was at fault, a critique easier for the government to swallow. It is important to note that the radical/reform distinction refers to different means of achieving a similar effect, and should not be confused with the underlying ideological basis and outcome. Both strategies seek to institutionalize government commitment to a similarly radical way of perceiving state responsibility under international law, which blurs the public/private divide (see Chapter 3).

TABLE 6.1. CAMPAIGN NETWORK HIERARCHY OF POLICY VALUES AND POLICY DEMANDS

Deep-core ideology: Protection from violence a fundamental women's right (Need Plus Structural Representation)	
Near-core policy values Asylum for all persecuted female claimants as soon as possible	**Radical policy demand** Change legislation to add "sex" or "gender" to the defintion of persecution, altering national use of international refugee law
Secondary-core policy values Asylum for as many persecuted female claimants as possible, as soon as possible	**Reform policy demand** Create policy mandating gendered reading of existing law
No policy change Asylum on a case-by-case basis under existing interpretation of the law	**Case-by-case reform demand (incremental)** Attain judicial or ministerial support under special procedures for rejected claimants

Pressure Tactics and External Responses

We know that the outcome of the campaigns was the secondary core, entailing interpretative change of existing legislation through the instatement of new policy guidelines. This brought an immediate though not ideal solution to a structural problem, providing a wide range of current and future asylum seekers with institutional options. How was this achieved? How did actors pressure for and negotiate between radical and reform strategies—what tactics were used? How did framing strategies and tactics evolve and change over the course of the campaigns?

The different policy demands were made using a combination of different tactics, and this combination strategically evolved and changed over the course of the campaigns in relation to state responses. At a most basic level we can distinguish between institutional and noninstitutional pressure tactics. Institutional tactics involve, foremost, inland refugee status determination systems that previous chapters have described internationally and in Canada (see in particular Figure 4.1 depicting multiple institutional paths asylum seekers may pursue in Canada). Asylum claims are heard in judicial settings with a number of levels to which claimants may appeal, drawing upon an elaborate framework of international and national law. Claimants must provide individual testimony and evidence of their inability to reside in the country of origin and are provided (or may hire) legal counsel. While awaiting decisions, they reside in Canada where they may access resources and rights typically available to citizens and residents, in addition to resources developed specifically for refugees and other international migrants. Resources include welfare and social services support, support by community organizations and NGOs, legal and civil rights. These resources help claimants by increasing opportunities to develop support networks, get the right information, make informed decisions, access legal rights, and ultimately make their claims and challenges.

Institutionalized claim making is important for policy because court decisions may either support the status quo or contribute to the growth of jurisprudence that changes the application of the law or even triggers change in the law itself. Through institutional claim making even the status determination process itself may be altered, as in the 1985 case of *Singh v. MEI* in which the Supreme Court of Canada granted the refugee claimant the right to a full oral hearing. This precedent, justified on the basis of the Canadian Charter of Rights and Freedoms (see Chapter 4; Knowles 1992:174), led to an overhaul of the Canadian refugee system from an administrative to a judicial model.

Institutional tactics supported important framing devices in the case studied. By using institutional tactics as far as possible before going public, actors not only made use of every resource but also protected their legitimacy. That is, rather than evading a refugee system inherently unfriendly to their claims (for instance by attempting illegal entry or fabricating claims on other grounds), they confronted and attempted to change the system to make their claims legitimate. If there were any doubt that such claims were sincere, one need only consider that it would be far more strategic for "illegitimate" refugees to fabricate stories of persecution on grounds readily recognized as legitimate, than to fabricate stories of persecution on grounds not merely outside the law but considered ludicrous by most refugee adjudicators. These asylum seekers presented themselves as working legitimately within a system they were entitled to utilize under international and national refugee law, but which was biased and violated Canadian norms of sexual equality and fairness.

Institutional tactics were essential both before and after instatement of the 1993 Guidelines, both among claimants who went public and those who did not, and often involved core supporters in important ways (having a lawyer, getting referrals to helpful organizations and individuals, getting moral, practical, and resource support). All claimants who used public pressure tactics went through the institutional refugee status determination process and received negative decisions. Many had appealed decisions before going public, in some cases going as high as the Federal Court. Most but not all had already been issued deportation orders by the time they joined campaigns. As IRB members later commented, the very existence of this claim making contributed to growing awareness within the IRB and inspired research by its internal Working Group on Refugee Women.[2] Several refugees and other campaigners also participated in other forms of institutional action after 1993 by speaking at national consultations between government and nongovernment groups aimed at shaping the application of the Guidelines and future legal developments. And between 1993 and 2003 significant judicial precedents were set that resulted in the 1996 revision of the Guidelines (see below).

However, more than jurisprudence was necessary to alter refugee policy. Rejected refugee claims also have value outside institutional status determination processes. Noninstitutional tactics may heighten awareness among the public, to positive or negative effect. Asylum seekers publicly declared defiance of deportation orders, mobilizing public pressure to challenge negative decisions on individual claims and demanding appropriate policy change. Asylum seekers participated in public press conferences, gave interviews to the mass media (radio, television, print), threatened to hold public demonstrations, and mobilized petitions and lobbying. Claimants going public and those in hiding to avoid deportation were clearly acting outside the normative institutional channels of refugee status determination processes. By going public, claimants and supporters aimed to generate political leverage that was not available in closed hearings, casting the legitimacy and aptness of court decisions into question, heightening the debate and mobilizing public support. The ability to create a public debate and raise domestic political support required rights and resources, such as rights of association, free speech, and access to necessary financial and legal resources. In noninstitutional tactics, framing devices became especially important and evolved through interactions with the public—from emphasis on the right to make claims and seek fair application of the law, to a much wider debate on the universality of national rights Canadian women take for granted.

Campaigns generally evolve in relation to the responses of the external environment, and these campaigns were no exception. The combination of a movement's stated goals and the tactics chosen to communicate them and to disrupt the public order to achieve them constitute strategic framing processes, or "signifying acts," and are instrument and effect of various publics' reactions (McAdam 1996). Table 6.2 presents a matrix of expected institutional responses to different combinations of radical/reform-oriented goals and institutional/noninstitutional pressure tactics in democratic contexts. This is adapted from McAdam (1996:342), who refers to "expected environmental responses" including the broader public.[3] Here, "institutional responses" refers to government responses within the institutionalized government bureaucracy. I suggest that expected institutional responses to movement goals/tactics differ from wider environmental responses (the public, nongovernmental groups). This is important, because policy actors wishing to influence the government often seek to influence the public in order to maximize effect. Thus institutional/public responses to goal/tactic combinations may differ from governmental responses, illuminating the possibility that one may influence the other.

Table 6.3 presents a matrix of expected public responses, referring to public and nongovernmental groups. This matrix is intended to convey how external responses hinge on "the degree of perceived threat conveyed by a movement's actions and tactics. . . . Taken together, the tactics and goals of the movement largely shape the reactions of various publics to the conflict" (McAdam 1996:341).

TABLE 6.2. EXPECTED INSTITUTIONAL RESPONSES TO MOVEMENT GOALS AND TACTICS

	Noninstitutional tactics	*Institutional tactics*
Radical goals	Repression	Indifference/surveillance and harassment
Reform goals	Heightened public attention/ polarized conflict	Indifference/minimal opposition and/or support

Source: Adapted from McAdam (1996:342).

TABLE 6.3. EXPECTED PUBLIC RESPONSES TO MOVEMENT GOALS AND TACTICS

	Noninstitutional tactics	*Institutional tactics*
Radical goals	Heightened public attention and polarized conflict especially across different publics	Indifference/moderate opposition and/or support
Reform goals	Heightened public attention and polarized conflict especially between publics and government	Indifference/minimal opposition and/or support (little or no debate)

Source: Adapted from McAdam (1996:342).

Together, the matrices of likely institutional and wider environmental responses depict strategic possibilities for collective action and offer a framework for analyzing the course of the campaigns, specifically the evolution of framing tactics used to legitimize demands. Different combinations of goals and tactics appeal differently to the government and public, and each combination has its own advantages and drawbacks. In both matrices, the lower right hand corner cell depicts "the least threatening and perhaps most common type of movement" (McAdam 1996:343). Pursued through institutional tactics, reform goals tend to evoke indifference, minimal opposition and/or support, both institutionally and in the wider environment. On the positive side, this indifference may at times enable activists to proceed incrementally, relatively unhindered. This combination was exhibited in the case studied in the use of case-by-case methods of incremental reform via the generation of jurisprudence.

In the scenario depicted in the upper-right-hand cell, radical goals pursued through institutional tactics tend to provoke institutional indifference or surveillance and harassment. In this scenario, authorities dismiss institutional tactics as illegitimate or irrelevant under the current system. Paradoxically, when actors with radical goals attempt to operate through proper institutional channels, as McAdam notes, dismissal may create greater room to maneuver but at the same time delegitimize actors. I suggest in Table 6.3 that wider external interest is, regardless, moderately heightened over the reform/institutional blend (whether in favor of or against proposed radical goals) due to the attention and time government spends attempting to delegitimize activists and legitimize their own actions. The institutional response acknowledges and thus raises attention to an issue conflict. This combination of goals/tactics was used in the case studied when one of the core network organizations (NOIVMW) submitted a report to the federal government prior to campaigning. It is possible that this report influenced a new IRB Working Group on Refugee Women, but this was not evidenced. As no government or public debate ensued, it appears the report was largely dismissed until noninstitutional tactics were adopted. Later, after the 1993 Guidelines had been instated, campaigners again advocated for radical policy change through cooperative institutional processes (the National Consultations) but did not succeed in changing Canada's 1976 refugee policy to insert "sex" or "gender" persecution.

The upper-left-hand cell of Table 6.2 depicts radical goals pursued through noninstitutional tactics as tending to provoke institutional repression. As McAdam explains, this combination may bring conflicting effects such as increasing public sympathy but reducing movement ability to operate. I additionally suggest that in this scenario, like the radical/institutional blend, authorities similarly attempt to paint demands as illegitimate in order to justify the current system, and that the wider external response (see Table 6.3) involves not only heightened public attention but also reflects split sympathies regarding campaigners' legitimacy. This serves to generate a higher degree of polarized conflict across different publics, compared to other goal/tactic combinations. The campaigns studied eventually transitioned into this combination and intensified both noninstitutional tactics and radical demands. The intensity of public support increased over time and ultimately compelled the government to make several key compromises.

The lower-left-hand cell depicts what McAdam describes as a "considerably rarer, but arguably more effective, blend of goals and tactics." Reform goals pursued through noninstitutional tactics tend to produce heightened institutional and external attention and polarized conflict between the two, generating support and/or opposition: "In their willingness and demonstrated ability to disrupt public order and, by extension, the realization of their opponents' interests, radical reform groups often come to be seen as powerful and threatening. Their adherence to moderate reform goals, however, bespeaks a respect for the broader system that invites support from various publics while simultaneously restraining the social control proclivities of opponents. This optimal mix of outcomes, however, is not easily achieved and must ultimately depend upon a highly developed and flexible capacity for framing" (McAdam 1996:344). I suggest in Table 6.3 that this combination produces *less* polarized conflict across the nongovernmental external environment than in the radical/noninstitutional blend, resulting in more clearly united public support with greater potential to influence the government. The campaigns studied emphasized this combination during the peak campaign period when they demanded immediate institutionalization of government's reform-oriented promises and achieved them within the month.

These matrices not only depict why a movement's aims and tactics may yield certain results, but why a movement may strategically choose and pursue certain blends. It complements Jenkins-Smith and Sabatier's (1994) concept of policy hierarchies, which while explaining why shifting policy aims are possible in relation to changes in the external environment (e.g., the emergence of new technical information or the prognosis for success), underexplores why coalitions strategically choose and combine particular aims with certain tactics at particular times, and thus why they may or may not be successful. We can also add to McAdam's depiction of movement-environment relations by specifying the possibility that, rather than one particular blend of goals/tactics making up the overarching campaign strategy, one movement can exhibit different combinations of goals and tactics simultaneously or at different times in the same campaign.[4] In the latter, campaigners may strategically change the combination over time as a public and institutional bargaining tool and as result of policy learning. The core campaign network here used each combination of goals and tactics, sometimes simultaneously but generally demarcating different campaign periods (generative, peak, decline). Government and external responses largely conform to the matrices presented. Two clarifications however are noteworthy. First, onlookers not sensitive to refugees' situation may see repression in this case as minimal and nonviolent. But efforts to silence dissidence by rejecting and deporting claimants back to their home countries is a harsh response indeed—rejected asylum seekers who genuinely fled persecution may be sent back to their death. Second, government efforts to delegitimize the issue may not always have been intentional, nor were they limited to one goals/tactics blend. For instance, adjudicators long dismissed and explicitly delegitimized refugee claims (saying gender issues were "irrelevant" to the refugee process) because they believed they were upholding the law. Government officials' public responses to campaign demands, on the other hand, both explicitly and consciously sought to delegitimize actors right up to the moment of capitulation.

Diversity of goals and tactics may be instrument and effect of the diversity of actors and by the time frame for achieving goals. Different actors' had different access to information, different degrees of political access, and different perceptions about the possibilities for success or risks associated with particular strategies (generally or over time). The time factor may shift actors' focus from one to another goal/tactic, depending upon responses elicited and the priority actors assign both to the time factor and to particular goals. As we will see, this emerges in actors' shift to reform demands during the peak period of campaigning, and their later shift into less effectual radical goals/noninstitutional tactics after the 1993 Guidelines were instated. Changing or simultaneous combinations may reduce or increase strategic diversity and influence.

Strategic Evolution and Influence

Having considered the campaign network's policy value hierarchy and described its basic goals and tactics in relation to possible state and nonstate responses, we can now observe the strategic evolution of the campaign in detail, the roles of asylum seekers and different framing tactics, and outcomes as a whole. The political and policy process is analyzed to show how tactics and policy aims evolved in relation to the government and publics, how they attracted media attention, framed the debate, mobilized public support, constrained the state's options, and attained a favorable response. This analysis additionally uncovers asylum seekers' and supporters' integral use of a range of rights and resources—concrete, symbolic/discursive, national, and international—to seek and achieve results.

Campaigns were organized around a series of individual claimants and

groups of claimants going public between 1991 and 1996. Strategies undertaken are analyzed in the pre-campaign period and in three distinct campaign periods: a low-intensity generative period; a period of high-intensity
or peak activism oriented around policy change; and a post-Guidelines period of decline characterized by institutional cooperation and limited activism geared toward monitoring, implementing, and improving the
Guidelines. Institutional actions were used throughout the campaigns and
expanded during the period of decline in response to concessions made by
the government. The nature and intensity of activism in each period both
provoked and responded strategically to government reactions and to the
changing political climate of the country.

The Pre-Campaign Period

Prior to 1991 gender-related refugee claims were made only through institutional status determination processes under existing law, challenging the limits of the law on a case-by-case basis. Like all asylum seekers in Canada, such
women had the right to make a claim, be heard in an oral hearing, and be
protected under the right of *nonrefoulement* (not returned to the country of
origin unless absence of persecution is established) often invoked to appeal
negative decisions. To back their claims, some drew upon a 1985 United Nations recommendation that the "social group" category of persecution in the
1951 Convention refugee definition may describe some persecuted women as
a social group.[5] Others used ad hoc and special procedures or attempted
entry on non-Convention status. Policy change was not demanded.
Claimants sought fair application of the law on a case-by-case basis, including gender-sensitive procedural measures (e.g., separate hearings for husband and wife, female interpreters). Acceptances could set precedents for
future claimants without changing the law but slowly reforming its interpretation and application. Such changes require a long-term time frame not
available to claimants in this study.

The number of acceptances through such procedures prior to 1993 is
unknown, as government data did not disaggregate refugee claims by type of
persecution or for sex/gender-based elements of persecution. Interviews with
refugee lawyers and organizations suggested women might have more commonly sought and attained residence on humanitarian and compassionate
grounds or Ministerial Permits rather than as Convention refugees (thus not
setting precedents). It is clear that acceptances in the "social group" category

were few and their precedents inconsistently followed. Of two cases noted by legal scholars, one was awarded on the basis of "political opinion" in opposing Iranian laws governing dress (*Shahabaldin v. MEI* [1987]) and the other on the basis of belonging to a "particular social group" comprised of "single women living in a Moslem country without the protection of a male relative (father, brother, husband, son)" (*Incirciyan v. MEI* [1987]). Yet after these two key precedents, claimants in this study included some with similar scenarios of persecution who were nonetheless rejected. Many had used the social group category, and one even drew on political opinion regarding Saudi Arabian laws governing dress. Notably, documented judicial justifications in these cases did not find the claimants to have presented false evidence; rather the claims were simply dismissed as irrelevant to the refugee determination process. In the pre-campaign period no debate was raised institutionally or in the public domain.

TABLE 6.4. PRE-CAMPAIGN PERIOD: INSTITUTIONAL CASE-BY-CASE REFORM

Claimant demand:	Fair application of the law on a case-by-case basis through traditional refugee categories or progressive use of the "social group" category for women; no policy change.
Campaign framing:	Right to seek asylum and to fairness in procedural issues; women as a "social group" recommended by UNHCR and endorsed by Canada
Institutional and public response:	Indifference/minimal opposition and/or support; two key precedents but mainly rejection of claims and inconsistent decision making; wider public not informed
Institutional framing:	Inconsistent judicial responses; claims largely labeled "irrelevant" to the refugee process; no discussion by government; no debate in the wider public.

The Generative Period: Opening Dialogue, Attracting Interest, Developing Debate

Inconsistent application of the UN recommendation provided impetus to challenge Canadian law. During the *generative period* between May 1991 and August 1992 four key developments occurred: (1) campaigners transitioned toward the use of noninstitutional tactics; (2) interest in the issue was generated among what became core supporters, who began working together through particular claimants; (3) dialogue with government was opened; and (4) campaigners strategically evolved their framing tactics and demands. These dimensions will be discussed as they developed around the changing political climate of the country and five key refugee claimants during that time.

Core supporters' participation was explained in Chapter 5 in relation to previous experience, ideology, and contact with asylum seekers. Looking now at the external environment, we see that interest emerged as free trade and constitutional debates (NAFTA and Charlottetown Accord) were drawing to a close in 1992. Many core organizations, such as NAC and the CCR, had devoted a sizable portion of their time and energy to these issues. Their activity around the newly emerging sex persecution issue evolved during the generative period and increased as other issues dropped off the agenda. During this time the first steps were taken to get secondary supporters' attention by bridging women's groups and immigrant and refugee advocates. At the same time dialogue with government was initiated and demands were developed. And two key strategic shifts occurred: campaigners gradually transitioned toward the use of noninstitutional tactics and the use of human rights discourses. These two strategies would not be put to full effect, however, until the peak campaign period.

Campaigns began with public calls for ministerial stays of deportation in two cases involving domestic violence. At a press conference called by Flora Tristan Shelter for Immigrant Women in 1991, shelter residents Ana (from Mexico) and Sandy (from Germany), both facing imminent deportation, went public to expose the injustice of a system that would grant refugee status to a man on the basis of persecution, grant residence to his wife only due to kinship, and deport the wife if she separated from her husband due to domestic violence. This type of situation was dubbed "sponsorship abuse" because women refugees unwilling to return to their home country remain captive to their abusive husbands in the host country. Invited to the press conference panel were the claimants' lawyers and the National Organization of Immigrant and Visible Minority Women of Canada (NOIVM), as well as the Quebec minister of immigration and culture and a representative of a federal subcommission on violence against women within Health and Welfare Canada.[6] The discussion in this well-rounded and strategically chosen panel of claimants, NGOs, lawyers, and government representatives solicited positive media attention.

At the press conference, Ana and Sandy asked publicly for the immigration minister to overturn their deportation orders using special ministerial powers and to grant them leave to remain on humanitarian and compassionate grounds. The deportation of women who break the sponsorship contract with an abusive sponsor was painted as discriminatory and unjust. Participants argued that government was insensitive to the problem of sponsorship abuse because the immigration and refugee status determination system was inherently gender-biased. They made recommendations based on the experiences of women residing at the Flora Tristan women's shelter and reports by NOIVMW and the Social Planning Council Coordinating Committee on Wife Assault. NOIVMW'S report, previously submitted to the federal subcommission on violence against women, recommended that immigrant women's dependency be broken by lessening work restrictions, developing more gender-sensitive procedures in the refugee hearing room, and using minister's permits in cases of sponsorship breakdown.[7] Appeals to the public were simple. These asylum seekers were fleeing domestic violence—something Canadian women could understand in their own country. In a 1993 survey, Statistics Canada found that one-quarter of women in Canada experience violence by current or past marital or common-law partners. Prior to the generative period government had already made clear commitments in its 1988 Initiative on Family Violence and 1990 Declaration on Family Violence. A 1993 National Action Plan on Family Violence later reified this commitment.

NOIVMW's report had also suggested broadening the refugee definition to include sex persecution (a radical/institutional tactic), but like the organization's other demands it was not earlier taken up by the government. During the press conference the question of changing the refugee definition to include sex as a grounds of persecution was raised in a response to a journalist but was otherwise peripheral to the main issue of sponsorship abuse under discussion. However, the comment triggered reaction among a broader and more powerful group of NGOs and initiated a transition to radical/noninstitutional goals and tactics, heightening government and public attention and polarizing debate. After the conference, these NGOs responded by asking the government to clarify its position on the persecution of women.

From the onset the government painted two paradoxical justifications for its position: refugee policy change was both threatening and unnecessary. State recognition of sex persecution was threatening, first, because it would destroy the traditional public/private demarcation in international law demarcating state responsibility and state sovereignty (see Romany 1993; Charlesworth, Chinkin, and Wright 1991; Cook 1994). Second, making "private" violence into an international "public" responsibility would question the rights of other states to choose their own culturally relevant practices. Opening the doors to abused women would be culturally judgmental, imposing Western gender roles on non-Western countries. Third, government suggested that accepting violence against women as persecution would open the "floodgates" for vast numbers of women around the world who face chronic structural violence and who lack protection and that Canada's refugee system and welfare state would not be equipped to deal with such an influx. National security and interests (economic, demographic, and international) were prioritized over the rights of women, suggesting that the former would be compromised by the latter; accepting even one case, it was posited, could open the floodgates. On the other hand, the federal government maintained that policy change was unnecessary because existing frameworks were based on the 1951 Convention, which itself does not include sex but is intended to be "gender neutral" and therefore capable of meeting females' needs. The gendered public/private distinction in international law was thus dismissed altogether and demands were painted as unreasonable and irrelevant.

A series of initial government responses capture these views. Activists widely regarded the first public response by Randy Gordan, assistant to the immigration minister, as triggering a campaign turning point. He stated that Employment and Immigration Canada (EIC) does not consider gender within the refugee definition and that accepting women such as those being publicized "would be opening a whole can of worms" (*NOW*, December 1992). This was interpreted to mean that the government would prefer to keep the issue closed despite a real underlying problem. Janet Dench from the CCR explained: "What he was saying had to do with violence against women and 'floodgates': that there is just far too much violence against women and therefore we cannot accept everybody who comes [on that basis]."[8] His statement provoked women's groups, was criticized in *NOW* magazine, and prompted the CCR to write a letter asking for the government to clarify its policy and moral position. At that time the CCR also adopted an internal resolution supporting gender-inclusive refugee policy. In a letter responding to David Matas, president of the CCR, Gordan stated that Canadian refugee policy is based on the UN Convention refugee definition in which "gender" does not appear as grounds of persecution. He also attempted to disassociate the powers and duties of the EIC and immigration minister from those of the IRB, saying: "decisions on refugee claims are made by independent, quasi-judicial, decision-makers. Neither the Minister, nor any member of his staff, can determine whether a claimant is a Convention refugee. Nor . . . can the Minister fetter the discretion of officers of Employment and Immigration Canada who exercise delegated authority with respect to humanitarian and compassionate review."[9]

Divorcing executive and administrative from judicial branches of government, Gordan ignored their shared responsibility in refugee policy development. He also appeared unaware of governmental research on the problem of sponsorship abuse.[10] He ignored the immigration minister's special powers to grant acceptance on humanitarian and compassionate grounds (via the minister Permit) despite negative IRB and EIC decisions, although Ana and Sandy had appealed for such intervention. While not granting Convention refugee status, making such exceptions *publicly* could place the refugee determination system and the law in question. The immigration minister avoided this possibility. Gordan was unable to steer the debate toward an administrative solution either specifically for sponsorship abuse or generally for the application of refugee policy. Rather, he gave further reason for refugee policy to be questioned. This was heightened when in the same letter Gordan stated that: "the position of the government with respect to the persecution of women is irrelevant to the refugee status determination process. Nonetheless, let me assure you that the Minister does not condone discrimination against, or persecution of, women." Despite efforts to avoid responsibility and delegitimize activists, when confronted with a politically charged question in a country with a strong humanitarian and women's rights reputation, Gordan was compelled to assert the government's moral conviction against the persecution of women. These correspondences and press statements elevated the issue from a question of administrative ineptness and gender insensitivity to one of structural persecution and gross state negligence. This marked an important evolution in framing tactics. Sponsorship was no longer the trigger issue. Subsequent cases were publicized with an emphasis on state responsibility for upholding gender inclusive women's human rights principles by amending refugee policy, and a wider range of types of female-specific violence was publicized as amounting to "persecution." The next three cases represented both public and private forms of violence. Those forms previously handled as administrative problems concerning either sponsorship (typically involving domestic violence) or the inconsistent application of the "social group" category (as recommended by the UN) both turned to question the basis of policy itself, rather than merely its fair application to women. And they increasingly used noninstitutional tactics to do so.

Between May 1991 and August 1992 campaigns were designed around Taramati, Dulerie, and Nada. Each had made refugee claims, had been rejected, and was facing deportation. Their cases heightened debate on a range of issues: whether female-specific forms of violence may ever amount to persecution or whether they are culturally relative; whether the Canadian government considered women's rights as understood in Canada to be human rights; whether some forms of violence against women may be considered persecution and not others; whether perpetrators must be traditional "state actors" or even located in the country of origin at the time of the claim.

Taramati, Dulerie, and Nada's claims (described in the Chapter 5 in relation to decisions to go public) differed from those of Ana and Sandy. Rather than relying on the issue of procedural fairness, they introduced the risk they faced in their country of origin if deported due to lack of state resources and willingness to protect. Both Nada and Dulerie had independently fled their countries of origin due to the violence they faced there. Taramati and her husband came to Canada together, she as his dependent. After two years in Canada she applied for refugee status on her own grounds and her husband was deported.

Dulerie and Taramati's cases involved domestic violence, a powerful image of torture and threat to life with which Canadians could more readily identify perhaps compared to other more culturally specific forms of violence against women. Taramati and Dulerie had resided in Canada with children since 1988, and both had fled to women's shelters. Both were in the final stages of the refugee status determination process between December and October 1992 after two years awaiting and appealing decisions. Dulerie's claim was processed through all the standard refugee status determination reviews, and in July 1992 she was ordered deported "because she fled to Canada to escape domestic violence instead of political oppression." Immigration department official Roger White defended his decision by citing a new family violence act passed in Trinidad in 1991 allowing abused women to lay charges and obtain protection orders. Dulerie's lawyers argued that the recent law was not being implemented: "You can have a written law, but the effect of it is a different thing altogether. If someone refuses to enforce the law, then what is one supposed to do? And that in effect is what the police [in Trinidad] are doing."[11] Dulerie formally appealed to the immigration minister and was refused. In Taramati's case, the IRB had found that domestic abuse was not a basis for a refugee claim although her husband had been deported back to their home country and was issuing death threats. Taramati applied for leave to remain in Canada on humanitarian and compassionate grounds after her refugee claim was rejected in January 1992 and a deportation order was issued. In August she was still awaiting a decision.

Nada's case involved "public" forms of violence against women. She made a refugee claim in 1991 based on her female-specific experience of persecution related to political opinion, in refusing to comply with discriminatory laws against women (a dress code) with severe physical punishment for infraction. Nada's rejection highlighted the IRB's general unreceptivity to female claimants and its gender biases in applications of refugee and human rights law, considering the precedent offered in the case of *Shahabaldin v. MEI* (1987), in which Convention refugee status was awarded on the basis of "political opinion" in opposing Iranian laws governing dress. After failing to win an appeal by the Federal Court, Nada was ordered deported, went into hiding, and sought NGO support. In August 1992 she appealed to the immigration minister and was refused.

By August 1992 these three claimants coincided in having exhausted most of their institutional options and simultaneously began preparing to appeal *publicly* to the immigration minister. They had attained the support of women's shelters and refugee and humanitarian groups. Diana Bronson (ICHRDD) describes some of the strengths of the core campaign network that started meeting on a biweekly basis: "Each of us was basically powerless as individuals, but each of us had organizations that could carry a lot of weight. The CCR is a coalition of 150 refugee groups across the country, NAC is some 500 women's groups, I am from an institution created by Parliament with a president who has a powerful public voice, and [Nada's lawyer] could connect with all the lawyers." She described their strategies as twofold: "one, we would try to draw media attention to this problem, and, two, we would have a consultation that would bring together NGOs, government and women's groups and so on, to talk about it."[12] Publicity was limited throughout the summer while groups concentrated on writing letters to the immigration minister and potential supporters and on introducing more radical demands by developing a human rights approach to arguing the cases. On 19 August 1992 the ICHRDD president wrote to the immigration minister, saying: "If [Nada] is forced to return to her country, Canada will be sending out a signal that it will not act to oppose the systematic violation of women's human rights, nor will it accord asylum to those who are victims of such violations. This would be most unfortunate, given the important initiatives that Canada has taken on behalf of gender equality and human rights in the Francophonie, the Commonwealth and the Organisation of American States. A failure to act decisively on the side of justice in this case would be most damaging, both domestically and internationally."[13] The ICHRDD's involvement with Nada raised human rights issues and Canadian responsibilities both at home and abroad; these became the touchstone of the campaign. It demonstrated the weight of domestic concern for the issue and domestic repercussions. Adopting the slogan "women's rights are human rights," the ICHRDD made clear the connection between Canadian women's rights and human rights of women elsewhere. The ICHRDD later explained: "The challenge for women is to use the language and mechanisms of international human rights law in a way that makes it relevant to their experiences. *The challenge for the human rights movement is to start taking the violations of women's rights as seriously as the violations of men's rights.* Women must use the paradigm that exists already and begin to forge a new one for the realities that the old language of human rights still cannot address."[14]

The question of radically changing refugee law was not taken up by the government. Instead, the IRB Working Group on Refugee Women suggested a draft policy guideline intended to alert adjudicators to gender issues and promote more consistent decision making in this area without in fact changing the law. It was circulated among the UNHCR–Canadian Division, CCR, ICHRDD, and other NGOs and lawyers. Although the guidelines received positive responses, they were also criticized for being reform in nature, excluding domestic violence as a form of persecution, and lacking a timeline for instatement. This combined with the immigration minister's openly adverse position on the issue did not bode well, suggesting government itself had split sympathies on the issue. The imminent deportation claimants faced and their accumulation of support ushered in the peak period of activism between September 1992 and March 1993.

TABLE 6.5. GENERATIVE PERIOD: REFORM GOALS PLUS NONINSTITUTIONAL TACTICS

Claimant demand:	Special reprieve from a biased law through ministerial powers; sex-specific procedural issues for women such as sensitivity in the hearing room; long-term need to achieve fairness under the law (no change in the law, only its application)
Campaign framing:	Domestic violence is a chronic structural problem and violation of women's rights under Canadian law; Canadian policy fosters "sponsorship abuse" and grants reprieve to criminals rather than victims; nonpublic transition toward use of human rights language to characterize violence against women
Institutional response:	Rejection of claims; heightened public attention; polarized conflict
Institutional framing:	Canadian refugee law is in accordance with international law in not recognizing gender or sex persecution; the government does not condone discrimination or persecution of women in Canada, but violence against women is a cultural issue

Peak Period: Polarizing the Debate and Mobilizing Public Support

The shift into the peak period was expressed through a dramatic increase in use of mass media, conferences, petitioning, and correspondence to the immigration minister. It served two main purposes: to heighten attention and to polarize the debate. A dialogue between government and nongovernment actors took place in which the latter provoked and responded strategically to the former and to the changing political climate of the country. In so doing, campaigners managed to successfully mobilize national support—the immigration and refugee community, women's groups, and the broader public—thus creating leverage to influence the government.

The campaign brought its new framing tactics squarely into the public sphere and intensively targeted radical policy change to include "sex" as one of six categories of persecution in the refugee definition. The debate took on rhetorical tones, eliciting provocative newspaper headlines such as "Is Sexual

Equality a Universal Value? Debate Rages over Giving Refugee Status to Abused Women" (*Montreal Gazette*, 15 February 1993), "Indivisible: Until Women's Rights Are Human Rights, We Have Far to Go" (*Montreal Gazette*, 3 November 1993), "Canada Not Planning to Widen Refugee Rules to Cover Sex Bias: Women Fleeing Abuse Would Strain System, [Immigration Minister] Valcourt Says" (*Globe and Mail*, 15 January 1993), and "NAC: Make Canada a Haven for Abused Women" (*Montreal Gazette*, 30 November 1992). The women's human rights issue exploded on the Canadian scene. It was asked whether the Canadian government considered women's rights to safety from violence to be culturally relevant or universal rights that transcend nations. Canada's potential role as an international leader on women's human rights and women refugee rights was flagged. Not only Canadian legislation was at stake; campaigners wanted the government to use its influence to promote the issue to the United Nations.

The campaign simultaneously framed these broad sweeping demands and critical questions in reference to a series of individual asylum seekers facing deportation. They argued for court decisions to be reversed in these cases and appropriate policy to be instated for future claimants. Taramati, Dulerie, and Nada went public and between September 1992 and March 1993 and were joined by an additional eighteen claimants who told their stories to the press, while many others made private appeals to the immigration minister.[15] Over the course of the campaigns, publicized cases involved claimants from eighteen different countries: Trinidad and Tobago, Saudi Arabia, Bangladesh, Iran, Lebanon, Peru, Russia, St. Vincent, Bulgaria, Guatemala, Zaire, Seychelles, Dominica, Cameroon, Mexico, Germany, Somalia, and Turkey. All were facing and many were defying deportation orders.

TABLE 6.6. REGIONAL AND ORGANIZATIONAL CAMPAIGN REPRESENTATION

Regional representation of asylum seekers	Canadian representation
• Africa • Latin America and the Caribbean • Eastern Europe and Russia • Middle East • South America • Southeast Asia	• Immigration and refugee lawyers • Women's shelters • National (umbrella) refugee advocacy NGO • Immigrant and refugee membership groups • Immigrant and refugee service groups • National (umbrella) women's organization • National human rights organization

These asylum seekers gained the increasing attention in part due to their timeliness; unfavorable aspects of political opportunity structure began to change. That same autumn, the Canadian public was shocked by international coverage of mass rape as a strategy of ethnic cleansing in the former Yugoslavia. This tragedy helped alert Canadians to the reality of acts of war targeting women. And domestically, Canada was shifting its focus considerably. It is perhaps no surprise that the most influential period of the campaign, from December to March, occurred just one month after NAFTA was signed and the Charlottetown Accord was rejected. Canadians were fed up with long-lasting debates on national unity and free from years of international trade debates. This not only provided a public space for other important issues, but also coincided with the onset of federal elections. As the issue gained public sympathy, politicians were compelled to state policy positions, and women refugees were on the agenda for the first time. In particular, Liberal members of Parliament lent their support to a number of individual refugee claimants who went public, and in January 1993 the Liberal government began making promises. Sheila Copps, deputy prime minister of the Liberal Party, promised that if the Liberals were elected a moratorium would be held on deportations of women claiming sex persecution in order to enable review of their cases under a fair determination system. Meanwhile the Conservative government began making moves to change party political leaders in an attempt to win back Canadian trust. During this period other immigration issues and problems were mounting. The last backlog clearance program came to an end and the unpopular new immigration bill (C-86) was poised to come into effect by February 1993, making Conservatives particularly vulnerable to public dissent on immigration matters.[16]

Between September and December 1992 Dulerie, Taramati, and Nada finally went public. At the same time the favorable result of another claimant's appeal to the Federal Court was publicized. Media use was at its highest, including newspapers, journals, and in-depth radio and television broadcasts. Public appeals were made primarily through press conferences involving claimants and called by lawyers and national and local women's, immigrant, and refugee organizations. One asylum seeker wrote a newspaper editorial and several spoke at conferences. Influential heads of organizations wrote editorials.

Dulerie went public after Immigration Minister Valcourt's refusal to intervene in her deportation. On 17 September, the *Toronto Star* published an article about Dulerie's rejection. The article, "Trinidad Can Protect Woman,

Ottawa Insists," raised the first wave of protest by human rights, refugee, and women's groups across the country. Bronson of the ICHRDD observed that the immigration minister's office was "flooded with faxes and calls" criticizing his nonintervention.[17] Less than one week later Valcourt reversed his decision. Headlines ran: "Abused Woman Allowed to Stay Here" (*Toronto Star*, 23 September 1992). But interestingly, Valcourt's decision did not give Dulerie the right to stay based on humanitarian and compassionate grounds, the status usually bestowed by ministers. It skirted questions of human rights violations or persecution that might suggest a chronic structural problem within Canada's refugee system and of whether future claimants should be awarded asylum on humanitarian and compassionate grounds or on Convention refugee grounds. Dulerie's case was to be handled through a legal loophole: she would be "shuffled." She would be deported, admitting no fault by the IRB, but rather than being returned to her country she would be sent to the United States and after a two-week period allowed to apply for immigrant status in Canada, with guaranteed acceptance. While recognizing a fundamental shortcoming of the refugee determination system this solution offered no structural corrective. Dulerie's lawyer explained: "it doesn't show any insight on the government's part as far as compassionate or humanitarian grounds,"[18] referring to its application to claims involving female persecution. It was, however, a direct response to public pressure suggesting government's vulnerability on the issue.

In early September Nada went public, giving her first interview. Bronson (ICHRDD) commented on forms of publicity sought and the significance of sympathetic and committed journalists, as well as networking among lawyers handling similar cases. "The first article Nada did was for the *Ottawa Citizen*, a detailed article by Jack Miller, a very good journalist, very committed to this issue. Then we helped Carol Offe from CBC Radio do a series of radio reports on it, for five nights in a row on *The World at Six*, different cases of women who had been refused refugee status. We had begun to get information from lawyers in Toronto who were facing similar problems . . . [such as] Dulerie's case."[19] Nada's case specifically asked that Convention refugee status apply to women facing female persecution. Still in hiding, Nada did not receive a direct response from the immigration minister until December.

As public pressure mounted, Taramati's application on humanitarian and compassionate grounds was rejected and in October she and her three children were ordered deported for a second time. After press conferences were held, the immigration minister agreed to delay deportation in order to review the case and determine whether humanitarian and compassionate grounds could be determined. This would not grant her Convention refugee status, but would mark a step toward recognizing the abuse she suffered as amounting to persecution, although falling outside the Convention definition. The decision on her case remained pending.

A further gain was made when another Trinidadian woman won an appeal to the Federal Court in November. The claimant had fled to Canada with her five children in 1986 after fifteen years of abuse by her husband in Trinidad. She reported that Trinidadian police typically took several hours to respond to her calls and then sided with her husband. After two years in Canada she applied for refugee status. After a delay of three years, an IRB tribunal found in January 1991 a "credible basis" to her refugee claim, "based on years of violent assaults, rapes and kidnappings at the hands of her estranged husband."[20] However the Justice Department then appealed the tribunal's decision, arguing that the claimant was not fleeing state persecution but domestic violence and that fear of assault by husband is not fear of persecution. Such women are not a "social group." On 11 November 1992 the Federal Court of Appeal determined that the argument was irrelevant, saying the tribunal that heard her case was responsible for determining not those issues but only whether a "credible basis" to her claim exists, giving her the right to apply for Convention refugee status, and credible basis had been found. This ruling did not automatically give the claimant refugee status nor did it determine whether women fleeing domestic violence meet the legal criteria for becoming refugees. Her lawyer explained: "They did not decide the broader issue of whether she is a member of a social group fearing persecution."[21] However, the decision paved the way for her acceptance on humanitarian and compassionate grounds and bolstered the legitimacy of the campaign as a whole. The *Montreal Gazette*'s headline ran: "Victim of Spousal Abuse Can Stay: Trinidadian Woman's Refugee Claim 'Credible'" (*Montreal Gazette*, 30 November 1992). The *Toronto Star* announced that an "abused woman" has grounds to apply for refugee status.

Following these examples, other claimants began appealing to the immigration minister, typically with the support of women's shelters where they were residing. After becoming involved through Nada and Taramati, NAC propelled the national debate with the slogan: "Make Canada a Haven for Abused Women," which was headlined in the *Montreal Gazette* on 30 November 1992. The image of Canada as a safe haven for abused women drew upon inroads toward understanding domestic violence and the fundamental role of women's shelters in Canada. NAC strategically called on the government to declare commitment toward abused women in refugee policy by 6 December 1992, the third anniversary of the shooting deaths of fourteen women in an antifeminist attack known as the Montreal Massacre, drawing parallels between violence against women elsewhere and Canada's own experience. In the 1989 massacre, Marc Lepine entered an engineering school, separated out the women and opened fire while screaming "I hate feminists." The massacre had become a powerful symbol and galvanizing moment in the women's antiviolence movement and its impact was still deep in Canadians'—and politicians'—minds.[22]

By December Nada's story was receiving sympathetic national coverage and support. Advocates were calling explicitly for refugee policy to include sex persecution. Nada's rejection by the IRB, the appeals court, and the immigration minister appeared more outrageous after exceptions had just been made for battered women. In particular the traditionally less radical public nature of the persecution Nada claimed she faced, and the well-documented treatment of women in Saudi Arabia, made her rejection appear increasingly unacceptable to the public. Bronson of the ICHRDD explained: "Nada was getting prime-time news, she was doing radio stations, the *Toronto Star* and other papers [were picking it up], there were various editorials about it, Michele Lansberg got on it, the human rights people from the editorialists across the country, all kinds of people were just outraged that Nada had be refused." Nada's campaign network included individuals with organizational backing of extensive influence and a variety of skills (see Chapter 5), who as Bronson noted, negotiated their tasks effectively: "This was something I always found myself explaining at our meetings . . . let us do what we are good at. We are not good at some things, and we are very good at other things. You are good at mobilizing women's groups; you do that. We are good at writing letters to the minister; we'll do that. And each compliments the other. I think that is what was so interesting about the way the group of us approached the problem. Everybody did what they were good at and we were all very clear about what it was we were good at."[23] Lawyers played important mobilizing and organizing roles. Nada's lawyer explained: "To win a case like that you have to pull strings, to push; anyone who knows anyone calls the person and so you need a network. You hopefully know someone who knows a reporter. You really need all those contacts and as an individual lawyer you can't do that, you just can't, and you have to work in a team. You have to work with human rights groups, women's groups, grassroots organizations. You *have* to do it that way. Which is something I suspected but in that case it revealed itself very clearly."[24]

In late December Edward Broadbent, president of the ICHRDD, wrote an editorial for the *Globe and Mail* and *La Presse*. Its impact, as Bronson explains, was profound: "It embarrassed the hell out of the government, they did not know what to respond to it. It was very good."[25] In a statement to the press Immigration Minister Valcourt responded by justifying the government's decision in Nada's case on the grounds of cultural relativism: "I don't think Canada should unilaterally try to impose its values on the rest of the world. Canada cannot go it alone, we just cannot" (*London Free Press*, 16 January 1993). Accepting Nada would imply condemnation of the laws of Saudi Arabia regarding culturally accepted roles and behaviors of women. Valcourt declared: "The laws of general application in countries of the world are not necessarily laws that we in this country would want to promote because of our values but will Canada act as an imperialist country and impose its values on other countries around the world?" (*The House*, CBC Radio, 16 January 1993). The rhetorical swing of the debate caught the government unprepared. Its responses were described as repressive, ignorant, and lazy, and ultimately furthered mass public support. Dench from the CCR described the radicalization of policy demands to include sex as a grounds of persecution, "as undoubtedly serv[ing] a useful rhetorical purpose. It is an easily communicated hook on which to hang demands for reform, demands which if fully spelt out would certainly not fit a newspaper headline or excite an uninitiated public."[26]

As a national umbrella group for immigrant and refugee organizations, the CCR has privileged insight into the activities and political culture of the advocacy community. Dench attributed the surge of interest to individuals within the community with particular interests relevant to the issue, claimants whose cases peaked the interest of the public, and the widespread perception that government was vulnerable on this issue. "I think certainly in the beginning of 1993 it was clear that this was an issue on which we were winning, under the old Conservative regime of Valcourt. This is something where we were getting a lot of favorable media attention. So if you were in the refugee advocacy community, this was a good vehicle to jump on. And the community that we have is said to be very open. . . . The scope of interest is quite broad."[27]

The view that Immigration Minister Valcourt contributed directly, though "unwittingly" to support for women's human rights, was widely held among activists. They repeatedly pointed to particular instances that were crucial to the movement's ability to attract favorable media coverage, generate antigovernment support, and by embarrassing the government, constrain its social control options. Bronson, public relations officer of the ICHRDD, explained: "Bernard Valcourt, the immigration minister at the time, at one point made a real mistake. He told the *Globe and Mail* and a group of reporters that it would be culturally imperialist for Canada to accept Nada. He said something about Canada not being able to pass judgment on 'other countries' cultures.' And saying also that Canada would be 'flooded' with women refugees."[28]

That the Conservative government was threatened by increasing Canadian malaise, skepticism, and cynicism, while national identity was fragile, made the immigration minister's potentially racist and sexist responses to questions regarding women's human rights indeed dire. Not only did he provoke women's and immigrant and refugee groups, but the wider public. He was painted as staining a great source of Canadian identity and pride, its progressive humanitarian reputation, while ignoring the rights and recognition won by Canada's feminist movement. In a public speech, the CCR's executive director Dench described the significance of the latter and the profound impact of Valcourt's comments: "It is widely understood [in Canada] that women have rights that are traditionally trampled upon, that violence against women is a problem we have never taken seriously enough, that attitudes need to change. In this context, it is more difficult to get away with patent insensitivity toward the oppression of women. . . . Into this trap fell the Minister of the day, Bernard Valcourt. . . . He contributed immeasurably and no doubt entirely against his will, to the cause of women refugees, by some ill-conceived public remarks. . . . The Minister was taken to task for suggesting that the rights of women are no more than a matter of cultural choice and that we should keep the door open for men, but slam it shut for women, lest too many come."[29] Groups responded immediately to Valcourt's statements, sending out press releases, letters, and faxes. Several more claimants were in the public eye, and the debate between universal and culturally relative human rights of women was increasingly polarized. The ICHRDD put out a press release two days later, as Bronson described, "saying that it was 'bizarre' that [the government] would say such a thing. . . . And two weeks later Nada was accepted. The heat was just too much . . . I was told that Bernard Valcourt's fax machine was just running off the hook, women really got angry across the country and started faxing him."[30]

Media attention was clearly favorable; the *Globe and Mail* reported: "No Plan to Accept Victims of Sex Bias" (16 January 1993), and the *Montreal Gazette* wrote: "Consider Gender: Persecuted Women should Have Refugee Status" (25 January 1993). Nada was the proverbial straw that broke the camel's back. Conceding to public pressure, Valcourt retracted his statements, granted Nada a stay of deportation on humanitarian and compassionate grounds and promised to go ahead with special policy guidelines to deal with similar cases and to consider changing Canada's Immigration Act to include gender or sex persecution by holding national consultations on the issue. In his press statement Valcourt underscored the influence of Broadbent's editorial advice: "In reaching my decision I took into consideration the comments made by the Honorable Edward Broadbent, President of the International Centre for Human Rights and Democratic Development." Speaking for the immigration minister, Randy Gordan additionally announced: "If there was a consensus on this gender issue in this country, and it was brought back to the government, the government could consider making representations on this issue to the United Nations" (*Ottawa Citizen*, 25 January 1993). Table 6.7 captures campaign demands and framing, institutional and public responses, and institutional framing during this peak period characterized by a radical/noninstitutional blend of goals and tactics.

Interestingly, in February 1993 campaigning heightened rather than declined after the government reversed its position, seen in a continuing pattern of provocation, government response, heightened activity, and media attention. Activists wanted the government to follow through with its promises, and quickly, not just make popular statements. The National Consultations on the feasibility of changing Canadian refugee law would take time, as would making representations to the United Nations. Activists wanted the government to initiate an immediate plan of action for these long-term promises and, more urgently, to enact an immediate solution that would address the pending deportations of women asylum seekers in Canada. Activists played the government's acceptance of the possibility of radical legislative change against the urgency of current asylum claims and life-threatening deportations. NAC president Judy Rebick explained to the press: "When they know it's going to go public and the heat goes on, they stay the deportation, but what about the cases that don't go public?" (*Montreal Gazette* 15 February 1993). David Matas of the CCR stated: "Sexual equality isn't a Canadian value, it is a universal value. The Minister is dragging his heels over something over which there is no need to drag his heels" (*Montreal Gazette*, 15 February 1993). Broadbent, president of the ICHRDD, stated: "We want a recognition by Canada, to lead internationally, that women are persecuted as women and that they should be recognized as part of the refugee process" (*Montreal Gazette*, 30 January 1993). The media continued to push provocative headlines such as "Is Sexual Equality a Universal Value?" (*Montreal Gazette*, 15 February 1993), which were strongly and consistently favorable.

TABLE 6.7. PEAK PERIOD: RADICAL GOALS PLUS NONINSTITUTIONAL TACTICS

Claimant demand:	Special reprieve from a biased law for individuals currently facing deportation (ministerial powers, federal appeals); change Canadian refugee law to achieve equality under the law; make representations to the United Nations to add "sex persecution" to the 1951 Convention Relating to the Status of Refugees
Campaign framing:	Violence against women is a chronic structural problem and violation of women's rights under Canadian law; Canadian refugee law condones human rights violations against women; "Sexual equality isn't a Canadian value, it is a universal value"; "Women's rights are human rights"; "Make Canada a haven for abused women"; debate polarized by implying government doesn't really believe in sexual equality
Institutional and public response:	Refusal to change the law; attempts to justify position; immigration minister initially rejects appeals; deportation orders continue to be issued; draft IRB guidelines developed, but do not progress; at height of campaigning, reversal of position and long-term promises (instate guidelines, hold consultations, and make representation to the UN); heightened attention and highly polarized conflict
Institutional framing:	Violence against women is irrelevant to the refugee process; Canadian refugee law is in accordance with international law; nevertheless, Canada does not support the persecution of women; violence against women is a cultural issue, Canada cannot "impose its values on the rest of the world"; reversal: "If there was consensus in this country . . ."

The thrust behind these demands and coverage was a spate of new refugee claims going public. Several claimants went public in February 1993 and were accepted by the immigration minister. NAC announced it was working with fifty refugee claimants, fourteen of whom went public in early March at simultaneous press conferences in Toronto and Montreal. NAC demanded a moratorium on all pending deportations of sex persecution claimants until an appropriate determination system could be instated. Campaigners demanded the instatement of the reform-oriented solution—the adoption of new policy guidelines—by the end of the month.

The government capitulated, announcing a moratorium on deportation of the fourteen women and a timeline for national consultations on the issue of including sex persecution in Canadian refugee policy, and that very month the IRB instated its policy guidelines on women refugees fleeing gender-related persecution. That summer the government presented its new Guidelines on Women Refugee Claimants Fearing Gender-Related Persecution at the Vienna Conference on Human Rights, formally introducing the persecution of women as relevant to refugee law and as a human rights issue and promoting the Canadian model (see Table 6.8).

TABLE 6.8. PEAK PERIOD: REFORM GOALS PLUS NONINSTITUTIONAL TACTICS

Claimant demand:	Immediately institutionalize special policy guidelines to ensure fair application of refugee law to women; delay deportations to reconsider claims under the guidelines; initiate plans and timelines for long-term promises
Campaign framing:	As earlier, but also: the government will be sending a small number of harmless women to their death; reform the law immediately to provide them asylum
Institutional and public response:	United public sympathies; little further government resistance; instead, capitulation to implementation demands—instatement of the 1993 Guidelines within the month, stays of deportation, timeline for national policy consultations, and promise of representation to UN
Institutional framing:	"If there was consensus in this country . . ."

The Canadian Guidelines on Women Refugee Claimants Fearing Gender-Related Persecution made explicit the legitimacy of a new category of refugees under the law, necessarily invoking women's rights as human rights in a controversial area commonly discussed as culturally relative. Once begun, domestic policy struggles were successful over a relatively brief period of time. In this the evolution of signifying acts that combined radical and re-form goals, framing tactics that highlighted both Canadian values and universal values and a combination of institutional and noninstitutional actions, all played important roles. Activists' strategic framing processes were provocative and timely—responding to and eliciting government responses, fueling antigovernment public support, and encouraging speedy instatement of the Guidelines. When the government dismissed or repressed demands, advocates radicalized the debate further and thus heightened public attention and mobilized antigovernment supporters, urging the government to take moderate demands more seriously. The final shift to reform goals combined with noninstitutional tactics and backed up by radical demands as a bargaining point, was quite effective, hinging on the ability of groups "to master the art of simultaneously playing to a variety of publics, threatening opponents, and pressuring the state, all the while appearing nonthreatening and sympathetic to the media and other publics" (McAdam 1996:344).

Why did activists shift strategies and push for immediate instatement of the Guidelines rather than increasing pressure for full legislative reform? Here we must look at the nature of the Guidelines and supporters' views of them. The Guidelines cut a compromise by mediating between immediate needs (safety for current asylum seekers) and long-term goals (long-term legislative change). Most fundamentally, they were developed in lieu of re-opening the 1951 Convention or Canadian Immigration Act to include gender or sex persecution. Instead, gender as a type of persecution may be "related" to any of the five traditional grounds of persecution (rather than solely social group). The Guidelines educate, aid, and mandate decision makers to provide "gender-inclusive" hearings and evaluations of claims, rather than subsuming refugee experiences under the traditional male model (Turley 1994).

Immigration and Refugee Board "guidelines" were only given statutory basis in Canada when amendments to the Immigration Act came into force on 1 February 1993. The gender persecution guidelines were therefore the first of their kind in Canada. This also weighed on the timeliness of the campaigns. IRB chairperson Nurjehan Mawani's immediate use of board guidelines to address female persecution and problems in the hearing room was considered a brilliant strategy by many. It negotiated between competing perspectives on need for, and shape of, policy change and helped make gender refugees legitimate in the face of deep controversy over a relatively brief period of time. The Guidelines use the human rights approach in refugee law, which is readily extendable to female persecution due to the gender neutral language of the Universal Declaration of Human Rights. They avoid outright condemnation of sending states by explicitly stating that some governments may lack sufficient resources to provide internal protection. The nonbinding nature of the Guidelines protects Canada's sovereignty but obliges adjudicators to take the Guidelines into account and give well-founded reasons for any decisions that deter from them, making the "burden of proof" more balanced for women asylum seekers. As "guidelines," they may be refined over time through relatively easy and swift procedures that circumvent the more tedious processes of outright legislative change. Agreeing that floodgate theory and cultural relativism are irrelevant, this pragmatic perspective maintains that by accepting such refugees Canada acknowledges and exposes the maltreatment of women in many countries and makes an international statement that women's rights are human rights rather than sexually, culturally, or racially determined.

Chairperson Mawani was awarded the American Immigration Lawyers Association (AILA) Humanitarian Award, "citing her ability to forge ahead with the gender agenda in times where the national mood of host states in the Western world is one typically characterized as increasingly restrictionist, not expansive" (MacMillan 1993). Her decision to forge ahead in drafting and preparing the Guidelines was impacted by the public pressure being brought to bear upon the immigration minister whose change of stance was crucial.

Core campaigners supported the resulting Guidelines, although to differing degrees regarding their long-term usefulness. Their work with individual asylum seekers facing deportation weighed heavily upon their opinion of the Guidelines. Weighing the potential for success given external responses (public support, elite sympathy, government position) over time, alongside policy values and time constraints, forced a shift in the hierarchy of policy priorities depicted earlier. What changed were expectations about institutional responses within specified time periods. Near-core aims take on a different time frame and subsequently become a long-term second tier priority. No supporters were willing to sacrifice the priority of campaigning asylum seekers' immediate needs for safety under strict time pressure. Shifting from long-term goals to short-term needs produced policy aims geared toward guaranteeing asylum to the greatest possible range of asylum seekers within the shortest possible time frame.

Supporters defended the shift as strategic and realistic given various goals and constraints, but to different degrees. Some accepted the compromise as a short-term solution only, while others essentially abandoned long-term policy aims. Aside from contact with asylum seekers facing deportation, the second most important reason for supporting the Guidelines was related to different levels of political access and knowledge of refugee law. The strongest supporters of the Guidelines were those with greater expertise about refugee law, such as the CCR, ICHRDD, and RAM. They accepted the idea of formally harnessing the law to the needs of women refugees without reopening the 1951 Convention to introduce "sex persecution," yet still transcending the social group category and "public" forms of persecution. They felt long-term policy change would be difficult to achieve, in part because reopening the 1951 Convention would also reopen other refugee issues for discussion during a period of increasing restrictions on migration worldwide. This could paradoxically erode other established protection mechanisms.[31] Bronson of the ICHRDD explained: "I think we have been persuaded by everybody, from [the CCR] to [IRB Chairperson] Mawani to the UNHCR that politically it is not a viable option because if you open up the Convention then you will never get another one signed, because of a very general climate of closing down borders and so on."[32] Nada's lawyer observed that the instated Guidelines might make the existing refugee definition work by changing attitudes and understanding: "This reinforces the statement that you did not need to change the law because you could have accepted women before; it was just a way of perceiving reality."[33] Supporters particularly emphasized the need to now work toward getting the Guidelines implemented at overseas refugee offices, as for inland status determination.

Least enthusiastic about the Guidelines as a longer-term solution were feminist organizations and those that tended to do more frontline service. Flora Fernandez from Women's Aid and NAC commented: "We think the directives of Madame Mawani are . . . good progress in the world. But to have a *real* solution we must put another point in the definition of 'refugee.' Within the five points we must add 'gender persecution.'"[34] Such groups did not believe the Guidelines would be enough in the long-term. Those that worked with refugee women on a day-to-day basis would witness whether the Guidelines were applied consistently or progressively. Yet women's shelters and NAC also stopped pressuring for radical policy change in the campaign period that followed.

Decline: Cooperation and Implementation

By accepting the Guidelines the campaign cycle entered a period of decline in which activism centered more on implementation than standard setting and on working cooperatively with government to develop plans for longer-term promises that had been made. The decline of public actions coincided with an increase in government-nongovernment cooperation. National consultations took place in which each sector was represented. These were initiated in June 1993 and involved nongovernment and government actors as well as refugees and were aimed at generating greater gender inclusivity in the refugee determination system, including discussion of the possibility of changing refugee law (Hathaway 1993).

Cooperation was a strongly emphasized goal of the first consultation, whose organization was spearheaded mainly by campaigners and represented by the TCMR. Glynis Williams from RAM described: "The consultations were incredible. It was . . . set up in a way that wasn't meant to be confrontational. It was meant to be exploratory. We had people who had lived the experience already, we had advocates, and we had government people. We all knew what everybody's position was, we didn't want to get in that position where everybody is just defending what they were doing. It was really hoped people would, through exposure to other views, become more conscious of the issues." The participation of refugees was frequently commented upon as both novel and powerful. Williams noted that their testimonies were also identified as one of the only real sources of controversy: "Liliana was quite emotional about her experiences at the board and how bad it had been. [Her testimony] was quite long. It was good, it was important, and she needed to do that. But the response was . . . a sort of rather defensive outburst; it was too bad. But it doesn't surprise me; it is the setting . . . where it is the NGO community putting [government] on the defensive, criticizing the system that is in place, and [where some individuals are] part of that system. And I'm sure [they feel] at times caught because . . . I'm sure they cared about the issue but these are things that people up until the Guidelines happily didn't think about."[35] This controversy describes IRB members caught between personal interest and support for the particular claimants, on one hand, and constraints imposed by institutional affiliation on the other. It also indicates the importance of elite supporters who worked against institutional constraints and were instrumental in developing and getting institutional support for the Guidelines to begin with. Janet Dench, executive director of the CCR, described: "As it turned out a lot of the individuals who were sitting at that table were quite radical in their way, not necessarily taking the defense of government line. So you've got things like the representative of Quebec government putting forth all sorts of ideas and confident that she would not be attributed because what she was saying was not necessarily representing the Quebec government point of view."[36]

Among issues discussed was need for more comprehensive and consistent decision making through the Guidelines; gender-awareness training of immigration and refugee officers and adjudicators; administrative changes in the refugee hearing room to enable women claimants to be heard; and encouraging new interpretations of gender-related persecution by developing a body of case law from which lawyers can draw. However, no consensus was reached regarding whether the Convention refugee definition should be expanded, although the view that Guidelines were inadequate was prevalent (Turley 1994). And during the consultation period neither follow-up nor monitoring occurred. After the final report from the consultations (1994) was issued, government stopped calling for meetings of the Steering Group on Gender and Refugee Issues. It was not apparent whether the Guidelines were being applied consistently, were sufficient in the depth of their analysis of the structural basis of claims, or could ever be applied to a broader range of cases.

TABLE 6.9. DECLINE: RADICAL GOALS PLUS INSTITUTIONAL TACTICS

Claimant demand:	Consider adding "sex" or "gender" persecution to refugee law and promote issue to the UN; monitor and ensure implementation of the Guidelines
Campaign framing:	Cooperation, discussion, and bridge building (versus demanding and pressuring) to achieve a gender-inclusive system
Institutional and public response:	Cooperative, consultative government response, but no outcome regarding policy change in now institutionalized debates; debate recedes from public domain
Institutional framing:	Government wants consensus and consultation to develop the most appropriate response on a national level

Nearly a year after peak activity in 1993, a more limited spate of noninstitutional actions were sparked by the rejection of asylum seekers with what advocates' considered strong claims, including several who had been involved in the peak campaign period. The three most publicized cases involved Taramati and Thérèse, both involved in earlier campaigning, and Ginette. Their publicized cases raised public debate concerning whether the Guidelines were being implemented properly or even went far enough. This activism differed from the peak period because there was no return to radical policy demands. Rather, it focused on reform goals and noninstitutional tactics (see Table 6.10).

The most powerful framing tactics emerged in Taramati's case. Tamarati's claim was rejected because while awaiting a decision, her ex-husband returned to Canada by marrying a Canadian. The woman's shelter where Taramati resided appealed to Quebec Immigration Minister Lucienne Robillard, saying: "The delay of 7 years [in processing her refugee claim] has been long enough for the ex-husband to apply for refugee status, have a seventh child, be deported back to Trinidad, remarry a Canadian citizen, reapply to Canada and finally be accepted as a permanent resident in our country." They compared the rights of persecutors and the persecuted: "To maintain this deportation order would raise the indignation of the Canadian people as they learn that our government gives exile to wife abusers and deports the victims. We are unable to give any credibility to the report from the Immigration services and the population will not be able to give him any credibility. The only message that Canada would hear from coast to coast is that Canada colludes with violent spouses at the detriment of the victims." Canada's international responsibility was also questioned: "It would be very embarrassing for our representatives at Beijing [the Fourth World Conference on Women, in September 1995] to be criticized about an unfavorable decision. How will they be able to explain that Canada favors wife abusers? We are convinced that this is not in the best interests of Canada."[37] No demand for radical policy change was made, simply demand for appropriate implementation of the Guidelines. Similarly, Thérèse and Ginette's cases primarily argued that domestic violence may amount to persecution, attempting to secure consistent application of the Guidelines and to expand them across complicated case scenarios.

The absence of radical demands for legislative change may be explained by several factors, most important the cooperative stance government had adopted and which it insisted it still maintained. This helped reduce conflict and controversy. It was accompanied by a new government strategy of conflict avoidance in particular cases, both those that went public during this period and those that made private appeals. By this time, the new Liberal government had learned to make neither private responses to particular claimants nor public statements in response to public demands in the cases studied until the latest possible moment before deportation. This strategy, seen under the new immigration minister Sergio Marchi, reduced conflict by avoiding the media and reducing activists' opportunities to make use of it. Thérèse's lawyer explained: "We went to the press, and the minister promised to look into the case again, personally. So that looked good. But he waited until the day before her planned departure to tell us 'No.' So we had remained kind of silent because, we reasoned, we have to collaborate, we have to give him a chance. . . . He waited until the very last minute so that we would not make too much noise."[38] Thérèse's case ultimately won through public pressure exerted when she reentered Canada after being deported and then detained and rejected at the third country option she had chosen in order to avoid her country of origin. Her case provides an example of changed government tactics and explains some of the heightened disagreement among supporters concerning the use of noninstitutional tactics, particularly between lawyers and women's shelter workers after cases were lost. Several shelter workers believed lawyers had waited too long to go public, having too much faith in the state and institutional approaches, and thus lost cases due to lack of public pressure. One lawyer explained: "It was often a process of explaining what you have done, then getting the impression that they don't understand what the work involves, that they doubt me, my competence, thinking that I don't do good work."[39] Nada's lawyer similarly observed that "[Nada] had a lawyer before me . . . a good lawyer who does good work. But sometimes when you lose a case, the client can say it was the lawyer's fault."[40]

During this period it also became apparent that the effectiveness of the media strategy was declining, a second change. The immigration minister overturned the court decision in only one out of the three public cases at that time. This had been a major concern among many activists: that media interest would wane or public responses and impact on government would degenerate. Williams from RAM commented that she was "concerned that as a strategy for the future it is already suffering from overwork."[41] During this period media interest was again intense, as the spate of coverage of Thérèse, Taramati, and Ginette's cases indicate, but the nature of its interest and impact changed. This was perhaps an offshoot of the government's new stance and the existence of the Guidelines. Provocative headlines that grabbed public attention in 1993 were no longer used as further refugee policy change was not being demanded. There was a return to the kinds of headlines seen early on in Dulerie's case and a refocusing of emphasis on implementing existing policy rather than changing it.

Other factors may also have been involved in declining influence. In particular, several of the largest and most influential supporting organizations, the ICHRDD, CCR, and NAC, were decreasing their involvement. The assistance they continued to offer was primarily information and advice to potential or current activists on how to campaign, although the CCR continued to work more directly in Thérèse's case. Thus, despite significant media attention and the involvement of a large number of previous and new supporting organizations, Ginette ultimately went into hiding to avoid deportation and Taramati was deported. Only Thérèse was accepted. Perhaps not surprisingly, Thérèse's acceptance occurred just after a major scandal within the ranks of Canada's peacekeeping force in Somalia, when Canada's humanitarian policies and actions were under intense scrutiny.

The failure of these domestic violence cases was significant. It did not effect further policy change at that time, but may have exerted additional pressure on the IRB to closely examine the implementation of the Guidelines and to consider revising them to help ensure better implementation.

TABLE 6.10. DECLINE: REFORM GOALS PLUS NONINSTITUTIONAL TACTICS

Claimant demand:	Revise and properly implement Guidelines; overturn negative decisions on domestic violence cases
Campaign framing:	The Guidelines are not being properly implemented and do not go far enough; "Canada favors wife abusers"; Canada will embarrass itself at the 1995 Beijing conference—it is not in Canada's interests to deport women refugees who flee domestic violence
Institutional and public response:	Heightened attention and polarized debate; more resistance to appeals in individual cases; attempts to avoid and minimize public debate; revision of the Guidelines in 1996 (see below)
Institutional framing:	Avoidance of public debate via cooperative public response; delayed decision making and private rejection of cases

Institutional Influence in the First Years

> *The first battle was over words and it has almost been won. . . . But if we*
> *make the mistake of being satisfied with words that are ultimately not*
> *respected, or phantom programs that are not really functional, we will*
> *really be no closer to our objective. We must not be satisfied with*
> *declarations, we must look at implementation. We must not be satisfied*
> *with the Guidelines, we must monitor their impact and be prepared to*
> *adjust if need be.*
> —Diana Bronson, ICHRDD 1994

In 1996 the IRB released a report concluding that an update to the Guidelines should be issued to better reflect the needs of women refugees. Later, IRB Chairperson Mawani stated that the 1996 "*Update* [to the Guidelines] was necessitated by the volume of jurisprudence that has emerged in the field of gender-related claims and also by the experience . . . gained with such claims since the issuance of the original *Guidelines*" (Mawani 1997). Perhaps the most significant expansion in the concept of gender-related persecution in the 1996 Update is the more explicit and elaborate effort to identify domestic violence and other forms of "private" violence by nonstate actors and to justify the use of the social group category of persecution in such cases. Previously violence "at the hands of private citizens" was left open to interpretation, and as seen in Taramati, Ginette and Thérèse's cases, this sometimes resulted in a narrow interpretation. More broadly, the update also addresses change of circumstances in sending countries and how cultural, economic, and religious factors may affect claimants' internal flight alternatives (see Mawani 1997).

The 1996 Update demonstrates the powerful if incremental policy influence of asylum seekers' institutional actions. With Canada's 1993 Guidelines in place, important new channels opened for asylum seekers to make claims that further shaped and expanded official recognition of the kinds of persecution females experience. The ways and extent to which such claims more specifically challenged traditional refugee law, as well as the Guidelines themselves, can be elaborated through qualitative analysis of "notable" cases that emerged in the first crucial years from instatement of the Guidelines in March 1993 to revision in November 1996. "Notable" cases are those that break legal ground, expand or challenge existing jurisprudence. Analysis of cases published during this period in RefLex, Canada's primary legal digest of notable refugee cases, illuminates evolutions in how refugee law was interpreted and implemented for women.[42] Decisions on claims exhibiting characteristics critical to the decision but not previously addressed in jurisprudence, or evoking different outcomes and justifications, constitute legal precedents. Landes and Posner explain, "In a legal system . . . in which legislative bodies confine themselves for the most part to prescribing general norms of conduct rather than highly specific rules, the published decisions of courts and administrative agencies interpreting and applying the legislative enactments are an important source of the specific rules of law. When the parties to a legal dispute are unable to agree on the meaning of the governing statute as applied to their dispute . . . that meaning will be an issue for the court to resolve. The court's resolution will define the specific requirements of the statute in the circumstances presented by the case and thus create . . . a specific rule of legal obligation applicable to like circumstances" (1976:249).

TABLE 6.11. GENDER-RELATED CLAIMS AND OUTCOMES IN THE EARLY YEARS

Gender-related claims identified by the IRB through December 1996[a]	1,200
Positive decisions	664
Negative decisions	363
Cases pending, withdrawn, abandoned, or discontinued	173
As a percentage of all refugee claims in Canada, annual average	1–2%
"Notable" gender-related claims (RefLex) through November 1996[b]	147
As a percentage of IRB identified gender-related claims	8.2%

[a] Source: IRB, Mawani 1997.
[b] Source: Analysis of RefLex cases. Does not include cases from December 1996 therefore 8.2% is an underestimate.

RefLex cases are, specifically, those in which (1) court decisions depict a "novel approach to law" set out in a clear and concise manner, (2) the application of established legal principle to a novel fact situation occurred, or (3) reasons for decisions are representative of a number of decisions on a specific issue from a particular country or decided by the IRB branch in a particular region of the Canada. In the time period studied, RefLex published 147 notable gender-related refugee decisions, including 20 decisions at federal trials and federal appeals levels (Table 6.11).[43] These notable cases constitute a significant 8.2 percent of the total number of gender-related claims reported by Immigration and Refugee Board to December 1996. This is likely lower than the total number of notable gender-related cases during that period since the RefLex compendium of cases is representative rather than inclusive of all notable cases during particular periods (RefLex Memorandum 1).[44]

Analysis of these notable cases uncovers six areas where gender-related claims expanded traditional interpretation of refugee law: (1) *Relations between persecutor and persecuted*, expanded to include family and extended family members, persecutors located either inland or overseas at the time of the claim, and family persecutors with special status in the community and/or state; (2) *involvement of children* of claimants, expanded to include implications for custody, rights, and evidence issues central to claims; (3) *claimant role in the persecution*, expanded to include not only claimant defiance of persecutory laws or customs, but also claimant adherence to or evasion of such laws, resulting in persecution; (4) *role of the state*, expanded to include not only commission, but also omission, that is, failure to protect individuals from persecution; (5) *structural causes of persecution*, expanded to encompass gender-inclusive and sex-specific causes of persecution, the latter captured particularly in the social group category; and (6) cross-cutting each of the above five areas are innovations regarding the locale in which persecution occurs (with related manifestations or forms of violence in each locale), stretching from the state level (violence perpetrated by officials of the state), to the community and family levels (traditionally "private" spheres) (see Appendix).

Arguably the most profound developments in this body of jurisprudence are those in which adjudicators equate novel *causes* of persecution with novel *forms* of violence that gender-related claims exhibit. Forms of violence that are the same for men and women (i.e., not novel) but were previously ignored among women, and forms particular to women but occurring for the same reasons as men (not novel), were least problematic and most consistently justified in the data set. For instance, sexual torture or rape in war by authorities for political or religious beliefs fell neatly within the categories of persecution on the grounds of political opinion or religion. Rape was a manifestation of violence but women's sex in itself was not the cause. Similarly, "persecution of kin," in which women are tortured in ways no different from men but due to the political opinions of a male relative rather then their own, fall under polit-

ical opinion. The real challenge emerges around cases involving forms of persecution *specific* to women that at the same time occur for reasons *different*
from men. To what structural causes did adjudicators attribute the newly recognized persecution in the jurisprudence considered?

The most striking trend emerges around use of the social group category
and the very large proportion of cases involving essentially similar forms of violence that fell into this category but were nevertheless each considered a notable case (Table 6.12). A total of 99 of the 147 gender-related RefLex cases, or
about 67 percent, invoked the social group category as a cause of persecution.
The most common novel form of violence under refugee law in this category
was family violence. Yet the reasoning behind application of the social group
category is wide-ranging, often inconsistent, and almost never identifies gender, sex, or women as a self-contained social group. Nevertheless, the use of social group and the precedents set in the area of family violence constitute the
greatest challenge to—and later expansion within—the Guidelines. The second, less common but novel form of violence associated with social group was
state-inflicted violence through laws that severely discriminate against women,
typically affiliated with religious doctrine interpreted to condone severe punishment for infringements of expected female behavior. However, this group of
cases often had a primary affiliation with a different category of persecution
and only a secondary affiliation with social group (e.g., religious persecution,
where women as a social group are particularly affected). Therefore I concentrate here on the main body of claims expressing a novel form of violence that
had social group as a primary affiliation—family violence.

TABLE 6.12 NOTABLE CLAIMS INVOLVING SOCIAL GROUP AND FAMILY VIOLENCE

Percentage of all claims involving family violence as the primary form of persecution experienced	33%
Percentage of all claims invoking social group	67%
Percentage of social group claims involving family violence as a primary or secondary form of persecution	54%
Percentage of social group claims with positive outcomes involving family violence[a]	56%

Source: Analysis of 147 RefLex cases
[a]Excludes Federal Court decisions

Family-violence-related claims constituted at least 33 percent of the
RefLex cases, and 54 percent of RefLex cases in which the social group was in-

voked. Family violence cases invoking social group also represent 56 percent of acceptances in the social group category. While these rates likely reflect editors' attempts to represent a balance of cases, the large number of these seemingly similar types of claims classified as notable compared to other types is striking. What does it indicate?

One reason for the sizable proportion of family-violence-related claims considered notable is the fact that, unlike the definition of family or "domestic" violence typically accepted by Western cultures, which refer to spousal or partner abuse, these claims may involve violence by family members other than spouses (e.g., parents, in-laws, even brothers). Each nontypical type of family violence encountered could set a precedent. Moreover, violence perpetrated by family members is often linked to causes of persecution that Western cultures might not commonly associate with domestic violence. Violence committed by family members might be legitimated by religious beliefs, for example, and invoke religious persecution. Very few family violence claims in the data set were interpreted as persecution occurring solely on the basis of race, religion, nationality, or political opinion. But almost all family violence cases described women of a particular race, religion, or ethnicity as making up a "particular social group." That is, women themselves are not the social group, but women of a particular race, religion, or political opinion may be. Without these added dimensions, the social group category fails. In addition, the number of precedents increases with the number of possible sending countries documented (case by case) as having discriminatory laws or lack of protection for women. Finally, the need to forge a link between gender-related persecution and nationality, race, ethnicity, religion, or political opinion in particular countries (where politicized ideas about cultural relativism come into play for many adjudicators) creates the last layer on a diverse and complex range of possible "social group" scenarios.

The multiple layers where precedents may be set in a single claim involving family violence in the social group category can be read as presenting multiple obstacles to making successful claims. These multiple layers also mean that the percentage rate of domestic violence cases invoking social group necessarily overlaps with that of other structural causes of persecution (race, religion, and so on). The most common grounds for persecution associated with social group and family violence in notable cases were nationality and race/ethnicity. Each case of family violence set a precedent regarding the country or culture in which the persecution occurred. While a similar method of setting precedents and applying them (i.e., by country) occurs in other nongender-related claims as human rights violations are discovered and documented, it may be more the case that some claims occur across a narrower range of sending countries—for example, Kurdish refugees fleeing ethnic persecution, or even (in the case of gender-related claims) those involving defiance of the dress code being limited to Islamic countries. In contrast, domestic violence is endemic to the majority of countries and cultures around the world, while state responses vary widely and often are not well documented. This results in a huge range of possible scenarios for family violence as persecution, as precedents on a country-by-country basis, which even later must be monitored to reflect changing conditions for women in different countries over time.

A few examples of the tremendous range of the social group category (including cases of family violence as well as other gender-related forms of violence) are illustrative. Looking only at social group cases receiving positive decisions, "social group" has been described variously as: "unwed mothers in China who have two children" in the case of a woman facing forced sterilization for transgressing the one-child policy (CRDD V94-01287); "Westernized Tajik women in a society moving towards Islamic orthodoxy, with no male protection" (CRDD V T93-04176); "Ecuadorian women subject to wife abuse" (CRDD U92-08714); "Ghanian women subject to forced marriage" (CRDD V95-00374); and "Sikh women fearing police harassment who cannot obtain state protection" (CRDD U95-02138). Two precedents emerged in which the named social group is simply "women" (i.e., CRDD T91-01497; T94-00416). Most commonly, women form a social group based on a particular nationality (i.e., "Syrian women," CRDD T93-11934). An additional indicator of complexities arising from the social group category, and also through cases of domestic violence invoking it, is the disproportionate number of such claims that reached federal trial and federal appeal levels; nine out of twenty of these levels in the RefLex data set involved domestic violence, and twelve out of twenty invoked the social group category.

This examination of notable cases enables comment on asylum seekers' use of, and impact on, the 1993 Guidelines. The range of cases that received positive decisions clearly cross family, community, and state dimensions regarding the locus, agent, as well as manifestation of forms of violence against women (see Figure 6.1). In all instances, lack of protection by, and linkages between, the three locales are crucial to proving well-founded fear of persecution, individuality and universality of the persecution, and lack of internal flight alternatives (the broad requirements of refugee eligibility). The range of cases examined suggests that prior to the 1996 Update, the Guidelines proved flexible and expandable. They were applied to a wide range of case scenarios involving complex and critical gendered dimensions. Positive outcomes applied across forms of violence against women understood in a cross-cultural setting. Successful and noteworthy cases expanded the interpretation and application of the Guidelines along a number of dimensions not explicitly excluded from the Guidelines, but left to elaboration in practice.

Figure 6.1. Interrelatedness of Locus and Agent in Manifestations of Violence Against Women. Revised from Margaret Schuler, 1992.

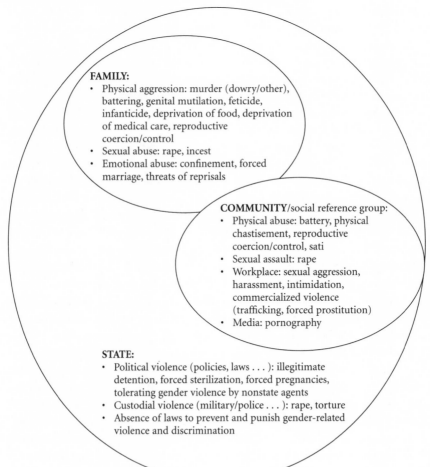

Conclusion: Noncitizens Claiming Universal Rights

We have explored the evolution of campaign strategies and policy influence, both noninstitutional and institutional, in relation to the wider external environment. In this the integral role of asylum seekers, despite their noncitizen status, has emerged, as has the evolution and use of key "signifying acts" representing a fusion of goals, tactics, and framing that pushed out the boundaries of rights.

Campaign aims were expressed and achieved both through policy demands and the policy change process itself. They prioritized participating asylum seekers' immediate need for safety as well as their structural representation. When near-core policy aims seemed unlikely to be attained quickly enough, secondary-core policy aims prioritized immediate need for safety. Shifting strategies responded to and provoked the external environment. Framing processes *combined* in the campaigns were each provocative and timely in their own way. They responded to and elicited government responses, fueled antigovernment public support, and encouraged speedy instatement of the Guidelines as a short-term solution. Near-core demands were an important bargaining tool, but campaigns evolved around a series of individual asylum seekers whose immediate needs were paramount. When government dismissed or repressed demands, advocates polarized the debate further and thus heightened public attention and mobilized antigovernment supporters, urging government to take moderate demands more seriously. The coexistence and changing combination of goals and tactics were both proactive and reactive; they were important strategies in themselves, as the evolving dialogue of conflict and negotiation between the campaign network and the environment indicates.

Interestingly, both human rights and citizenship rights (despite asylum seekers' noncitizen status) legitimated and facilitated asylum seekers in making claims for protection and in then challenging the limits of those rights. The dialectics between citizenship and human rights of both theoretical and substantive kinds were played off one another in the framing of policy demands, to become mutually enhancing and legitimating. In this, asylum seekers who went public were the primary vehicles for the expression of campaign goals. This brought many opportunities and needs for public pressure, creating a staggered effect of numerous concentrated actions over a relatively brief period of time. Each case was fought individually and also referred to a group. Asylum seekers were advocates in their own cases and representatives of the persecuted group. As cases were publicized one after another, pressure mounted. In this the basic messages and tactics of persuasion conveyed through asylum seekers' participation, as *actors* as taking part in institutional and noninstitutional tactics and as *signifiers* of campaign ideals, were crucial to campaign success.

As *actors* who had made refugee claims and been rejected, asylum seekers who went public clearly worked outside the institutional system, pressuring for inclusion by attempting to change it. Their institutionalized rights to status determination processes and oral hearing were upheld through the Canadian Charter of Rights and Freedoms and their human rights upheld in refugee policy. The citizenship and human rights asylum seekers could access provided building blocks for noninstitutional tactics and demands for policy change. They also supported the legitimacy of demands and mobilized a wide range of public interest and positive media coverage, creating sufficient domestic pressure to outweigh the states' perceived risks of policy reform. By "going public" they gave human faces as well as the evidence of their testimonies and strength of their convictions to the body of claimants they represented. This was crucial for attracting media attention, primarily of a positive kind, polarizing the debate, gaining public support and embarrassing government, and constraining social control options of the latter. Asylum seekers' noninstitutional actions affected bystander publics.

Asylum seekers' roles as *signifiers* of campaign ideals most fundamentally entailed aligning human rights with the citizenship rights of women in Canada regarding safety from female-specific violence. These two simultaneous discursive and ideological frames—international human rights and national citizenship values—were the linchpin for goals and demands. But to move the public, asylum seekers appeared paradoxically as both symbols and exceptions. This played to two different publics—those supportive of broad institutional change as the right thing to do regardless of consequences and those afraid institutional change in this area would overwhelm the refugee system. By playing to both sides the campaign network mobilized broad public support. As *symbols*, these asylum seekers represented a structurally persecuted group. This raised the question of Canada's international human rights obligations, drew attention to structural failures of Canada's refugee regime, and polarized the debate. Arriving from Latin America and South America, the Caribbean, Russia, the Middle East, Eastern Europe, Africa, and Southeast Asia, they represented a range of forms of structural violence experienced by women around the world. These asylum seekers all ultimately exhausted institutional channels. They raised the question of whether human rights are universal or culturally relative and put into question Canada's responsibility for upholding human rights dear to Canadians (and subsequently upholding its humanitarian reputation), as well as corresponding citizenship rights. As *exceptions*, asylum seekers mobilized the public through the reverse tactic. They were individuals who against all odds sought asylum in Canada. This strategy emphasizes their individual humanity, drawing upon Canadians' sympathy and upon Canada's beneficent humanitarian reputation and privileged position as an advanced democratic country with ample resources. It is not Canada's legal obligation to accept them, but its moral duty. The campaign kept the issue extremely local and visible by constantly referring to individuals and to Canada's failure rather than sending-country or sending-culture failures. Making appeals for *individual needs* sometimes entailed framing individual cases as isolated occurrences. It played down long-term implications for refugee policy and for future asylum seekers, making humanitarian acceptance of individual cases as nonthreatening to Canadians as possible. As Janet Dench from the CCR describes: "it seemed like big government against a small number of largely defenseless harmless women who simply wanted to be allowed to live in Canada." Crucial to this approach was the argument that women around the world tend to lack means and opportunities to seek asylum in the first place: no floodgates would be opened by making exceptions for a few cases or by altering refugee policy to accommodate their needs. By contrasting the powerful state against the harmlessness of a few women, the campaigns also played on Canadians' concurrent antigovernment sentiments, "provid[ing] a new angle on the popular theme of the incompetence and heartlessness of the reigning government."[45] In the long-term this view proved correct; gender-related refugees have constituted under 2 percent of Canada's annual intake of refugees since instatement of the Guidelines.

Focusing on individuals gave names, faces, and individual stories to the abstract concepts, legal issues, and moral dilemmas they represented. It elicited public sympathy *both* on structural grounds and as exceptions to the rule. It appealed to Canadian's who took as basic Canada's humanitarian identity, as well as the right of women resident in Canada to be protected from violence, whether public or private, with whom these asylum seekers could be equated. Canadian women were invited to compare their own positions, privileges, expectations and fears of violence, and assumed rights to protection with those of a few stateless women from other cultures who were being denied the same help in Canada. One of the most powerful sources of antistate sentiment arose as implications for *Canadian* women were emphasized: Canadian women may have rights at home, but even they did not have privilege to human rights in the abstract sense. If the right to safety from the kinds of torture and degradation that battered women experience is not a human right, it is a right at risk in a global society. The sympathy elicited was overwhelming, including not only refugee advocates but women's organizations, politicians, and residents. These moral and legal arguments represent a fusion of feminism, citizenship, and human rights.

The policy reform that occurred satisfied core policy values, cutting a compromise between the two key values in the belief system hierarchy: immediate safety for asylum seekers and an ideologically radical interpretation and application of human rights law. It dramatically expanded state responsibilities for human rights protections by blurring traditional notions of the "public" and "private" spheres. Strategically, demands for radical policy change when supported by the public made acceptance of more moderate policy reform easier for the state to swallow. Mediation between radical and reform goals, institutional and noninstitutional actions, played an important role in the nature and extent of influence that asylum seekers and advocates were able to achieve within a short time frame. Advocates tolerated political compromise in accepting shorter-term solutions but continued to challenge and expand the Guidelines.

The birth of the 1993 Guidelines on Women Refugee Claimants Fearing Gender-Related Persecution, the first and most comprehensive policy guidelines worldwide for women persecuted as women, may thus be better understood through the conflicting forces and grassroots actions shaping them, including the important roles of asylum seekers both through institutional and noninstitutional means, and the weighting of value priorities when compromises had to be made.

Chapter 7
Making Sex Persecution Matter

When we become able to conceive of the humanity of distant human beings, of their dignity and their needs, we at least begin to ask the hard questions about the contingency that affects people's lives more than any other, the contingency of birth location.

—*Martha Nussbaum,* Sex and Social Justice, *1999*

What are the global impacts of the refugee movement studied, for policy and theory? In conclusion I illuminate the development and entrenchment of women's human rights in refugee policy at international, regional, and national levels, as impacted by the Canadian model. I then consider the theoretical implications of the political process studied, revisiting explanations and implications of new noncitizen rights in particular and the broader means through which new human rights are made viable.

Asylum Policy for Women: International Developments

UNHCR

The Canadian Guidelines necessarily built on upon previous advances in knowledge about women's rights generally and women refugees specifically, but marked a fundamental and radical turning point, becoming a model for other countries as well as regional and international bodies. The highest level impact was felt in the UNHCR, which took on board the human rights implications shortly after the Canadian Guidelines were instated in 1993. Executive Committee Conclusion No. 73, "Refugee Protection and Sexual Violence" (1993) adopts explicit and forceful human rights language to address sexual violence in particular as persecution, stating that the UNHCR Executive Committee (ExCom):

Strongly condemns persecution through sexual violence, which not only constitutes a gross violation of human rights, as well as, when committed in the context of armed conflict, a grave breach of humanitarian law, but is also a particularly serious offence to human dignity;

Supports the recognition as refugees of persons whose claim to refugee status is based upon a well-founded fear of persecution, through sexual violence, for reasons of race, religion, nationality, membership of a particular social group or political opinion;

Recommends that in procedures for the determination of refugee status, asylum-seekers who may have suffered sexual violence be treated with particular sensitivity.

Over the following years the Executive Committee worked toward the adoption of guidelines similar to the Canadian model. ExCom, currently made up of sixty-eight member states, meets in Geneva annually to review and approve the UNHCR's programs and budget, advise on international protection, and discuss a wide range of other issues with UNHCR and its intergovernmental and nongovernmental partners. Its discussion and negotiation of this issue was consequently wide reaching, and its conclusions reflect substantial international consensus. Its 1995 General Conclusion on International Protection (No. 77g [XLVI]) exceeded the 1993 conclusion by specifically calling on the High Commissioner, "to support and promote efforts by States towards the development and implementation of criteria and guidelines on responses to persecution specifically aimed at women, by sharing information on States' initiatives to develop such criteria and guidelines, and by monitoring to ensure their fair and consistent application. In accordance with the principle that women's rights are human rights, these guidelines should recognize as refugees women whose claim to refugee status is based upon well-founded fear of persecution for reasons enumerated in the 1951 Convention and 1967 Protocol, including persecution through sexual violence or other gender-related persecution." Over the next years the Executive Committee reiterated its call in a series of conclusions, recommendations, and reports, including its report *Sexual Violence Against Refugees: Guidelines on Prevention and Response* (UNHCR 1995); and its statements within its General Conclusion on International Protection in 1996, 1997, and 1999.[1] In the latter, ExCom broadened its call to "encourage States, UNHCR and other concerned actors to promote wider acceptance, and inclusion in their protection criteria of the notion that persecution may be gender-related or effected through sexual violence; further encourage UNHCR and other concerned actors to develop, promote and implement guidelines, codes of conduct and training programmes on gender-related refugee issues, in order to support the mainstreaming of a gender perspective and enhance accountability for the implementation of gender policies."

The March 2001 report of the Inter-Agency Lessons Learned Conference Proceedings, *Prevention and Response to Sexual and Gender-Based Violence in Refugee Situations*, and the outcomes of the second track of the Global Consultations on International Protection in 2001, in particular its *Summary Conclusions—Gender-Related Persecution*, furthered international negotiations. They were taken into account in the UNHCR's January 2000 "Position Paper on Gender-Related Persecution," which also notes the "valuable guidance provided by various States and other actors," naming Canada and the two countries to next instate comprehensive policy guidelines, the United States (in 1995) and Australia (in 1996). In 2002 the position paper was replaced by the formal Guidelines on International Protection: Gender-Related Persecution Within the Context of Article 1A(2) of the 1951 UN Convention and/or Its 1967 Protocol Relating to the Status of Refugees (HCR/GIP/02/01, 7 May 2002). These guidelines closely reflect the core elements and key principles outlined in the Canadian model, incorporating female specific forms and causes of harm, violence by state and nonstate actors, the explicit nexus between human rights and gender-related violence, the elaboration of gender-related forms and causes of persecution within each of the five existing 1951 Convention grounds of persecution, and the identification of gender appropriate determination processes. This is well captured in article B(9):

While female and male applicants may be subjected to the same forms of harm, they may also face forms of persecution specific to their sex. International human rights law and international criminal law clearly identify certain acts as violations of these laws, such as sexual violence, and support their characterization as serious abuses, amounting to persecution. In this sense, international law can assist decision-makers to determine the persecutory nature of a particular act. There is no doubt that rape and other forms of gender-related violence, such as dowry-related violence, female genital mutilation, domestic violence, and trafficking, are acts which inflict severe pain and suffering—both mental and physical—and which have been used as forms of persecution, whether perpetrated by State or private actors.

Europe

In Recommendation 1374 (1998)[1] Situation of Refugee Women in Europe, the Council of Europe calls on the Committee of Ministers to instruct its committees to "hold exchanges of views and experience on the subject" of gender persecution; "examine the question of the recognition of gender-related persecution as a basis for refugee status"; and "implement Recommendation 1371, adopted 23 April 1998 by the Assembly aimed at prohibiting and punishing sexual mutilations of women" (6.i a–c). Among other measures it calls on member states to recognize "as refugees women whose claim to refugee status is based upon well founded fear of persecution for reasons enumerated in the 1951 Convention and 1967 Protocol relating to the status of refugees, including persecution through sexual violence or gender-related persecution" (6.vi.c); "ensure that the authorities responsible for refugee status determination procedure are well informed about the overall situation" in applicants' countries of origin, "in particular concerning the situation of women, possible gender-related persecution and its consequences" (vi.c); and "adopt criteria and guidelines dealing with women seeking asylum, in order to enhance a gender-sensitive approach and ensure that women's specific needs are met, particularly at ports of entry" (vi.i).

This culminated in two new European Union Council directives in April 2004, known as the Qualification Directive[2] and the Asylum Procedures Directive.[3] The Qualification Directive specifically includes calls for states to assess each application on an individual basis taking into account factors such as gender (art. 3, para 3c), acts including sexual violence and "of a gender-specific . . . nature" (art. 9, para. 2a, 2f), and stating that "a particular social group might include a group based on a common characteristic of sexual orientation. . . . Gender related aspects might be considered" (art. 10, para. 1d).

States

A number of states have instituted measures specifically addressing female persecution. In Europe some were instated before Recommendation 1374 in 1998, and most occurred before the 2004 European Union Council directive. In Europe and elsewhere, most also occurred before the UNHCR formalized its guidelines in 2002. These national policies have taken a variety of forms ranging from soft to hard law measures and are termed differently in accordance with the political, judicial, and administrative systems of different national contexts, as "considerations," "directives," "guidelines," and "legislation." Some are more extensive and detailed, and many are considered initial steps toward more concrete measures. The existence of prior national-level policies on this issue reinforces the importance of national developments for later international-level consensus building.

Interestingly, gender-specific measures developed or proposed in European Union states prior to the 2004 EU directive also went beyond it, while non-EU countries have developed measures without any regional directives as of yet. These include guidelines developed in the United Kingdom in 2000 and 2004,[4] considered the most progressive in Europe and advancing far beyond the EU directive;[5] in Sweden in 2001;[6] the United States in 1995,[7] and Australia in 1996.[8] Other progressive measures have been adopted by states that specifically identify "sex," "gender," and/or "sexual orientation" as grounds for claiming refugee status within refugee legislation, as in Ireland[9] and, outside of Europe, South Africa,[10] although without guidelines for implementation their success is varied. Other states have identified gender-related points within their refugee status determination procedures and directives, as in Austria,[11] the Czech Republic,[12] Finland,[13] Germany,[14] Lithuania,[15] the Netherlands,[16] Norway,[17] Switzerland,[18] and (in draft) in Belgium.[19] Many of these countries refer to specific forms of gender-related persecution rather than, or in addition to, providing an additional ground of persecution. The year the EU directives were issued, the UNHCR reported that seventeen European countries had recognized sexual violence in particular as a form of persecution (Crawley and Lester 2004). Outside Europe, Guatemala specifically identifies sexual violence as a form of persecution,[20] while Panama[21] and Venezuela[22] refer specifically to "gender" or "sex" as grounds of persecution.

Here I concentrate on measures adopted by the United States and Australia, as the first countries to follow Canada, and by South Africa, which in 1998 instituted more radical policy change. Of course, policy and legislation do not automatically translate into adequate implementation, and certainly there is ample room for improvement in this area in each of the states considered. However, here I am concerned first with the preliminary and indeed groundbreaking step of adopting the necessary rules and regulations for later implementation.

In 1995, the United States became the second country to adopt a comprehensive policy on gender-related persecution. The "Considerations for Asylum Officers Adjudicating Asylum Claims from Women" (Immigration and Naturalization Service, Office of International Affairs, 26 May 1995; hereafter U.S. Considerations) describe developments in U.S. refugee law in this area as "a natural and multi-faceted outgrowth" of a number of international and national developments, specifically citing UNHCR recommendations up to 1995 and the 1993 Canadian Guidelines. They make special mention of the nature and development of the Canadian Guidelines as a key contribution to policy in this area, stating: "On March 9, 1993, the Canadian Immigration and Refugee Board (IRB) issued the ground-breaking 'Guidelines on Women Refugee Claimants Fearing Gender Related Persecution.' The Canadian guidelines attracted considerable interest both in the United States and other countries because they are the first national guidelines to formally recognize that women fleeing persecution because of their gender can be found to be refugees. In developing the guidelines, the IRB carried out extensive consultations with interested governmental and non-governmental groups and individuals. More than two years after their release, the Canadian guidelines remain a model for gender-based asylum adjudications" (1995:3).

The U.S. Considerations explicitly recognize that "forms of harm . . . that are unique to or more commonly befall women have included sexual abuse, rape, infanticide, genital mutilation, forced marriage, slavery, domestic violence, and forced abortion. The form of harm or punishment may be selected because of the gender of the victim." It classifies gender persecution as occurring through rape and other forms of sexual violence as persecution, and through violation of fundamental beliefs as persecution (beliefs about gender roles and relations, and harsh criminal punishment for violation of cultural practices, for example violations of gender dress codes). Similar to the Canadian Guidelines, the U.S. version attempts to identify the nexus between gender-specific forms and causes of persecution and the five traditional grounds of persecution identified in the 1951 Convention. This includes specifying gender aspects of "actual or imputed political opinion" and "membership in a particular social group." It also takes into consideration emerging case law on public and private forms of violence and government commission versus omission of protection. In 2000, the U.S. Department of State additionally issued Gender Guidelines for Overseas Refugee Processing.

In 1996 the Australian Department of Immigration and Multicultural Affairs issued Guidelines on Gender Issues for Decision-Makers, building on Canadian and American work in this area as well as a report of the Australian Law Reform Commission on Violence and Women's Refugee Status. The Australian government was reportedly working on a revision of its gender guidelines since September 2003. In a comparative analysis of Canadian, American, and Australian approaches, Audrey Macklin writes, "The U.S. Considerations and the Australian Guidelines bear striking resemblance to the Canadian Guidelines; indeed, the Considerations explicitly acknowledge the latter's influences. . . . All deal with the process by which women's claims are heard, as well as the substance of the refugee definition as it applies to women making gender-based claims. Beyond this, the content of the directive is also very similar, although the distinctive administrative, legal and jurisprudential landscape of each jurisdiction affects the interpretive space available to the drafters of the directives" (1999:275). The United States, like Canada, also recognizes "the contribution of non-governmental organizations (NGOs), scholars, and activists" and describes the product as a "collaborative effort" (US Considerations 1995; see Macklin 1999:275). All three approaches lay out forms of persecution that are unique to women or which are predominantly inflicted upon women, including sexual violence, genital mutilation, forced abortion, and domestic violence. They address in detail the question of how women may constitute "a particular social group" under the 1951 Convention as well as the possibility of persecution perpetrated either directly by a state, or by private actors in states unable or unwilling to intervene (Macklin 1999:274).

Developments in the Republic of South Africa are the most surprising and far reaching. The National Consortium on Refugee Affairs (NCRA 1999) explains that "South Africa is in the unique position of having included gender within the definition of 'social group' in the Refugees Act. Most states which have recognized gender persecution have chosen not to amend existing legislation, but rather to provide non-binding guidelines on how gender may be incorporated into the category of 'social group' persecution. By including the category of gender within its legislation and giving it legally binding status, South Africa has made a real commitment towards the recognition of women's rights and gender equality." Under chapter I.1 (xxi) of the 1998 Refugees Act (No. 130), South Africa's national refugee legislation, "social group" is stated to include "a group of persons of particular gender, sexual orientation, disability, class or caste." Without doubt the highest legislative adaptation to date, South Africa has nevertheless found the need to also develop more elaborate policy guidelines to aid decision makers and ensure that the status determination process is undertaken through gender-sensitive procedures. Interestingly, like the Canadian policy campaigns examined in this book, the National Consortium on Refugee Affairs' proposed Gender Guidelines for Asylum Determination (1999) draws explicitly on the South African Constitution for legitimation, specifically regarding the right to equality. It states: "The right to equality in the South African Constitution, when applied to refugee determination procedures, requires that women who fear for their lives and security be assessed according to their own specific and unique circumstance inherent to their gender. In the context of South African refugee statistics (as well as those of most other refugee-receiving states), where the very low number of women seeking asylum is overwhelmingly disproportionate to the actual number of women refugees worldwide, the failure to account for and incorporate women's experiences within the determination procedures amounts to widespread infringement of their right to equality." The purpose of the proposed South African guidelines is to elaborate the meaning and interpretation of the specific clause on gender persecution in the 1998 Refugees Act and to promote sensitive and appropriate approaches to evidentiary hearings for women's cases, thus creating a "blueprint by which to evaluate such cases." In so doing, the NCRA also finds necessary the need "to deconstruct assumptions concerning the 'universal' refugee," and in so doing, "to try to reflect the totality of human experiences, and to extend the *opportunity* for protection to all asylum seekers on the basis of gender equality" (NCRA 1999).

Theoretical Implications: Negotiating National and International Rights

Asylum seekers' challenge to traditional conceptions of human rights underpinning refugee policy reflects changing relationships between individuals, groups, and states in a global system. On one hand, the parameters of citizenship and state sovereignty can no longer prevent or adequately control noncitizens making successful claims upon states for the protections associated with membership—or even for membership itself. Instead, various forms of identity-driven politics are finding opportunities and means to push out the boundaries of state responsibility, and in this recourse to international human rights plays no small role. On the other hand, national rights and values in strong states are fundamental for the continuing growth of just what we think of as human rights and to whom they apply. In the case studied, noncitizens played an important role in bringing national values and international human rights face to face, challenging the limits of both.

The previous chapters unraveled the relationships between theory, opportunity, and practice shaping interpretations of persecution and refugee status eligibility and subsequently shaping state responsibilities for systematic, structural human rights violations related to sex or gender. Dynamics of these relationships, revealed as part of the very institutional logic of asylum seeking that women asylum seekers in this study faced, set structural barriers against female claimants and also opportunities for overcoming them. The study illuminated the international and Canadian structural contexts and how asylum seekers actually navigated and influenced their developing dynamics.

These asylum seekers had access to a range of rights, resources, and political opportunities at national and international levels, enabling them to challenge policy through both institutional and noninstitutional means. The rights they drew upon included citizenship and human rights of formal and substantive kinds (linked to membership status, as well as regardless of status) in an interesting dialectic between institutionalized norms, codes, and practices that were at times conflictual and at times mutually supportive. These rights provided asylum seekers with powerful strategic *framing tactics*, lending legal and moral legitimacy to their claims. They also provided claimants authorized and informal access to a variety of resources and *mobilizing structures* necessary to push their claims forward. Among crucial resources accessed were those institutionalized in status determination processes, as well as national rights available through residency and those stemming from the noninstitutional support of a range of influential individuals and organizations located inside Canada. These rights and resources could be best put to use given changing *political opportunities structures*. These included a refugee system with a strong humanitarian reputation that nevertheless became unable to efficiently manage claims, and a domestic political environment that had become particularly vulnerable to public dissent on women's and multicultural issues. Canada was at that time emerging from its own identity crisis involving gender and multicultural and global dimensions. These arose from, in particular, national debates over women's equal rights in the Canadian Charter of Human Rights and Freedoms in the 1980s and deeply divisive national debates about multiculturalism in Canada's bilingual population and its position in NAFTA. Asylum seekers' claims and the public dissent they triggered cast Canada's multicultural, humanitarian, and women's rights reputation into conflict. At the same time, the campaigns coincided with the onset of federal elections, making contending parties particularly sensitive to public dissent.

We saw how women facing deportation exhausted institutional avenues and how they strategically used noninstitutional tactics—going public—to mobilize public support for radical policy demands, namely to change

Canada's use of the internationally standard-setting 1951 Convention Relating to the Status of Refugees. The campaign network systematically provoked, responded to, and raised the stakes for the government, and their "signifying work" (McAdam 1996) carefully played a combination of framing tactics together. As negative decisions on asylum seekers' claims were institutionally overturned in what were first portrayed as exceptional cases settled outside refugee law, examples were set and expectations raised about decisions on similar cases and the need for legislative change to accommodate them. When the Guidelines on Women Refugee Claimants Fearing Gender-Related Persecution came into effect, claim making tested their flexibility and application, sometimes resulting in further noninstitutional actions being taken and ultimately encouraging revision of the Guidelines at the end of 1996 to include a wider range of human rights abuses against women. Examination of a legal database of "notable" claims and court decisions during the period studied isolated a sizable pool of gender-related cases and illuminated the range and nature of the challenges such claims posed to traditional ways of thinking about and implementing refugee law. It also suggested further policy change may be in order to explicitly recognize "sex" as a category of persecution alongside, rather than within, the existing categories of persecution in refugee law (race, religion, nationality, political opinion, and social group) in years to come. South Africa took a significant step in this direction by writing sex and gender explicitly into its 1998 refugee legislation, though again within the definition of social group. And interestingly, legislation without accompanying policy "guidelines" also appears insufficient to ensure implementation. The international community's diverse use of terms such as "sex persecution," "gender persecution," and "gender-related persecution" in recommendations and policy directives, using powerful human rights language and typically referring beyond the "social group" category, suggests that a new dialogue is emerging around the notion that individuals are often persecuted on the grounds of sex or gender alone, just as they are often persecuted on the grounds of race. National precedents in this case have even "trickled up" to regional and UN-level policies.

Asylum seekers acted not solely upon need (as "forced migrants") but as actors seeking alternatives, weighing the risks associated with political action in the receiving country, and making decisions. They not only made use of political opportunities, but also helped shape them. They influenced the internal political culture of the campaign network by mobilizing participants and affecting policy aims. They were integral to the success of public pressure tactics to influence government. Many engaged directly with the media, act-ing as both symbols of structural persecution and as exceptions to asylum-seeking trends. They helped bridge the gap between the public understanding of women's citizenship rights in Canada and human rights globally. They also shaped policy strategies, which shifted over time between radical and reform. The Guidelines, while achieving campaigners' goals, were in fact a compromise, targeting the greatest range of asylum seekers possible within the shortest time possible. But their impact was both deep and far-reaching; it was the Canadian Guidelines that opened the way for similar pol-icy developments underpinned by progressive human rights interpretations in other national and regional contexts and in the United Nations. By help-ing to shape Canadian policy these asylum seekers subsequently helped shape the structural context of asylum seeking as well as a broader understanding of human rights.

All these aspects illustrate that asylum seekers can play explicitly politi-cal roles in the policy change process and that as *noncitizens* their negotiation of national and international rights and values drove crucial national debates that ultimately expanded conceptions of human rights in concrete institu-tional terms. Historically, the evolution of refugee women's rights has re-flected the conflict between static traditional and newly emerging ideals of women's rights, mirroring international and national debates on women's rights that have had both biological stereotypes and cultural relativist under-pinnings. Asylum seekers addressed these conflicts head on and, in so doing, helped shape their own eligibility criteria for membership in Canada and women's international rights to protection. Claimants' drew on both human rights foundations of refugee policy and on substantive citizenship rights in Canada as they made claims, awaited decisions, and challenged them, bring-ing conflicting sets of ideologies face to face: Canada's domestic policies con-demning violence against women and promoting social and legal interventions; and Canada's foreign policy, treating violence against women as a "private" or nonstate issue, remaining silent on the maltreatment of women in many countries, and failing to provide refuge for women fleeing female persecution. In an unusual twist, Canadian women's rights, though more progressive, were condemned as culturally relative rather than univer-sally upheld by their own state. The campaign highlighted this larger situa-tion and called on the Canadian government to rectify it. These noncitizens invoked human rights to protection through national rights associated with residence and national values, ultimately expanding state responsibilities for the human rights of noncitizens. By changing the application of refugee policy, Canada explicitly recognized that women's rights are human rights, regardless of where women live.

The policy outcomes of the campaigns attracted international attention and were widely recognized as promoting a radical expansion in state responsibilities for women's human rights. Yet the national processes driving these internationally significant effects, and their theoretical implications, were previously unexplained. Here noncitizen asylum seekers' roles in policy-making processes and the ways they invoked not only human rights but also national rights and values have been illuminated, explaining for the first time how noncitizens made sex persecution matter.

It is clear that the asylum-seeking process and the unusually explicit challenge asylum seekers faced and posed here was a grave matter. Asylum seekers were indeed desperate and often traumatized by their experiences of persecution. But they were also politically active individuals who formed a structural group ultimately able to bring identity and rights together in a significant way. Some were highly articulate about their political consciousness. All were integral to the policy process. It is also apparent that these asylum seekers could not have done it alone. Asylum seekers' participation was a necessary but insufficient condition for policy change. Their participation and influence was enabled by previous international developments in relevant policies and human rights discourses, alongside the salience of women's rights ideologies and increasing opportunities to migrate and reside in host countries while seeking refugee status. It was also enabled by the particular Canadian context for asylum seeking and political dissent and by Canadian residents' explicit support. Globalization affected all of these dimensions, increasing the interaction between national and international levels, culturally specific and universal rights, and changing the dynamic between them regarding interstate protection.

What are the theoretical implications of asylum seekers' demonstrated negotiation and successful attainment of national and international rights? Several particularly striking processes drove the expansion of international protection in this case and consequently shed light on current theories of human rights change, to which we now return. These include: the noncitizen core of campaign structure and agency, in which asylum seekers as resident transnational actors were enabled to play key political and strategic roles; the criticality of strategic transnational signifying acts, in which actors played national and international rights off one another; and the power of deeply entrenched national values and rights in a strong sovereign state offering crucial political space for existing articulations of human rights to be debated and transcended and new formulations to be triggered in the international arena. These dimensions were deeply intertwined and fundamentally facilitated by globalization.

These findings pose a challenge to current thinking about human rights change, which evolves around the critical question of how tensions between human rights and state-defined citizenship rights are played out, and whether sovereign states are losing the ability to determine who ultimately enjoys "rights to rights." The following analysis considers theoretical implications for the fundamental citizenship–human rights paradox that plagues human rights both in theory and in practice, and consequently for models of human rights change. As one corrective it advocates the use of social movement theory and analyzes findings that result: the significance of strong states, national values, and noncitizens for triggering international human rights expansions, and the relationships between refugee policy, noncitizens, and the creation of international cultural legitimacy.

The Citizenship–Human Rights Paradox: Toward "Human Equality of Membership"

Human rights change is widely believed to involve both a powerful international normative element and an international agency element. Both are facilitated by globalization, which brings new pressures to bear upon states and is increasingly said to be undermining state sovereignty. Specifically, human rights are increasingly believed to challenge nationally specific traditions of citizenship. States can no longer violate the dignity and security of their citizens without invoking moral judgment by the international community, because the formalization of the international human rights regime in the mid-twentieth century generated individual rights above and beyond national-level rights. But one group, perhaps more than any other, has consistently fallen through the cracks of the human rights safety net— noncitizens. It is one thing for states to be pressured to better protect their own citizens and quite another for states to take on the task of protecting individuals not considered national members. In a sense, noncitizens, both those within host countries and in the world outside their borders, are the last frontier of human rights. The reality of noncitizens' situation epitomizes the fundamental paradox of human rights: human rights are meant to transcend states, while relying precisely on states, which typically care only for their citizens, for implementation. Individuals lacking citizenship (in their own country or abroad) lack access to citizenship rights, which remain the primary vehicle for the national implementation of human rights. Noncitizens are doubly rightless.

The rise of noncitizen rights in Western countries since World War II has subsequently become a particular focus within human rights scholarship. Academic work on the rights of nonnationals expresses a keen interest in the ways policy making around noncitizen rights brings state sovereignty and domestic norms toward citizens face to face with international human rights norms and institutions (Habermas 1994b). And this is precisely because these two bodies of norms often do not coalesce neatly, and more often than not are considered conflictual (see Donnelly 2004). Noncitizens' increasing (if still limited) access to national rights in Western countries, seen for example in guest workers' and long-term illegal migrants' access to public services (e.g., education and health benefits) and to many civil and political rights (e.g., freedom to organize and freedom of religious expression) has in recent years been taken to further evidence that the institution of citizenship is being undermined and in some accounts even replaced by more global terms of membership embodied in human rights (Soysal 1994; Jacobson 1996; Sassen 1996; Baubock 1997). The concepts of nationality and national membership, it is said, are being recast under more universal notions of personhood. In resulting postnational (Soysal 1994) and transnational (Baubock 1997) models of membership, noncitizen rights are driven by the growing salience of global human rights and the international pressures exerted by human rights institutions and by noncitizens using judicial systems to claim human rights (Soysal 1994, 1996; Sassen 1996; Jacobson 1996). Positive outcomes of this process further the absorption of existing human rights into national contexts, undermining national practices and citizenship parameters and thus weakening state sovereignty. Many of the most influential academic works on this issue convey the decline-of-citizenship theory explicitly in their titles, for example Jacobson's *Rights Across Borders: Immigration and the Decline of Citizenship*, Soysal's *Limits of Citizenship: Migrants and Post-national Membership in Europe*, and Sassen's *Losing Control? Sovereignty in an Age of Globalization*.

In *Rights Across Borders* (1996), Jacobson contends that changing relations between individuals' rights and states in the global system are devaluating citizenship. Taking the case of illegal immigration, he argues that

"Transnational migration is steadily eroding the traditional basis of nation-state membership, namely citizenship," and "contribut[ing] to the increasing importance of international human rights codes" (9). Jacobson suggests that the "devaluation" of citizenship is not decreasing the role of states in proportion to "a supranational polity." Rather it is increasing the role of the state as a "mechanism essential for the institutionalization of international human rights" (1996:11), while simultaneously weakening states' decision-making capacities and sovereignty. While citizenship and nationality may be in a process of being recast, the rights of individuals in relation to states and benefits of membership are growing through the national institutionalization of existing human rights codes.

Jacobson's analysis supports Soysal's earlier work *Limits of Citizenship* (1994), which argued that a new form of postnational membership is arising. Building on the example of guest workers' incorporation into European countries, she elaborates a postnational model as a replacement for the citizenship model. Guest workers have been incorporated into host countries in various ways corresponding to different national incorporation regimes and by drawing upon human rights discourses to legitimate and facilitate claim making. Soysal explains: "membership and the rights it entails are not necessarily based on the criterion of nationality. In the postnational model, universal personhood replaces nationhood; and universal human rights replace national rights. The justification for the state's obligations to foreign populations goes beyond the nation-state itself. The rights and claims of individuals are legitimated by ideologies grounded in a transnational community, through international codes, conventions, and laws on human rights, independent of their citizenship in a nation-state. Hence, the individual transcends the citizen. This is the most elemental way that the postnational model differs from the national model" (1994:142).

Soysal suggests that the state maintains or strengthens its role in implementing human rights, but the *justification* for rights is increasingly postnational and state decision making and national values are bowing to international norms. Not all residents are "citizens," thus their experience does not correspond to traditional citizenship models. Different legal status types, rules of entry, and degrees of access to rights persist, corresponding to different immigration regimes and patterns of incorporation. Yet the experience of international migrants today demonstrates that an expansion of state responsibilities toward noncitizens is occurring through recognition of their international human rights. This gives noncitizens new legitimacy and agency; they can evoke institutionalized discourses and norms of universal personhood to advance claims and undermine state sovereignty.

Other studies on the incorporation of international migrants into host societies observe similar trends and even prescribe new membership parameters to further facilitate it, including some that give greater emphasis to the importance of established citizenship traditions. Baubock (1997, 1998) refers to the new forms of membership as *transnational* in nature, maintaining the importance of host-country and sending-country citizenship rights while explicitly drawing on human rights and transnational state responsibilities to explain states' declining ability to deny rights to noncitizens. More recently, Benhabib (2004) has taken a more moderate view, criticizing decline-of-citizenship theories and suggesting that human rights are transfiguring but not undermining citizenship. In this, international human rights and noncitizen claims feed into an iterative process whereby states reconfigure their existing national values and rights, expanding them to encompass new populations and rights, creating more robust and deep forms of citizenship in a global world. Citizenship is not at an end; as a form of political community, it has never been static and unchanging, but has evolved and is continuing to do so under human rights, absorbing postnational terms of membership. But in this state sovereignty is still perceived as being fundamentally undermined or "frayed" (Benhabib 2004:1) due to states' decreasing ability to refuse or prevent expansions of citizenship driven by more progressive human rights.

One reason studies of human rights change around noncitizens have been so widely discussed may be their focus on advanced industrial countries, which suggests even the economically and politically powerful states of Europe and North America are succumbing to the power of human rights. This supports broader human rights scholarship, which has developed theories of human rights change based predominantly upon the experiences of poorer and less politically powerful countries, whose inability to resist international pressures to comply with human rights may seem less surprising when it occurs. Both areas of scholarship identify similar factors to explain human rights change, and both take for granted the normative dominance of supranational over national rights and focus on cases that support this assumption.

On the surface, such trends might suggest that the outcome of the Canadian cases was similarly a decline of citizenship and state sovereignty, since government went from strongly resisting a national policy change to embracing one that incorporated human rights. But closer examination revealed a different process at play, with substantially different implications. Here, not only were human rights critical to the extension of national rights to noncitizens, but national rights were critical to a substantive expansion of human rights. To better understand this, we must return to a policy debate that pre-dates the human rights discussion: the robustness of the institution of citizenship as a gateway through which individuals can access civil, political, and social rights in particular national contexts. Public policy analysts have long noted that disparities in the enjoyment of social, economic, and political citizenship rights are shaped by factors such as nationality, race, gender, age, class, and health (see Bulmer and Rees 1996), while noncitizen integration into host countries, particularly visible in increasing access to public services, contradicts the notion that formal citizenship status is really (or ought to be) required for access to national rights.

Interestingly, T. H. Marshall's path-setting conceptualization of citizenship as the route to civil, political, and social rights in *Citizenship and Social Class* (1950) is concerned less with national allegiance (Rees 1995) or formal legal status of the kind arising through birth, allegiance, and/or residency, all factors commonly equated with citizenship, and more with a social and qualitative kind of status bestowing equality of rights to social integration as "full members of a community" (Marshall 1963:87). Marshall underscored this in a later publication in 1992 (Marshall and Bottomore 1992). In so far as citizenship becomes a *means* of achieving such social integration, it is a "developing institution" between state and society created by investing citizenship status with "rights and duties" (Marshall 1963:87). Society creates "an ideal citizenship against which achievement can be measured and towards which aspiration can be directed," expressed through rights and duties that come to embody the *institution* of citizenship; citizenship is a "status bestowed." Ideally it confers what Marshall termed "human equality of membership" (Marshall 1963:87, 124).

Marshall went on to reveal successive stages in the expansion of this developing institution, each stage marked by the growth of a different type of citizenship right. According to his periodization of history, civil and political rights developed in the eighteenth, and nineteenth centuries respectively, culminating in social rights championed by twentieth-century welfare states. The idea, said Marshall, was that citizenship rights and the state-citizen dialogue accruing from those rights would equalize people of different social classes by enabling them to become full members of a community, that is, enjoying full citizenship. The working classes could be integrated into what Marshall called "civilized" society not by being lifted out of their class, but through equality of civil, political, and social rights and the general quality of life these rights could foster. Marshall argued that the growth of social rights embodied in the welfare state need not conflict with the social class system and the rise of capitalism. He believed the inherent tension between democratic and welfare rights on one hand and the distribution of power and incomes by the market on the other could be managed. Significantly, he considered this tension within nation-states, not across them.

Marshall's conception of citizenship was much discussed and in many ways taken for granted until the 1980s, when it came under attack on several grounds: its inherent parameters of inclusion and exclusion, its Englishness, its basis in the experience of Caucasian males, and its sweeping historical analysis and periodization of rights. Marshall's conceptualization was subsequently expanded in some important respects, key to which was explicit recognition that the ideal and institution of citizenship involves both formal and substantive elements. Marshall, and much work after him, focused primarily on the substantive rights element, largely ignoring formal citizenship status and taking the state as the most logical political unit for implementation, and neglecting the question of *which* state individuals may make claims upon (Marshall and Bottomore, 1992).

The conflict and complexity that arises when formal status and substantive rights of citizenship are treated synonymously emerges in the case of massive immigration in the late twentieth century. Brubaker's influential work (1989, 1992) illuminated changing relationships between formal and substantive elements. Brubaker (1992:38) explains: "The 'sociologization' of the concept of citizenship in the work of Marshall and Bendix and theorists of participation has indeed been fruitful [but] it has introduced an *endogenous* bias into the study of citizenship. Formal membership of the state has been taken for granted. . . . But the massive immigration of the last quarter-century to Western Europe and North America, leaving in its wake a large population whose formal citizenship is in question, has engendered a new politics of citizenship, centered precisely on the question of membership in the nation-state." Brubaker's comparison of immigration and citizenship demonstrates that citizenship status is derived differently in countries with different immigration traditions. The "politics of citizenship" varies across countries because it bears various relations to conceptions of nationhood.

Immigration raises questions about criteria for access to civil, political, and social citizenship rights, both formally and informally. Two significant gray areas in the relation between formal and substantive citizenship emerge: "That which constitutes citizenship—the array of rights or the pattern of participation—is not necessarily tied to formal state-membership. Formal citizenship is *neither a sufficient nor a necessary condition* for substantive citizenship" (Brubaker 1992:36, emphasis added).

In the first gray area, formal citizenship is not a *sufficient* condition for substantive rights and participation, because "one can possess formal state-membership yet be excluded (in law or in fact) from certain political, civil, or social rights or from effective participation in the business of rule in a variety of settings" (Brubaker 1992:36). Women, racial and ethnic minorities, youths and the elderly, the mentally ill and the disabled—all have been discriminated against at different times and in countries around the world, often attaining formal citizenship rights in a very different (and slower) chronological order than white males and to very different extents and capacities, as many public policy analysts have shown (Pinker 1971; O'Connor 1973; Evans and Ungerson 1983; Land 1989; Pateman 1988, 1989; Walby 1990; Williams 1989; Cohen 1985; Gordon 1989). The functioning of citizenship was thus revealed as faulty through historical analyses demonstrating that many citizens have been treated as second class or "denizens" (Hammar 1990), excluded from various rights and benefits.

The second gray area, which Brubaker notes is "less clear," arises when formal citizenship "is not a *necessary* condition of substantive citizenship," "while formal citizenship may be required for certain components of substantive citizenship (e.g., voting in national elections), other components . . . are independent of formal state-membership. Social rights, for example, are accessible to citizens and legally resident noncitizens on virtually identical terms, as is participation in the self-governance of associations, political parties, unions, factory councils, and other institutions" (Brubaker 1992:36–38). Thus many long-term residents and guest workers can claim an array of benefits despite being noncitizens (Brubaker 1992; see also Rees 1995; Bulmer and Rees 1996; Boeri, Hanson, and McCormick 2002). Ultimately, *formal* citizenship status is neither a full guarantee nor an absolute condition for rights and benefits of national membership.

The inequalities revealed by many public policy analysts bolstered calls for access to substantive citizenship rights to be explicitly extended to new populations by rethinking the social and intellectual assumptions underlying citizenship rights, reinvesting such rights with values that, in essence, broaden the concept of citizenship: "to adapt our social and political institutions to a new and more inclusive idea of citizenship that reflects the interconnected social world we live in" (Glennerster 1983:222). The race and gender movements in Europe and North America in the 1970s were no doubt influential here, and the emergence of more gender, racial, and capability appropriate policies began to quicken in many advanced industrial countries. In the 1990s, academic work on *expanded* forms of citizenship burgeoned, the most groundbreaking perhaps being work on European citizenship. It also included a range of more visionary forms of citizenship identified with transnational issues—rights of cultural, ecological, corporate, and global citizenship, to name just a few (for example, Turner 1994; Van Steenbergen 1994; Meehan 1993; Falk 1994). These tend to be less concerned with formal citizenship status and admissions processes, and more with state-led substantive rights for more expansive and diverse populations, including residents lacking formal status. That is, in ideal terms citizenship is increasingly considered more as a bundle of rights, and less as a formal status that might be used to justify the exclusion of either denizens or noncitizens. Marshall's original formulation of citizenship as conferring "human equality of membership" with little concern for formal status or national allegiance is prescient here. Recent work comes full circle, this time explicitly emphasizing possibilities of expanding citizenship rights across countries.

This explanation is also relevant to the case studied in this book, since noncitizens ultimately won rights to protection that already existed in Canada's citizenship tradition. However it does not account for the simultaneous role of human rights, which was so apparent. Human rights scholarship contributes to the sociologization of the concept of citizenship by adding a new layer of theorizing about the sociopolitical influence of international human rights norms under conditions of globalization. But its unidirectional view that states are compelled to respect human rights due to international pressures is equally one-sided. The study in this book exclusively fits neither of these two approaches, the former depicting a substantive expansion of existing citizenship values to wider populations in order to confer a more globally relevant "human equality of membership" within the state, the latter depicting new pressures on membership by more progressive human rights. Instead, by bridging these two discourses, new implications emerge. At times, states may choose to respect international human rights due to the moral weight of their own evolving citizenship traditions, which at times may actually be more progressive than international rights. In some cases, by framing national rights and values as "universal" they may even set international precedents that impact the global human rights agenda. These *international trigger cases* affect substantive understandings of international human rights and reach previously neglected populations on a world scale.

Human Rights Change and Social Movement

International trigger cases depict greater interaction and symbiosis between citizenship and human rights and alert us to different drivers, actors, and outcomes. As such, this book has argued that they may require a different analytical approach. The dominant theory of human rights change is built upon empirical studies in cases involving geographic rather than substantive expansions of human rights. These support the theory that Transnational Advocacy Networks (Keck and Sikkink 1998; Risse, Ropp, and Sikkink 1999) exert essential international pressure for states to absorb human rights into national practice. TANs are said to bolster domestic actors through "simultaneous activities [of actors] at four levels": (1) interactions among transnationally operating international nongovernmental organizations (INGOs), international human rights regimes and organizations, and Western states; (2) domestic society in the norm-violating state; (3) links between the societal opposition and the transnational networks; and (4) national governments of norm-violating states (Risse, Ropp, and Sikkink 1999:18–19). The "spiral model" of political change (Risse, Ropp, and Sikkink 1999) describes the stages of human rights socialization under the influence of TANs.[23]

Political explanations of *substantive* human rights expansions, which have developed in international relations theories of "norm emergence" more generally, similarly incorporate the essential involvement of TANs, but lack detailed empirical studies. In particular, they do not explain actual political processes of persuasion (Bob 2005), which should include "norm resistance" (Elgström 2000) as well as close attention to the national level. Instead they generally chart the genealogy of states' implementation of "emerging" norms alongside sweeping genealogies of national and international campaigns. In this, the substance of these novel norms is taken for granted, and the dialectical processes through which the new norms were articulated and conceptualized by different political actors is overlooked. To explain how some states become "norm leaders" ahead of the international community and potentially even international law, "international norm entrepreneurs" are simply said to involve TANs in persuading states to adopt the proposed rights (see Finnemore and Sikkink 1998). But in substantive human rights change, the very process of early norm articulation and pressure for implementation of novel ideas about rights may well differ from the relatively simpler implementation of existing human rights norms.

Indeed, the substantive human rights change studied in this book did not involve TANs.[24] Canada institutionalized novel human rights protections for women refugees without interference or pressure by foreign states, intergovernmental bodies, or international nongovernmental organizations abroad.[25] Perhaps this was due to the location of the processes studied, since human rights change in wealthy democratic countries is underresearched. In these countries noncitizens may not need international organizations to pressure the violator state into compliance, but rather simply refer to existing norms and institutions. Interestingly, empirical studies supporting the postnational membership model, which necessarily concentrate on advanced industrial countries, fail to note the involvement of TANs. So TANs may be less relevant for politically and financially powerful advanced industrialized countries. Equally plausible, TANs may simply not be required for *substantive* human rights change at the stage studied in the book, when states set international human rights precedents. This study therefore questions the generalizability of theories of human rights change based on TANs. It offers a much needed empirical study of political processes at the national level in a case involving the creation of a state "norm leader," whose national example ultimately triggered international debate and substantive human rights change.

How then are substantive expansions of human rights first generated in national contexts? Why and how do states articulate nationally conceived rights as viable subjects for human rights in the global arena? What are the pressures and political processes driving such trigger cases? This book has suggested that well-established theories of social movement, if used more consistently, can offer more rigorous explanatory accounts of human rights change. Social movement theory is not organized around necessary levels of actors and rights, nor necessary norms and institutions; but rather around the *changes* that occur within and across relevant components of the political arena and the subsequent evolution, forms, and processes of political and strategic agency. It can be used to identify changing opportunities for agency and actors' use of them—namely changing political opportunity structures, mobilizing structures or vehicles, and framing tactics (McAdam, McCarthy and Zald 1996)—regardless of where actors and rights are located. Actors' national or transnational location and organization will differ in different successful cases, as will the level of dominant rights applied (national or international); what is at issue is actors' changing access, opportunities, and abilities to use old and new resources and strategies for change to positive effect in particular times and places.

Social movement theory applies particularly well to contentious political processes of human rights change that occurs around collective identities. Although human rights are articulated around the "individual," they nevertheless find expression in terms of individuals' common experiences of abuse stemming from power inequalities. Human rights adhere around commonly felt needs for human dignity and human security. Individuals' human rights are subsequently elaborated around their association with collective identities whose human dignity and human security may be violated on common grounds—association with a particular class, race, religion, nationality or citizenship (or lack thereof), ethnicity, sex, political opinion, age cohort, ability, and so on. Indeed, a plethora of human rights treaties have evolved around such identity groups, seen in conventions and declarations on the rights of minorities, ethnic and religious groups, children, women, indigenous people, refugees and the stateless, workers and the poor, to name but a few. These collective identities transcend nation-states and cross citizenship boundaries and their rights may be pursued within or across states.

Social movement theory explains political processes in the case studied in this book, in the absence of TANs and prior international norms on sex persecution. It facilitated the illumination of stable and changing opportunities for actors to make claims and influence their environment, within and across the particular institutional, normative, political, and structural systems that comprise their environment. For asylum seekers whose shared collective identity was persecution based on sex or gender, this environment included an elaborate network of international and national migration systems, rights, and resources (both tangible and intangible or symbolic). Globalization was impacting upon and changing this environment, and asylum seekers made use of changing political opportunities that emerged.

Because social movement theory does not preconceive key actors and levels of norms and activity (international versus national), it avoids normative assumptions about a one-way influence of human rights standards upon national contexts and can better account for the symbiosis between citizenship and human rights as well as the role of nontraditional actors such as noncitizens. By applying to a broader set of cases social movement theory can offer a corrective to the false dichotomies underlying dominant theories of human rights and globalization, thus generating new theoretical outcomes. This does not render invalid other explanations of human rights change that invoke global to national human rights impacts. New international pressures and norms do seem to be influencing territorially defined forms of political community and influencing states in some important ways, and neither advanced industrial or less developed countries are immune to this. However, it does limit their generalizability and presents a more comprehensive picture of human rights change in the context of globalization. The consistent use of a common and more broadly applicable theoretical framework in future empirical studies of human rights change would also help illuminate which factors are essential in what types of cases, why human rights change is successful in some contexts and times and not others, and what these trends herald.

Human Rights Expansion: Strong States, National Values, and Noncitizens

In the case studied, social movement theory uncovered lessons from refugee and noncitizen politics as a new area for research in human rights scholarship. It is clear that in the absence of targeted international norms that could be grafted onto the national context under the influence of transnational actors, a different political process was at play. An unusual combination of noncitizens and national values in a strong sovereign state emerged as key drivers of international substantive and domestic institutional human rights expansions. Therefore in the human rights debate over state sovereignty, findings of this study agree more with the dissonant views of Welch and Monshipouri (2001) and Donnelly (2004). According to Donnelly, "The reshaping of sovereignty by human rights has left states today no less sovereign than they were fifty, a hundred, or three hundred and fifty years ago" (Donnelly 2004:1). He takes to task the methodologies behind perceived conflicts between human rights and state sovereignty. He argues that treatments of state sovereignty inaccurately confuse state control with state authority. State sovereignty has in practice historically described state authority over a territory, while state abilities to actually control all aspects and influences upon a territory have never been absolute. What we may now be witnessing is a continuing process in the historical transformation of state sovereignty under globalization in terms of what states can control.[26] States cannot always control or prevent international influences, which affect them in new ways. But in this, states may remain very much sovereigns as they make decisions, even under pressure, about the ways and extent to which they will implement or reject human rights. In fact, even under a great deal of international pressure many states persist in violating human rights (Welch and Monshipouri 2001:375). The continuing resistance to ratifying many international treaties, and the large-scale human rights abuses that continually occur even in signatory states, are indicative.[27] This view of state sovereignty does not negate observations of the power of international human rights norms to exert pressures on states and in some cases alter state behavior. Rather, it agrees more with globalization theorists that take a moderate "transformationalist" approach (Held and McGrew 2000, 2003). Globalization is transforming world politics, but state sovereignty need not conflict with human rights. The findings of this study lend empirical evidence to this interpretation and extend it further.

When a state justifies a decision to extend citizenship rights to noncitizens by referring to international human rights, several outcomes may result. First, agreeing with postnational and nationalization approaches, citizenship rights, national values, and state sovereignty may be undermined or transformed by human rights; national rights may be substantively expanded (to cover additional rights) or extended (toward previously excluded populations), limiting state abuses of power and individuals' freedom to practice harmful traditions. Second, nationalist backlashes may occur, resulting in states simultaneously strengthening and entrenching nationally conceived values and parameters for membership as a defense against global pressures.

Third, national rights and values may be expanded in ways consistent with states' culturally rooted ideologies and interests, reflecting broader international norms without being undermined. In some cases national rights may even be expanded *regardless* of international human rights norms; the latter may support, bolster, and reinforce expanded national rights but not constitute a key causal factor or basis of expanding national rights. In some advanced industrialized countries with multicultural populations, national values have been in a long process of adapting to more diverse constituencies and may subsequently play key roles in driving expansions of rights to noncitizens and diverse cultures within the national context. Such growth may be part of a state's citizenship tradition. Indeed, as noted earlier, until recently scholarship on expanding citizenship rights did not refer to "human rights" at all. So while human rights norms may be increasingly referred to, and in some cases even begin to trigger national changes, processes earlier set in motion ought not to be underplayed. In such scenarios, citizenship rights may not be inferior to human rights or in decline, rather human rights may gain importance alongside them, sometimes even after the fact. Indeed, without certain preexisting citizenship rights, many human rights (as such) might never gain a foothold in national contexts at all.

Fourth, progressive citizenship rights in strong sovereign states may be envisioned more broadly as appropriate for international or "universal" values—getting projected into international human rights debates and agendas. They may expand current conceptualizations of international human rights, as in this book, to justify or reify the extension of citizenship rights to new populations. The extension of national rights to noncitizens through human rights expansions may serve state interests in promoting national values. In this, the transformation of world politics under globalization, by increasing and intensifying interaction between cultures and states, human rights and domestic norms, brings not only threats to states but also opportunities to influence international standards and practices. These developing opportunities may alter the ways the international human rights agenda is set.

Each of the above scenarios may shape noncitizen access (or lack thereof) to substantive rights in host countries despite lack of formal citizenship. Scenarios three and four present alternative explanations for cases often described as evoking new rights of postnational membership. This suggests that the dominance of human rights norms in the postnational membership model may be undemonstrated in cases in which *substantive* citizenship rights are extended to noncitizens (rights without status). However we might speculate that the model is more robust in explaining why some noncitizens may gain *formal* membership status (rights to citizenship or permanent resident status). This may be the purest application of the postnational model, requiring examination of cases involving *status-seeking* migrants, and would be no clearer than in the case of refugees, whose eligibility or membership criteria are explicitly guided by human rights interpreted and applied at national levels. At the moment, institutionalized legal rights to claim formal membership on the grounds of human rights is still reserved for refugees. In this context citizenship becomes a vehicle for the institutional protection of human rights on human rights grounds. Indeed, refugee policies and applications have been expanding in some important ways since the 1960s. They *increasingly* draw upon human rights principles to identify persecution and legitimate refugee status (Hathaway 1991a:104–105). Asylum seeking is a rich yet underresearched example of the changing dynamic between human rights and citizenship rights, changing access to citizenship rights and changing processes and pressures on national policy making in an increasingly global community. "Human equality of membership," to use Marshall's conceptualization of the ultimate aim of citizenship, constitutes the equal right among human beings to be "admitted to a share in the social heritage." This is a right individuals possess first as beings with rights to full membership in the human community, and second as persons institutionally circumscribed by a state or other governing structure. The aim of citizenship to achieve human equality of membership can be interpreted in a global world. Indeed, in later works Marshall (1963) stated that nationality is too large a binding concept; he subsequently held more of a minimal conception of citizenship in this regard, describing persons related through common rules and jurisdictions regulating their conduct and opportunities (rather than through homogeneity of cultural and historical background) and not excluding jurisdictions larger than the state (see Parry 1991). Citizenship achieves human equality of membership through the institutionalizing vehicle of the state, and as we are increasingly seeing, it does so by drawing on both international and national rights and the interaction between the two.

But postnational membership studies have not drawn on cases of status-seeking migrants. Rather, they draw specifically on cases of *established* migrants (legal and illegal) seeking not formal status but formal access to substantive rights through human rights claims. In the much discussed French "headscarf affair," for example, Muslim immigrants drew on human rights to religious freedom in order to counter national laws banning the wearing of religious symbols in public institutions in France. To do this, established migrants needed access to some substantive citizenship rights to begin with (freedom of speech, association, right to public services) in order to lay claim to or transform others to their cultural preferences. Similarly guest workers and other noncitizens may build on existing residence rights by layering in human rights, in this way attaining (for example) new rights to health care, education, and even limited local voting. In this setting, minority group claims draw on universal human rights frameworks for legitimacy in multicultural societies, while the ability of majority cultures in host countries to maintain their own culturally relativist rules to control minority populations is cast into question. Linklater (1998) remarks that citizenship is a well-established "moral resource" upon which more universal rights can be grafted, and others recognize the importance of states with the capacity to nationalize and enforce international rights, but generally the inferiority of national rights in the supranational arena is assumed.

In contrast, this study did capture processes involving *status-seeking* migrants, whose purpose in making claims on the state was to establish legally the right to residence. But here the postnational membership model in what I have referred to as its pure form was not applicable. These migrants' first point of access to rights was through the human right to seek asylum (a "pure" postnational justification). This route failing, their second point of access was through the states' sovereign right to interpret the 1951 UN refugee convention in a manner suitable to the national context. Their third point of access was derived through temporary residence (e.g., financial resources, social services, civil society links, constitutional rights to freedom of speech, association, public protest) as inland asylum seekers awaiting decisions on their claims. This enabled them to pressure for the use of established national rights and values in order to reshape national interpretations of international human rights and international refugee law. National rights explicitly expanded refugees' human rights; without this expansion, these noncitizens would not have gained rights to residence. This is not surprising considering that in receiving countries, established citizenship rights that are of at least an equivalent order to human rights are essential if refugees are to be protected. States do not typically grant refugees any protection that their own citizens lack (see Smith 2003:9). Refugees move to countries where they can find better protections through substantive citizenship rights already in existence there. This study shows how in some cases citizenship rights may be a vehicle for expanding institutionalized norms or readings of what constitutes human rights. New types of noncitizen claims are being made that may enlarge the pool of human rights from which refugees can draw, enlarge the interpretation of what constitutes human rights violations, or increasingly blur human rights and citizenship categories together and transform them. When states define human rights based membership eligibility on their own terms, they help to shape and set precedents for human rights and directly impact noncitizens' potential for international protection. In the case studied, national rights transcended and influenced the human rights basis of eligibility for membership and international protection.

The main differences therefore between the characteristics of this noncitizen case compared to those considered in the postnational model were status-seeking subjects and national rights that transcended human rights. The postnational model rightly addresses the transformation of citizenship as a process of conflict and negotiation between noncitizen and citizen groups, describing how the struggle between cultural relativism and universalism may be played out in ethnically mixed populations, but always in cases where human rights are perceived as broader or more inclusive than citizenship rights. This sets the stage for the more one-way interaction observed in which human rights influence national rights and thus expand their reach across the globe. While this does not necessarily make observations inaccurate, it does not address the question of how human rights norms themselves are articulated newly and made viable. Human rights are not static, complete, or unchanging. And the greatest influences on human rights historically include internationally precedent-setting, nationally conceived rights, which triggered international attention and debate and ultimately gained international legitimacy (e.g., 1776 American Declaration of Independence, 1789 French Declaration of the Rights of Man and the Citizen, 1791 U.S. Bill of Rights). In the more recent context of globalization, we continue to observe cases in which national rights clearly transcend understandings and applications of international rights at particular historical moments, ultimately gaining authority and legitimacy beyond national boundaries by taking on international forms. Women's movements have had a particularly visible, profound, and sustained impact over the past forty years. Other recent human rights developments preceded by national developments include the Convention on the Rights of the Child (1989), its Optional Protocols (2000, in force 2002), the Declaration on the Elimination of Violence Against Women (1993), Declaration on the Right to Development (1986) and the Declaration on the Rights of Indigenous Peoples (2007). These recent declarations signal that many deeply entrenched interpretations of human rights have been limited, as evidenced more broadly in the repeated need for articles of the Universal Declaration of Human Rights to be elaborated through a proliferation of conventions and declarations, some of which have challenged deeply held and long-standing assumptions about human rights from the early days of the UDHR. Looking closely at how new human rights are developed, we see an iterative process in which existing human rights and citizenship values interact and transform one another. This may occur first in countries that prize the rights in question and reframe them as suitable for the international level and second in intergovernmental forums where the rights are proposed and debated. As countries such as

India and China gain world economic and political power, their non-Western views of group rights, for example, become increasingly pertinent and influential. Rather than being undermined when states implement human rights (new or old) on their own terms, their national values and rights may have a deep impact upon the world human rights stage. The obvious counterargument, that the UDHR is amenable to such expansions or reinterpretations, fails to answer how such expansions occur and what such processes say about current conceptualizations of universal rights. Currently limited human rights may be expanded, and in this national precedents and practices need not be a threat to universal rights, but a key.

Refugee Policy, Noncitizens, and Cultural Legitimacy

That human rights expansions in this case occurred around developments in refugee eligibility criteria is significant here, and it is worth revisiting refugee policy as one key site through which globalization brings national and international rights and values face-to-face and shapes their cultural legitimacy and to expand upon the role of noncitizens in this process. Refugee scholars have shown how host countries, by accepting asylum seekers, can send powerful political messages to the international community and to sending countries about human rights violations.[28] Refugee policy also, and most obviously, serves a fundamental role in protecting human rights by essentially transferring responsibility for persecuted individuals from one state to another, at least temporarily and often permanently. Unfortunately, despite the apparent importance of refugee policies for human rights, the political processes shaping refugee policy development remain poorly understood (Loescher 1989; Hollifield 2000). In this, the making of refugee policy that breaks new ground in human rights protection is also neglected.

Global pressures are increasingly seen as undermining state control over international migration—particularly the world economy, international trade and labor agreements, and the international human rights regime, which sets standards and legitimates the rights of noncitizens (see Sassen, 1988, 1996, 1998). In analyses of refugee policy development, theories of receiving-country policy responses have moved beyond push-pull theories that characterize refugee policy as purely reactive. Resulting "migration systems" theories offer more complex, explanatory accounts of the pressures and strategic interests that shape national responses to refugee flows. They tend to focus on international politics such as sending- and receiving-country relations (economic, political, historical) and foreign policy aims shaping the strategic formation of national refugee policy. Zolberg, Suhrke, and Aguayo (1989) and Hathaway (1991b) remind us that asylum seekers play a fundamental role in alerting the international community to the occurrence of human rights abuses by what Hathaway refers to as "voting with their feet." But migration scholars have given little attention to political processes underlying policy struggles among domestic constituencies (see Baubock 1998), and these are further limited to citizens and established residents, overlooking the role of asylum seekers themselves. These invisible actors in refugee policy change are perceived largely as a "forced" actors, leaving the political nature of the asylum-seeking and claim-making process untheorized. This is surprising given the institutional logic of the asylum-seeking process, which requires asylum seekers to make claims often in adversarial judicial settings and to prove the "well-foundedness" of their fear of persecution within national and international legal parameters. National refugee policy pivots fundamentally on a complex set of national and international rights, values, and interests, which must be negotiated and can be challenged, though not all challenges will be successful. It depends fundamentally therefore not only on established institutions and laws, but upon the structural agency of actors working within them, of whom asylum seekers are prominent. From time to time, refugees make claims whose rejection triggers national debates, often with ideological underpinnings that potential host countries care less or more about, as we have seen over the years regarding whether specific groups should be granted refugee status. This includes so-called economic refugees of many nationalities and ethic groups seeking asylum in North America and Europe over the years; groups fleeing generalized situations of conflict (rather than individually targeted persecution as required under the 1951 Convention) as in the Sanctuary Movement involving Salvadoran asylum seekers in the United States in the 1980s, and in hunger strikes by Afghan refugees seeking asylum in countries such as Australia and Canada in the 1990s. The 1990s also saw new debates around individuals seeking asylum on claims that they were discriminated for being HIV positive, gay or lesbian, and of course the refugees of this study.

The institutional logic of the refugee system actually requires asylum seekers to draw on human rights, while at the same time inland asylum seekers can access an array of citizenship rights as they await decisions on their claims. Therefore the claim-making process itself, in which noncitizens are primary actors and national debates are sometimes triggered, makes refugee policy development fertile ground for some of the fundamental debates of our times. In this, debates about culturally specific versus universal rights and values are paramount and intensified by increasing intercultural and international interactions under globalization. A significant aspect of the asylum-seeking and refuge policy development process is therefore its role in the evolution of interstate responsibilities. While refugee regimes may expand and contract in the liberalness of their approach over time, the debates and political conflicts that asylum seeking can provoke sit at the frontiers of human rights. This underscores the significance of asylum seekers as *nonnational* local actors in host countries. Without acts of seeking asylum, refugee policy becomes irrelevant, and without untraditional or controversial claims being made, refugee policy would not need to expand. Like other nonnationals in host countries, the making of relevant policies pits state sovereignty and national values against emerging human rights norms and institutions. But more explicitly than other types of nonnationals, asylum seekers *inevitably* straddle international human rights and national citizenship institutions and norms. And the representative nature of their claim making in foreign national contexts, in which they are required to demonstrate belonging to a particular persecuted group, raises political conflicts between international human rights and culturally bound national rights.

Inland asylum seekers may extrapolate culturally relative rights of citizens in host countries to thicken the use of human rights principles in their cases. In practice, cultural relativism underpins interpretations of the universal standards upon which refugee policy is based. Refugee policy change raises moral and political debates in receiving countries regarding *which* culture, *which* country, and *which* rights will ultimately be used as touchstones for interpretations and applications of human rights. And asylum seekers can help determine the outcome of such debates. One useful way of looking at the conflict between universalism and cultural relativism in moral debates over whether or not to grant asylum is the right of individuals to choose which "universal cultural morality" they believe in. The right of a sovereign state to commit, condone, or ignore human rights violations should never be considered a culturally relative right in the international domain if violated individuals reject it. Asylum seekers make an expressly political choice by seeking membership in a foreign country, appealing to internationally accepted human rights standards, or to "nationally universal" moral underpinnings of citizenship rights in receiving countries, and lending external cultural legitimacy to them. Asylum seekers, as noncitizens, underscore the contestability of assignations made or upheld by states regarding who should enjoy what kind of human rights and in what places, justified by reference to different cultural and citizenship traditions. In an increasingly global society, it is unsurprising that some individuals and groups will question the inevitability of their social-political structural environment, even as others move more toward preserving it. It is also unsurprising that in an increasingly interconnected world, residents with nationally upheld citizenship rights would want to safeguard their rights as particular structural groups (women, ethnic minorities, children, gays and lesbians, etc.) on a world scale. When citizen and noncitizen constituencies join forces, a stronger case can be made for internationalizing national values and state responsibilities.

This was clearly portrayed in the case studied. Fundamental rights enjoyed by women in Canada were considered citizenship rights in practice and theory, but not human rights. Canada's judgment on the rights that women should be able to expect in other countries corresponded with existing citizenship rights in those countries, even if those rights were of a much lower standard. The question raised was why such judgment should not be made according to Canada's values. Why should some citizenship rights be considered human rights, while others are not? In Canada violence against women is considered not only physically and psychologically harmful to females, but also an obstacle to their full participation in society and thus a detriment to society as a whole and the equality of its members. Canada's commitment to ending violence against women is explicitly legitimated through citizenship discourses and rights. A federal government report on violence against women states: "These assaults on the person, dignity and rights of women as equal citizens undermine the values Canadians revere and upon which they are trying to build a tolerant, just and strong nation. It is the responsibility of every individual, institution and level of government to acknowledge the gravity of this problem and to work in partnership to prevent it and to improve society's response to the problem" (CACSW 1991:1). Canada has evolved an elaborate network of legislation and social programs enacted through the voluntary sector and eight government departments in order to prevent and eradicate violence against women, drawing on national social, civil, and political rights. Asylum seekers requested these same protections through the right to make refugee claims, facilitated by international human rights principles, Canadian refugee policy, as well as aliens' constitutional rights in Canada. Asylum seekers were also able to draw on individual rights as well as structural rights as women and as refugees, in different legal contexts.

The legal and moral force of asylum seekers' argument was bolstered by the inherent compatibility between Canadian citizenship rights pertaining to women's equality and safety from violence and more general human rights principles. Traditional applications of universal human rights could be merged with these more progressive, explicit, and already institutionalized Canadian citizenship rights. Here the use of citizenship and human rights is a two-way street. In refugee systems, the claim to citizenship rights is made by appeal to human rights, while the claim to human rights may be made by appeal to rights developed in a country's particular citizenship tradition.

These asylum seekers combined citizenship and human rights differently from migrants in postnational membership studies, and they had different aims. Asylum seekers clearly wanted Canadian citizenship rights, aiming to formalize their entry eligibility in order to gain the desired rights to protection from violence, and established citizenship rights were fundamental to their claims. Canada made institutionally viable a comprehensive refugee policy for women pivoting around human rights and later promoted the approach internationally. Canada's policy change, and policy changes that later occurred elsewhere, reified Canadian values and rights.

Asylum seekers were fundamental to these changes, largely driving the interaction between national and international rights. They participated in political processes in the host country before attaining citizenship or permanent resident status, and in some cases even after they were issued deportation notices and declared illegal. They helped enumerate new eligibility frameworks in refugee policy, actually shaping their own group rights to entry in institutional terms. Noncitizens' ability to make claims and raise key debates about international rights in national settings was the linchpin for the changes that occurred.

Migration theory must increasingly come to terms with the nature of "refugee" eligibility as a political and social construct. It is shaped not only by national interests and interstate relations, but also by increasingly deterritorialized relations between groups and states in a global system, within which are asylum seekers themselves. Consequently, national refugee policy making is a fertile area for contests between culturally specific and more universally defined rights and inevitably involves noncitizens.

The case studied does not suggest that all asylum seekers can or will influence national debates and refugee policy to such dramatic effects, nor does it describe the predominant means for such success. Asylum seekers here illustrate one of perhaps many ways the human rights–citizenship dialectic may be strategically used to shape state responsibilities toward more ideal rights, a broader membership base, and wider justification for "rights to rights." National policies are prone to new noncitizen-state relationships as new international influences emerge under globalization. Noncitizens can help shape expanded human rights protections by triggering debate and lending external cultural legitimacy to national values, as one illustration of new ways global influences impact what we think of as human rights and who is responsible for them. Noncitizens, whose numbers are quickly and dramatically increasing and whose capacities to participate in host country politics are apparently increasing, can put a cross-cultural check or endorsement on national debates about the potential universality of nationally envisioned rights and values.

Noncitizen influence is relevant not only in shaping substantive rights, but in shaping a human right to national membership—"rights to rights" (Arendt 1973). In advanced democratic countries the institutional logic of migration systems combined with changing opportunities to seek asylum may be enabling atypical claims that raise new debates and negotiate new boundaries. The combination of increasing global interdependency involving global-level rights of persons and concurrent unevenness in acceptance and enforcement of rights poses a new challenge for national welfare systems in particular. The irony is that while welfare states are under attack, they are also facing pressures to extend their responsibilities toward more transnational issues and beneficiaries and greater interstate cooperation (Deacon 1997).[29] Advanced welfare states offer implementation mechanisms for social, cultural, and economic rights that are as yet poorly addressed at the international level of human rights, which instead tend to prioritize civil and political rights. Similarly, while national refugee regimes are becoming increasingly restrictive in many important respects, some are also broadening their coverage as new types of claims emerge, as in the case of gender-related refugees.

New Vistas for Human Rights Research

Human rights scholarship must be more attentive to new pressures upon the limits of human rights. As much as the globalization of human rights norms may impact upon states by extending the reach of human rights into national territories, globalization also brings new pressures and opportunities for states to project their own national values globally, facilitating an expansion of national rights and values into international human rights agendas. Fundamental to this process is the fact that citizenship's experimentations in different countries can enable internationally novel conceptions and practices of rights to develop. Transformations of political community are thus occurring on a two-way street; globalization invites us to consider new conceptualizations of citizenship *and* human rights and may be providing new tools for them to be played off one another in a symbiotic rather than hierarchical relationship.

This study contrasts with the dominant focus on decline of citizenship and state sovereignty in human rights scholarship, instead underlining their criticality for the continuing evolution of international human rights. Further research is needed that avoids either polarizing citizenship and human rights, or subsuming one in the other, keeping an eye on the problem of distinguishing between formal status and substantive rights. Such an approach concentrates on citizenship and human rights as mutually reinforcing ideals with distinct though interdependent institutionalizing vehicles. This is important because, as Donnelly (2003) so clearly articulated, human rights are most valuable precisely when one does not have them. In countries like Canada where women enjoyed powerful rights upheld through citizenship, there was no pressing need for a struggle to achieve recognition of women's rights as human rights. In asylum seekers' countries of origin, on the other hand, there was inadequate room for national struggle by women to attain higher citizenship rights, not to mention human rights. Canada offered crucial political space in which foreign nationals could pressure for the projection of host-country values onto the human rights agenda. The presence of these two powerful legitimating forces—citizenship and human rights—was essential to expand human rights and state responsibilities toward noncitizens.

Human rights scholarship also needs to further explore how individuals and groups actually drive such developments through the new opportunities for political agency that globalization affords. The interaction and expansion in the case studied would not have occurred without noncitizens' agency. Asylum seekers brought nationally specific citizenship discourses and rights regarding females face-to-face with human rights, strategically drawing on the most helpful established elements within each tradition and attracting substantial popular support that no doubt was fundamental to their success. As one emerging pressure on the limits of human rights, noncitizen politics heralds a very important source of legitimacy for nationally and culturally specific values. Noncitizen politics can force a negotiation of international and domestic standards and help to develop new norms. In particular, noncitizens can add a crucial layer of *external* support that helps to select those national values that may be more worthy of internationalization. Noncitizen politics therefore offers a new avenue for exploration in human rights studies, and as international migration intensifies under globalization, it may well become increasingly important. How are differences and similarities between international and national rights and values negotiated by noncitizens in other cases? What enables noncitizens to negotiate these rights? How are existing citizenship rights and values affected? How are existing human rights norms affected?

The case studied suggests that new and developing patterns of interaction that globalization encourages offer new infrastructures for agency and action that further drive globalization and reshape national and international actions. Asylum seekers' grassroots social change occurs within institutionalized cultural contexts that lend legitimacy and opportunity to individual and collective actions (Meyer 1994; Powell and DiMaggio 1991), and which are marked by increasing interaction between national and world-level institutionalized cultural rules and norms, as part of the process of globalization.[30] It may also be described as furthering this interaction. The developing dynamic provides legitimacy and mobilizing vehicles for individual political action within an increasingly transnational community. While national and transnational institutional frameworks are mutually reinforcing in some respects, the conflicts and contradictions between them also make the political actorhood of noncitizens viable and subsequently exert new pressures for states to expand their social responsibilities. This emerges regarding the conflicts between the citizenship and human rights of particular groups such as women. Women's rights are powerfully supported in many national and international legal codes and enjoy widespread and diverse support by many different publics, even compared to many other social rights. But in the case studied *both* the stronghold and pervasiveness of ideas about women's rights and their continuing unevenness in substance, implementation, dispersion, and rate of development across the world, were driving forces, as with many issues affected by globalization today (see Held and McGrew 2003).

The complexity of the unfolding dialectic between citizenship and human rights suggests we need to more closely engage with broader consequences of globalization. We must consider different citizenship–human rights dynamics developing under globalization to account more explicitly for substantive human rights expansions. Of course, the projection of national rights onto the international human rights agenda can also move in a more exclusive direction, an effect fraught with as much danger as inward-looking cultural relativist approaches that deny universal validity altogether. Realists and positivists have long regarded states as the central influence on human rights, and even some human rights universalists see state influence on the human rights agenda in negative terms. But we must also be alert to positive outcomes and the changing paths of influence as globalization opens new avenues for national political debate, for new actors to take part in or even drive such debates, and for states to project their visions internationally. Through national struggles, states generate models of rights from which the international community can draw to formulate and elaborate global standards. Indeed, non-Western countries today are asserting cultural rights perceived to have been sidelined when key human rights instruments were developed under the influence of more powerful Western states. For instance, collective or group rights advanced by developing countries with deeply entrenched collective values long seen by human rights scholars as antithetical to individual rights are gaining ground. This is occurring not by undermining the individual basis of human rights, but by incorporating individual rights to membership in a group (Donnelly 2003). At the same time, Western countries such as the United States continue to go their own way when their perceived needs conflict with international norms. In both cases, states no longer contest the notion of human rights, rather they argue that their nationally specific choices are more enlightened than current human rights formulations and ought to be part of the human rights agenda. They attempt to assert their legitimacy within human rights. From an optimistic viewpoint, deeply entrenched citizenship rights that are truly broader or deeper than existing human rights norms may trigger reflection and debate about the proper scope of human rights and may themselves even be refined to take on more universal aspects in originator states.

This evolution of human rights under globalization has implications for theories of human rights standard setting, which need to be further developed and refined. Legal analyses of intergovernmental negotiations during treaty drafting and adoption have largely ignored the creation of knowledge about what rights ought to be considered universal. And philosophical analyses of the substance of human rights prescribe but do not offer empirical studies of political processes that actually shape moral debates into legal outcomes. Political analyses in the "norm emergence" literature need more and better empirical studies rather than relying on those that essentially entail human rights implementation. If human rights are envisioned and shaped through historically contingent political processes, theories of human rights change need to account for the more diverse ways that human rights can and should continue to evolve. In particular, they should engage with variations in national rights as the petri dish of rights experimentation. The case studied here reaffirms the importance of national variation in rights that emerges from cultural differences. New human rights, such as right to protection from sex-based violence, are made viable through processes including the use of national rights to lend legitimacy to proposed international values. Theories of human rights standard setting need to better understand political processes through which nation-states frame their national values as internationally relevant norms to support expansions in the substance of human rights, involving multiple actors who negotiate different rights. They therefore also need to account for greater variation among actors. As human rights have gained international legitimacy and the public has become more educated about them, national processes may increasingly occur on a broad grassroots basis, moving away from the more top-down "dictatorship of the enlightened" that could be said to have dominated human rights developments during the first critical years of human rights in the 1940s and 1950s.

While the vigorous drive among human rights supporters to promote human rights as "universal" and morally superior may be important for growing the legitimacy of human rights worldwide, a more flexible understanding of human rights is essential in order to ensure continuing human rights expansions. The first challenge is to enable flexibility while guarding against regressive interpretations of human rights that undo progress made so far. The second challenge is the need for more open dialogues among states regarding their often very different and culturally rooted national rights traditions as essential for the continuing evolution of human rights; indeed, many of the world's most controversial debates about cultural relativism still need to be closely considered. The third challenge is to develop mechanisms for such dialogues to take place on a more balanced playing field between states and cultures that have historically wielded very different power in the world community, putting prescriptive approaches in political philosophy to the test. To find the means of addressing these challenges, we need a wider variety of empirical studies at both intergovernmental and national levels.

The political process studied in this book supports the view that human rights expansions depend precisely upon strong sovereign states with the political clout to advance new human rights formulations, particularly those with cultural legitimacy in the eyes of the most powerful Western states. For non-Western states with different cultural traditions, this poses a serious problem. For Western states, the risk lay in an unknown future when new power balances develop. Without effective and democratic global governance or other mechanisms to level the playing field and thereby ensure real global dialogue, human rights challenges in the future could take either positive or negative turns. As one defense mechanism, states ought to take noncitizen politics more seriously, for in a sense each nation faces a world of noncitizens outside its borders, not to mention a growing population of noncitizen residents within, emboldened by international and national rights and enabled by globalization. This is becoming increasingly apparent in new global movements such as the antiglobalization and global justice movements and in the national public protests by noncitizens in Europe and the United States (as in 2006). This study of asylum seekers' compelling human rights expansions in foreign states marks a step toward better understanding the theoretical and policy implications of noncitizen politics upon the evolution of human rights and state responsibilities. Noncitizens constitute an important moral resource keenly available to host countries.

Refugee movement is of course far from an ideal way of universalizing either citizenship or human rights, since refugees are always a product of structural persecution that should ideally be prevented from occurring in the first place. Asylum seekers cannot *easily* influence policy, nor should policy respond immediately to reflect all claims. Indeed, rising panic about the unmanageability of international migration, and refugee flows in particular, has brought worldwide tightening of border controls and increased controversies about "illegitimate" and "illegal" international migrants. Rather, this book has explored the political processes in an internationally significant case with implications for human rights, under the recognition that there are now and will likely always be refugees fleeing injustice and persecution. This reveals asylum seekers' use of changing dynamics between citizenship and human rights to justify national membership, with subsequent influence upon refugee policies and human rights. The study also suggests that listening better to asylum seekers can create a fairer refugee system without compromising the rigor of selection systems. International protection eligibility criteria can be negotiated to more accurately reflect the wide range of social injustice that exists in the world, while narrowing in on those most in need within each category. Listening to noncitizens can also open up new vistas for those trying to understand the current transformations and future potential of a more truly global responsibility for human welfare and human rights.

Appendix: Comprehensive and Novel Aspects of Gender-Related Claims

I. Perpetrator relation, location, status
   A. Relation to claimant
      1. Member of immediate "social world" of claimant (especially family, community)
      2. "Outside" immediate social world of claimant
   B. Location at time of victim's claim
      1. Receiving country (principle applicant, spouse/dependent, or none)
      2. Sending country (as in traditional refugee claims)
   C. Status
      1. Public official (government, military, law or enforcement)
      2. Kinship or close connection with public officials
      3. State or religious sanctioned status and behavior of males toward females generally
      4. Unofficially condoned (customary state, religious, cultural practices) status and behavior of males toward females
II. Claimants with children
   A. Status and protection issues
      1. Children born in country of origin
         a) Custody issues in country of origin under religious or customary law
         b) Custody issues due to father's position of authority in country of origin
      2. Children born in receiving country
         a) Custody issues in country of origin (above) that endanger children if deported with mother
         b) Custody issues in receiving country that may endanger children if mother is deported
   B. Rights issues
      1. Child's right to nationality versus right to have a mother

    2. Claimant's right to motherhood and family

   C. Evidence in children's case affecting mother's claim

     1. Evidence of child abuse

     2. Having children as an infraction of the law or social code

     3. Responsibility for protection of children adding weight to the mother's claim

III. Claimant activism

   A. Defiance of cultural, religious, and/or state sanctioned norms regarding social roles and behaviors

   B. Adherence to cultural, religious, and/or state sanctioned norms that are inherently discriminatory and persecutory; in some cases claimants have been prevented, under threat of persecution, from defying or seeking internal protection from cultural, religious, and/or state sanctioned norms

   C. Familial relation to political activist, resulting in political opinions being imputed to the claimant

IV. State role in persecution

   A. Active enforcement of government legislation that severely discriminates against females and/or imposes severe sanctions for transgressions of these laws

   B. Government legislation or unofficial cultural codes (as above) not actively or regularly enforced by the government but by family and community in the context of lack of state protection

   C. State unwillingness or inability to enforce existing legislation that bans or provides protection from social practices harmful to females

   D. Existing legislation that bans or provides protection from social practices harmful to females is insufficient even if fully implemented

V. Gender-inclusive and sex-specific structural causes of persecution

   A. Women persecuted *as women* and/or *in a manner specific to women*, by members of their own race, religion, nationality, political opinion, or social group, as part of traditional practices and repressing women as a group

   B. Women persecuted *as women* and/or in a *manner specific to women*, by nonmembers of their own race, religion, nationality, political opinion, or social group, as part of intergroup tensions and as a way to harm the larger group

Source: Analysis of RefLex cases, 1993–1996. See Chapter 6 for a discussion.

Notes

Chapter 1. Introduction: The Sex Persecution Campaigns

Note to epigraphs: Thérèse, refugee claimant and board member of Refugee Action Montreal (RAM). Interview, Montreal, 19 July 1995. Nada, cited in the *Ottawa Citizen*, 11 March 1993. Randy Gordan, assistant to the immigration minister, letter to the ICHRDD, 7 September 1992. Bernard Valcourt, immigration minister, cited in *London Free Press*, 16 January 1993.

1. See, for example, research cited by the University of California at Hastings project on gender persecution, http://sierra.uchastings.edu/cgrs/law/articles.html (at February 2008), and the 2005 UNHCR bibliography on refugee women.

2. Exceptions are limited to descriptive paragraphs on political process in Macklin (1999), Kuttner (1997), and Gilad (1999), and a policy paper by Young (1994), which analyzes an asylum claim from the campaign period studied. Summary accounts of legal developments in this area are generally positivist, nationally focused, and short-term, concerned neither with explaining developments nor how entrenched gender bias in human rights was overcome. In a 1994 speech, Janet Dench, executive director, CCR, observed refugee women's importance to policy changes that occurred but was not concerned with explaining their participation or resulting human rights expansions. I was grateful for the opportunity to interview Dench and Young along with other key actors, whose personal experience and insights were invaluable to this study.

3. These are examined in Chapter 3.

4. IRB chairperson's memorandum, "Procedures for the Guideline-Making Process s.65(3) and (4) of the Immigration Act." IRB guidelines were given statutory basis in Canada when amendments to the Immigration Act came into force on 1 February 1993.

5. Ireland, Refugee Act, 1996; South Africa, Refugees Act, 1998. See Chapter 7 for an analysis of legislation and policy in other countries and regions.

6. Known cases emerged earlier in Canada and other countries but did not gain public visibility or attain the critical mass or influence of the movement studied here. See DeNeef (1984) and Kelson (1997).

7. International refugee law is considered part of the corpus of broader international human rights law.

8. Later chapters document policy attitudes on this issue and public and

governmental recognition of movement actors and organizations in driving the policy change.

9. Randy Gordan, assistant to the immigration minister, letter to the ICHRDD, 7 September 1992; Bernard Valcourt, immigration minister, cited in *London Free Press*, 16 January 1993.

10. Government statements cited in *Ottawa Citizen*, 25 January 1993.

11. See Chapter 7 for details.

12. In Canada this included new preflight visa requirements, higher fees, and a new, increasingly complicated bureaucratic refugee processing system, as Chapter 4 describes.

13. Among the most influential early works were by Charlesworth, Chinkin, and Wright (1991), on gender bias in international treaties, and Cook (1994), on violence against women as a human rights violation.

14. Marie-Louise Côté, refugee lawyer, quoted in *Montreal Gazette*, 17 November 1994.

15. Such attention to the neglected national level has been described as a major gap in the study of international relations.

16. Randy Gordan, interview, *NOW* magazine (Toronto: NOW Communications), 1992.

17. Again, here I refer to domestic human rights developments that explicitly transcend international human rights law (e.g., women's rights as human rights) and not to domestic rights developments that do not explicitly engage with international human rights even though they may set examples that later influence human rights.

18. What some have called "third-wave" feminism covering the period in this book is described as an expansion of feminist space for women not descended from Europeans, East Asians, Arabs, or Jews, and is focused on rallying young feminists. Its roots are in the mid-1980s with feminist leaders from the second wave including women of color, who called for a new race-related subjectivity in feminist voice.

19. Benhabib discusses the thickening of citizenship through international cosmopolitan principles, but underscores the "fraying of state sovereignty" and argues for new international forms of political membership through cosmopolitan federalism that reflects the moral universalism of human rights.

20. The concept of transnational signifying acts that I use here builds on McAdam's (1996) concept of "signifying acts," the latter not being explicitly international in nature.

Chapter 2. Human Rights, Social Movement, and Asylum Seeking

1. Work specifically on the "globalization" of human rights differs from the larger, more diverse body of work on the "internationalization" of human rights.

2. The principle corollaries of states' sovereignty comprise: (1) a jurisdiction, prima facie exclusive, over a territory and the permanent population living there; (2) a duty of nonintervention in the area of exclusive jurisdiction of other states; and (3) the de-

pendence of obligations arising from customary law and treaties on the consent of the obligor (Brownlie 1990:287).

3. Donnelly argues these claims are based on historically inaccurate definitions of state sovereignty ("control" versus "authority") and are therefore overblown. Rather, state sovereignty may be transformed by, but not necessarily clash with, international human rights. He is not concerned with how states are compelled to respect human rights, but implications of such pressures on states.

4. Krasner (1999b) argues that Westphalian sovereignty "can be compromised through invitation as well as intervention." The latter is obvious and well understood, whereas "Invitation occurs when a ruler voluntarily compromises the domestic autonomy of his or her own polity. . . . Regardless of the motivation or the perspicacity of rulers, invitations violate Westphalian sovereignty by subjecting internal authority structures to external constraints." He also argues that modern violations of sovereignty are not new because sovereignty has never "been a stable equilibrium from which rulers had no incentives to deviate." Rather, the "Westphalian" brand of state sovereignty has historically always been undermined (Krasner 1999b in Steiner and Alston 2000:576, 577).

5. Moral and political philosophies in human rights scholarship may suggest or envision relevant mechanisms, but they do not analyze actual political processes.

6. The Western tradition of natural rights is widely believed to have laid key foundations for human rights; see Donnelly 2003.

7. These are typically more comparative in nature than global.

8. In contrast, policy-making models tend to offer highly structural and institutional accounts of the policy-change process without closely examining the dynamics of the conflict between actors (Ham and Hill 1984, 1997). They tend to neglect important factors in the *generative* stage of policy conflicts, such as the identification of grievances as structural (versus individual) by potential actors, the formation of collective identities around grievances, the development and use of appropriate ideologies, and the actual mobilization of actors into a collectivity, which social movement theory identifies. They do not consider noncitizens as policy actors.

9. Mansbach and Vasquez (1981) added a "co-operation" dimension between states, which can also facilitate refugee policy development. Hastedt and Knickrehm (1984) observed that receiving-state response patterns typically correspond with their stances toward particular "issue areas." Refugee flows raise central issues within the context of preexisting interstate relations, such as ex-colonial relationships or populations with common or divergent bonds or ideologies, which may facilitate or constrain policy decisions around particular groups of refugees characterized.

10. Zolberg, Suhrke, and Aguayo (1989) propose that to address refugee problems, greater emphasis must be placed on the role of external parties and regional peace systems in addition to conflict reducing institutional reforms.

11. This should not be confused with studies of settled immigrant communities' impact on national and local politics.

12. See Olson (1965) on "selective" and "solidary" incentives, which help explain the free-rider problem in social movement participation.

13. "International refugee law" applies to refugee-related conventions and treaties

and the human rights standards to which they conform. The standard for treaties and state policy is the UN 1951 Geneva Convention Relating to the Status of Refugees and the 1967 New York Protocol.

14. On lack of documentary evidence for women refugees, see Martin-Forbes (1992) and OLAP (1994). Canada's 1993 Guidelines note problematic evidentiary matters including the "particularized evidence rule," lack of "statistical data on the incidence of sexual violence in the country of origin," indirect state involvement in persecution by failing to protect, and special problems facing women at status determinations, that is, cultural barriers in disclosing sexual violence (8–9).

15. Incentives and abilities to migrate have been mainly explored among immigrants on the micro level through social networks linking them to established migrant communities in receiving countries (see Price 1963; Boyd 1989). Migration cycles across generations of families are said to link international migrants of various types—refugees may be followed by extended family members as immigrants.

16. Also relevant, Jenkins-Smith and Sabatier (1994) explain that policies can be mapped on the same canvas as "belief systems" and that policy actors cohere in coalitions for policy change through a "hierarchy of policy values" from deep level beliefs to preferred policy instruments and aims.

17. Yin describes "the distinctive need for case studies" arising out of "the desire to understand complex social phenomena. In brief, the case study allows an investigation to retain the holistic and meaningful characteristics of real-life events" (1994:3). The analytical framework for this study was indeed generated through an iterative relationship with the empirical work. In this process of explanation building, an initial proposition is compared to findings of case studies and revised (Yin 1994).

18. See bibliography of interviews cited. Interviews were conducted at each core organization with the exception of the Canadian division of Amnesty International, which took a more marginal role in orchestrating campaigns, although providing an important source of legitimacy for the campaigns. Several lawyers were unavailable or could not be located but the majority was interviewed (six lawyers who handled thirteen of twenty cases that went public).

19. See media sources in bibliography. Use of media sources was not intended to compare coverage.

20. I am particularly grateful to Nancy Dory from the IRB Montreal Division; the Montreal IRB Documentation Centre archivists; Valerie Woods, a regional coordinator of RefLex; and Sarah Morgan, who responded to my queries through the Access to Information Act.

Chapter 3. Global Challenges and Opportunites for Sex-Based Asylum Seeking

1. This approach is used in Canada; see IRB Preferred Position Paper 1992; and OLAP REF6-1, 1994:4.

2. Violence against women subsequently became a serious social policy concern in many countries, where domestic responsibility ideally consists of prevention, protec-

tion, and prosecution. These policy aims are built upon state obligations to promote the well-being and full integration of all members of society; and upon the idea that violence against females is a "public" matter for communities and the state as a product and promoter of women's sociopolitical inequality (Status of Women Canada 1991).

3. This was upheld in the UN Draft Code of State Responsibility, which asserts that acts by individuals or a group not acting on behalf of the state are not considered acts of the state; see Romany 1993:111.

4. The UN Declaration on the Elimination of Violence Against Women was adopted in 1993, but has not yet reached convention status.

5. Celina Romany describes women as "the paradigmatic alien subjects of international law. To be an alien is to be an *other*, and *outsider*. Women are *aliens* within their states and *aliens* within an exclusive international club of states which constitutes international society" (1993:87).

6. OLAP 1994, case study cited by Australia Law Reform Commission, NSW, Submission 588 (69).

7. Flora Liebich, IRB member and chairperson of the Working Group on Women Refugee Claimants in Canada, explains that in Canada adjudication looks to both Canadian case law and to international human rights instruments for guidance in determining what constitutes persecution (1993).

8. Sponsorship abuse is a particular concern for "foreign domestics" (domestic servants) who are contractually bound to employers for a number of years before they can acquire permanent residence. Women's shelters have been key in revealing sponsorship abuse since the late 1980s. In 1990 a report was produced on needs and services for battered immigrant and refugee women, based on a survey and consultations with women's shelters across Canada.

9. In Canada, this gained some recognition in the late 1980s when the IRB formed an internal Working Group on Women Refugee Claimants. Members produced reports on specific needs of refugee women in hearing room processes due to gender cultural barriers. They showed that by allowing male heads of families to speak for females, the refugee determination system reflects the assumption that women are dependents and do not have claims of their own (Leibich 1987).

10. Marie-Louise Côté, refugee lawyer, interview, Montreal, 13 January 1995.

11. Instruments targeting the claim-making process for women generally would include official recognition of need for sensitivity (cultural and gender) to barriers in the hearing room that may hinder female refugees from presenting convincing claims; appropriate theoretical frameworks by which adjudicators may decide claims; relevant documentation pertaining to country-specific conditions as well as individual experiences as evidence; and a support structure in the receiving country to promote the interests of women refugees and help them make claims.

12. I draw on primary documents in a comprehensive historical analysis, complemented by secondary sources. For analysis of jurisprudence in the Canadian context specifically I draw on IRB documentation and interviews with refugee lawyers.

13. The fall in numbers of refugees, to the lowest level in almost a quarter century, is attributed to the end of some major conflicts, the repatriation of major populations

and increasing restrictions on refugee movement (GCIM 2005). The rise in number of people "of concern" to UNHCR reflects differing patterns of movement among refugees, civilians who have repatriated but still need help, internally displaced persons (IDPs), asylum seekers, and stateless people. There were large increases in the number of IDPs and stateless persons.

14. A particular focus of study has been female migrants' roles in low and unpaid labor in ethnic small businesses, and in family and education for "reproducing and maintaining ethnic languages and cultures and resisting racism" in receiving countries, thus strengthening ethnic communities and furthering the migratory cycle (Castles and Miller 1993:8 and 32; see also Phizacklea 1983).

15. See Oakley (2000) on gender methodologies and typologies.

16. These have been particularly well documented by Martin-Forbes (1992).

17. European Parliament, Resolution on the Application of the 1951 UN Convention Relating to the Status of Refugees, report by the Ministry of Social Affairs and Labour 1984, see p. 64–64.

18. See Advisory Committee on Human Rights and Foreign Policy (1987) for opinions of Dutch members supporting a social group interpretation, and objections of dissenting states.

19. See Advisory Committee on Human Rights and Foreign Policy (1987), Appendix 1.

20. Adjudicators maintain discretion as to how detailed their report will be, but generally negative decisions receive lengthy reports, and positive decisions do not.

Chapter 4. Moving In

1. Edelman (1971) refers to signs and signals that the establishment may be vulnerable to influence, and the timely convergence of ideas and opportunities for their transformation into strategies, as "social cueings." Similarly, McAdam (1982) describes social cueings in relation to expanding political opportunities for potential actors' mobilization.

2. Section 95, British North America Act, now the Constitution Act, 1867.

3. NGO participation in immigration consultations is regarded both as significant to democratic processes of policy making and as an effective mechanism for government to manage opposition, providing a forum for NGO cooperation without actual decision-making power.

4. This contrasts markedly with the experience of the United States and Australia, which early on boasted large associations as coordinating bodies and forums for exchanging ideas and information for voluntary activity with good working relationships with government (Hawkins 1972:304).

5. During the period studied, three years of residence was required to apply for Canadian citizenship.

6. For analysis of the women's movement to include gender provisions in the Cana-

dian Charter of Rights and Freedoms, see Naomi Black, "Ripples in the Second Wave," in Backhouse and Flaherty (1993).

7. Sylvie Piriou, refugee lawyer, interview, Montreal, 30 October 1996.

8. Barbara Jackman, president, Ontario Lawyer Association, and refugee lawyer, interview, Toronto, 22 November 1994.

9. Described in the previous chapter, these were *Shahabaldin v. MEI* (1987) and *Incirciyan v. MEI* (1987).

10. On restrictive aspects of Bills C-84 and C-86, see Dirks (1995); on Bill C-55 see Young (1997).

11. Rivka Augenfeld, president, Table de Concertation des Organismes de Montreal au Service des Personnes Réfugiées et Immigrantes (TCMR), interview, Montreal, 22 August 1995.

12. Ibid.

13. Ibid.

14. Ibid.

15. With the exception of Amnesty International, whose development followed international trends. Characteristics and development of campaign organizations are described in annual reports (ICHRDD 1994; TCMR 1995), special reports, and unpublished organizational documents (RAM, CCR, Flora Tristan), and interviews with representatives of the organizations. For detailed historical and organizational overviews of NAC, see Vickers, Rankin, and Appelle (1993); for other organizations, see Schreader (1990) and Agnew (1996).

16. Flora Fernandez, NAC Executive Committee, Violence Against Women Unit, Women's Aid director, member, NOIVMW of Canada, interview, Montreal, 24 August 1995.

Chapter 5. *"Use My Name"*

Note to epigraph: Thérèse, refugee claimant and board member of Refugee Action Montreal (RAM), interview, Montreal, 19 July 1995.

1. I draw on detailed asylum seeker case histories and in-depth interviews with supporters and claimants.

2. Inconsistency of outcomes was due in part, at the time, to (1) technical and administrative difficulties due to cases having begun before the Guidelines were instated, and (2) cases being forerunners of certain interpretations of cases, both before and after instatement of the Guidelines.

3. Flora Fernandez, interview, Montreal, 24 August 1995; *Montreal Gazette*, 30 November 1992.

4. The confidentiality of claimants was protected in this study. See Chapter 2 on methodology.

5. Thérèse, interview, Montreal, 19 July 1995.

6. Ibid.

7. Ibid.

8. See the insightful analysis of Nada's claim in the policy paper by Young (1994), which includes an informal translation of the refugee hearing.

9. Diana Bronson, information officer, ICHRDD, interview, Montreal, 25 January 1995.

10. Ibid.

11. See the *Montreal Gazette*, November 1992.

12. See also Paul (1992:15) and the discussion in Chapter 3.

13. NAC press packet, February 1993; and Fernandez, interview, Montreal, 24 August 1995.

14. NAC press packet, February 1993.

15. Fernandez, interview, Montreal, 24 August 1995.

16. Thérèse, interview, Montreal, 19 July 1995.

17. Ginette, cited in Norris, *Montreal Gazette*, 7 December 1994.

18. Bronson, interview, Montreal, 25 January 1995.

19. See Chapter 2 for a list of all countries and claimants in this study.

20. Thérèse, interview, Montreal, 19 July 1995.

21. Social movement literature discusses these processes in the formation of collective identity for movement development and mobilization. Whether before or through contact with other actors or potential actors, the politicization of identity and aims must eventually occur.

22. Claims made public were not the first involving sex persecution to be accepted, contrary to portrayals in many media reports. However they received inconsistent treatment, perhaps inciting public campaigning. See Chapter 3.

23. Ginette, quoted in Wilton, *Montreal Gazette*, 6 December 1994.

24. Tamarati, quoted in Norris, *Montreal Gazette*, 10 February 1995.

25. Dulerie, quoted in Wilkes, *Montreal Gazette*, 23 September 1992.

26. Basdaye, quoted in the *Montreal Gazette*, 11 February 1993.

27. "Lee," court statement quoted in *Toronto Star*, 11 November 1992.

28. Miranda, quoted in *Toronto Star*, 11 February 1993.

29. Sylvie Piriou, refugee lawyer, interview, Montreal, 30 October 1996.

30. Thérèse, interview, Montreal, 19 July 1995.

31. Ibid.

32. Ibid; Bronson, interview, Montreal, 25 January 1995.

33. Thérèse, interview, Montreal, 19 July 1995.

34. Glynis Williams, coordinator, Refugee Action Montreal (RAM), interview, Montreal, 28 July 1995.

35. Bronson, interview, Montreal, 25 January 1995.

36. Ibid.

37. Rivka Augenfeld, president, Table de Concertation des Organismes de Montreal au Service des Personnes Réfugiées et Immigrantes (TCMR), interview, Montreal, 22 August 1995.

38. Diane Belanger, refugee lawyer, cited in Wilton, *Montreal Gazette*, 6 December 1994.

39. Anonymous refugee lawyer, interview, Montreal, 1995.

40. Anonymous women's shelter informant, interview, 1995.

41. Anonymous NGO informant, interview, 1995.

42. Ibid.

43. The social movement literature describes factors such as ideological support (or predisposition), previous organizational support, and past participation or previous experiences (personal and work) contributing to the "mobilization potential" of potential actors. See Kriesi (1992).

44. Augenfeld, interview, Montreal, 22 August 1995.

45. Bronson, interview, Montreal, 25 January 1995.

46. Ibid.

47. Ibid.

48. Fernandez, interview, Montreal, 24 August 1995.

49. Ibid.

50. Ibid.

51. Augenfeld, interview, Montreal, 22 August 1995.

52. Elizabeth Montecino, director, Flora Tristan (Montreal shelter for immigrant women), interview, Montreal, 31 January 1995.

53. Fernandez, interview, Montreal, 24 August 1995.

54. For example, author's questionnaire (1996) respondents: Nellies Hostel; Harmony House; Maison d'Amite (5 percent yearly increase, 1993 to 1995).

55. Montecino, interview, Montreal, 31 January 1995.

56. Williams, interview, Montreal, 28 July 1995.

57. Ibid.

58. Marie-Louise Côté, refugee lawyer, interview, Montreal, 13 January 1995.

59. Ibid.

60. Diane Belanger, refugee lawyer, interview, Montreal, 11 July 1995.

Chapter 6. Universalizing National Rights

1. I draw on interview data, institutional campaign documents (annual reports, correspondence, memos, and other documentation), and documentary evidence from mass media.

2. Nancy Doray, adjudicator, member of the IRB Working Group on Women Refugee Claimants, interview, Montreal, 30 January 1995.

3. McAdam uses the term "revolutionary" rather than "radical" goals. I use the latter to steer clear of narrow readings of revolutionary. McAdam distinguishes between revolutionary and reform goals "depending on whether or not they require a major redistribution of wealth and/or power," and observes that, "the emphasis . . . on a *democratic context*, cannot be understated. Given the very different legitimating philosophy that underlies nondemocratic systems, the interaction between movements and other sets of actors is expected to conform to very different dynamics than those evident within ostensibly democratic systems" (1996:341).

4. This differs from the "radical flank effect" (Haines 1988) although it shares cer-

tain commonalities. The RFE explains benefits of movement fragmentation for more moderate groups. McAdam explains, "a movement stands to benefit when there is a wide ideological spectrum among its adherents . . . The existence of radicals makes moderate groups in the movement more attractive negotiating partners to the movement opponents. Radicalness provides strong incentives to the state to get to the bargaining table with the moderates in order to avoid dealing with the radicals. In addition, financial support flowing to moderate groups in the movement increases dramatically in the presence of radicals" (McAdam 1992). In the case studied, the movement was not fragmented; rather, as a group, members strategically shifted goals and tactics over time. Also on the RFE, see McAdam, McCarthy, and Zald (1996); Tarrow (1998); McAdam et al. (2001).

5. This recommendation in turn was based on a 1985 Dutch Refugee Council directive. See Chapter 3 for a genealogy of soft law in this area.

6. Maison Flora Tristan 1991; *Journal de Montreal* 2 May 1991.

7. Institutional documents, NOIVMW, Report 18.

8. Janet Dench, executive director, CCR, interview, Montreal, 20 December 1994.

9. Randy Gordan, assistant to the Canadian immigration minister, letter to CCR president David Matas, 8 July 1992.

10. Particularly the IRB Working Group on Refugee Women. The CACSW and the QCCI (Provincial immigration) had also produced reports on sponsorship problems since the late 1980s.

11. Cited in *Toronto Star*, 17 September 1992.

12. Bronson, interview, Montreal, 25 January 1995.

13. Edward Broadbent, ICHRDD president, in a letter to Immigration Minister Bernard Valcourt, 19 August 1992.

14. Bronson, ICHRDD presentation to the CCR, 12 May 1993.

15. Including both major and minor case histories of those who went public, and excluding three claimants with whom campaigners worked to attain appeals but who did not go public, as well as two claimants who only went public at the earlier generative stage. See Chapter 2 describing the twenty-six asylum seekers in this study and Chapter 4 describing when claimants went public.

16. See Chapter 4 for discussion of the political climate at the time, including controversial aspects of bills first introduced in the 1980s.

17. Bronson, interview, Montreal, 25 January 1995.

18. Cited in *Toronto Star*, 23 September 1992.

19. Bronson, interview, 25 January 1995.

20. *Montreal Gazette*, 11 November 1992.

21. Cited in *Montreal Gazette*, 11 November 1992.

22. The Canadian Broadcast Corporation wrote: "For 45 minutes on Dec. 6, 1989 an enraged gunman roamed the corridors of Montreal's École Polytechnique and killed 14 women. Marc Lepine, 25, separated the men from the women and before opening fire on the classroom of female engineering students he screamed, 'I hate feminists.' Almost immediately, the Montreal Massacre became a galvanizing moment in which mourning turned into outrage about all violence against women." Police found Lepine's written confession in which he railed against females and had drawn up a list of

women whom he hoped to kill, including his mother. CBC Digital Archive, "The Montreal Massacre."

23. Bronson, interview, Montreal, 25 January 1995.

24. Marie-Louise Côté, interview, Montreal, 13 January 1995.

25. Branson, interview, Montreal, 25 January 1995.

26. Janet Dench, executive cirector, Canadian Council for Refugees (CCR), speech to Boston College Law School, 1994.

27. Dench, interview, Montreal, 20 December 1994.

28. Bronson, interview, Montreal, 25 January 1995.

29. Dench, speech to Boston College Law School, 1994.

30. Ibid.

31. Ibid.

32. Bronson, interview, Montreal, 25 January 1995.

33. Côté, interview, Montreal, 13 January 1995.

34. Fernandez, interview, Montreal, 24 August 1995.

35. Williams, interview, Montreal, 28 July 1995.

36. Dench, interview, Montreal, 20 December 1994.

37. Secours aux Femmes, letter to the immigration minister, February 1995.

38. Côté, interview, Montreal, 13 January 1995.

39. Diane Belanger, interview, Montreal, 11 July 1995.

40. Côté, interview, Montreal, 13 January 1995.

41. Williams, interview, Montreal, 28 July 1995.

42. The objectives of RefLex are (1) to disseminate information on immigration and refugee protection to decision makers and staff; (2) to inform decision makers of decisions rendered by their colleagues across the country, which may be of assistance and may be referred to in their own reasons; this will further the goal of consistency in IRB jurisprudence; (3) to create a bank of jurisprudence to facilitate legal research; and (4) to foster a better understanding of IRB jurisprudence. See Chapter 2 for further information.

43. RefLex cases do not separate out "gender-related" cases as a distinct category, therefore these cases were identified through coding and analysis of cases.

44. In the novel area of gender-related claims, the 1993 Guidelines facilitate more consistent decision making by providing a framework for justifications of decisions. Lack of relevant jurisprudence prior to 1993 means that whether the special characteristics of subsequent cases do or don't "fit" the Guidelines, or involve expanded or narrowed interpretations of less clear areas of the Guidelines, the decision is likely to be notable. This is significant, as other areas of law with substantial jurisprudence are less likely to set precedents simply for being in accordance with the law.

45. Dench, speech to Boston College Law School, 1994.

Chapter 7. Making Sex Persecution Matter

1. UNHCR ExCom, General Conclusion on International Protection No. 79(o), 1996; No. 81(t), 1997; and No. 87(n) 1999.

2. European Union. Council Directive 2004/83/EC on minimum standards for the qualification and status of third country nationals or stateless persons as refugees or as persons who otherwise need international protection and the content of the protection granted.

3. Ibid., Amended Proposal for a Council Directive on minimum standards on procedures in Member States for granting and withdrawing refugee status, 30 April 2004.

4. United Kingdom, Immigration Appellate Authority, Asylum Gender Guidelines, November 2000; and Home Office, Asylum Policy Instructions, *Gender Issues in the Asylum Claim*, March 2004.

5. See also *Asylum Rules Eased for Women* and the Refugee Women's Legal Group's earlier, proposed Gender Guidelines for Determination of Asylum Claims in the UK (1998).

6. Sweden, Migration Board, *Gender-Based Persecution: Guidelines for Investigation and Evaluation of the Needs of Women for Protection*, March 2001.

7. U.S. Department of Justice, Immigration and Naturalization Service, memorandum from Phyllis Cover, Office of International Affairs, "Considerations for Asylum Officers Adjudicating Asylum Claims from Women," 26 May 1995.

8. Australia, Department of Immigration and Multicultural Affairs, Refugee and Humanitarian Visa Applicants, Guidelines on Gender Issues for Decision-Makers, July 1996.

9. Ireland, Refugee Act, 1996. Section I defines membership of a particular social group as including "persons whose defining characteristic is their belonging to the female or the male sex or having a particular sexual orientation." In 2000, guidelines were proposed by the Irish Council for Civil Liberties Women's Committee (Gender Guidelines for Female Refugees and Asylum Seekers, 2000) in order to facilitate actual implementation.

10. South Africa, Refugee Act, 1998. Members of a particular social group can include persons persecuted because of their "gender, sexual orientation, class or caste."

11. Austria, Ministry of Interior, Order No. 97.101/10/SL III/95, 1995. Specifically, rape may constitute a basis for asylum under the 1991 Asylum Law if motivated by one of the Geneva Convention grounds of persecution.

12. Gender is included in policies on *nonrefoulement* or temporary/complementary protection. See Asylum Aid (2005).

13. New legislation in Finland mentions female asylum seekers, and refugee status determinations are required to take a gender perspective in all decisions. See Asylum Aid (2005).

14. Germany provides adjudicators with a handbook on the definition of gender-related persecution, and its general refugee status determination handbook mentions special issues in interviewing female asylum seekers. See Asylum Aid (2005). It identifies rape specifically and prohibits *refoulement* of aliens facing persecution because of their gender.

15. Lithuania's manual for refugee status determination includes gender within the definition of "particular social group," reference to women who do not conform to social and religious mores, and to assessing claims by vulnerable applicants such as women. See Asylum Aid (2005).

16. Netherlands, Immigration and Naturalization Service, Work Instruction No. 148: Women in the Asylum Procedure (UNHCR translation, reprinted in Spijkerboer 2000).

17. Norway, Guidelines, 1998. The Norwegian Organization for Asylum Seekers notes that in Norwegian practice, gender-related persecution is a valid basis for seeking asylum. Guidelines effective 15 January 1998 recognize gender-related persecution, characterized as situations where women through their actions, omissions, and statements violate written and unwritten social rules that affect women particularly, regarding dress, right to employment, and so on. If punished with sanctions constituting persecution in accordance with the 1951 UN Convention, asylum should be granted. Legislation in draft would, according to Municipal Minister Erna Solberg, make it "easier for refugees who are exposed to gender-based persecution to obtain asylum in Norway." See *Women's Asylum News*, 33, 12 June 2003.

18. Guidelines within Switzerland's refugee status determination handbook include a directive stating that same-sex interviewers should be provided where possible and automatically in cases of gender-related persecution, while its annex addresses gender issues relating to interviewing and credibility. Gender is also included in policies on *nonrefoulement* or temporary/complementary protection. See Asylum Aid (2005).

19. Gender-sensitive directives in draft. See Asylum Aid (2005).

20. Guatemala, Government Accord No. 383-2001, 14 September 2001, article 11(d).

21. Panama, Executive Decree No. 23, 10 February 1998. Article 5 includes "gender."

22. Venezuela, National Assembly Decree October 2001. Article 5 adds the ground of "sex" to the refugee definition.

23. Keck and Sikkink's (1998) depiction of the "boomerang effect" in human rights change, a process by which local actors engage transnational actors, leads to the formation of TANs.

24. The current study was not constructed to evidence or disprove the need for TANs in human rights change; rather the absence of TANs in this case became evident during the course of fieldwork, and this both negated the possibility of using models of human rights change that rely on the existence TANs and generated critical questions.

25. The few international NGOs involved were Canadian, working on international issues while located within Canada. Only one was a national branch of a larger INGO (Amnesty International), which was marginally involved and did not receive support from international headquarters in London.

26. Krasner (1999b) takes a different view, concluding that Westphalian state sovereignty has always been and is currently being violated; that is, state sovereignty can be violated or transformed without undermining its defining features.

27. Zimbabwe is a current example of this.

28. See Teitelbaum (1984:433) on the relation between foreign policy and international migration.

29. On the EU, for example, see Meehan (1993).

30. While there are numerous and contested definitions, that offered by Held and McGrew (2000, 2003) is one of the most widely regarded and is adopted here. See Chapter 2.

Bibliography

Abusharaf, R. (ed.). *Female Circumcision in Multicultural Perspective.* Philadelphia: University of Pennsylvania Press, 2006.

Aceves, William J. "Relative Normativity: Challenging the Sovereignty Norm Through Human Rights Litigation." *Hastings International and Comparative Law Review* 25, no. 3 (Summer 2002): 261–278.

Adelman, Howard, Allan Borowski, Meyer Burstein, and Lois Foster (eds.). *Immigration and Refugee Policy: Australia and Canada Compared.* Vol. 1. Toronto: University of Toronto Press, 1994.

Adler, Emanuel. *The Power of Ideology: The Quest for Technological Autonomy in Argentina and Brazil.* Berkeley: University of California Press, 1987.

Advisory Committee on Human Rights and Foreign Policy (Netherlands). "Threatened Women and Refugee Status." Advisory report no. 6. The Hague, 9 December 1987.

Agnew, V. *Resisting Discrimination: Women from Asia, Africa, and the Caribbean and the Women's Movement in Canada.* Toronto: University of Toronto Press, 1996.

Al-Omari, G. "The Legal Protection of Refugee Women." *RPN* 20 Oxford: Refugee Participation Network (November 1995).

Anderson, B. *Imagined Communities.* London: Verso, 1983.

Anderson, G. M., and W. Marr. "Immigration and Social Policy." In Shankar A. Yelaja (ed.), *Canadian Social Policy.* 2nd edition. Waterloo, Ontario: Wilfred Laurier University Press, 1987.

An-Naim, Abdullahi (ed.). *Human Rights in Cross-Cultural Perspectives: A Quest for Consensus.* Philadelphia: University of Pennsylvania Press, 1992.

Arendt, Hannah. *The Origins of Totalitarianism.* New York: Harcourt, 1973.

Ashworth, Georgina. *Of Violence and Violation: Women and Human Rights.* London: CHANGE Thinkbook II, 1986.

Asylum Aid. *Gender Issues in Assessing Asylum Claims: Spreading Good Practice Across the European Union.* Briefing by the Refugee Women's Resource Project, tabled by the United Kingdom at the Intergovernmental Committee Asylum Working Group, Geneva, 15–16 November 2005.

Ayoob, M. "Humanitarian Intervention and State Sovereignty." *International Journal of Human Rights* 6, no. 1 (Spring 2002): 81–102.

Bachrach, P., and M. Baratz. "The Two Faces of Power." *American Political Science Review* 56, no. 4 (1962): 947–952.

Bader, V. (ed.). *Citizenship and Exclusion.* Basingstoke, England: Macmillan, 1997.

Barnett, M., and M. Finnemore. *Rules for the World: International Organizations in Global Politics.* Ithaca, N.Y.: Cornell University Press, 2004.

Baubock, Rainer. "Citizenship and National Identities in the European Union." 1997. http://www.jeanmonnetprogram.org/papers/97/97-04-.html.

———. *Immigration and the Boundaries of Citizenship.* Warwick, England: Centre for Research in Ethnic Relations, 1991.

———. "International Migration and Liberal Democracies: The Challenge of Integration." Paper delivered at the Third International Metropolis Conference, Zichron Yaacov, Israel, December 1998.

Baubōck, Rainer, Agnes Heller, and Aristide R. Zolberg (eds.). *The Challenge of Diversity: Integration and Pluralism in Societies of Immigration.* Aldershot, England: Avebury 1996, for European Centre, Vienna.

Beasley, M. E., and D. Q. Thomas. "Domestic Violence as a Human Rights Issue." In M. A. Fineman and R. Mykitiuk (eds.), *The Public Nature of Private Violence: The Discovery of Domestic Abuse.* New York: Routledge, 1994.

Beneria, Lourdes. *Women and Development: The Sexual Division of Labor in Rual Societies.* New York: Praeger, 1982.

Benhabib, Seyla. *The Rights of Others: Aliens, Residents and Citizens.* Cambridge: Cambridge University Press, 2004.

Bettati, Mario. "The International Community and Limitations of Sovereignty." *Diogenes* 44, no. 4 (Winter 1996): 91–109.

Bhabha, Jacqueline. "Enforcing the Human Rights of Citizens and Non-Citizens in the Era of Maastricht: Some Reflections on the Importance of States." *Development and Change* 29 (1998): 697–724.

Birnie, P. W., and A. E. Boyle. *International Law and the Environment.* Oxford: Clarendon Press; New York: Oxford University Press, 1992.

Black, Naomi. "Ripples in the Second Wave." In Constance Blackhouse and David H. Flaherty (eds.), *Challenging Times: The Women's Movement in Canada and the United States.* Montreal: McGill-Queen's University Press. 1992.

Blanck, Amanda. "Domestic Violence as a Basis for Asylum Status: A Human Rights Based Approach." *Women's Rights Law Reporter* 22 (Fall–Winter 2000): 47–75.

Bob, C. *The Marketing of Rebellion: Insurgents, Media, and International Activism.* Cambridge: Cambridge University Press, 2005.

Boeri, Tito, Gordon Hanson, and Barry McCormick (eds.). *Immigration Policy and the Welfare System: A Report for the Fondazione Rodolfo Debenedetti.* Oxford: Oxford University Press, 2002.

Bohning, W. R. *Studies in International Labor Migration.* London: Macmillan, 1984.

Bonnerjea, L. *Shaming the World: The Needs of Women Refugees.* London: CHANGE, 1985.

Boserup, Ester. *Women's Role in Economic Development.* London: Allen and Unwin, 1970.

Boutang, Y. M., and D. Papademetriou. "Typology, Evolution and Performance of Main Migration Systems." In *Migration and Development: New Partnerships for Co-operation.* Paris: OECD, 1994.

Boyd, Monica. "Canada's Refugee Flows: Gender Inequality." *Canadian Social Trends* 30 (Spring 1994): 7–10.

————. "Family and Personal Networks in Migration." *International Migration Review* (Special Silver Anniversary Issue) 23, no. 3 (1989): 638–671.

————. "Migrant Women in Canada: Profiles and Policies." Employment and Immigration Canada, 1987.

Boyd, Monica, and Chris Taylor. "Canada." In Charles Nam, William Serow, David Sly, and Robert Weller (eds.), *Handbook on International Migration*. Westport: Greenwood Press, 1990.

Brecher, Jeremy, and Tim Costello. *Global Village or Global Pillage: Economic Reconstruction from the Bottom Up*. Boston: South End Press, 1994.

Bronson, D. "Violence Against Women as a Human Rights Issue." *Refuge* 13, no. 4 (July–August 1993).

Brownlie, I. *Principles of Public International Law*. 4th edition. Oxford: Oxford University Press, 1990.

Brubaker, Rogers. *Citizenship and Nationhood in France and Germany*. Cambridge, Mass.: Harvard University Press, 1992.

Brubaker, William Rogers (ed.). *Immigration and the Politics of Citizenship in Europe and North America*. Lanham, Md.: University Press of America, 1989.

Bryman, A. *Quantity and Quality in Social Research*. London: Unwin Hyman, 1988.

Brysk, Alison (ed). *Globalization and Human Rights*. Berkeley: University of California Press, 2002.

————. *Human Rights and Private Wrongs: Constructing Global Civil Society*. New York: Routledge, 2005.

Brysk, Alison, and Gershan Shafir (eds.). *People Out of Place: Globalization, Human Rights, and the Citizenship Gap*. New York: Routledge. 2004.

Buijs, G. (ed.). *Migrant Women: Crossing Boundaries and Changing Identities*. Oxford: Berg, 1993.

Bulmer, Martin, and Anthony M. Rees (eds.). *Citizenship Today: The Contemporary Relevance of T. H. Marshall*. London: UCL Press, 1996.

Bunch, Charlotte. "Organizing for Women's Human Rights Globally." In Joanna Kerr (ed.), *Ours By Right*. Ottawa: North-South Institute, 1993.

————. "Women's Rights as Human Rights: Toward a Re-Vision of Human Rights." *Human Rights Quarterly* 12, no, 4 (1990): 486–498.

Bunch, Charlotte, and Roxanna Carillo. *Gender Violence: A Development and Human Rights Issue*. Dublin: Attic Press, 1990.

Bunch, Charlotte, and Niamh Reilly. *Demanding Accountability: The Global Campaign and Vienna Tribunal Women's Human Rights*. Center for Women's Global Leadership and the United Nations Development Fund for Women, 1994.

Burbach, Roger, Orlando Nuñez, and Boris Kagarlitsky. *Globalization and Its Discontents: The Rise of Postmodern Socialisms*. Chicago: Pluto Press, 1997.

Burgess, R. G. *In the Field: An Introduction to Field Research*. London: Allen and Unwin, 1984.

Butenhoff, Linda. "Localizing Human Rights in an Era of Globalization: The Case of Hong Kong." In M. Monshapoori, N. Englehart, A. J. Nathan, and K. Philip (eds), *Constructing Human Rights in the Age of Globalization*. Armonk, N.Y.: M. E. Sharpe, 2003.

Byrnes, A. "Toward More Effective Enforcement of Women's Human Rights Through the Use of International Human Rights Law and Procedures." In R. Cook (ed.), *Human Rights of Women: National and International Perspectives.* Philadelphia: University of Pennsylvania Press, 1994.

CACSW. *Male Violence Against Women: The Brutal Face of Inequality.* Brief to the House of Commons Subcommittee on the Status of Women: Violence Against Women. 13 February 1991.

Cairns, Alan C. "Citizens (Outsiders) and Governments (Insiders) in Constitution-Making: The Case of Meech Lake." *Canadian Public Policy* 14 (September 1988): 121–145.

Camus-Jacques, Genevieve. "Refugee Women: The Forgotten Majority." In Gil Loescher and Laila Monahan (eds.), *Refugees and International Relations.* Oxford: Oxford University Press, 1989.

Canadian Council for Refugees (CCR). Letter from CCR President David Matas to Immigration Minister Bernard Valcourt. 20 December 1991.

———. Letter to Laura Chapman, director General of Policy and Program Development, EIC, 20 January 1993.

———. Press release, 20 January 1993.

———. Press release, 2 February 1993.

———. Working Group on Refugee Women. *Goals and Activities Summary, November 1985–July 1990.* Canadian Council for Refugees. 1989.

Cardenas, Sonia. "National Human Rights Commissions in Asia." In John D. Montgomery and Nathan Glazer (eds.), *Sovereignty Under Challenge.* New Brunswick, N.J.: Transaction Publishers, 2002.

Castells, M. *The Power of Identity.* Malden, Mass.: Blackwell, 1997.

Castles, S., and M. J. Miller. *The Age of Migration.* London: Macmillan Press, 1993.

Chapman, L. "Main Features of the Immigration System in Canada." In *Migration and Development: New Partnerships for Co-operation.* Paris: OECD, 1994.

Charlesworth, Hilary. "What Are 'Women's International Human Rights'?" In Rebecca J. Cook (ed.), *Human Rights of Women.* Philadelphia: University of Pennsylvania Press, 1994.

Charlesworth, Hilary, Christine Chinkin, and Shelley Wright. "Feminist Approaches to International Law." *American Journal of International Law* 85 (1991): 613, 624.

Chinkin, C. M. "The Challenge of Soft Law: Development and Change in International Law." *International and Comparative Law Quarterly* 38, no. 4 (1989): 850–866.

Clapham, Christopher. "Sovereignty and the Third World State." *Political Studies* 47, no. 3 (1999): 522–538.

Cohen, S. "Anti-Semitism, Immigration Controls and the Welfare State, *Critical Social Policy* 13 (1985).

Community Legal Education Ontario. *Immigration Fact Sheet, 1994.* Ontario: CLEO, 1994.

Cook, Rebecca J. (ed.). *Human Rights of Women: National and International Perspectives.* Philadelphia: University of Pennsylvania Press, 1994.

Cox, D., and P. Glenn. "Illegal Immigration and Refugee Claims." In Howard Adelman et al. (eds.), *Immigration and Refugee Policy: Australia and Canada Compared.* Vol. 1. Toronto: University of Toronto Press, 1994.

Multi-Femmes. Quebec and Canadian Coalition for Ginette Ngvego and Daughter. Letter to Immigration Minister Sergio Marchi, request for ministerial intervention, 12 December 1994.

———. Letter to supporters, 12 December 1994.

Counsel for Zahra. Letter to manager of Hearings and Appeals, Canada Immigration Centre in Vancouver, on Pre-Removal Humanitarian and Compassionate Review. 13 October 1992.

Crawley, H. "Women and Refugee Status: Beyond the Public/Private Dichotomy in UK Asylum Policy." In D. Indra (ed.), *Engendering Forced Migration: Theory and Practice*. Oxford: Berghahn Books, 1999.

Crawley, Heaven, and Trine Lester. *Comparative Analysis of Gender-Related Persecution in National Asylum Legislation and Practice in Europe.* Geneva: UNHCR, 2004.

Critcher C., D. Waddington, and B. Dicks. "Qualitative Methods and Welfare Research." In F. Williams, J. Popay, and A. Oakley (eds.), *Welfare Research: A Critical Review*. London: UCL Press, 1999.

Dacyl, J. *Between Compassion and Realpolitik: In Search of a General Model of the Responses of Recipient Countries to Large-Scale Refugee Flows with Reference to the South-East Asian Refugee Crisis.* Stockholm: Stockholm University, 1992.

Davidson, S. *Human Rights*. Buckingham: Open University Press, 1993.

Deacon, B. *Global Social Policy: International Organizations and the Future of Welfare.* London: Sage, 1997.

Dench, Janet. "Does Gender a Refugee Make?" Speech to Boston College Law School, Owen M. Kupferschmidt Holocaust Human Rights Project. Transcript, Canadian Council for Refugees, 23 March 1994.

———. "Report to Consultation on Gender Issues and Refugees." Canadian Council for Refugees, 1993.

DeNeef, C. *Sexual Violence Against Women Refugees: Report of the Nature and Consequences of Sexual Violation Suffered Elsewhere.* The Hague: Netherlands Ministry of Social Affairs and Employment, 1984.

DeSwaan, A. (ed.). *Social Policy Beyond Borders*. Amsterdam: Amsterdam University Press, 1994.

Dirks, G. *Controversy and Complexity: Canadian Immigration Policy During the 1980s.* Montreal: McGill-Queen's University Press, 1995.

Dobash, R. Emerson, and Russell P. Dobash. *Women, Violence, and Social Change.* London: Routledge, 1992.

Donnelly, Jack. *The Concept of Human Rights.* New York: St. Martin's Press, 1985.

———. "Human Rights and Human Dignity: An Analytical Critique of Non-Western Conceptions of Human Rights." *American Political Science Review* 76 (1982): 303–316.

———. *International Human Rights.* 3rd edition. Boulder, Colo.: Westview Press, 206.

———. "International Human Rights: A Regime Analysis." *International Organization* 40 (Summer 1986): 599–642.

———. "State Sovereignty and Human Rights." Working paper no. 21. Graduate School of International Studies, University of Denver, June 2004.

————. *Universal Human Rights in Theory and Practice* 2nd edition. Ithaca, N.Y.: Cornell University Press, 2003.

Dutch Refugee Association. "Oppression of Women and Refugee Status." Discussion paper for the international Seminar on Refugee Women, May 1985.

Easton, D. A. *Systems Analysis of Political Life.* New York: Wiley, 1965.

Edelman, Murray. *Politics as Symbolic Action: Mass Arousal and Quiescence.* Chicago: Markham, 1971.

Elgström, Ole. "Norm Negotiations: The Construction of New Norms Regarding Gender and Development in EU Foreign Aid Policy." *Journal of European Public Policy 7,* no. 3 (September 2000): 457–476.

Elliot, J. L., and A. Fleras. "Immigration and the Canadian Ethnic Mosaic." In P. Li (ed.), *Race and Ethnic Relations in Canada.* Toronto: Oxford University Press, 1990.

Engle, K. "International Human Rights and Feminism: When Discourses Meet." *Michigan Journal of International Law* 13 (1992): 517.

Enloe, C. *Bananas, Beaches and Bases: Making Feminist Sense of International Politics.* London: Pandora, 1989.

Equality Now. *Annual Report: Gender-Based Asylum in Canada: October 1992–January 1993.* New York: Equality Now, 1993b.

Esping-Andersen, Gøsta. *The Three Worlds of Welfare Capitalism.* Cambridge: Polity, 1990.

————. (ed.). *Welfare States in Transition: National Adaptations in Global Economies.* London: Sage, 1996.

Evans, Mary, and Clare Ungerson (eds.). *Sexual Divisions: Patterns and Processes.* London: Tavistock, 1983.

Evans, P. B., D. Rueschemeyer, and T. Skocpol. *Bringing the State Back In.* Cambridge: Cambridge University Press, 1993.

Evans, Tony. *The Politics of Human Rights: A Global Perspective.* 1st edition. Stirling, Va.: Pluto Press, 2001.

————. *The Politics of Human Rights: A Global Perspective.* 2nd edition. London: Pluto Press, 2005.

Evans, Tony, and Jan Hancock. "Doing Something Without Doing Anything: International Law and the Challenge of Globalization." *International Journal of Human Rights* 2, no. 3, (1998): 1–21.

Faist, Thomas. "Immigration, Integration, and the Welfare State: Germany and the USA in Comparative Perspective." In Rainer Bauböck, Agnes Heller, and Aristide Zolberg (eds.), *The Challenge of Diversity: Integration and Pluralism in Societies of Immigration.* Aldershot, England: Avebury, 1996.

Falk, Richard. "The Making of Global Citizenship." In B. VanSteenbergen (ed.), *The Condition of Citizenship.* London: Sage, 1994.

————. *On Humane Governance: Toward a New Global Politics.* World Order Models Project Report of the Global Civilization Initiative. University Park: Pennsylvania State University Press, 1995.

Fawcett, J. T. "Networks, Linkages and Migration Systems." *International Migration Review* (Special Silver Anniversary Issue), vol. 23, no. 3 (1989): 671–680.

Fawcett, J. T., and F. Arnold. "Explaining Diversity: Asian and Pacific Immigration Systems." In J. T. Fawcett and B. V. Carino (eds.), *Pacific Bridges: The New Immigration from Asia and the Pacific Islands.* New York: Center for Migration Studies, 1987.

Feller, E., T. Volker, and F. Nicholson (eds.). *Refugee Protection in International Law: UNHCR's Global Consultations on International Protection.* Cambridge: Cambridge University Press, 2003.

Fincher, Ruth, Lois Foster, Wenona Giles, and Valerie Preston. "Gender and Migration Policy." In Howard Adelman et al. (eds.), *Immigration and Refugee Policy: Australia and Canada Compared,*Vol. 1. Toronto: University of Toronto Press, 1994.

Finnemore, Martha. "International Organizations as Teachers of Norms: The United Nations Educational, Scientific and Cultural Organization and Science Policy." *International Organization* 47 (Autumn 993): 565–598.

Finnemore, Martha, and K. Sikkink. "International Norm Dynamics and Political Change." *International Organization* 52 (1998): 887–917.

Flanagan, Scott C. "Changing Values in Advanced Industrial Societies: Inglehart's Silent Revolution from the Perspective of Japanese Findings." *Comparative Political Studies* 14 (1982): 403–444.

———. "Value Change in Industrial Society." *American Political Science Review* 81 (1987): 1303–1319.

Forsythe, David P. *Human Rights and World Politics.* 2nd edition. Ithaca, N.Y.: Cornell University Press, 1989.

———. *The Internationalization of Human Rights.* Lexington Mass.: Lexington Books, 1991.

Friedman, Elisabeth. "Women's Human Rights: The Emergence of a Movement." In Julie Peters and Andrea Wolper (eds.), *Women's Rights, Human Rights: International Feminist Perspectives.* London: Routledge, 1995.

Gamson, W. A. *The Strategy of Social Protest.* Homewood, Ill.: Dorsey. 1975.

GCIM (Global Commission on International Migration). *Migration in an Interconnected World: New Directions for Action.* Switzerland: SRO Kundig, 2005.

Gerlach, Luther P., and Virginia H. Hine. *People, Power, Change.* New York: Bobbs-Merrill, 1970.

Giddens, A. *The Consequences of Modernity.* Cambridge: Polity Press, 1990.

Gilad, Lisa. "The Problem of Gender-Related Persecution: A Challenge of International Protection." In Doreen Indra (ed.), *Engendering Forced Migration: Theory and Practice.* Oxford: Berghahn Books, 1999.

Giles, W. Speech transcript. International Women's Day. Gender Unit at the Centre for Refugee Studies, York University, 5 March 1996.

Glennerster, H. (ed.) *The Future of the Welfare State: Remaking Social Policy.* London: Heinemann, 1983.

Goldberg, Pamela. "Analytical Approaches in Search of Consistent Application: A Comparative Analysis of the Second Circuit Decisions Addressing Gender in the Asylum Law Context." *Brooklyn Law Review* 66 (2000): 309–360.

Gordon, P. *Citizenship For Some? Race and Government Policy.* London: Runnymede Trust, 1989.

Grant, Rebecca, and Kathleen Newland. *Gender and International Relations.* Milton Keynes: Open University Press, 1991.

Greatbatch, J. "The Gender Difference: Feminist Critiques of Refugee Discourse." *International Journal of Refugee Law* 1 (1989): 518.

Grotius, H. *De Jure Belli ac Pacis Libri Tres (The Law of War and Peace).* 1625. Translated by Francis W. Kelsey. New York: Oceana, 1964.

Haas, Ernst B. *When Knowledge Is Power: Three Models of Change in International Organizations.* Berkeley: University of California Press, 1990.

Habermas, J. "Citizenship and National Identity." In Bart van Steenbergen (ed.), *The Condition of Citizenship.* London: Sage, 1994.

———. "Struggles for Recognition in the Democratic Constitutional State." In Amy Gutman (ed.), *Multiculturalism: Examining the Politics of Recognition.* Princeton, N.J.: Princeton University Press, 1994.

———. *The Theory of Communicative Action, Vol. II.* Cambridge: Polity Press. 1987.

Haines, herbert H. *Black Radicals and the Civil Rights Mainstream, 1954–1970.* Knoxville: University of Tennessee Press, 1988.

Hall, P., H. Land, R. Parker, and A. Webb. *Change, Choice and Conflict in Social Policy.* London: Heinemann Educational, 1975.

Ham, Christopher, and Michael J. Hill. *The Policy Process in the Modern Capitalist State,* 1st edition. Brighton, England: Wheatsheaf, 1984.

———. *The Policy Process in the Modern State.* New York: Prentice-Hall, 1997.

Hammar, T. *Democracy and the Nation State: Aliens, Denizens and Citizens in a World of International Migration.* Aldershot, England: Avebury, 1990.

Hammar, T., G. Brochmann, K. Tamas, and T. Faist (eds.). *International Migration, Immobility and Development: Multidisciplinary Perspectives.* Oxford: Berg, 1997.

Hardcastle, Leonie, Andrew Parkin, Alan Simmons, and Nobuaki Suyama. "The Making of Immigration and Refugee Policy: Politicians, Bureaucrats and Citizens." In Howard Adelman et al. (eds.), *Immigration and Refugee Policy: Australia and Canada Compared.* Vol. 1. Toronto: University of Toronto Press, 1994.

Hastedt, G., and K. Knickrehm. "Predicting Refugee Flows: The Response Patterns of Receiving States." Paper presented at the International Studies Association Meeting, Atlanta, Georgia, March 1984.

Hathaway, James C. *The Law of Refugee Status.* Toronto: Butterworths, 1991a.

———. "Recommendation to Gender Consultations, Agenda Setting Meeting." National Gender Consultations, Ottawa. 1993.

———. "Reconceiving Refugee Law as Human Rights Protection." *Journal of Refugee Studies* 4, no. 2 (1991b): 113–131.

Hawkins, Freda. *Canada and Immigration: Public Policy and Public Concern.* Montreal: McGill-Queen's University Press, 1972.

———. *The Critical Years in Immigration: Canada and Australia Compared.* Montreal: McGill-Queen's University Press, 1989.

Heise, Lori L. "International Dimensions of Violence Against Women." *Response* 12, no. 1 (1989): 3–11.

Held, D. *Democracy and the Global Order: From the Modern State to Cosmopolitan Governance.* Cambridge: Polity, 1995.

Held, David, and Anthony McGrew. *The Global Transformations Reader: An Introduction to the Globalization Debate.* 1st edition. Cambridge: Polity Press, 2000.

———. *The Global Transformations Reader.* 2nd edition. Cambridge: Polity Press, 2003.

Held, David, Anthony McGrew, David Goldblatt, and Jonathan Perraton. "Rethinking Globalization." In David Held and Anthony Mcgrew (eds.), *Global Transformations Reader.* 2nd edition. Cambridge: Polity Press, 2003.

Henkin, Louis. "That 'S' Word: Sovereignty, and Globalization, and Human Rights, Et Cetera." *Fordham Law Review* 68, no. 1 (October 1999): 1–14.

Hill, Michael (ed.). *The Policy Process: A Reader.* London: Harvester-Wheatsheaf, 1993.

Hollifield, James. "How Can We Bring the State Back In?" In Caroline B. Brettell and James F. Hollifield (eds.), *Migration Theory.* New York: Routledge, 2000.

Howard-Hassmann, R. E. "Culture, Human Rights, and the Politics of Resentment in the Era of Globalization." *Human Rights Review* 6, no. 1 (October–December 2004): 5–26.

———. "The Flogging of Bariya Magazu: Nigerian Politics, Canadian Pressures, and Women's and Children's Rights." *Journal of Human Rights* 3, no. 1 (March 2004): 3–20.

———. "The Second Great Transformation: Human Rights Leapfrogging in the Era of Globalization." *Human Rights Quarterly* 27, no. 1 (2005): 1–40.

Howard-Hassmann, Rhoda E., and Claude E. Welch, Jr. (eds). *Economic Rights in Canada and the United States.* Philidephia: University of Pennsylvania Press, 2006.

"Hunger Strike Day." Press release issued by legal counsel for Fard Radjai and Firoozeh Radjai, and Iranian Immigrant and Refugee of (IIRBC). 1 March 1993.

"Hunger Strike Day 9." Press release issued by legal counsel and the IIRBC. 3 March 1993.

Hunter, A. "Globalization from Below? Promises and Perils of the New Internationalism." *Social Policy* (Summer 1995): 6–13.

Immigration Ministry, Canada. Dossier prepared for Immigration Minister Sergio Marchi. January 1995.

Immigration and Refugee Board (IRB). *Guidelines on Women Refugee Claimants Fearing Gender Related Persecution: Backgrounder.* Press release issued 6 August 2003. Accessed 10 January 2007 at http://www.irbcisr.gc.ca/en/media/back ground/back_women2_e.htm.

———. Immigration Minister, letter to Ed Broadbent, ICHRDD, 29 January 1993.

———. Press release issued by the Immigration Minister's office, 29 January 1993.

———. Randy Gordan, assistant to Immigration Minister, letter to David Matas, 8 July 1992.

International Center for Human Rights and Democratic Development (ICHRDD). *Annual Report 1993–1994.* ICHRDD, 1994.

———.ICHRDD president Ed Broadbent, letter to Immigration Minister Bernard Valcourt, 19 August 1992.

———. ICHRDD president Ed Broadbent, letter to Immigration Minister Bernard Valcourt, 11 February 1993.

————. Letter to Immigration Minister Bernard Valcourt, and MPs. March 25, 1993.

————. Letter to potential supporters, 13 August 1992.

————. Press release, 18 January 1993.

————. Press release, 29 January 1993.

Ignatieff, M. *Human Rights as Politics and Ideology.* Princeton, N.J.: Princeton University Press, 2001.

Indra, Doreen. (ed.). *Engendering Forced Migration: Theory and Practice.* Oxford: Berghahn, 1999.

————. "Gender: A Key Dimension of the Refugee Experience." *Refugee* 6 (February 1987): 3–4.

Jacobsen, Michael, and Stephanie Lawson. "Between Globalization and Localization: A Case Study of Human Rights Versus State Sovereignty." *Global Governance* 5, no. 2 (April–June 1999): 203–219.

Jacobson, D. *Rights Across Borders: Immigration and the Decline of Citizenship.* Baltimore: Johns Hopkins University Press, 1996.

Jayawardena, K. *Feminism and Nationalism in the Third World.* London: Zed Press, 1986.

Jenkins-Smith, Hank, and Paul Sabatier. "Evaluating the Advocacy Coalition Framework." *Journal of Public Policy* 14, no. 2 (1994): 175–203.

Jordan A. G., and J. J. Richardson. *Governing Under Pressure.* Oxford: Martin Robertson, 1979.

Kandiyoti, D. (ed.). *Women, Islam and the State.* Basingstoke, England: Macmillan, 1990.

Katzenstein, P. J. *The Culture of National Security: Norms and Identity in World Politics.* New York: Columbia University Press, 1996.

Kearns, Temple Fett. "Breaking the Shackles of the Past: The Role and Future of State Sovereignty in Today's Human Rights Arena." *Nova Law Review* 25, no. 2 (Winter 2001): 502–524.

Keck, M., K. Sikkink. *Activists Beyond Borders: Advocacy Networks in International Politics.* Ithaca, N.Y.: Cornell University Press, 1998.

Kelson, Gregory A. "Gender-Based Persecution and Political Asylum: The International Debate for Equality Begins." *Texas Journal of Women and the Law* 6 (1997): 181–213.

Kerr, Joanna (ed.). *Ours by Right: Women's Rights as Human Rights.* London: Zed Books, 1993.

Klare, Karl E. "The Public/Private Distinction in Labor Law." *University of Pennsylvania Law Review* 130, no. 6 (1982): 1358–1422.

Kleinman, M., and D. Piachaud. "European Social Policy: Conceptions and Choices." *Journal of European Social Policy* 3, no. 1 (1993): 1–19.

Klotz, A. *Norms in International Relations: The Struggle Against Apartheid.* Ithaca, N.Y.: Cornell University Press, 1995.

Knop, K. "Beyond Borders: Women's Rights and the Issue of Sovereignty." In Joanna Kerr (ed.), *Ours by Right: Womens' Rights as Human Rights.* London: Zed Books, 1993.

Knowles, V. *Strangers at Our Gates: Immigration and Immigration Policy, 1540–1990.* Toronto: Dundurn Press, 1992.

Korey, W. *NGOs and the Universal Declaration of Human Rights: A Curious Grapevine.* New York: St. Martin's Press, 1998.

Krasner, Stephen D. "Globalization and Sovereignty." In D. A. Smith, D. S. Solinger, and S C Topik (eds.), *States and Sovereignty in the Global Economy.* London: Routledge, 1999a.

———. *Sovereignty: Organized Hypocrisy.* Princeton, N.J.: Princeton University Press, 1999b.

———. "Think Again: Sovereignty." *Foreign Policy* 122 (January–February 2001): 20–29.

Kriesi, Hanspeter. "The Rebellion of the Research 'Objects.' " In Mario Diani and Ron Eyerman (eds.), *Studying Collective Action.* London: Sage, 1992.

Kuhn, T. *The Structure of Scientific Revolutions.* 2nd edition. Chicago: University of Chicago Press, 1970.

Kuttner, S. "Gender-Related Persecution as a Basis for Refugee Status: The Emergence of an International Norm." *Refugee* 16, no. 4 (October 1997): 17–21.

Kymlicka, W. *Finding Our Way: Rethinking Ethnocultural Relations in Canada.* Toronto: Oxford University Press Canada, 1998.

Land, H. "The Construction of Dependency." In Martin Bulmer, Jane Lewis, and David Piachaud (eds.), *The Goals of Social Policy.* London: Unwin Hyman, 1989.

Landes, William M., and Richard A. Posner. "Legal Precedent: A Theoretical and Empirical Analysis." *Journal of Law and Economics* 19, no. 2 (August 1976): 249–307.

Landry, D., and G. MacLean (eds.). *The Spivak Reader.* New York: Routledge, 1996.

Lapidoth, Ruth. "Redefining Authority." *Harvard International Review* 17, no. 3 (Summer 1995): 8–13.

Laumann, M., D. V. Marsden, and D. Prensky. "The Boundary Specification Problem in Network Analysis." In R. S. Burt and M. J. Minor (eds.), *Applied Network Analysis: A Methodological Introduction.* London: Sage, 1983.

Lauterpacht, H. *International Law and Human Rights.* Hamden, Conn.: Archon Books, 1968 [1950].

Layton-Henry, A. (ed.). *The Political Rights of Migrant Workers in Western Europe.* London: Sage, 1990.

Leiss, Anne, and Ruby Boesjes. *Female Asylum Seekers: A Comparative Study Concerning Policy and Jurisprudence in the Netherlands, Germany, France, the United Kingdom, also Dealing Summarily with Belgium and Canada.* Amsterdam: Dutch Refugee Council, 1994.

Levin, P. *Making Social Policy: The Mechanisms of Government and Politics, and How to Investigate Them.* Buckingham, England: Open University Press, 1997.

Lewis, J. "Gender and the Development of Welfare Regimes." *Journal of European Social Policy* 2, no. 3 (1992): 159–173.

Liebich, Flora. "Gender Issues and Refugee Determination." Presented at Conference on Gender Issues and Refugees: Development Implications. York University, Toronto, 9 May 1993.

———. Report on Needs of Refugee Women in the Hearing Room. IRB, 1987.

Linklater, Andrew. "Cosmopolitan Citizenship." *Citizenship Studies* 2 (1998): 23–41.

Lister, R. *Citizenship: Feminist Perspectives.* London: Macmillan Press, 1997.

Loescher, G., and L. Monahan (eds.). *Refugees and International Relations.* Oxford: Oxford University Press, 1989.

Lukes, S. *Power: A Radical View.* London: Macmillan, 1974.

Lutz, Ellen L. "Strengthening Core Values in the Americas: Regional Commitment to Democracy and the Protection of Human Rights." *Houston Journal of International Law* 19, no. 3 (Spring 1997): 643–657.

Lyons, Gene M., and James Mayall. "Stating the Problem of Group Rights." In G. M. Lyons and J. Mayall (eds.), *International Human Rights in the 21st Century: Protecting the Rights of Groups.* Lanham: Rowman and Littlefield, 2003.

MacEoin, G. (ed). *Sanctuary.* San Francisco: Harper and Row, 1985.

Macklin, Audrey. "A Comparative Analysis of the Canadian, US and Australian Directives on Gender Persecution and Refugee Status." In Doreen Indra (ed.), *Engendering Forced Migration: Theory and Practice.* Oxford: Berghahn Books, 1999.

———. "Women Refugees and the Imperative of Categories." *Human Rights Quarterly* 17 (1995): 213.

MacLeod, L., and M. Shin. *Isolated, Afraid and Forgotten: The Service Delivery Need and Realities of Immigrant and Refugee Women Who Are Battered.* Ottawa: Health and Welfare Canada, National Clearinghouse on Family Violence, 1990.

MacMillan, Leanne. "Reflections on the Gender Guidelines." *Refuge* 13, no. 4 (July–August 1993): 2–3.

Maison Flora Tristan. *Annual Report, 1993–1994.* Montreal: Maison Flora Tristan, 1994.

———. "Compte rendu: Femmes immigrantes victimes de violence conjugale en attente de Statut de parrainage et parrainees." Unpublished institutional document. May 1991.

Malarek, V. *Haven's Gate: Canada's Immigration Fiasco.* Toronto: Macmillan, 1987.

Mander, Jerry, and Edward Goldsmith (eds.). *The Case Against the Global Economy: And for a Turn Toward the Local.* San Francisco: Sierra Club Books, 1996.

Mansbach, Richard W., and John A. Vasquez. *In Search of Theory: A New Paradigm for Global Politics.* New York: Columbia University Press, 1981.

March, J. G., and J. P. Olsen. "The New Institutionalism: Organizational Factors in Political Life." *American Political Science Review* 78, no. 3 (1984): 743–749.

Marsh, D., and R. A. W. Rhodes (eds.). *Policy Networks in British Government.* Oxford: Oxford University Press, 1992.

Marshall, T. H. *Citizenship and Social Class and Other Essays.* Cambridge: University Press, 1950.

———. *The Right to Welfare and Other Essays.* London: Heinemann, 1981.

———. *Sociology at the Crossroads and Other Essays.* London: Heinemann, 1963.

Marshall T. H, and Tom Bottomore. *Citizenship and Social Class.* London: Pluto Press, 1992.

Martin-Forbes, S. *Refugee Women.* London: Zed Books, 1992.

Maslow, Abraham. *Motivation and Personality.* New York: Harper and Row, 1970.

Matthews, R. "Refugees and Stability in Africa." *International Organization* 26 (1972): 62–83.

Mawani, Nurjehan. "Chairperson's Message." Presentation for the IRB Conference on International Women's Day, Montreal, 6 March 1997.

———. "Chairperson's Message." Presentation for the IRB International Women's Day, Montreal, 8 March 1999.

———. "The Convention Definition and Gender-Related Persecution: The IRB Perspective." IRB presentation to the Conference on Gender Issues and Refugees: Development Implications. York University, Toronto, 10 May 1993a.

———. "Emerging Human Rights Issues in Refugee Protection." IRB chairperson's presentation to the International Judicial Conference on Asylum and Procedures, London, 1 December 1995a.

———. "The Factual and Legal Legitimacy of Addressing Gender Issues." *Refuge* 13, no. 4 (July–August 1993b): 7–10.

———. "IRB Guidelines on Gender Related Persecution: First Anniversary Address." IRB chairperson's address to the National Indo-Canadian Council, Montreal, 9 March 1994.

———. "Violations of the Rights of Women in the Refugee Context." IRB chairperson's address to the Human Rights Centre, University of Ottawa, 20 November 1993c.

———. "Women and Asylum: Canadian Experiences." In Robert A. Dahl, *Polyarchy*. New Haven, Conn.: Yale University Press, 1971.

———. "Women, Culture and the Law." IRB chairperson's presentation to the Seventh Appellate Judges Conference, 27 September 1995b.

McAdam, D. "The Framing Function of Movement Tactics: Strategic Dramaturgy in the American Civil Rights Movement." In D. McAdam, J. D. McCarthy, and M. N. Zald, *Comparative Perspectives on Social Movements: Political Opportunities, Mobilizing Structures, and Cultural Framings*. New York: Cambridge University Press, 1996.

———. *Political Process and the Development of Black Insurgency, 1930–1970*. Chicago: University of Chicago Press, 1982.

———. "Studying Social Movements: A Conceptual Tour of the Field." Seminar, Presidents and Fellows of Harvard College 2003–2005, Harvard, 11 March 1992.

McAdam, D., J. D. McCarthy, and M. N. Zald. *Comparative Perspectives on Social Movements: Political Opportunities, Mobilizing Structures, and Cultural Framings*. New York: Cambridge University Press, 1996.

McAdam, D., S. Tarrow, and C. Tilly. *Dynamics of Contention*. Cambridge: Cambridge University Press. 2001.

McCarthy, J. D., and M. N. Zald (eds.). *The Dynamics of Social Movements: Resource Mobilization, Social Control and Tactics*. Cambridge: Winthrop Publishers, 1979.

Meehan, E. *Citizenship and the European Community*. London: Sage, 1993.

———. "European Citizenship and Social Policies." In Ursula Vogel and Michael Moran (eds.), *The Frontiers of Citizenship*. London: Macmillan, 1991.

Melander, G. "The Concept of the Term 'Refugee.'" In A. C. Bramwell (ed.), *Refugees in the Age of Total War*. London: Unwin Hyman, 1988.

Melucci, A. *Nomads of the Present: Social Movements and Individual Needs in Contemporary Society*. London: Hutchinson, 1989.

Meyer, J. W. "Rationalized Environments." In W. Richard Scott and John W. Meyer, *Institutional Environments and Organizations: Structural Complexity and Individualism*. London: Sage, 1994.

Meyer, J. W., J. Boli, and G. M. Thomas. "Ontology and Rationalization in the Western Cultural Account." In W. Richard Scott and John W. Meyer, *Institutional Environments and Organizations: Structural Complexity and Individualism*. London: Sage, 1994.

———. "Ontology and rationalization in the Western Cultural Account." In G. M. Thomas, J. W. Meyer, F. O. Ramirez, and J. Boli, *Institutional Structure: Constituting State, Society, and the Individual*. Newbury Park, Calif.: Sage, 1987.

Meyer, J. W., J. Boli, G. M. Thomas, and F. Ramirez. "World Society and the Nation-State." *American Journal of Sociology* 103, no. 1 (1997): 144–181.

Midgley, J. *Social Welfare in Global Context*. London: Sage, 1997.

Mills, Kurt. *Human Rights in the Emerging Global Order: A New Sovereignty?* New York: St. Martin's Press, 1998.

Mishra, R. *Globalization and the Welfare State*. Cheltenham, England: Edward Elgar, 1999.

Mitchell, C. "International Migration, International Relations and Foreign Policy." *International Migration Review* (Special Silver Anniversary Issue), vol. 23, no. 3 (1989): 681–708.

Mohanty, C. T., A. Russo, and L. Torres. *Third World Women and the Politics of Feminism*. Bloomington: Indiana University Press, 1991.

Morokvasic, Mirjana. "Birds of Passage Are Also Women." *International Migration Review* 18, no. 4 (1984): 886–907.

Moser, Caroline. "Gender Planning in the Third World: Meeting Practical and Strategic Needs." In R. Grant, and K. Newland (eds.), *Gender and International Relations*. London: Open University Press, 1991.

Musalo, Karen. "Irreconcilable Differences? Divorcing Refugee Protections from Human Rights Norms." *Michigan Journal of International Law* 15 (1994): 1179.

———. "Revisiting Social Group and Nexus in Gender Asylum Claims: A Unifying Rationale for Evolving Jurisprudence." *DePaul Law Review* 52 (2003): 777–808.

NAC. Letter to Immigration Minister Bernard Valcourt. February 26, 1993.

———. Press package on fourteen women seeking stay of deportation. March 1993.

———. Press release. 16 November 1994.

Nadelmann, Ethan A. "Global Prohibition Regimes: The Evolution of Norms in International Society." *International Organization* 44 (1990): 479–526.

National Consortium on Reguee Affairs (NCRA). *Gender Guidelines for Asylum Determination*. NCRA, South Africa 1999.

Nedelmann, Birgitta. "New Political Movements and Changes in Processes of Intermediation." *Social Science Information* 23, no. 6 (1984).

Nevitte, N. *The Decline of Deference: Canadian Value Change in Cross-National Perspective*. Peterborough, Ont.: Broadview Press, 1996.

Newland, K. "From Transnational Relationships to International Relations: 'Women in Development and the International Decade for Women.'" In R. Grant, and K.

Newland (eds.), *Gender and International Relations*. London: Open University Press, 1991.

Nussbaum, Martha C. "Capabilities and Human Rights." *Fordham Law Review* 66 (1997): 273–300.

———. *Sex and Social Justice*. New York: Oxford University Press, 1999.

Nussbaum, Martha C., and Amartya Sen (eds.). *The Quality of Life*. Oxford: Clarendon Press, 1993.

O'Connor, J. *The Fiscal Crisis of the State*. New York: St. Martin's Press, 1973.

Oakley, A. *Experiments in Knowing: Gender and Method in the Social Sciences*. New York: New Press, 2000.

Oberschall, A. *Social Conflict and Social Movements*. Englewood Cliffs, N.J.: Prentice-Hall, 1973.

OECD. *Migration and Development: New Partnerships for Co-operation*. Paris: OECD, 1994.

Offe, C. "New Social Movements: Challenging the Boundaries of Institutional Politics." *Social Research* 52, no. 4 (1985) 817–68.

Olson, Mancur. *The Logic of Collective Action*. Cambridge, Mass.: Harvard University Press, 1965.

Ontario Lawyers Assistance Program. Research Facility (Law Society of Upper Canada). *Refugees: Gender Related Persecution*. OLAP, 1994.

Onuf, N. G., and V. peterson. "Human Rights from an International Regime Perspective." *Journal of International Affairs*, 37 (1984): 329–333.

Panikkar, R. "Is the Notion of Human Rights a Western Concept?" *Diogenes* 120 (1982): 75–102.

Parekh, B. "Rethinking Humanitarian Intervention." *International Political Science Review* 18, no. 1 (1997): 49–69.

———. "Three Theories of Immigration." In S. Spencer (ed.), *Strangers and Citizens: A Positive Approach to Migrants and Refugees*. London: Rivers Oram Press, 1994.

Parry, Geraint. "Paths to Citizenship." In Ursula Vogel and Michael Moran (eds.), *The Frontiers of Citizenship*. London: Macmillan, 1991.

Pateman, Carole. *The Disorder of Women: Democracy, Feminism, and Political Theory*. Cambridge: Polity Press, 1989.

———. *The Sexual Contract*. Cambridge: Polity Press, 1988.

Paul, K. "Granting Refugee Status for Gender-Based Persecution and Attitudes and Behavior in the Hearing Room." UNHCR Promotion of Refugee Law Unit, Division of International Protection, presentation for the IRB/CRDD workshop *Working Group on Women Refugee Claimants: Determination Issues in Refugee Claims Made by Women*, Toronto, 19 March 1992.

Peters, Julie, and Andrea Wolper (eds.). *Women's Rights, Human Rights*. New York: Routledge, 1995.

Peterson, V. Spike, and Anne Sisson Runyan. *Global Gender Issues*. Boulder, Colo.: Westview, 1993.

Phizacklea, Annie (ed). *One Way Ticket: Migration and Female Labor*. London: Routledge, 1983.

Pinker, R. *Social Theory and Social Policy*. London: Heinemann Educational, 1971.

Plender, R. *International Migration Law.*, 2nd edition. London: Nijhoff, 1988.

————. *The Right of Asylum.* The Hague Academy of International Law, Centre for Studies and Research in International Law and International Relations, Netherlands: Martinus Nijhoff Publishers, 1989.

Pollitt, C., S. Harrison, D. J. Hunter, and G. Marnoch. "No Hiding Place: On the Discomforts of Researching the Contemporary Policy Process." *Journal of Social Policy* 19, no. 2 (1990): 169–190.

Pope, L., and F. Stairs. "No Place Like Home: Assaulted Migrant Women's Claims to Refugee Status and Landings on Humanitarian and Compassionate Grounds." *Journal of Law and Social Policy* 6 (Fall 1990): 148–225.

Portes A. *The Economic Sociology of Immigration: Essays on Networks, Ethnicity, and Entrepreneurship.* New York: Russell Sage Foundation, 1995.

Portes, A., and J. Borocz. "Contemporary Immigration: Theoretical Perspectives on Its Determinants and Modes of Incorporation." *International Migration Review* 23 (1989): 83.

Portes, A., and R. G. Rumbaut. *Immigrant America: A Portrait.* Los Angeles: University of California Press, 1990.

Powell, Walter W., and Paul J. DiMaggio (eds.). *The New Institutionalism in Organizational Analysis.* Chicago: University of Chicago Press, 1991.

Power, S. *"A Problem from Hell": America and the Age of Genocide.* New York: Basic Books, 2002.

Price, C. *Southern Europeans in Australia.* Melbourne: Oxford University Press, 1963.

Rawls, J. *Political Liberalism.* New York: Columbia University Press, 1996.

Rees, A. M. "The Other T. H. Marshall." *Journal of Social Policy* 24, no. 3 (1995): 341–362.

Reisman, W. M. "Remarks." *Proceedings of the American Society of International Law* 82 (1988): 373–377.

Renteln, A., and A. Dundes. *International Human Rights: Universalism vs. Relativism.* Newbury Park, Calif.: Sage, 1990.

Riggs, R., and J. Piano. *The United Nations: International Organization and World Politics.* Homewood, Ill.: Dorsey Press, 1988.

Risse, Thomas, Stephen C. Ropp, and Kathryn Sikkink. *The Power of Human Rights: International Norms and Domestic Change.* New York: Cambridge University Press, 1999.

Robertson, R. *Globalization: Social Theory and Global Culture.* London: Sage, 1992.

Romany, Celina. "State Responsibility Goes Private: A Feminist Critique of the Public/Private Distinction in International Human Rights Law." In Rebecca J. Cook (ed.), *Human Rights of Women: National and International Perspectives.* Philadelphia: University of Pennsylvania Press, 1994.

————. "Women as Aliens: A Feminist Critique of the Public/Private Distinction in International Human Rights Law." *Harvard Human Rights Journal* 6 (Spring 1993): 87–125.

Rosenau, James N. "The Relocation of Authority in a Shrinking World." *Comparative Politics* 24, no. 3 (1992): 253–271.

Rosenau, J. N., and W. M. Fagen. "A New Dynamism in World Affairs: Increasingly Skillful Citizens?" *International Studies Quarterly* 41 (December 1997): 655–686.

Roth, Kenneth. "Domestic Violence as an International Human Rights Issue." In Rebecca J. Cook (ed.), *Human Rights of Women: National and International Perspectives*. Philadelphia: University of Pennsylvania Press, 1994.

Ruddick, E. "The Selection and Management of Immigration to Canada." In OECD *Migration and Development: New Partnerships for Co-operation*. Paris: OECD, 1994.

Sabatier, Paul, and Hank Jenkins-Smith (eds). *Policy Change and Learning: An Advocacy Coalition Approach*. Boulder, Colo.: Westview Press, 1993.

Sassen, Saskia. *Globalization and Its Discontents*. New York: New Press, 1998.

———. *Losing Control? Sovereignty in an Age of Globalization*. New York: Columbia University Press, 1996.

———. *The Mobility of Labor and Capital: A Study in International Investment and Labor Flow*. Cambridge: Cambridge University Press, 1988.

Schaffer, Haley. "Domestic Violence and Asylum in the United States." *Northwestern University Law Review* 95 (Winter 2001): 779.

Schenke, T. S. "A Proposal to Improve the Treatment of Women in Asylum Law." *Global Legal Studies Journal* 2, no. 1 (1996): 301–344.

Scholte, J. A. "Beyond the Buzzword: Toward a Critical Theory of Globalization." In E. Kofman and G. Youngs (eds.), *Globalization: Theory and Practice*. London: Pinter, 1996.

———. *Globalization: A Critical Introduction*. New York: St. Martin's Press, 2000.

———. "Globalization and Collective Identities." In Jill Krause and Neil Renwick (eds.), *Identities in International Relations*. New York: St. Martin's Press, 1996.

Schreader, Alicia. "The State Funded Women's Movement." In Roxana Ng, Gillian Walker, and Jacob Muller (eds.), *Community Organization and the Canadian State*. Toronto: Garamond Press, 1990.

Schuler, Margaret (ed.). *Freedom from Violence: Women's Strategies from Around the World*. New York: Women INK; OEF International; UNIFEM Widbooks, 1992.

Schwab, Peter, and Adamantia Pollis. "Globalization's Impact on Human Rights." In Adamantia Pollis and Peter Schwab. (eds.). *Human Rights: New Perspectives, New Realities*. Boulder, Colo.: Lynne Rienner Publishers, 2000.

Secours aux Femmes. Letter to immigration officials and supporters, 23 November 1992.

Sen, A. "Capability and Well-Being." In M. Nussbaum and A. Sen (eds.). *The Quality of Life*. Oxford: Clarendon Press, 1993.

Sen, Gita, and Caren Grown. *Development, Crises and Alternative Visions: Third World Women's Perspectives*. London: Earthscan, 1988.

Seton-Watson, H. *Nations and States*. London: Methuen, 1977.

Shen, J. "National Sovereignty and Human Rights in a Positive Law Context." *Brooklyn Journal of International Law* 26, no. 2 (2000): 417–446.

Shor, Elizabeth. "Domestic Abuse and Alien Women in Immigration Law: Response and Responsibility." *Cornell Journal of Law and Public Policy* 9 (2000): 697–713.

Sikkink, K. "Human Rights, Principled Issue Networks, and Sovereignty in Latin America." *International Organization* 47, no. 3 (1993a): 411–441.

———. *Ideas and Institutions: Developmentalism in Brazil and Argentina.* Ithaca, N.Y.: Cornell University Press, 1991.

———. "The Power of Principled Ideas: Human Rights Politics in the United States and Western Europe." In J. Goldstein and R. O. Keohane (eds.), *Ideas and Foreign Policy.* Ithaca, N.Y.: Cornell University Press, 1993b.

Simeon, Richard. "Federalism in the 1980s." In Paul W. Fox and Graham White (eds.), *Politics: Canada.* 6th edition. Toronto: McGraw-Hill Ryerson, 1987.

Smith, Lynn, and Eleanor Wachtel. *A Feminist Guide to the Constitution.* Ottawa: CACSW, 1992.

Smith, Rhona K. M. *Textbook on International Human Rights.* Oxford: Oxford University Press, 2003.

Snow, David A., and Robert D. Benford. "Ideology, Frame Resonance, and Participant Mobilization." In Bert Klandermans, Hanspeler Kriesi, and Sidney Tarrow (eds.), *From Structure to Action: Comparing Social Movement Research Across Cultures.* Greenwich, Conn.: JAI Press, 1988.

———. "Master Frames and Cycles of Protest," in Aldon D. Morris and Carol Mc-Clurg Mueller (eds.), *Frontiers in Social Movement Theory.* New Haven: Yale University Press, 1992.

Soysal, Y. N. "Changing Parameters of Citizenship and Claims-making: Organized Islam in European Public Spheres." European University Institute, Badia Fiesolan, EUI Working paper EUF No. 4, 1996.

———. *Limits of Citizenship: Migrants and Postnational Membership in Europe.* Chicago: University of Chicago, 1994.

Spencer, S. (ed.). *Strangers and Citizens.* London: Rivers Oram Press, 1994.

Spijkerboer, Thomas. *Gender and Refugee Status.* Aldershot, England: Ashgate, 2000.

Spivak, Gayatri. "Can the Subaltern Speak?" In C. Nelson and L. Grossberg (eds.), *Marxism and the Interpretation of Culture.* Urbana: University of Illinois Press, 1988.

Statistics Canada. "Violence Against Women Survey." *Canadian Social Trends.* Autumn 1994.

Steiner, Henry, and Philip Alston. *International Human Rights in Context: Law, Politics, Morals.* Oxford: Oxford University Press, 2000.

Sunstein, C. R. *Free Markets and Social Justice.* Oxford: Oxford University Press, 1997.

Sylvester, C. *Feminist Theory and International Relations in a Postmodern Era.* Cambridge: Cambridge University Press, 1994.

Tarrow, Sidney. *Power in Movement: Social Movements and Contentious Politics.* Cambridge University Press, 1998.

TCMR. *Annual Report 1994/95.* Montreal: TCMR, 1995.

———. *Consultations on Refugee Women Claimants.* Montreal: TCMR, 1993.

Teitelbaum, Michael S. "Immigration, Refugees, and Foreign Policy." *International Organization* 38, no. 3 (Summer 1984): 429–450.

Thérèse. Speech delivered at the IRB Conference for International Women's Day, Montreal, 8 March 1995.

Tilly, Charles. *From Mobilization to Revolution*. Reading, Mass.: Addison-Wesley, 1978.

Touraine, A. *The Voice and the Eye: An Analysis of Social Movements*. Cambridge: Cambridge University Press, 1981.

Tranter, L. "A Step Forward in Protecting Human Rights: *Canada v. Ward*." *Refuge* 13, no. 4 (July–August 1993): 16–18.

Tuitt, Patricia. *False Images: Law's Construction of the Refugee*. London: Pluto Press, 1996.

Turley, E. *Consultations on Gender Issues and Refugees: Final Report*. Ottawa, March 1994.

Turner, B. (ed.). *Citizenship and Social Theory*. London: Sage, 1993.

Turner, B. "Postmodern Culture/Modern Citizens." In Bart van Steenbergen (ed.), *The Condition of Citizenship*. London: Sage, 1994.

Ungerson Clare, and Mary Kember (eds.). *Women and Social Policy: A Reader*. Basingstoke, England: Macmillan, 1997.

UN High Commissioner for Refugees. *News Stories*. "UNHCR Hails Tenth Anniversary of Canada's Guidelines on Gender-Related Persecution." 7 March 2003.

———. *Prevention and Response to Sexual and Gender-Based Violence in Refugee Situations. Inter-Agency Lessons Learned Conference Proceedings, 27–29 March 2001, Geneva*. March 2001.

———. *Selected Bibliography on Refugee Women*. Geneva, 2005.

van Hoof, F. "International Human Rights Obligations for Companies and Domestic Courts: An Unlikely Combination?" M. Castermans-Holeman, F., van Hoof, and J. Smith (eds.), *The Role of the Nation-State in the 21st Century: Human Rights, International Organisations, and Foreign Policy: Essays in Honour of Peter Baehr*. The Hague: Kluwer Law International, 1998.

van Steenbergen, Bart (ed.). *The Condition of Citizenship*. London: Sage, 1994.

Vickers, Jill, Pauline Rankin, and Christine Appelle. *Politics as if Women Mattered: A Political Analysis of the National Action Committee on the Status Of Women*. Toronto: University of Toronto Press, 1993.

Vincent, R. J. *Human Rights and International Relations*. Cambridge: Cambridge University Press, 1986.

Vogel, Ursula, and Michael Moran (eds.). *The Frontiers of Citizenship*. London: Macmillan, 1991.

Von Sternberg, Mark. "Battered Women and the Criteria for Refugee Status." *World Refugee Survey* (2000): 40–47.

Walby, S. *Theorizing Patriarchy*. Oxford: Basil Blackwell, 1990.

Walker, R. B. J. "Social Movements/World Politics." *Millennium: Journal of International Studies* 23, no. 3 (1994): 669–700.

Watson, J. S. "A Realistic Jurisprudence of International Law," *Yearbook of International Affairs* 30 (1976): 265–285.

Weiss, Thomas G., and Jarat Chopra. "Sovereignty Under Siege: From Intervention to Humanitarian Space." In G. M. Lyons, and M. Mastanduno (eds.), *Beyond Westphalia? State Sovereignty and International Intervention*. Baltimore: Johns Hopkins University Press, 1995.

Welch, C. E. *NGOs and Human Rights: Promise and Performance.* Philadelphia: University of Pennsylvania Press, 2001.

Welch, C. E., and R. E. Howard-Hassmann (eds.). *Economic Rights in Canada and the United States.* Philadelphia: University of Pennsylvania Press, 2006.

Welch, Claude E., and Mahmood Monshipouri. "The Search for International Human Rights and Justice: Coming to Terms with the New Global Realities." *Human Rights Quarterly* 23, no. 2 (May 2001): 370–401.

Wheeler, Nicholas J. *Saving Strangers.* Oxford: Oxford University Press, 2000.

Williams, F. *Social Policy: A Critical Introduction.* Cambridge: Polity Press, 1989.

Women's Aid. Letter to Immigration Minister Bernard Valcourt and MPs. November 1993.

Yee, A. S. "The Causal Effects of Ideas on Policies." *International Organization* 50, no. 1 (1996): 69–108.

Yin, R. K. *Case Study Research: Design and Methods.* 2nd edition. London: Sage, 1994.

Young, M. "Bill C-55: A New Refugee Status Determination System." Legislative Summary LS-6E, Library of Parliament Research Branch, Law and Government Division, Ottawa, 29 May 1997.

———. "Gender-Related Refugee Claims." Background paper BP-370E, Library of Parliament Research Branch, Law and Government Division, Ottawa, March 1994.

Yuval-Davis, N. *Gender and Nation.* London: Sage, 1997.

Yuval-Davis, N., and F. Anthias. *Woman-Nation-State.* London: Macmillan, 1989.

Zolberg, Aristide R., Astri Suhrke, and Sergio Aguayo. *Escape from Violence: Conflict and the Refugee Crisis in the Developing World.* Oxford: Oxford University Press, 1989.

International Instruments

American Convention on Human Rights. OAS Treaty Series No. 36, 1144 UNTS 123, (1969), entered into force 18 July 1978.

Beijing Declaration and Platform of Action. A/CONF.177/20 (1995) and A/CONF.177/20/Add.1 (1995).

Convention Against Torture and Other Cruel, Inhuman or Degrading Treatment or Punishment. G.A. res. 39/46, annex, 39 UN GAOR Supp. (No. 51) at 197, UN Doc. A/39/51 (1984), entered into force 26 June 1987.

Convention Governing the Specific Aspects of Refugee Problems in Africa. 1001 UNTS 45 (1969), entered into force 20 June 1974.

Convention on the Elimination of All Forms of Discrimination Against Women, G.A. res. 34/180, 34 UN GAOR Supp. (No. 46) at 193, UN Doc. A/34/46 (1979), entered into force 3 September 1981.

Convention on the Rights of the Child. G.A. res. 44/25, annex, 44 UN GAOR Supp. (No. 49) at 167, UN Doc. A/44/49 (1989), entered into force 2 September 1990.

Convention Relating to the Status of Refugees. 189 UNTS 150 (1951), entered into force 22 April 1954.

Council of Europe. Parliamentary Assemby Recommendation 1374 (1998) on the *Situation of Refugee Women in Europe*. 26 May 1998.

Declaration on Territorial Asylum. G.A. res. 2312 (XXII), 22 UN GAOR Supp. (No. 16) at 81, UN Doc. A/6716 (1967).

Declaration on the Elimination of Violence Against Women. G.A. res. 48/104, 48 UN GAOR Supp. (No. 49) at 217, UN Doc. A/48/49 (1993).

Declaration on the Right and Responsibility of Individuals, Groups and Organs of Society to Promote and Protect Universally Recognized Human Rights and Fundamental Freedoms. G.A. res.53/144, annex, 53 UN GAOR Supp., UN Doc. A/RES/53/144 (1999).

Declaration on the Right to Development. G.A. res. 41/128, annex, 41 UN GAOR Supp. (No. 53) at 186, UN Doc. A/41/53 (1986).

Declaration on the Rights of Indigenous Peoples. G.A. Res. 61/295, UN Doc. A/RES/47/1 (2007).

Draft Code on State Responsibility. Report of the International Law Commission to the General Assembly, A/135/10, 1980.

European Convention for the Protection of Human Rights and Fundamental Freedoms. (ETS 5), 213 UNTS 222 (1950), entered into force 3, September 1953.

European Parliament. Resolution on the application of the 1951 UN Convention Relating to the Status of Refugees. 13 April 1984.

————. Motion for a resolution pursuant to Rule 47 of the Rules of Procedure on the revison on the Geneva Convention Relating to the Status of Refugees. [1–545/82] 28 July 1982.

European Union Council. Amended proposal for a council directive on minimum standards on procedures in Member States for granting and withdrawing refugee status. 30 April 2004.

————. Directive 2004/83/EC on minimum standards for the qualification and status of third country nationals or stateless persons as refugees or as persons who otherwise need international protection and the content of the protection granted. 29 April 2004.

Inter-American Convention on the Prevention, Punishment, and Eradication of Violence Against Women. 33 I.L.M. 1534 (1994), entered into force 5 March 1995.

International Covenant on Civil and Political Rights. G.A. res. 2200A (XXI), 21 UN GAOR Supp. (No. 16) at 52, UN Doc. A/6316 (1966), 999 UNTS 171, entered into force 23 March 1976.

International Covenant on Economic, Social and Cultural Rights. G.A. res. 2200A (XXI), 21 UN GAOR Supp. (No. 16) at 49, UN Doc. A/6316 (1966), 993 UNTS 3, entered into force 3 January 1976.

Nairobi Forward Looking Strategies for Advancement of Women. A/CONF/ 1116/28, 1985.

Organization of American States Convention on Territorial Asylum. 1438 UN 129, OAS Treaty Series, No. 19. 28 March 1954.

Protocol Relating to the Status of Refuees. 606 UNTS 267, entered into force 4 October 1967.

Report of the International Law Commission to the General Assembly. UN Doc. A/35/10 (1980).

Statute of the Office of the United Nations High Commissioner for Refugees. G.A. res. 428 (V), annex, 5 UN GAOR Supp. (No. 20) at 46, UN Doc. A/1775 (1950).

———. *Summary Conclusions—Gender-Related Persecution.* Global Consultations on International Protection, Second Track, San Reap, 6–8 September 2001.

United Nations Centre for Social Development and Humanitarian Affairs. *UN Report on Violence Against Women in the Family.* UN Doc. ST/SCDHA/2.UN, 1989.

United Nations Charter. 26 June 1945. 59 Stat. 1031, T.S. 993, 3 Bevans 1153, entered into force 24 October 1945.

United Nations High Commissioner for Refugees. "Asylum Under Threat." In *The State of the World's Refugees: The Challenge of Protection.* Geneva, 1993.

———. Guidelines on International Protection: Gender-Related Persecution within the Context of Article 1a(2) of the 1951 Convention and Its 1967 Protocol Relating to the Status of Refugees, UN Doc. HCR/GIP/02/01, 7 May 2002.

———. Guidelines on the Protection of Refugee Women. UN Doc. EC/SCP/67, 22 July 1991.

———. Position Paper on Gender-Related Persecution. Geneva, January 2000

———. Prevention and Response to Sexual and Gender-Based Violence in Refugee Situations. Proceedings of the Inter-Agency Lessons Learned Conference, 27–29 March 2001, Geneva.

———. "Refugee Women and girls: Surviving Violence and Neglect." In *The State of the World's Refugees: In Search of Solutions.* Geneva, 1995.

———. Roundtable Discussion on Refugee Women and Sexual Violence. Geneva, 1980.

United Nations High Commissioner for Refugees, Executive Committee. Conclusion No. 54 on Refugee Women. Report of the 39th Session. 1988.

———. Conclusion on Refugee Women and International Protection. Report of the 36th Sessino. (A/AC.96/67) October 1985.

———. Conclusion on Refugee Protection and Sexual Violence. No. 73 (XLIV). 1993.

———. Conclusions on the Development of Appropriate Guidelines. 1995.

———. General Conclusion on Internaitonal Protection. No. 79(o) 1996, No. 81(t) 1997, and No. 87(n) 1999.

———. General Conclusion on International Protection. No. 77g (XLVI), 1995.

———. Note on International Protection: Summary. Report of the 41st Session. 27 August 1990.

———. Note on Refugee Women and International protection. EC/SCP/39, 8 July 1985.

———. Note on Refugee Women and International protection. EC/SCP/59, 28 August 1990.

———. Progress Report on the Implementation of the UNHCR Policy on Refugee Women. 17 July 1991.

———. Report on Refugee Women. A/AC.96/727, 19 July 1989.

———. Sexual Violence Against Refugees: Guidelines on Prevention and Response. Geneva, 1995.

———. UNHCR Roundtable, Helping Refugee Women Help Themselves, Geneva, 1985.

Universal Declaration of Human Rights. G.A. res. 217A (III), UN Doc. A/810 at 71 (1948).

Vienna Declaration. World Conference on Human Rights, Vienna, 14–25 June 1993, UN Doc. A/CONF.157/24 (Part I) at 20 (1993).

National Instruments

Australia. Department of Immigration and Multicultural Affairs. Refugee and Humanitarian Visa Applicants: Guidelines on Gender Issues for Decision-Makers. July 1996.

Austria. Ministry of Interior. Order No. 97.101/10/SL III/95. 1995.

Canada. Citizenship and Immigration Canada (CIC). *Declaration on Refugee Protection for Women.* 1 June 1994.

———. Citizenship and Immigration Canada (CIC). *Refugees, Immigration and Gender: Report of the Standing Committee on Citizenship and Immigration.* 1995.

———. Employment and Immigration. *Gender Issues in the Refuge Status Determination Process in Canada.* Paper for Agenda Setting Meeting for National Consultations. June 1993.

———. Employment and Immigration. Refugee Affairs. *Gender Issues and Refugees.* Policy Discussion Paper. June 1993.

———. Employment and Immigration. *Report on Consultations on Gender Issues and Refugees.* Fall 1993.

———. Immigration and Refugee Board. Preferred Position Paper. *Membership in a Particular Social Group as a Basis for a Well-founded Fear of Persecution.* Ottawa, March 1992.

———. Immigration and Refugee Board. *Compendium of Decisions: Update to the Guidelines for Women Refugee Claimants Fearing Gender-Related Persecution Guidelines.* February 2003.

———. Immigration and Refugee Board. *The Gender Action Plan of the Immigration and Refugee Board.* Ottawa, May 1994.

———. Immigration and Refugee Board. Guidelines on Women Refugee Claimants Fearing Gender-Related Persecution (Pursuant to section 65(3) of the Immigration Act). 9 March 1993.

———. Immigration and Refugee Board. Update to the Guidelines on Women Refugee Claimants Fearing Gender-Related Persecution Guidelines (section I.3), effective 13 November 1996.

———. Status of Women Canada. *Living Without Fear: Everyone's Goal, Every Woman's Right.* November 1991.

———. Canadian Charter of Rights and Freedoms. 1982.

———. Canadian Human Rights Act. 1977 (amended 1983, 1993).

———. Immigration Act. 1976, 1993.

———. Multiculturalism Act. 1988.

Danish Refugee Council. Information and Documentation Department. *Women and Asylum.* Conference report on gender-related persecution. June 1997.

France. Declaration of the Rights of Man and the Citizen. 1789.

Guatemala. Government Accord No. 383-2001. 14 September 2001.

Ireland. Irish Council for Civil Liberties Women's Committee. Gender Guidelines for Female Refugees and Asylum Seekers. 2000.

Ireland. Refugee Act. 1996.

Netherlands. Dutch Refugee Council. Policy Directive to the 1985 Proceedings of the International Seminar on Refugee Women, 1985.

————. Immigration and Naturalization Service. Work Instruction No. 148. *Women in the Asylum Procedure*. UNHCR translation, reprinted in Spijkerboer 2000.

Norway. Royal Ministry of Justice and the Police. Guidelines for Determining Refugee Status in Norway. 15 January 1998.

Panama. Executive Decree No. 23. 10 February 1998.

South Africa, Republic of. Refugees Act. No. 13 of 1998.

Sweden. Migration Board. Gender-Based Persecution: Guidelines for Investigation and Evaluation of the Needs of Women for Protection. March 2001.

United Kingdom. Asylum Policy Instructions. *Gender Issues in the Asylum Claim*. London: Home Office, March 2004.

————. Immigration Appellate Authority. Asylum Gender Guidelines. November 2000.

United States. Department of Justice. Immigration and Naturalization Service, Office of International Affairs. "Considerations for Asylum Officers Adjudicating Asylum Claims from Women." 26 May 1995.

Venezuela. National Assembly. Decree of October 2001.

Interviews Cited

Asimaliopulos, Julie. Staff member, Multi-Femmes (Montreal shelter for ethnically diverse women). Interview, Montreal, 28 February 1995.

Augenfeld, Rivka. President, Table de Concertation des Organismes de Montreal au Service des Personnes Réfugiées et Immigrantes (TCMR). Interview, Montreal, 22 August 1995.

Belanger, Diane. Refugee lawyer. Interview, Montreal, 11 July 1995.

Bronson, Diana. Information officer, International Centre for Human Rights and Democratic Development (ICHRDD). Interview, Montreal, 25 January 1995.

Brunet, Arienne. International Centre for Human Rights and Democratic Development (ICHRDD). Interview, Montreal, 21 December 1994.

Côté, Marie-Louise. Refugee lawyer. Interview, Montreal, 13 January 1995.

Dench, Janet. Executive director, Canadian Council for Refugees (CCR). Interview, Montreal, 20 December 1994.

Doray, Nancy. Adjudicator; member of the Working Group on Refugee Women; Immigration and Refugee Board (IRB) adjudicator. Interview, Montreal, 30 January 1995.

Duquette, Pierre. Refugee lawyer. Interview, Montreal, 20 July 1995.

Fernandez, Flora. National Action Committee on the Status of Women (NAC), Executive Committee, Violence Against Women Unit; director, Women's Aid (Montreal shelter for immigrant women); member, National Organization of Immigrant and Visible Minority Women of Canada. Interview, Montreal, 24 August 1995.

Heyeur, Sonia. Refugee lawyer. Interview, Montreal, 2 February 1995.

Jackman, Barbara. President, Ontario Lawyer Association; refugee lawyer. Interview, Toronto, 22 November 1994.

LaCroix, Marie. Member, Coalition Aux Réfugiées, Montreal (CAR). Interview, Montreal (phone), 27 August 1995.

Martha. Staff member, Auberge Transition (Montreal women's shelter). Interview, Montreal (phone), 17 January 1995.

Montecino, Elizabeth. Director, Flora Tristan (Montreal shelter for immigrant women). Interview, Montreal, 31 January 1995.

Piriou, Sylvie. Refugee lawyer. Interview, Montreal, 30 October 1996.

Ramkisson, Suhk. Refugee lawyer. Interview, Toronto, 18 October 1996.

Thèrése. Refugee claimant. Interview, Montreal, 19 July 1995.

Williams, Glynis. Coordinator, Refugee Action Montreal (RAM). Interview, Montreal, 28 July 1995.

Young, Margaret. Library of Parliament, Research Division, Law and Government. Interview, Ottawa (phone), 23 August 1995.

Press Coverage

Caribbean Camera. 21 June 1996. "Lesbian Gets Walking Papers."

———. 26 August 1996. "Guyanese Granted Refugee Status."

Christian Science Monitor. 9 March 1994. M. Clayton, "Afflicted Women Find Hope in Canada's Refugee Rules."

Economist. 20 March 1993. "Women's Refuge."

Globe and Mail. 15 January 1993. Estanislao Oziewicz, "Canada Not Planning to Widen Refugee Rules to Cover Sex Bias: Women Fleeing Abuse Would Strain System, Valcourt Says."

———. 16 January 1993. Estanislao Oziewicz, "No Plan to Accept Victims of Sex Bias."

———. 21 December 1993. Edward Broadbent, "Prisoners in Their Own Homes." Editorial.

———. 8 February 1995. Canadian Press. "Deportation Order Fought."

Guardian (London). 22 March 1993. "One Giant Step for Women in Search of Asylum."

Hamilton Spectator. 30 January 1993. Canadian Press. "Persecuted Due to Her Sex, Woman Will Stay in Canada."

———. 11 February 1993. Canadian Press. "Deportation Order for Abused Woman Under Review."

———. 6 March 1993. Canadian Press. "Follow Canada's Policy on Women Refugees Group Says."

Hour Magazine. 5–11 January 1995. Jennifer Feinberg, "Cameroonian Woman Threatened from the Grave."

Journal de Montreal. 2 May 1991. "Retourner dans leur pays ou continuer d'être maltraitées."

———. 8 February 1995. "Immigration Canada accusée de déporter une femme battue."

Montreal Gazette. 11 November 1992. Stephan Bindman, "Victim of Spousal Abuse Can Stay: Trinidadian Woman's Refugee Claim 'Credible.' "

———. 30 November 1992. LuAnne LaSalle, "Make Canada a Haven for Abused Women: NAC."

———. 25 January 1993. David Scanlan, "Consider Gender: Persecuted Women Should Have Refugees Status."

———. 25 January 1993. "Rape and war: They Go Together, Experts Say."

———. 30 January 1993. Canadian Press. "Persecuted Woman Gets Refugee Haven."

———. 3 February 1993. David Scanlan, "Women's Groups Say Abuse Is Ground for Refugee Status."

———. 6 February 1993. Canadian Press. "Valcourt Stays Deportation fo Trinidad Woman."

———. 10 February 1993. Jane Miller. "Battered Montreal Mother Fears for Life if Deported to Bangladesh."

———. 15 February 1993. Peggy Curran, "Is Sexual Equality a Universal Value?"

———. 5 March 1993. Janet Bagnall, "Stop Deporting Female Refugee Claimants: NAC."

———. 8 March 1993. Janet Bagnall, "Battered Bangladeshi Woman Can Stay."

———. 10 March 1993. Peggy Curran, "Ottawa Eases Way for Women Seeking Refugee Status."

———. 11 March 1993. Edward Broadbent, "Indivisible: Until Women's Rights Are Human Rights, We Have Far to Go."

———. 17 November 1994. Lisa Fitterman, "Woman Gets Eighteen-Day Delay on Deportation: Seychelles Native Fears Estranged Husband Will Kill Her if She's Sent Home."

———. 17 November 1994. "Woman Fears Death If Deported Tomorrow."

———. 17 November 1994. Elena Cherney, "Can't Shelter All Battered Refugees."

———. 17 November 1994. >Susan Semenak, "Marchi Stops Deportation of Abused Woman and Two Children."

———. 6 December 1994. Katherine Wilton, "Pleading to Stay."

———. 7 December 1994. Alexander Norris, "Woman Hides from Deportation: Says In-Laws Will Kill Her in Cameroon."

———. 11 January 1995. Sarah Binder, "Cameroon Woman in Hiding Tests New Immigration Guidelines."

———. 2 February 1995. Alexander Norris, "Battered Woman Kicked Out."

———. 8 February 1995. Alexander Norris, "Ottawa Ruling Angers Women's Groups."

———. 10 February 1995. Alexander Norris, "Battered Woman to be Deported Today: Immigration Rejects Last-Ditch Plea to Allow Trinidadian to Stay."

———. 12 July 1995. Katherine wilton, "Woman Had Reason to Flee Ghana: Threat of Genital Mutilation Justifies Her Appeal to Stay, Court Rules."

———. 28 December 1998. Amanda Jelowicki, "Deportee Fears for Her Life."

Montreal Mirror. 5 January 1995. "Hiding out, waiting, hoping."

Ottawa Citizen. 30 January 1993. "Feminist Refugee Can Stay: Strong Message to Decision Makers."

———. 11 March 1993. Nada. "A Serious Step Toward Accepting Female Refugees."

La Presse, Montreal. 8 February 1995. François Berger, "Ottawa déporte une immigrant battue . . . mais accepte l'ex-mari agresseur."

———. 10 February 1995. François Berger, "Les groups de feemes demandent à Québec de bloquer la déportation d'une famille e Trinidad."

———. 11 February 1995. François Berger, "Enfants appréhendés en vue de l'expulsion de leur mère."

Quarter Libre. 20 December 1994. Calmels, Didier. "Entre la mort et la clandestinité."

Record (Kitchener-Waterloo). 30 January 1993. Canadian Press. "Entry East for Abused Refugee Women: Saudi Who Wouldn't Wear Veil Can Stay in Canada."

Toronto Star. 17 September 1992. Canadian Press. "Trinidad Can Protect Woman, Ottawa Insists."

———. 23 September 1992. Jim Willkes, "Abused Woman Allowed to Stay Here."

———. 11 November 1992. Special. "Court Allows Refugee Bid by Abused Woman."

———. 1 December 1992. M. Landsberg, "Immigrant Keeps Terrorist in, Kicks Women Out Our Door."

———. 11 February 1993. Allan Thompson, "Women Fleeing Abuse to Qualify as Refugees.

———. 11 February 1993. Canadian Press. "Valcourt to Review Case of Bangladeshi Woman."

———. 6 June 1993. Allan thompson, "Woman Given Refugee Status After Fleeing Spouse's Beatings."

Toronto Sun. 26 August 1996. Tom Godfrey, "Battered Wife Can Stay Here."

Westmount Experience (Montreal). 23 November 1994. "Westmounters Backing Seychelles Refugee: Petition to Prevent Deportation of Threatened Woman Available for Signing at Church of the Advent."

———. November 1994. Clare Harting, "Un sursis de 18 jours ne rassure en rien la famille Sabadin: Une mère et ses deux enfants vivent dans la peur."

———. December 1994. Glynis Williams, "Success for Refugee Action Montreal."

———. February 1995. "Irrégularités dans la déportation d'une mère et de ses deux enfants."

Index

Advocacy network, core, 76, 79, 80

Asylum, right to, 60, 108. *See also* persecution; refugees

Australia, 12, 93, 113, 228, 230, 256, 275–76, 282, 285, 288

Austria, 12, 230, 282

Bangladesh, 74, 145, 147, 197

Beijing, Fourth World Conference on Women, 212, 214

Boomerang effect, 17, 42, 283

Bride burning, 92

Bulgaria, 74, 147, 197

Cameroon, 74, 150, 151, 197

Canadian Advisory Council on the Status of Women (CACSW), 106, 116, 258, 280

Canadian Charter of Rights and Freedoms, 112, 121, 132

Canadian Council for Refugees (CCR), 125–26, 128, 132, 154–55, 160, 170, 172–73, 189, 191, 194–95, 202, 204, 209, 211, 214, 224, 271, 277, 280, 281

Canadian Human Rights Act, 117, 119

Case study method, 27, 71–72

Children of refugees, 95, 120, 132, 144–45, 147–48, 153–55, 158, 161, 193, 199–200, 217, 220, 248, 258, 267–68

Citizenship, 14–16, 23–25, 37, 44–45, 48, 62, 66–70, 105, 107, 115, 118, 222–25, 233–34, 236, 238–46, 248, 250–54, 256–63, 265, 272, 276

Claim-making process, refugees: 48, 64, 73, 75, 88–89, 108, 122, 127, 256, 275; and going public, 64, 72, 130–32, 136–38, 141–42, 144–46, 148–49, 152–53, 155–58, 168, 176, 180–82, 187, 206, 223, 234

Collective action, 47, 65, 137, 152, 169, 183, 262. *See also* social movement

Constructivist, 15, 37, 38, 39, 42

Convention Governing the Specific Aspects of Refugee Problems in Africa, 65

Convention on the Elimination of All Forms of Discrimination Against Women (CEDAW), 13, 101

Convention on the Political Rights of Women, 21

Convention on the Rights of the Child, 254

Convention Relating to the Status of Refugees (1951 Convention), 2, 4, 7, 10, 12, 14, 16, 60, 65, 70, 75, 82–84, 87, 97–101, 103, 114, 178, 187, 191, 205, 207, 209, 227–29, 231–32, 235, 256

Cultural legitimacy, 35, 42, 45–46, 238, 255, 257, 260, 265

Cultural relativism, 16, 46, 67, 97, 142, 202, 208, 219, 236, 254, 257, 263, 264

Custodial violence, 221

Czech Republic, 12, 230

Decapitating, for adultery, 96

Declaration on the Elimination of Violence Against Women, 14, 254, 275

Declaration on the Right to Development, 254

Declaration on the Rights of Indigenous Peoples, 254

Denizens, 118, 244–45

Deportation, 63–64, 89, 91, 123–24, 127, 130, 132, 143, 145–48, 154–55, 162, 164–65, 181–82, 189–90, 193–95, 197–98, 200, 204–6, 208–9, 212–14, 234, 259

Domestic violence, 3, 5–6, 8–9, 13, 16, 23, 92, 107, 127, 130, 144, 148, 150–52, 155, 161, 164–67, 189–90, 193, 195–96, 200–201, 212, 214–15, 219–20, 228, 231–32

Dominica, 74, 147, 197

Donnelly, Jack, 17, 23, 31, 33–35, 41–43, 239, 249, 261, 263, 273

Dowry deaths, 14

Dress code violations, punishment for, 6, 9, 13, 87, 141–42, 194

Employment and Immigration, Canada (EIC), 122, 173, 191–92
European Union (EU), 230, 284

Female genital mutilation, 91, 150, 228
Female persecution, definition, 10. *See also* persecution; refugees
Feminization of migration, 92–94
Feticide, of girls, 221
Finland, 12, 230, 282
Flora Tristan Shelter for Immigrant Women, 126, 164–65, 189–90, 277, 279–80
Forced abortion, 84, 95, 223–24
Forced marriage, 92, 220–21, 231
Forced sterilization, 220–21
Foreign policy, 2, 17, 37, 53, 55, 59, 62, 86, 236, 256, 283
Framing: cultural, 10, 26–28, 81, 89, 92, 107, 175; tactics, processes, strategies, 19, 27, 28, 39, 47–49, 58, 60, 65, 92, 152, 175, 180, 182–83, 185–86, 188–89, 192, 196, 204, 205–7, 210, 212, 214, 222, 224, 234–35, 246–47; cognitive, 20; structures, 26, 60, 112; institutional, 188, 196, 205–6, 210, 212, 214
France, 45, 102, 252

Gender-related persecution, Canadian definition, 5–7, 10–11. *See also* persecution; refugees
Germany, 12, 74, 102, 189, 197, 230, 282
Global Commission on International Migration (GCIM), 25, 44–45, 276
Globalization, 16–18, 22–26, 29, 30–44, 48, 50, 52, 55–58, 66–67, 69, 71, 93, 104, 106, 237–39, 245, 248–51, 254–55, 257, 260–65, 272; definition, 31; transformationalists, 250
Group rights, 115, 255, 259, 263
Guatemala, 12, 74, 147, 152, 197, 230, 283
Guest workers, 24, 239, 240, 244, 252
Guidelines for Refugee Women Fleeing Gender-Related Persecution, analysis of contents, 4–8; Update, 215, 220

Hard law, 94, 229
Headscarf affair, 252
Hearings, refugee, 29, 87, 90–91, 123, 167, 190, 211, 278

HIV/AIDS, 256
Homosexuality: lesbians, 256, 309; gays, 256
Honor killing, 14
Housing, 59, 61
Human rights: substantive change, 17–18, 22, 26, 28, 35–36, 39, 42–44, 46, 62, 222, 234, 236, 242–47, 249–51, 253, 260–61, 263; standard setting, processes, 18, 21–22, 34–38, 40, 44, 210, 263–64; standard-setting precedents, 20; international trigger cases, 4, 14, 16, 20–22, 27, 39, 238, 246–47, 251, 254; geographical expansion, 17, 21, 25–26, 144; universal rights, 45–46, 67, 197, 222, 237, 253, 255, 257; origins, theories of, 42–43

Identity, 46–49, 56–58, 64, 68–71, 73, 109, 115, 117, 119, 133, 135–36, 138–42, 146–49, 158, 168–69, 175, 203, 224, 233–34, 237, 248, 278
Illegal migrants, 64, 120, 239
Immigration Act, Canada, 4, 7, 65, 102, 114–15, 121, 204, 207, 271
Immigration and Refugee Board, Canada (IRB), 4, 7–8, 13, 23, 76–78, 80, 103, 110, 122–23, 170, 173, 181, 184, 192, 194–95, 199–201, 205–7, 209, 211, 214–16, 231, 271, 274–75, 279–81
Indigenous rights, 248, 254
Infanticide of girls, 221
Institutionalist, 42, 46
International Centre for Human Rights and Democratic Development (ICHRDD), 126, 128, 132, 143, 147, 154, 156, 160–61, 164, 167, 170, 173, 194–95, 199, 201–3, 205, 209, 214–15, 271–72, 277–78, 280
International development, gender in, 95–96
International trigger cases, 4, 14, 16, 20–22, 27, 39, 238, 246–47, 251, 254. *See also* human rights
Iran, 74, 147, 197
Ireland, 8, 12, 271, 282

Lebanon, 74, 197
Legal Aid, 59

Marshall, T. H., 242–43, 245, 252
Membership: national, 239, 244, 260, 265; postnational, 239–40, 247, 251–54, 259; transnational, 239
Mexico, 74, 189, 197
Migration system: theory, 26, 49, 52, 61, 63,

69, 255; institutional logic of, 49, 260; national level, definition of, 51; and human rights change, 60–71; migration policy, definition, 51–52
Mobilizing vehicles, 48, 60, 112, 262
Multiculturalism Act, Canada, 116–17

Nairobi Forward Looking Strategies for Advancement of Women (Nairobi Conference), 101, 106
National Action Committee on the Status of Women (NAC), 126, 129, 132, 138–39, 145–46, 160–64, 171–73, 189, 194, 197, 200–201, 204, 206, 209, 214, 277–78
National Organization of Immigrant and Visible Minority Women (NOIVMW), 126, 129, 132, 154, 171–73, 184, 190, 277, 280
National rights, 21–24, 28, 37, 40–44, 46, 70, 112, 175, 182, 233–34, 236–37, 239–42, 246, 250–65
National values, 14, 17, 22, 24, 26, 29, 42, 44–46, 233, 236, 238, 240–41, 249–51, 255, 257–58, 260–62, 264
Nationality, 2, 4, 5, 7, 10, 12, 64, 78, 82, 83, 87, 102, 138, 219, 220, 227, 235, 239, 240, 242, 248, 252, 268, 269
Netherlands, 12, 98, 102, 230, 283
Network, see *advocacy network.*
New social movement theory, 47–8
Noncitizens, 15–17, 23, 25, 27–28, 37, 45–46, 66–67, 69, 111, 122, 168, 174, 222, 233, 236–41, 246, 244–45, 247, 249–62, 265–66, 273
Norms: norm cascade, 17, 19, 21; norm diffusion, 14, 19; norm entrepreneurs, 19–20, 38, 246; norm resistance, 19, 39, 246; and precedents, 17, 20–22, 26; normative bias, 17, 22; supra/international, 14, 17, 19, 20, 26, 30, 35, 37–39, 43, 238, 240, 248–50, 263; national, 18, 20, 70
Norway, 12, 230, 283

Panama, 12, 283
Persecution: definition, 10, 82–84; and human rights, 10; and women's experience, 84–92; public/private divide, 84–86; gender persecution, definition, 10; gender-related persecution, Canadian definition, 5–7, 10–11; female persecution, definition, 10. *See also* refugees
Persecution of kin, 5, 217

Peru, 74, 147, 152, 197
Policy values, 136, 169, 177–79, 186, 208, 225, 274; deep core values, 159, 177–79; near-core values, 177–79, 208, 222; secondary-core values, 177–79, 222
Political opinion, 2, 4, 5, 7, 10, 12, 82–83, 102, 138, 188, 194, 217, 219, 227, 231, 235, 248, 269
Political opportunities, 27, 47–49, 59, 60, 65, 69–70, 81, 112, 133, 234, 235, 248, 276
Pornography, 221
Positivist, 3, 18, 22, 37, 271
Push-pull theory, 50, 63, 255

Race, 2, 4, 5, 7, 10, 12, 81–83, 85, 97, 102, 109, 112, 119, 138, 219, 228, 235, 242, 245, 248, 268, 272
Rape, 5, 9, 13, 87, 92, 96, 98, 103, 140–41, 151, 198, 217, 221, 228, 231, 282
Realist, 14, 42, 79
RefLex, 77–78, 150, 215–18, 220, 269, 274, 281
Refugee Action Montreal (RAM), 126, 128, 132, 156, 165–66, 170, 173, 209–10, 213, 271, 277–78
Refugee regime: international definition, 51; national definition, 51; and refugee actors, 49–71; and strategic opportunities, 66; and human rights, 60–72, 257
Refugees: definition of, 4–5, 82; defining, 2, 49–50, 55, 82–84; pathways to determination, Canada, 122–23; principle applicants, 93, 130, 267; sponsored, or Family Class, 88–89, 93–94, 114, 127, 130, 132, 153; public/private distinction, 84–86; as actors, 49–71; and human rights change, 60–71; forced versus voluntary, 26, 28, 50, 54, 56, 62–63, 65, 69–70, 72, 135, 137, 148, 158, 168, 235, 256
Religion, 2, 4–5, 7, 10, 12, 81, 82–83, 85, 87, 97, 112, 138, 217, 219, 227, 235, 248, 268, 269
Resource mobilization theory, 47–48
Russia, 9, 74, 147, 197, 223

Sanctuary movement, 256
Saudi Arabia, 1, 74, 141–44, 152, 160, 166, 197, 201–2
Sexual exploitation, 98, 100
Seychelles, 74, 141, 147–48, 155, 197
Signifying acts, or work, 24, 27, 69, 141, 175–76, 182, 207, 222, 235, 237, 272
Slavery, 87, 231

Social group, 2, 4–8, 10, 12, 64, 78, 82–83, 87,
    97–102, 138, 167, 187–88, 193, 200, 207, 209,
    215, 217–20, 227, 229, 231–32, 235, 269, 276,
    282–83
Social movement, 26, 28, 30, 46–49, 57, 71,
    176, 238, 246–49, 272–73, 278–79. *See also*
    collective action
Soft law, 28, 92, 94, 96, 109, 280
Somalia, 74, 197, 214
South Africa, 8, 12, 230, 232, 235, 271, 282
Spiral model, 17, 246
Sponsorship abuse, 88, 165, 189–90, 192, 196,
    275
St. Vincent, 74, 147, 197
Standard setting, human rights: processes, 18,
    21–22, 34–38, 40, 44, 210, 263–64; prece-
    dents, 20; international trigger cases, 4, 14,
    16, 20–22, 27, 39, 238, 246–47, 251, 254. *See
    also* human rights
State sovereignty, 3, 17, 23–24, 33–35, 37, 41,
    44, 46, 62, 66, 71, 97, 100, 117, 191, 208, 233,
    238–41, 249–50, 257, 261, 272–73, 283
Sweden, 12, 65, 230, 282

Table de Concertation des Organismes de
    Montréal au Service des Personnes
    Réfugiées et Immigrantes (TCMR),
    125–26, 128, 156, 160, 163, 170, 172–73, 210,
    277, 278
Torture, 9, 82, 87, 96, 143, 151, 193, 217, 221,
    225, 304
Trafficking, 33, 221, 228
Transnational advocacy networks, 17, 24, 37,
    38, 40, 246
Trinidad and Tobago, 74, 147, 197

Turkey, 74, 147, 197

United Kingdom, 12, 102, 121, 230, 282
United Nations Charter, 85
United Nations High Commissioner for
    Refugees (UNHCR), 3, 4, 12, 51, 65, 81, 89,
    93–94, 98–102, 170, 172–73, 188, 195, 209,
    226–30, 271, 276, 282–83
United States, 12, 25, 45, 105, 113, 117, 199, 228,
    230–32, 256, 263, 265, 276
Universal Declaration of Human Rights
    (UDHR), 60, 81–83, 85, 208, 254–55
Universalism, 83, 254, 257, 272; universalist,
    41, 42

Venezuela, 12, 230, 283
Vienna Declaration, World Conference on
    Human Rights, 206
Violence against women: 6–7, 9, 11, 13–14, 18,
    23, 30, 85–87, 92, 96, 100–101, 103–11, 127,
    146, 163, 189–91, 193–94, 196, 201, 203, 205,
    220–21, 236, 254, 258, 272, 274–75, 277, 280;
    and family honor, 91; state omission and
    commission, 6, 217, 231; locus, agent, and
    manifestation, 220–21; and the Guidelines,
    2

Welfare, 55, 59–61, 95, 115, 118, 126, 147, 180,
    189, 191, 242–43, 260, 266
Women's movement, 62, 92, 105, 119, 254, 276;
    feminism, 18, 23, 28, 92, 104, 105, 109–10,
    119, 203, 209, 225, 272, 280; women's
    human rights movement, 103–7, 110, 119

Zaire, 74, 147, 197

Acknowledgments

My heartfelt thanks to the people who participated in this study, giving generously of their time and special insight. In particular I would like to thank Thérèse and the other asylum seekers whose role in the political process studied was part of a far more important and courageous fight for survival. Many refugee and feminist activists and lawyers also gave generously of their time and special insight to make this study possible—their participation was invaluable and their dedication to women's rights work inspiring. A big thank you goes to many other people, in particular Barbara Nichols, who inspired me to pursue this work and gave me many tools to do so; as well as Howard Glennerster, Mark Hoffman, Jane Lewis, Yasmine Soysal, Ann Oakley, and the readers for the University of Pennsylvania Press, who provided crucial comments and feedback. To my parents, my deep thanks for their amazing support, encouragement, and understanding during this long project. Last but not least, a very special thank you goes to my sunshine, Nuno, for just about everything.